# Literature and Consolation

# Literature and Consolation

*Fictions of Comfort*

Jürgen Pieters

EDINBURGH
University Press

Edinburgh University Press is one of the leading university presses in the UK. We publish academic books and journals in our selected subject areas across the humanities and social sciences, combining cutting-edge scholarship with high editorial and production values to produce academic works of lasting importance. For more information visit our website: edinburghuniversitypress.com

© Jürgen Pieters, 2021, 2023

Edinburgh University Press Ltd
The Tun – Holyrood Road, 12(2f) Jackson's Entry, Edinburgh EH8 8PJ

First published in hardback by Edinburgh University Press 2021

Typeset in 11/13 Adobe Sabon by
IDSUK (DataConnection) Ltd

A CIP record for this book is available from the British Library

ISBN 978 1 4744 5655 5 (hardback)
ISBN 978 1 4744 5656 2 (paperback)
ISBN 978 1 4744 5657 9 (webready PDF)
ISBN 978 1 4744 5658 6 (epub)

The right of Jürgen Pieters to be identified as the author of this work has been asserted in accordance with the Copyright, Designs and Patents Act 1988, and the Copyright and Related Rights Regulations 2003 (SI No. 2498).

*Contents*

| | |
|---|---|
| Acknowledgements | vi |
| Introduction: Fictions of Comfort | 1 |
| 1. The Classical Regime of Literary Comfort: From Homer to Aristotle | 23 |
| 2. The Christian Regime of Literary Comfort: From Boethius to Dante | 62 |
| 3. Towards a Modern Regime of Literary Comfort: Shakespeare and the Failure to Console | 110 |
| 4. The Religion of Despair: George Sand and Gustave Flaubert on Reading and Writing | 193 |
| 5. Novels of Comfort: Woolf, Winnicott and the Work of Consolation | 225 |
| 6. Fragments of a Consolatory Discourse: Sontag, Riley, Proust, Barthes | 256 |
| Epilogue: The Library of Comfort | 282 |
| Bibliography | 287 |
| Index | 304 |

## *Acknowledgements*

There is comfort in true friendship and in the encouraging company of benevolent colleagues. In the decade during which this book continued to develop, I had the good fortune to be able to discuss it with a number of fellow travellers. Some of them read drafts of chapters in progress, while others allowed me to entertain them on the topic of literary consolation over lunch or during coffee breaks. For their generous feedback and warm encouragement, I would like to thank, in no particular order, Mieke Musschoot, Sandro Jung, Russell Palmer, Stijn Bussels, Bram Van Oostveldt, Ben Dhooge, Youri Desplenter, Veronique Christophe, Liliane Haegeman, Kate Briggs, Julian Wolfreys, Kornee Van der Haven, Kristoffel Demoen, Steven Vanden Broecke, Wim De Jonge, Tom Laureys, Christophe Madelein, Jakob Deroover, Wim De Brock and Siegfried Bracke. Special words of thanks are due to Catherine Belsey, Neil Badmington, Roland Greene and Marisa Galvez, Mark Phillips, Frans-Willem Korsten and Willy Roggeman. Each of them, in their own right, continues to serve as a mentor in good writing and good thinking. I will forever be indebted to them and remain thankful for their inspiration and the example they all set.

I am grateful for having been able to discuss the project that resulted in this book with audiences at the universities of Lille, Cardiff, Surrey and Leiden, where I was kindly invited by Fiona MacIntosh-Varjabédian, Rob Gossedge, Neema Parvini and Frans-Willem Korsten, respectively. For the past three years, I have been able to discuss some of the materials in this book with the students of my Poetics course at Ghent University. Their response and enthusiasm have fed into this project in ways that may be less visible but remain decisive. Some of the texts I discuss in the book's chapters I had the pleasure of teaching at non-academic institutions of adult education in Ghent, Bruges and Mechelen (Amarant, Vorming Plus, Background Education). The feedback that I received on these occasions made me realise all the more that the topic at hand is of potential interest to a broader audience.

Some fifteen years ago, I was ever so proud to be able to publish a book with Edinburgh University Press. The encouragement of Jackie Jones and Michelle Houston made all the difference as I was writing this new book. I am grateful to the anonymous reviewers who considered my initial proposal worthy of publication, and to Emma Caddy for help with the index. Thanks are also due to copy editor Fiona Screen for her editorial accuracy in the production of the final typescript and to James Dale for his smooth organisation of the book's production. Working with them has been a real pleasure.

I owe gratitude (and am more than willing to extend it) to the Federal Research Fund (FWO-Vlaanderen) and the Research Committee of Ghent University's Faculty of Arts for providing the means for the sabbatical which enabled me to finish the book. The project came to final fruition during the spring 2020 COVID lockdown. The latter half of the book I managed to write in the course of three months when I was surrounded 24/7 by my family. The children's online teaching and my wife's working from home banished me from the study where I usually write to our dining room table. Memories of that disturbingly viral spring will always be mixed in my mind with the pleasurable recollection of precious family time. To them – Nancy, Lukas, Emma and Anna – I would like to dedicate this book. And to my parents, Chris and Wilfried, for their unwavering support.

# Introduction: Fictions of Comfort

> Always comforting to assume there is a secret
> behind what torments you.
>
> Anne Carson, Nox[1]

On my writing desk sits a randomly organised stack of books whose titles immediately betray a common concern: *How Dante Can Save Your Life* (2015), *Jane Austen's Guide to Modern Life's Dilemmas* (2012), *Les livres prennent soin de nous* (2015), *Lesen als Medizin* (2015), *The Novel Cure* (2013), *The Western Lit Survival Kit* (2012), *The End of Your Life Book Club* (2012), *How Literature Saved My Life* (2013), *Petit guide de lectures qui aident à vivre* (2010), *Doktor Erich Kästners Lyrische Hausapotheke* (2016).[2] Judging by their title pages, each of these books is concerned with the wholesome effect the 'perusal' of literary writings may have on those reading them. Their common point can hardly be misunderstood. Literary authors have the power to save lives. Their books can serve as guides that help one either to survive or die well. In the end, poems and stories are, well, just about the best medicine possible.

What these books also have in common, as the years of their publication indicate, is a shared moment of production. Apart from the last title in the above list – its first edition (1936) predates the Second World War – all of these books were written and published in the course of the decade that precedes my current reflections. Their number continues to increase. As I was drafting the first version of this introduction, several new titles began to land on top of the ever-growing stack on my desk: Viv Groskop's *The Anna Karenina Fix: Life Lessons from Russian Literature* (2018), William Sieghart's *The Poetry Pharmacy* (2017) and *The Poetry Pharmacy Returns* (2019), Laura Freeman's *Reading Cure: How Books Restored my Appetite* (2019), Michael McGirr's *Books that Saved my Life* (2018) and Katharine Smyth's *All the Lives We Ever Lived* (2019).[3] The latter's alliterative subtitle – *Seeking Solace in*

*Virginia Woolf* – makes clearer than the book's main title why it belongs here as well. The soul-saving strength of books, Smyth seems to suggest, is synonymous with the success of their consolatory force. (In this, she appears to agree with McGirr, the subtitle of whose book – *Reading for Wisdom, Solace and Pleasure* – points in the same direction.)

I bought most of these books in my favourite bookshop in the Flemish town where I work. While the town harbours a middle-large university, the bookshop does not primarily target an academic readership. Its clientele consists of amateur-readers, mainly. To be clear: I'm using that term in the most positive sense possible; these amateurs are true book lovers, well-informed ones at that. The shop has a large literature section, offers good coffee and cakes (so I am told), and also specialises in children's literature and books on cooking and gardening, sections whose contents I browse only on rare occasions.

I found most of the books mentioned above, at regular intervals over the past few years, on the same table in the corner of the shop's literature section. The table caters for readers who are not simply interested in the latest quality fiction, but also in other books, non-fictional mostly, that conceive of the reading of literature in terms of a way of living, an 'ars vivendi atque legendi', the living of one's life with and among books. 'Bibliophiles', one could call these readers, though not in the traditional, technical sense of that word. The works that I just listed are neither rare nor precious, and they are not particularly expensive either. The lovers of books whom my local bookstore aims to serve have an interest in a diverse array of topics that bear on the distinct pleasures involved in reading, cherishing and collecting books. Its literature section will also have on display books about bookshops (Jen Campbell's *Weird Things Customers Say in Bookshops* (2012), for instance, or her later *The Bookshop Book* (2014)), books about the history and the future of the book (Amaranth Borsuk's *The Book* (2018)), books about how writers organise their personal libraries (Leah Price's *Unpacking my Library: Writers and their Books* (2011)), books containing witticisms about books (*The Book Lovers' Anthology* (2015)), and, finally, little notebooks or diaries in which readers can take down their most personal ideas about whatever new novel they just want everybody to know they love.[4] As it happens, these notebooks come in a dazzling variety of shapes, colours and titles – I have seen Edgar Allan Poe notebooks ('Get inspired to write your spookiest horror tales'), Alice in Wonderland notebooks ('It's small enough to fit with you when you fall down the rabbit hole, too') and *Logophile* notebooks ('This journal is made to look like an authentic library check-out card – what could be better?').

The books whose titles I started by singling out are a distinct subset of the broader range of the 'bibliophilia' to which I just referred. Each of them defines the love ('philia') of the book ('biblion') in terms of the healthy impact reading may have on the individual reader's state of mind. Books are good for us, the writers of these works suggest, and that is why we should keep reading them. Each of the above titles deals with the curative force of literature, with the therapeutic value of reading the right novel or poem at the right time. In *How Dante Can Save Your Life*, for instance, Rod Dreher tells the poignant story of how his reading of the *Divine Comedy* helped him come out of the severe depression that hit him sometime around the middle of his life, 'nel mezzo del cammin', as Dreher's thirteenth-century Italian guide put it. Will Schwalbe's *The End of Your Life Book Club* recalls and no doubt also stages sessions of shared reading between the author and his dying mother, in which the books – and, even more so, their readers' heartening conversations about them – turn out to be really helpful for both members of this very special book club. Katharine Smyth, finally, shows how her youthful fascination with Virginia Woolf's *To the Lighthouse* – a favourite since her junior year in Oxford – developed into a deeper understanding of the novel and its place in both her and its author's life, as the book helped her come to terms with her father's alcoholism and accompanying prolonged and fatal illness. Woolf's novel, Smyth comes to see in a more fundamental way, is really about the absence of a parent, a feeling that its author, unfortunately, knew all too well.

### Bibliotherapy

Each of these three titles, together with the other books that I mentioned earlier, belong to the specific branch of 'bibliophilia' that is commonly labelled 'bibliotherapy' – the gentle art of healing by means of the books that one reads.[5] The term (a mere neologism at the beginning of the previous century, even though the practice to which it refers can be said to be age-old) is by now usually taken to stand for two separate, yet clearly interlinked, meanings. It refers to both a serious (psycho-)medical practice that involves the use of literary texts to help patients come to terms with specific aspects of their medical condition and to an often more ironically self-conscious critical practice that involves the prescription of reading materials in a more informal context of self-help and self-improvement. In the definition offered by *Webster's International Dictionary*, in which the word first features in 1961,[6] bibliotherapy is said to refer to either '[t]he use of selected reading materials as therapeutic adjuvants in medicine and psychiatry' or, in a more general way, to other non-clinical forms of 'guidance in the solution of personal problems through directed reading.'[7] Natalia Tukhareli, author of one of the few recent scholarly monographs on the subject,[8] puts it like this:

> 'Bibliotherapy' is an umbrella term that covers a wide variety of clinical (therapeutic) and non-clinical (developmental, creative, social) interventions involving books, reading, and communication around texts. In the broadest sense of the term, bibliotherapy is the systematic use of books to assist individuals in dealing with mental, physical, emotional, developmental, or social problems.[9]

'Bibliotherapy', Jacqueline Stanley writes in a slightly older book, 'is the therapeutic use of books in the treatment of illnesses or personal problems.'[10]

In neither of the two meanings distinguished above should practitioners of 'bibliotherapy' be seen to be representing the latest methodological development in literary scholarship, in the way that, for instance, scholars working in the fields of animal studies, ecocriticism, cognitivist scholarship or digital humanities have recently been said to open up new perspectives in the academic discipline of literary studies. In the first meaning of the word, bibliotherapy as an institutionalised clinical practice, it generally appears to belong to the domain of specialists in the fields of medicine and psychiatry, even though interdisciplinary collectives of bibliotherapeutic endeavours, operating in the wider domain of the so-called medical humanities, will usually have connections with scholars or librarians working in the field of literature. The earliest instances of this institutionalised practice go back to the beginning of the twentieth century, as doctors and librarians in military hospitals in the United States worked together in prescribing the reading of specific books to soldiers coming back from the First World War.[11]

In English, the word is said to have been used for the first time in a satirical essay by the Unitarian minister Samuel McChord Crothers, published in *The Atlantic Monthly* in the September issue of 1916.[12] 'A Literary Clinic', the essay is called. In it, the author stages a conversation with his minister-friend Bagster who in his church organises sessions of 'Book Treatment',[13] prescribing specific writings (literary and other) to patients who suffer from one or other form of mental discomfort. 'During the last year', Bagster tells his interlocutor, 'I have been working up a system of Biblio-therapeutics. I don't pay much attention to the purely literary or historical classifications. I don't care whether a book is ancient or modern, whether it is English or German, whether it is in prose or verse, whether it is a history or a collection of essays, whether it is romantic or realistic. I only ask, "What is its therapeutic value?"'[14] 'The true function of a literary critic', he goes on to conclude, 'is not to pass judgement on the book, but to diagnose the condition of the person who has read it. What was his state of mind before reading and after reading? Was he better or worse for this experience?'[15]

In the course of the century that separates us from Crothers, the literature on bibliotherapy has developed exponentially, especially in academic journals of medicine, library studies and psychiatry, in which an ever-growing number of research reports testify to the success of the clinical practice for patients (and their relatives and loved ones) all over the world. In the second meaning of the term, bibliotherapists similarly prescribe books to be read or reflect otherwise on the therapeutic value of reading, but in this case the practice stands for a distinctly non-clinical critical endeavour, likewise centring on the concerns of the common reader, whose interests, many think, have not been served at all well by the literary scholarship of the past decades. In this case, bibliotherapists are not real doctors with an actual clinical training, but like their (presumed) patients are amateur-readers themselves. The logic that underlies their therapeutic practice is that their 'pretence' prescriptions would definitely not work if they were couched in the specialist jargon that according to some has come to dominate literary studies in the recent past. This form of bibliotherapy thrives on the pleasures of reading, and the treatment that it aims for needs to increase that pleasure, not downplay or kill it.

Also, the practice is generally sustained by the presumed solidarity between 'doctor' and 'patient', in the sense that the former is supposedly able to personally vouch for the effectiveness of the medicine prescribed. While real doctors need not have taken the drugs they administer to be certain of their effectiveness, 'book doctors' will definitely have read the books whose healing powers they proclaim – at least, their reading advice is premised on the promise that they have. William Sieghart, to give an example, in his collection of 'prescriptions' that make up *The Poetry Pharmacy*, keeps reminding his readers that the poems he selected for people who came to him for reading advice worked for him personally, in trying circumstances that he shared with his interlocutors. Hence the adjectives with which the book's subtitle opens: *Tried-and-True Prescriptions for the Heart, Mind and Soul*. Sieghart's pharmaceutical library is made up of poems, he writes, 'which I know from experience will help people through most conceivable difficulties of day-to-day life: through the various faces and frustrations of love, grief, work and all the other concerns that dominate our thoughts.'[16]

## Literature and Consolation

Let me make clear from the outset that the present book is not itself an attempt at bibliotherapy. Neither is it a book that explains what bibliotherapy is, what it can do, or what it needs to do in order to become (more) effective. This book's relationship to bibliotherapy is at once tangential and fundamental. The chapters that follow touch upon the subject only marginally, but they do so in a way that goes to the heart of bibliotherapy's central claim: the conviction that literary writings have the power to heal. More specifically, I will be dealing throughout in what follows with the idea that I singled out earlier with reference to Katharine Smyth's book about Virginia Woolf: the idea that the therapeutic value of literary writings is related to (or even boils down to) the fact that books offer solace. Laura Freeman's *The Reading Cure* – which, incidentally, also has a chapter on Woolf – seems to underscore Smyth's point. 'I want to write about the solace of reading', Freeman exclaims at the end of the chapter that introduces her readers to the story of her struggle with anorexia, a story which revolves around the books that helped (and still help) her come to terms with that disorder.[17] While Smyth and Freeman are not really concerned with what it is, exactly, in the books that helped their recovery, nor with how best to describe or analyse what they consider the 'consolations' of reading, they seem to agree that the curative effect of their encounters with specific texts can be summed up by that keyword: 'solace'. (To be clear: Smyth and Freeman do not 'prescribe' the books that have helped them in their search for mental comfort; they reflect on what it is in these books that worked therapeutically for them.)

Generally, attempts to sustain the claim that reading books can truly have a healing effect sooner or later (sooner rather than later, usually) refer to the consoling power of literary writings. Quite often, as in Smyth and Freeman, the suggestion seems to be that consolation is, actually, what the healing force of reading is all about. Bibliotherapy, the French philosopher Marc-Alain Ouaknin writes in an etymological reflection on the word's Greek roots, is *therapeia*, not *iatrikè*[18] – it is not a practice that pretends to have the power to heal people physically, in the way that 'true' medicine is said to do. *Therapeia* involves mental caretaking, *cura animarum* as it was called in Latin, careful and caring attempts to repair a state of mind and enable people who suffer to return to a more healthy situation.[19] The practice of consolation also does all of those things, obviously, which is exactly why the healing power of books and the consolatory force of reading are generally treated as nearly synonymous, as Tukhareli also makes clear in her book on bibliotherapy. Like other forms of art therapy, she writes, 'bibliotherapy emphasizes the idea of the healing, consoling power of art through its various forms'.[20] To be healed, in this specific case, equals being consoled.

In the past few years, it has struck me on several occasions that, both in reviews of books and in everyday conversations with both specialist and 'amateur' readers, the suggestion that a book can and does offer consolation occurs with surprising and increasing regularity. More often than not, the suggestion serves not just as a signal of the specific effect that books can have on readers and reviewers, but also as a signal of the quality of these books. A novel is often said to be great *because* it brings comfort. Conversely, the power to bring comfort is increasingly seen as one of the prime effects (and, indeed, tasks) of good literature. I will limit myself to one example here, because it brings together several of the arguments that we will have occasion to deal with more extensively in the remainder of this book. Reviewing *Zero K*, Don DeLillo's 2016 novel, for the *New York Times*, Joshua Ferris praised the author's novelistic output by pointing out the unique consolatory force of his books. 'Don DeLillo's novels generally offer consolation simply by enacting so well the mystery and awe of the real world', Ferris claims, 'by probing deeply and mystically into so much, and by offering the pleasures of his unique style.'[21] As will become clearer later, literary solace is no less a matter of an author's stylistic and formal prowess than of the specific moral depth of their worldview.

In a survey article that was published on the website of *Times Higher Education* and that deals with what its author calls 'the rise of the medical humanities', Belinda Jack refers in a central paragraph of her text – one in which she tries to elaborate on what she sees as a 'less obvious role' for poetry to play in the disciplinary field of the medical humanities – to the power of poems to 'console, teach, amuse, enlighten, mimic, disconcert and so much more'.[22] What is striking in this list of poetry's tasks is not so much the presence of that first verb, but the fact that Jack puts it there first, as the indication of poetry's foremost goal, so to speak, one that comes before the double Horatian imperative of teaching (*docere*) and amusement (*delectare*), the classical mixture of what is useful with what is pleasant. In the same paragraph, Jack further elaborates on what she sees as the specific consolatory function of poems. She does so primarily (and not entirely unexpectedly, of course) by referring to the public use of poems at funeral services. There, poems serve as individual and collective occasions for all of those present, so that, in Jack's words, '[e]ach of us can ponder what the poem conjures for us, bringing something felt into clearer and thus more comforting focus. Often the poem will be one that allows us to reconsider the absolute nature of death.' In other words: the comfort that the poem brings resides in the fact ('thus' being the signal of that specific causal relationship) that the poem's language and formal make-up allow us to see and understand more clearly something that we have been knowing and feeling all along (ideas about the absolute and inevitable nature of mortality), something that marks us as individuals, but which at the same time binds us together, collectively.

The poet Don Paterson, in his preface to the *Picador Book of Funeral Poems* that he edited, describes the consolation provided by this type of poem in strikingly similar terms. Paterson also singles out the specific consolatory function of quite a significant and representative group of poems as their prime goal. This is how he puts it:

> In our deepest grief we turn instinctively to poetry – to comfort and solace us, or to reflect our grief, give it proper public expression, or help us feel less alone in our experience of it. These poems [the ones in Paterson's collection], drawn from many different ages and cultures, remind us that the experience of parting is a timelessly human one: however lonely the loss of someone close might leave us, our mourning is also something that deeply unites us.[23]

Paterson's reflections on the principle of solidarity that underlies the central mechanism involved in the giving and receiving of solace (in order to feel comforted we need to feel understood, that is, we need to get the feeling that our comforters understand our suffering for what it is, so that they can properly share in it) find an echo in Belinda Jack's analysis of the consolatory force of funeral poems: 'Faced with some of life's most painful moments poetry can reassure us that we are not alone – others have suffered too.' A further truism implied by the solidarity of solace is the assertion that our own experiences may become more meaningful when we come to understand them through the experience of another. The feeling of comfort very often arrives when we begin to properly understand our pain – at a distance, as it were, the distance provided by someone else's perspective.

## Some Preliminary Examples

Katharine Smyth on Virginia Woolf provides good illustrative backing. What Smyth learns from *To the Lighthouse* cannot follow from a plain and full identification with either Woolf or the novel's narrator. The solace of reading that she experiences requires a more nuanced bifocal perspective that allows her to see both differences and similarities between her own situation (her struggle, first with her father's alcoholism and then with his death) and the differently similar situations in which the author and protagonists of *To the Lighthouse* find themselves – Woolf losing both her parents at a young age and Mrs Ramsay's children losing their mother in the course of the novel's narrative. Whenever Smyth relates a passage from the novel (or from Woolf's biography for that matter) to her own life story, she does so with a clear awareness of the dual ratio that lies behind what I just labelled a bifocal perspective – things are similar though different, and therein, precisely, lies the consolatory effect of her new and better understanding of the novel. 'Such is the nature of Woolfian failure', Smyth writes at one point, 'which, despite my urge to conflate them, turns out to be a different breed from my father's own'.[24] Smyth is always on the outlook for possibilities of identification, be it with the author or one of the novel's protagonists – 'I longed for Woolf's genius, yes, but I also longed for Mrs Ramsay herself, for her as my mother, for her as my friend; I wanted to *be* her'[25] – and comes to realise that more is to be learned (and more comfort to be had) from a reading that encourages further reflection on the difference between what we read and who we are. In that difference – in the very possibility of difference – the experience of consolation can come into being.

The ultimate solace of *To the Lighthouse*, in Smyth's experience, is related to a crucial insight that Woolf, almost in passing, visits on one of the novel's protagonists, James Ramsay, who begins to learn that all things in life (objects as much people) refuse to be given a single meaning: 'For nothing was simply one thing', the young man comes to realise at one point.[26] Smyth herself, re-reading Woolf's novel, comes to understand that its prime contribution lies in the fact that it makes clear to the reader (to this particular reader, at least) what she calls 'the complexities and contradictions of human experience'.[27] 'It was Woolf's genius', Smyth concludes, 'to express this richness, to never gloss over intricacy or inconsistency, to communicate through her characters her ongoing struggle to find truth and meaning in a world where are both are infinitely shifting.'[28] The fact that meaning does have the potential to shift (and, indeed, the habit of shifting) is what brings comfort in times of grief and pain: the awareness that what ails us bitterly can be seen differently, from another perspective. Coupled to that essential insight, in Smyth's experience, is the no less consoling thought that readers of Woolf's novel find themselves not to be lone sufferers – 'the deliciousness of feeling known and understood'[29] is how Smyth labels this special feeling that readers of novels, judging by the examples of the books that I mentioned earlier, often get more easily from the books they read than from their relatives or friends. 'No book has ever given me a look up and down and said, "You look better"', Laura Freeman writes in her bibliotherapeutic account of her struggle with anorexia: 'I always took this badly. "You're looking better" to me meant: "You're definitely fatter."'[30]

Writing about her own discovery of Woolf's work, Freeman concurs with Smyth's account of the particular – and particularly personal – bond readers can have with their cherished books: 'Here – and what a deliverance it was to discover her – was a writer who allowed me to say, not that I was not mad, for I felt very mad indeed at the time, but that I was not the only one.'[31] Solace, as we will see later, is related – in ways that need to be further probed – to solidarity, to the feeling that our grief can genuinely be shared with others and, by consequence, also alleviated. One further aspect singled out by Katharine Smyth in her analysis of the comfort that she derives from reading Woolf has to do with the aesthetics of the work of literature. As we will also see in the remainder of this book, there seems to be a fundamental link between the experiences of consolation and of beauty. '[A]t the very moment I believed my father to be dying', Smyth writes, 'my mind alighted, quite involuntarily, upon the pages of my favourite novel, taking solace not just in its lessons but its language, in the rhythm and beauty of phrases as familiar to me as the sound of the waves that break in Rhode Island'.[32] Bibliotherapeutic reflections of all kinds – whether in scholarly reports, non-academic essays or even in readers' comments on GoodReads or other bookish websites – draw the same conclusion at one point or another: the comfort of literature lies not just in *what* is being said, but also (and more importantly) in *how* things are being said.

Literary comfort, of course, comes in different forms and shapes and its effects are unpredictable. In this, it works (or not, as the case may be) like any other type of comfort. The book that almost single-handedly put bibliotherapy high on the agenda of literary studies – Ella Berthoud and Susan Elderkin's *The Novel Cure: An A–Z of Literary Remedies* – offers further proof of the critical equation between the healing potential of literature and its consolatory powers. Originally published in English in 2013, *The Novel Cure* now has editions in several major languages: I have found references to French, Italian, Spanish, German, Turkish, Portuguese, Russian, Chinese and Dutch editions. Most of these are more than simply translations of the English original. They also contain new 'literary prescriptions' based on novels in the respective editions' target languages. What Berthoud and Elderkin do in *The Novel Cure* is offer reading suggestions of novels for readers suffering from a wide array of possible complaints, verging from moderately innocent forms of mental discomfort (not being able to 'find a decent cup of coffee', for instance, or 'not knowing what novels to take on holiday') to grief caused by a broken heart or the death of a loved one. In the latter case, readers are advised to read John Berger's *Here Is Where We Meet*. Those suffering from one or other form of identity crisis, Berthoud and Elderkin further claim, should definitely have a look at Kafka's 'Die Verwandlung' ('The Metamorphosis'), while readers who complain about insomnia or depression are offered an undosed prescription of Pessoa's *Book of Disquiet* or Sylvia Plath's *The Bell Jar*, respectively.

In an interesting analysis of *The Novel Cure*, Josie Billington labelled Berthoud and Elderkin's approach as a 'half-joking' one.[33] The qualification is quite apt, I feel. The book, not unlike some others in the list that I started out with, is openly self-ironic about the presumed healing powers of literary writings. Of course, readers who pay a visit to the book doctor know very well that reading *Jane Eyre* will not really mend their broken hearts. And yet, when pressed on the issue, those same readers generally admit that they remain convinced of the curative powers of reading good literature. '*The Reading Cure* will speak to anyone who has ever felt pain and found solace in a book' reads one of the endorsements on Laura Freeman's memoir. What is it exactly that readers find so consoling in specific texts? And what does this say about their ideas about literature, or about consolation, for that matter?

In the brief preface to their book, a mere one-and-a-half pages long, Berthoud and Elderkin immediately admit that the 'cure' of their book's title is obviously not a real medicinal remedy. Interestingly, for our purposes, the word 'consolation' is invoked quite rapidly. It is mentioned in a paragraph in which Berthoud and Elderkin describe the effects of the literary prescriptions that the book as a whole lists: 'Whatever your ailment,' they assure us, in the parlance of real doctors, 'our prescriptions are simple: a novel (or two), to be read at regular intervals. Some treatments will lead to a complete cure. Others will simply offer solace, showing you that you are not alone. All will offer the temporary relief of your symptoms due to the power of literature to distract and transport.'[34] The logic of the passage is quite straightforward: the fact that literature 'simply' provides comfort – and the sort of comfort that it provides – is coupled with the literary text's power 'to distract and transport' us, rather than confront us with an absolute and threatening reality. Judging on several of the literary prescriptions that *The Novel Cure* offers, it would not be a farfetched idea to suggest that the literary solace that Berthoud and Elderkin are thinking of can be seen as a form of escapism, one which, however, procures the same effect as the funeral poems that both Belinda Jack and Don Paterson write about – the solace is a shared one, it results in the comforting thought 'that you are not alone'.

## Towards a Topology of Literary Comfort

The function of objects of art to console is also conspicuously present in *Art as Therapy* by John Armstrong and Alain de Botton, in the context of whose School of Thought the editors of *The Novel Cure* give actual sessions in bibliotherapy. In their introduction to the co-authored book, De Botton and Armstrong write: 'This book proposes that art (a category that includes works of design, architecture and craft) is a therapeutic medium that can help guide, exhort and console its viewers, enabling them to become better versions of themselves.'[35] What I'm interested in, in the remainder of this book, are questions that seem of lesser concern to the authors of *Art as Therapy* and *The Novel Cure* and that probe issues that seem to be taken as self-evident by them: what is it, exactly, that we mean if we say – as they do, like many other readers, reviewers, authors and critics nowadays – that art consoles? What is this consolation by a work of art or by a fictional character? Why do we allow ourselves to be comforted by fictional characters when in real life we find it hard to be consoled by the words and deeds of those surrounding us? In what does this fictional consolation consist precisely? Is it related to art's power to confront us with the real or to its power to help us escape from it? What is it exactly in these works that consoles us? Does the beauty of the work of art, its formal shape, have anything to do with this, and if so, to what extent and on the basis of which textual and affective mechanisms? How, to come back to the sentence that I just quoted from De Botton and Armstrong, is a consoled person a better version of themselves, especially a person who allows themselves to be consoled by a work of art?

I admit from the onset that these questions are too broad and general to be answered in a satisfactory way. As we will see, there is no single answer to the question of what, precisely, literary comfort boils down to. Also, it would be counter-intuitive, to say the least, to hope for such a single, homogeneous answer. Having described, with Katharine Smyth and *To the Lighthouse*'s James Ramsay, the experience of consolation as one that makes clear to us that 'nothing [is] simply one thing', it would make little sense to see that very thing as 'simply one'. Nevertheless, it is my intention in what follows to provide a systematic analysis of the arguments that have been used and are still being used in discussions surrounding the consolatory potential of literary writings. As I hope to show, these arguments are historically motivated and structurally related. It is my conviction that an analysis of their relatedness – historically as well as conceptually – will result in a better understanding of what it is that books do when we say, intuitively, that they bring comfort, or that we find ourselves consoled by them.

The idea that literary texts can be a source of consolation for those reading them is a founding topic in the history of Western literature, as I want to show in the remainder of this book. From the very beginning, the therapeutic effect of literary writings has been defined in terms of their consolatory force. This is still the case today, increasingly so even, as I just made clear. Numerous are the references to the comforting potential of literature, both in popular forms of criticism and in scholarly explorations of the values of reading. By focusing on a number of significant moments in the interlocking histories of the book's two central concepts, I want to open up the critical topos of 'literary consolation' so that readers can become aware of the premises that underlie the assumption that literary writings can bring comfort. What exactly do we mean when we make this often heard claim? What is it in literary texts that provides this special experience and how does the comfort that we derive from reading literary texts differ from other types of consolation? Conversely, how does literature (fiction?) help us to understand what consolation means and what effects it has? While this book does not pretend to offer a full historical trajectory of the inter-relationships between literature and consolation, it does take a historical perspective. Both 'literature' and 'consolation' are notions the meaning of which changes over the centuries (in the latter case even quite drastically). My historicist perspective, however, remains focused on the present. By looking at a number of significant moments where the histories of the book's two central concepts intersect (from Homer, through Dante, Shakespeare and Flaubert, to Woolf and more recent authors), I want to gain a deeper understanding of the meaning and values of literature and consolation today. (That is why, in the first four chapters, my historically inspired reflection on the texts at hand is related to a recent publication in which those texts are the occasion of a contemporary bibliotherapeutic reflection.)

The central argument of this book is that the histories of literature and consolation are mutually illuminating. I want to argue that we will understand the peculiar phenomenon of bibliotherapy better if we manage to grasp more fully the inter-relationships between the history of literature and the history of consolation. The two *Begriffsgeschichten*, and their numerous intersections, will be the central subject of the book. As I want to show in the course of this book, the grand narrative of the topos of 'literary comfort' is defined, from its beginning, by the inter-relationship of two extreme positions, which are opposed but historically related to each other: either it is argued that texts that are literary are meant to give comfort and that they are successful in doing so, or these texts are being derided because they cannot provide real consolation. Picking up on the medical metaphors that are central to the practice of bibliotherapy, one could say that literary writings as purveyors or mediators of consolation can be considered a *pharmakon* in the two oppositional meanings which Derrida reminded us are inherent in the original Greek word: they work as either true medicine or mere poison – they either offer the authentic insight of real consolation or its counter-productive variant, the illusion of comfort.[36]

As I hope to make clear in the chapters that follow, there are two reasons why these two positions are generally co-present (albeit in varying degrees of dominance and subordination) in most discussions that centre around the consolatory potential of literary writings – as indeed they seem to be in *The Novel Cure*. The first one, *pace* Derrida, is that literary comfort – the consolation provided by literary texts – is the outcome of writing, the prime *pharmakon* as the author of 'La pharmacie de Platon' has argued. Writing, in its capacity of remedy/poison, is characterised by an ambiguity that is not only unsettling, but also cannot be settled – it either delivers its promise to bring comfort or undermines that very promise by the simple act of making it. The second reason has to do with the fact that the specific samples of writing that I will discuss in the remainder of this book are implicated in two conceptual histories: that of 'literature' and that of 'consolation'. The two concepts undergo significant semantic changes in the course of the centuries. In the case of the former, these changes will be self-evident to students of literature reading this book: the works of Homer (Chapter 1), Dante (Chapter 2), Shakespeare (Chapter 3) and Flaubert (Chapter 4) were produced in very different cultural circumstances, in which the pragmatics of the literary 'text' and the tasks of the 'author' producing those texts were conceived of in different and often mutually contradictory ways. To give just one example: for Dante, literature's prime task was moral (i.e. religious) edification; for Flaubert, literature could serve no other cause than that of being a form of art. This basic difference in viewpoint with respect to the desired effect of literary writings will obviously play a role in discussions related to the question of literature's consolatory power.

It may be less self-evident that our Western ideas of what consolation was and how it functioned also changed considerably over time. We all have intuitions about which thoughts are comforting and which are not, but it suffices to read a letter of consolation that was written centuries ago to see that these intuitions are not at all universal. In the chapters that follow I will be distinguishing, in broadly defined terms, between three different 'regimes of consolation' – a classical one (Chapter 1), a Christian one (Chapter 2), and a modern one (Chapters 3 to 6). In the classical era, as we will see in the first chapter of this book, the practice of consolation was generally defined in terms of an appeal to reason, an injunction to overcome one's emotions, the excess of which was considered blinding: in a state of distress we no longer see the real for what it is, classical consolatory writings argue. In these texts, the logic of consolation aims for a decisive change of perspective, a return to the common sense: to be comforted involves being reminded of how things actually are. Parents who mourn the loss of a child, for instance, are urged to remember the way of all flesh and to find comfort in the happiness that the child brought before it passed away. In the Christian regime, as we will see in the second chapter, the state of comfort is seen as the righteous outcome of authentic belief – the goal of the Christian regime was the acceptance of God's providential design. However painful life on earth could be, mankind had to realise that it suffered for a just cause and that happiness awaited true believers in the after-life. Christian words and practices of consolation served as a reminder of that divinely ordained cause. If a young child was taken away, parents should come to understand – and find comfort in that understanding – that whatever happened did so because God willed it to happen.

In the modern era (Chapters 3 to 6), neither religious faith nor absolute belief in an unshakeable common rationality could continue to support the logic and rhetoric of consolation. Modern ideas of consolation are caught in the double-bind that is central to the German philosopher Hans Blumenberg's analysis of the phenomenon: man is a creature in need of comfort, but in essence this need can never be truly quenched – *Trostbedürfnis* (the 'need for comfort') and *Untröstlichkeit* (the 'impossibility of comfort') are the joint keywords in Blumenberg's analysis.[37] Modern reflections on comfort stress the difficulty of finding true comfort instead of the self-evident success of consolatory attempts that underlies the classical and Christian discourses on the topic. To be clear, the chapters that follow are not an attempt to analyse these different discursive regimes – had I wanted to do that, my focus would have been on texts other than the ones that are central to this book: not on literary writings, but on classical letters of consolation, for instance, or Christian treatises on spiritual comfort or older and more recent texts on philosophical and psychological aspects of consolation. My approach in what follows centres on literature because I want to find out how these specific writings – in their capacity of being literary, that is – represent, stage and reflect upon the phenomenon of consolation, either directly or by offering the reader room for that reflection. My ultimate aim is not a mere thematic one, as I hope to have made clear: in reading passages from texts by Homer, Dante, Shakespeare, Flaubert and more recent authors, in which consolatory encounters occur (scenes of comfort one could call them) and in correlating these passages both to the historical development of the concept of consolation and to that of literature, I want to arrive at a better and more proper understanding of the complex interplay of the intuitions that sustain our conviction that reading literature brings comfort – intuitions about what consolation is and should be, about what literature is and should be, and about the relationship between the two.

## Organisation of the Book

In the book's first three chapters, the identification of three successive 'regimes' of consolation – the classical, Christian and modern regimes – is related to the close reading of a number of scenes of comfort that I have taken from canonical texts which date from the respective periods: Homer's *Iliad*, Dante's *Divine Comedy* and a number of plays by Shakespeare. Chapter 1 ('The Classical Regime of Literary Comfort: From Homer to Aristotle') begins by focusing on what I consider to be Western literature's first major scene of comfort: the scene, towards the end of *Iliad* 24, in which Priam is comforted for the loss of his son by Achilles, who was single-handedly responsible for the death of that son. Coupled to a scene from Sophocles' *Electra* where consolation is rejected rather than embraced, the fragment from Homer serves as the occasion for a survey of classical ideas of consolation. Having outlined the principles underlying that regime – to bring comfort is to appeal for reasonable thought and behaviour, in which the emotions are generally allowed to play a moderate part (*metriopatheia*); the logic of comfort is one of solidarity and common-sense thinking and it is a logic whose efficiency and success is presented as self-evident and unproblematic – I round off the chapter with a reflection on classical debates on the values and limits of literary representation. As soon as ideas on consolation move from the literary to the philosophical genre of the *consolatio*, the question becomes how the philosophical critique of the limits and powers of literary mimesis (in Plato and Aristotle, respectively) affects later ideas surrounding the critical topos of 'literary comfort'. Until now, I believe, discussions on the question have revolved around positions already announced in the classical period. If we want to argue that literature brings comfort to the extent that it can be shown to provide genuine insight into core experiences of our individual and collective being (a position close to Aristotle's analysis of *katharsis*), we need to be wary of the possibility that literature tells lies and results only in escapism (Plato's position).

The scene of comfort that is central to the first half of Chapter 2 ('The Christian Regime of Literary Comfort: From Boethius to Dante') is the famous opening scene of Boethius' *De consolatione philosophiae*. In it, the Muses of Poetry are shooed away from the narrator's sickbed by Lady Philosophy. Poetic comfort, the scene seems to suggest, will never turn out to be effective, because it is ultimately self-deceptive. Opposed to philosophy proper, poetry is false medicine: because the

Muses of Poetry both target and feed on the prisoner's emotions, his attachment to them is bound to keep him sick, Lady Philosophy keeps claiming in the text's opening scene. In its entirety, though, Boethius' text offers a much more complex reflection on the healing comfort of literature. In her apology for philosophy, as we will see, Lady Philosophy makes use of so many literary tropes and techniques, inserting numerous references to literary writings, that it becomes impossible to take her critique of poetry at face value. As I want to show, the critique of poetry in Boethius' text gradually develops into an apology for a specific type of poetry, a species of literature that belongs to the domain of moral philosophy and has a positive consolatory effect on its readers, provided that it is being read properly – the sort of poetry, in other words, for which Dante continued to plea throughout his œuvre.

In the second part of my second chapter, I want to argue that the discovery of Boethius' text helped Dante in his lifelong search for a form of poetry that could become truly, that is, positively, consolatory. This development begins with the early intuition in the *Vita Nuova* that the poet should be able to find, as he puts it in Chapter 31 of his text, 'solace in sorrowful words'. It moves on to an important reflection that turns this intuition into a fully-fledged theoretical programme in the second book of the *Convivio*, where Boethius' example (together with that of Cicero) seems to inspire a form a writing that couples a 'sweet' rhetoric (*dolcezza*) to the production of true meaning under the guise of fiction. The theory of *Convivio* culminates in the consolatory poetry of the *Commedia*. More explicitly than Boethius' treatise, as we will see, Dante's poetry is steeped in the Christian regime of consolation. In that new regime, several guiding classical ideas of consolation return, but the overarching framework of the Christian religion offers a new foundation to consolatory arguments: our suffering is willed by God, a sign of His grace in anticipation of our final salvation.

In Chapter 3 ('Towards a Modern Regime of Literary Comfort: Shakespeare and the Failure to Console'), I discuss several scenes of comfort in five different plays by Shakespeare's plays. The scenes have one thing in common: in each of them, the practice of consolation fails. I take this failure to be representative of the modern regime of consolation. The scenes that I have selected come from *Hamlet*, *Richard II*, *Measure for Measure*, *Romeo and Juliet* and *The Tempest*. In discussing them together, I want to point out how Shakespeare's understanding of comfort is based on a thorough knowledge of the classical theories that were highlighted in my first chapter. But while in those theories it is taken for granted that the practice of comfort is always successful, Shakespeare shows us the failure of consolation. This failure, as I see it, is related to a heightened awareness of the duplicity of rhetoric and to the new, early modern understanding of the individual self. Shakespeare's characters fail to be comforted because they are no longer convinced that their inner experiences relate unproblematically to the common sense upon which theories of comfort were traditionally founded. Inconsolable characters like Hamlet and Queen Isabel (in *Richard II*) fail to feel like everybody else, which is, basically, what people who are being comforted are expected to do. Also, the Christian rhetoric of consolation that is central to Dante's *Divine Comedy* and to numerous early modern consolatory writings (Catholic as well as Protestant) is either absent in Shakespeare's scenes of comfort (as in *Hamlet*, for instance), or exposed as blatant lies (in *Measure for Measure* and in *Romeo and Juliet*). As I want to argue, Shakespeare's analysis of the failure of comfort is indicative of the modern regime of consolation, in which the difficulty and ultimate 'impossibility' of consolation (Blumenberg) are central.

Chapters 4 to 6 pursue the relationship of literature to the modern regime of consolation. From Dante to Shakespeare, we move from an aesthetics that considers good literature to be consolatory per se (Dante) to one that conceives of the artist's task as one of testing the limits of that ideal, and in doing so, exposing the possible failure of the moral good (Shakespeare). In Chapter 4 ('The Religion of Despair: Gustave Flaubert and George Sand on Reading and Writing') these two positions are the subject of an epistolary discussion between Gustave Flaubert and his friend George Sand. As Flaubert sees it, the chief aim of literary writing is not 'consolation' but 'desolation'. Real writers, Flaubert argues, should refrain from wanting to provide their readers with the sort of moral comfort that Sand still considers central to their task; they will instead confront their readers with reality as it is, desolate and cruel. While Sand sees it as her main task to make her readers happy and colour over the world with the hue of comfort, Flaubert wants to open his readers' eyes and show them how things really stand. The discussion between Flaubert and Sand not only revolves around the function of literature, it also brings into play the discussion of what consolation is meant to do: is it meant to show things as they really are and to confront the person in need of consolation with a state of affairs that is the cause of pain or sorrow, or is it meant to embellish this state of affairs and show the person in need of comfort that things are not as bad as they think they are?

The irony of Flaubert's scathing critique of what Sand called 'literature of consolation' is that his own work soon came to be seen as itself an example of false comfort. I begin Chapter 5 ('Novels of Comfort: Woolf, Winnicott and the Work of Consolation') by addressing the fact that, with specific respect to the question of literary consolation, Flaubert's call for an autonomous consideration of literature resulted in the critique that in the modernist tradition that his work opened up, style began to function as what David James calls 'an aesthetic salve'. In his recently published *Discrepant Solace* (2019), James deals with the work of a number of contemporary Anglophone writers (Ian McEwan, J. M. Coetzee, Marilynne Robinson, Joan Didion, . . .) who want to move beyond that critique and come up with a form of writing that questions, thematically as well as stylistically, the idea of consolation as necessarily soothing. James' thorough analysis of these writers' contribution to the historiography of literary consolation enables me to query the function of form in discussions of the healing power of literary writings. My case is Virginia Woolf, whose *To the Lighthouse* is the book that is central in Katharine Smyth's particularly interesting bibliotherapeutic memoir that I discuss more extensively in this chapter. My discussion of it results in an exploration of the idea that in bibliotherapy, books function as what the British psychoanalyst Donald Winnicott calls 'transitional objects'.

In my final chapter ('Fragments of a Consolatory Discourse: Sontag, Riley, Proust, Barthes'), I relate French philosopher Michaël Fœssel's analysis of the language of consolation – in a work that has been an important companion in the course of the writing of this book – to the question that underlies every bibliotherapeutic claim. If literature, as that claim goes, has healing powers (powers of comfort, in my reading of that curative potential), what is it in their specific use of language that sustains or even makes up that power? Starting from qualities of the discourse of consolation singled out by Fœssel, I have organised Chapter 6 around the examples of the inconsolable Susan Sontag, Denise Riley's analysis of the time of mourning and Proust's insights in the pleasures of solitary reading. My final (though in no way conclusive) case is the one that started me off on this project: Roland Barthes' brief reflections on the consolation of reading in the texts that serve as a lasting tribute to his mother, *Mourning Diary* and *Camera Lucida*.

As I have mentioned, the historical reflection that this book has to offer on the development of the critical topos of literary comfort is targeted to the present. My central question, throughout, is where our current (and currently fashionable) intuition that literature has the power to console comes from – by which historically determined ideas about literature and consolation (and the relationship between them) it is underpinned and shaped. In order to highlight the presentist nature of my historicist pursuit, I have included in each of the book's chapters a reflection on recent works that take as their central topic the healing or consolatory power of the work of the canonical authors that I deal with in these chapters. Whether it be a professor of literature working on Homer or Dante (Daniel Mendelsohn and Joseph Luzzi in Chapters 1 and 2), a murder convict reading Shakespeare (Larry Newton in Chapter 3), a retired doctor with a strange obsession for Flaubert (Julian Barnes' Geoffrey Braithwaite in Chapter 4) or a young woman mourning the loss of her father while reading Woolf (Katharine Smyth in Chapter 5), each of these readers serves as a convincing witness of the consolatory powers that we attribute to the literary writings that many of us continue to cherish so deeply.

## Notes

1. Carson, *Nox*, n.p.
2. Dreher, *How Dante Can Save Your Life*; Smith, *Jane Austen's Guide to Modern Life's Dilemmas*; Detambel, *Les livres prennent soin de nous*; Gerk, *Lesen als Medizin*; Berthoud and Elderkin, *The Novel Cure*; Newman, *The Western Lit Survival Kit*; Schwalbe, *The End of Your Life Book Club*; Shields, *How Literature Saved My Life*; Golomb, *Petit guide de lectures qui aident à vivre*; Kästner, *Doktor Erich Kästners Lyrische Hausapotheke*.
3. Groskop, *The Anna Karenina Fix*; Sieghart, *The Poetry Pharmacy*; Sieghart, *The Poetry Pharmacy Returns*; Freeman, *The Reading Cure*; McGirr, *Books that Saved my Life*; Smyth, *All the Lives We Ever Lived*.
4. Campbell, *Weird Things Customers Say in Bookshops*; Campbell, *The Bookshop Book*; Borsuk, *The Book*; Price, *Unpacking my Library*; *The Book Lovers' Anthology*.
5. For a good survey of the history and theories of bibliotherapy, see the contributions to the first section of Sarah McNicol and Liz Brewster (eds), *Bibliotherapy*. An important recent survey of theoretical and empirical work on the relationship between books and issues of mental wellbeing can be found in Josie Billington (ed.), *Reading and Mental Health*.
6. Sweeney, *Reading Is My Window*, 278n52.
7. Quoted in Ouaknin, *Bibliothérapie*, 12.
8. Tukhareli, *Healing Through Books*.
9. Tukhareli, 'Bibliotherapy-based Wellness Program for Healthcare Providers', 44.

10. Stanley, *Reading to Heal*, 3. Andrea Gerk cites a German medical dictionary in defining bibliotherapy as 'Form der Psychotherapie, bei der der Pat. durch die Lektüre einer gezielten Auswahl geeigneter Literatur darin unterstützt werden soll, seine Probleme zu verbalisieren, klarer zu reflektieren u. evtl. Die Begrifflichkeit des Therapeuten besser zu verstehen.' ['Type of psychotherapy in which patients are prescribed a specific selection of literary sources, the reading of which is meant to support their attempts to articulate personal problems and reflect more clearly on them. A further intended outcome is the improved understanding of the therapist's practice.'] Gerk, *Lesen als Medizin*, 91, my translation.
11. Bonnet, *La bibliothérapie en médecine générale*, 20.
12. McChord Crothers, 'A Literary Clinic'.
13. McChord Crothers, 'A Literary Clinic', 291.
14. McChord Crothers, 'A Literary Clinic', 292.
15. McChord Crothers, 'A Literary Clinic', 292–3.
16. Sieghart, *The Poetry Pharmacy*, xvii.
17. Freeman, *The Reading Cure*, 14.
18. Ouaknin, *Bibliothérapie*, 11–17.
19. Ouaknin, *Bibliothérapie*, 12–13. See also Pietrobelli, 'Soigner par les lettres'.
20. Tukhareli, *Healing Through Books*, i.
21. Ferris, review of Don DeLillo, *Zero K*.
22. Jack, 'The Rise of the Medical Humanities'.
23. Paterson (ed.), *The Picador Book of Funeral Poems*, xiii.
24. Smyth, *All the Lives We Ever Lived*, 114.
25. Smyth, *All the Lives We Ever Lived*, 67.
26. Smyth, *All the Lives We Ever Lived*, 89.
27. Smyth, *All the Lives We Ever Lived*, 89.
28. Smyth, *All the Lives We Ever Lived*, 89.
29. Smyth, *All the Lives We Ever Lived*, 186.
30. Freeman, *The Reading Cure*, 29.
31. Freeman, *The Reading Cure*, 129.
32. Smyth, *All the Lives We Ever Lived*, 186–7.
33. Billington, *Is Literature Healthy?*, 105.
34. Berthoud and Elderkin, *The Novel Cure*, 2.
35. De Botton and Armstrong, *Art As Therapy*, 5.
36. Derrida, 'La pharmacie de Platon'.
37. Blumenberg, 'Trostbedürfnis und Untröstlichkeit des Menschen'.

Chapter 1

# The Classical Regime of Literary Comfort: From Homer to Aristotle

These then are the duties of comforters: to do away with distress root and branch, or allay it, or diminish it as far as possible, or stop its progress and not allow it to extend further, or to divert it elsewhere. There are some who think it the sole duty of a comforter to insist that the evil has no existence at all, as is the view of Cleanthes; some, like the Peripatetics, favour the lesson that the evil is not serious. Some again favour the withdrawal of attention from evil to good, as Epicurus does; some, like the Cyrenaics, think it enough to show that nothing unexpected has taken place. Chrysippus on the other hand considers that the main thing in giving comfort is to remove from the mind of the mourner the belief already described, in case he should think he is discharging a regular duty which is obligatory. There are some too in favour of concentrating all these ways of administering comfort (for one man is influenced in one way, one in another) pretty nearly as in my Consolation I threw them all into one attempt at consolation; for my soul was in a feverish state and I attempted every means of curing its condition.
Cicero, Tusculan Disputations[1]

## Mendelsohn and Manguel on the Comforts of Reading Homer

Daniel Mendelsohn's *An Odyssey* (2017) is a title that I did not list in the opening pages of the introduction. Still, the book definitely belongs among the bibliotherapeutic reading memoirs on my desk.[2] The work's subtitle – *A Father, a Son and an Epic* – does a good job at indicating what Mendelsohn's book is about: it presents the author and his father who are reading and exploring Homer's *Odyssey*, thinking about the relevance of this centuries-old text to their respective lives, as fathers as well as sons. In what turned out to be, unfortunately, the last year of his life, Mendelsohn's father, a retired mathematician, asked if he could sit in on the undergraduate Homer seminar that his son was teaching at Bard College. An 81-year-old among freshmen, Mendelsohn's father proved an entertaining yet slightly domineering presence in the course of the sixteen weeks that the seminar ran, between late January and early May 2011.

After the seminar had ended, the Mendelsohns continued their joint exploration of Homer's text, as they went on a Mediterranean cruise ('Retracing the *Odyssey*') that in the course of ten days took its participants to several of the places Ulysses landed on during his journey of a decade between Troy and Ithaca. Interweaving scenes from the Bard classroom with scenes aboard the cruise ship, Mendelsohn's memoir keeps a steady eye on the elucidation of Homer's text, the epic that starts off, as the author reminds us in one of the first pages of his book, as the story of 'a son gone in search of an absent parent'.[3] From the book's very beginning, Mendelsohn's reader is made aware that the story does not end well at all for the author's father. Not too long after the end of the cruise, the old man is the victim of an unspectacular but nevertheless fatal fall in the parking lot of a California supermarket where he is shopping for a Thanksgiving meal. The fall leads to several complications that result in a massive stroke, about a year after the beginning of the seminar that started off the story.

In more than one way, Daniel Mendelsohn's book is a touching elegy for his father. As such, it also reflects, on several occasions, on the healing potential of literary writings, Homer's in particular. Let me pick out one example among many. About halfway through the book, Mendelsohn recalls a memorable conversation that he had on the cruise ship with an elderly Flemish man, who was accompanied on this journey by his daughter. Noticing a distinct scar on his leg (indeed, like Ulysses himself!), Mendelsohn thinks that the old man must be a war victim. He soon finds out, though, that the scar was not the result of any heroic military exploit. It was caused by a deep cut from an axe while chopping wood as a teenager. When, as a result, he fell seriously ill during the final winter of the war, the man's private tutor read to him the *Odyssey* in Greek. As the old man tells Mendelsohn, more than sixty years after the events:

> He read to me the *Odyssey* in Greek! He spoke to me in Latin! He was reciting the Classics all the time, just to have the sound in my head. I should say that I understood a good bit, since I had been studying classical languages with him already for two years. And I think that hearing that sound, the sound of a human voice reciting poetry, helped me to heal. Yes, I do think that is true. So I feel in some way the *Odyssey* saved my life.[4]

The anecdote – including the old man's final words that embody its message for Mendelsohn most centrally – not only stands as a testimony to the lasting impression that the Homeric epic may have on its readers, but also of the conviction – intuitive though it may be – that is the focal point of this study.

Before we move on to a more thorough exploration of the Homeric text in light of that central conviction, I want to present, briefly, a second anecdote that may help us on our way. This one is taken from Alberto Manguel's 'Biography' of the *Iliad* and the *Odyssey* that was published in the series 'Books that Shook the World'.[5] In the book's introduction, Manguel lists a number of indications of Homer's lasting appeal. As he sees it, that appeal must be mainly due to the fact that the Ancient Greek epics represent universal and timeless emotions. In doing so, it is inevitable that these texts continue to speak to us, Manguel claims, however unclear our relationship to them may feel. 'Achilles' anger or Ulysses' longing will somehow succeed in moving us,' Manguel writes, 'reminding us of our own endeavours, touching something in us that is not just our own but mysteriously common to humankind.'[6]

To illustrate this sense of a deeper universality, Manguel offers the story of an initiative, taken by the Colombian Ministry of Education, of a system of travelling libraries meant for inhabitants of faraway, mainly rural regions. On a regular basis, books of different sorts ('technical works, agricultural handbooks, collections of sewing patterns and the like, but a few literary works were also included'[7]) were being sent to numerous small villages, where their distribution was overseen by a local 'librarian'. After a few weeks, the books were generally duly returned. There was one memorable occasion, though, where the villagers refused to return a book they had been given: a Spanish translation of the *Iliad*. The Ministry in the end allowed the villagers to keep the book, but they were keen to find out why they considered that specific book so very special. In the words of one of the local librarians that Manguel quotes: 'Homer's story reflected their own: it told of a war-torn country, in which mad gods mix with men and women who never know exactly what the fighting is about, or when they will be happy, or why they will be killed.'[8] Clearly, the Colombian peasants recognised themselves in the stories of the Ancient Greeks, which they apparently also saw as some sort of moral beacon in times of uncertainty and potential meaninglessness. Homer's epic gave them the feeling that literature often seems to give to readers who feel comforted by the words of authors or fictional characters: 'we are not alone'. As Manguel puts it in his tentative conclusion of this anecdote: 'To Achilles, and perhaps to Priam, and perhaps to their readers in the Colombian sierra, this is consolation.'[9]

## Comforted by the Enemy: *Iliad* 24

Manguel invokes the story of the Colombian villagers by way of an introduction to the famous consolatory scene that dominates the closing book of the *Iliad*. I want to begin my analysis of the historical foundations of the topos of 'literary comfort' with a discussion of that memorable encounter. To be sure, Homer's epics contain plenty of scenes in which clearly recognisable acts of comfort are being performed and true words of consolation spoken. In his early reflection on Homer's rhetorical qualities, Quintilian (1st century AD) pointed out that his mastery not only shows in passages in which characters receive verbal applause or counsel, but also in monologues that are meant to bring comfort. '[Homer's] eloquence', Quintilian writes in the tenth book of his *Institutio Oratoria*, 'shows in praise, exhortation, and consolation'.[10]

Still, the most touching of Homer's scenes of comfort (as Manguel seems to agree, writing '[i]t is one of the most moving, most powerful scenes I know'[11]) is no doubt the one that dominates the very last book of the *Iliad*, Book 24. The scene, as one may recall, stages an unexpectedly serene confrontation between Achilles, the epic's Greek warrior-hero, and the Trojan king Priam, whose son, Hector, Achilles killed in the course of the events narrated in the *Iliad*'s Book 22.[12] Quintilian was a great admirer of the scene, as the remainder of the passage from the *Institutio Oratoria* that I just quoted shows: 'as for perorations', he wonders (the question is a rhetorical one, obviously), 'what can ever be equal to the prayers which Priam addresses to Achilles when he comes to beg for the body of his son?'[13] Indeed, judging by the logic of the epic's preceding events, the scene's two protagonists ought to be each other's worst enemies. But here, at the end of the classic war story that continues to pitch Greeks and Trojans against each other, their final encounter shows them in a different state of mind, one in which they manage to treat each other with the greatest mutual respect – the sort of respect that true acts of consolation would appear to require.

The consolation that Achilles has on offer for Priam in this moving scene results from the only possible insight which the bringer of comfort can be expected to have: the suffering of the person in need of comfort has to be treated with the utmost respect. In a modern interpretation of the phenomenon, the pain of the one in need of comfort has to be understood for what it is and treated as such. Ancient Greek ideas of consolation are not entirely compatible with our contemporary view on the subject, as we will soon see, but this is not where the difference lies.

By granting his enemy the right to be comforted, Achilles will have been seen by the earliest generations of Homer's readership to behave like a friend rather than an adversary. Interestingly, in the definition that he gives of friendship in Book 9 of the *Nicomachean Ethics*, Aristotle draws a connection between the tasks of friends and those of comforters: 'for a friend, if tactful, can comfort us with look and word', Aristotle writes, 'as he knows our characters and what things give us pleasure and pain'.[14]

The scene of comfort starts when Priam enters Achilles' tent (lines 471–2 of Book 24). Achilles has just finished his meal: he is sitting alone by himself, even though he is being attended by two of his company, Automedon and Alkimos. The text identifies them as 'those whom Achilles / most honored of all his comrades now Patroklos was dead' (lines 574–5).[15] Priam has brought a ransom to his enemy in order to reclaim the body of his son, Hector. The Trojan king wants to bury his son honourably, in accordance with his people's traditional rites. Hector's death resulted from the obsessive feelings of revenge that in Book 16 of the *Iliad* begin to function as the central impetus behind Homer's narrative: Hector had to pay with his life because he had single-handedly killed the person dearest to Achilles' heart.

Before we can move on to the actual scene of comfort that takes up the second half of the *Iliad*'s final book, we need to have a closer look at how Homer prepares for it in the book's opening section. The first lines of Book 24 give us a clear idea of the very depth of Achilles' feelings of revenge against the murderer of his beloved Patroklos. The narrator begins by stressing Achilles' protracted sadness at his great loss ('Achilles wept and wept, / thinking of his dear comrade, so that sleep the all-subduing / got no hold of him' (3–5)) and then relates how he maims Hector's corpse, dragging it behind his chariot and circling the mound of Patroklos' grave no less than three times. Achilles' cruel behaviour immediately provokes feelings of pity among the gods, especially in Apollo, who stresses the importance of a proper burial and argues that the bodily remains of the Trojan prince need to be protected 'from all unseemly decay / even in death' (19–20). Some of the other gods follow suit and suggest that Hermes 'steal the corpse' (24) so as to protect it from further defamation. But Hera, Poseidon and Athena, driven by an ancient hatred 'for sacred Ilion' (Homer's name for Troy), seem to veto the plan.

It is their protest that causes Apollo to speak out in the clearest of terms against 'the ruthless Achilles' (39). Apollo is appalled by the fact that some of his fellow gods want to defend the vindictive Greek warrior. Clearly, Apollo states, Achilles' 'mind's out of proper order and the will in his breast / inflexible – his nature's turned savage' (40–1). Achilles cannot contain himself, Apollo points out: he 'has lost all pity, and has no respect in him' (43). Men who have lost someone dear to them, he argues, ought to bury together with the body of their departed the tears that are merely the outward signs of their sadness. Achilles, in other words, should have stopped all wailing once he had given Patroklos his final resting place – 'for it's an enduring heart the Fates have given to mortals' (49).

Apollo's stern admonition is immediately countered by Hera, who accuses the god of poetry and light of lacking in respect for Achilles. The mortal hero is, after all, the son of a goddess, a daughter of Hera's moreover. The quarrel among the two gods is brought to an end by Zeus, who decides against the stealing of Hector's corpse. Instead, he sends for Achilles' mother, the sea-goddess Thetis, who is urged to convince her son that he needs to accept the ransom Priam is about to bring in exchange for Hector's body. The three-hundred lines that follow and that separate us from the actual scene of comfort serve as a preparation for the meeting of Priam and Achilles. First, the narrator makes clear how Thetis manages to convince Achilles of doing what Zeus has demanded from her and then he goes on to show how Priam, protected in his turn by the god Hermes, succeeds in stealing his way into the heart of the Greek enemy camp.

## *Eleos* and the Distance of Consolation

Homer's original audience will have had no difficulty in recognising the central message that the opening section of the *Iliad*'s closing book wants to convey. Time and again, we are reminded in the epic that whatever happens in the realm of the mortals should be seen as the outcome of some or other divine design. That central idea, as we will soon see, is also the basis of the consolatory arguments that Priam will hear later in the scene. As Achilles reminds him, there is no use in continuing to mourn what the gods have decided must happen.

Clearly, Achilles is slightly taken aback when he sees the old king of Troy enter his tent. Even though his mother had warned him about his enemy's imminent arrival, Priam's entry still strikes Achilles with surprise. Achilles' feelings are the subject of one of the epic's memorable Homeric comparisons: 'As when blind delusion possesses a man to murder / someone in his own country, and he flees to an alien people, / to some wealthy man's house, and wonder grips those who see him – / so Achilles was amazed at the sight of godlike Priam' (480–3). As soon as he has entered Achilles' tent, Priam kneels down in front of his enemy, the murderer of his son, no less. To reveal the state of mind in which he has come, he embraces Achilles' knees while kissing, in the words of the narrator, 'those terrible / murderous hands, that had killed so many of his sons' (478–9).[16]

To the self-evident gesture of his submission Priam adds a supplication that does not fail to move Achilles. He begins by begging the Greek warrior to call to mind his own father. The intended analogy is unmistakable: like the king of Troy, Achilles' father too is 'on old age's deathly threshold', as Priam puts it with reference to himself (487). To Priam, that is also where the analogy stops. Unlike the king of Troy, Achilles' father still has good hopes of welcoming the safe return of his son. Priam had no less than fifty sons, the text says, but most of these 'had their limbs unstrung by impetuous Ares', the merciless god of war (497). Now that Achilles has killed '[t]he one / true son I had left me to guard the city and its people' (498–9), Priam confesses to be beyond despair. 'Revere the gods, Achilles', he implores,

and to me show pity,
remembering your own father: but I'm the more pitiable,
for I've borne what no other mortal on earth has yet endured:
I've brought to my lips the hand of the man who killed my son.
(503–6)[17]

Priam's words are obviously meant to provoke pity, and judging by the description that we get of Achilles' response they seem not to miss their effect. 'So saying, he stirred in Achilles the urge to weep for his father' (507), as Homer's narrator puts it, in lines that give us more insight into the subtle workings of the psychological mechanism which the ancient Greeks labelled 'eleos', a state of mind to which the text refers explicitly: 'Revere the gods, Achilles, and to me show *pity*' (503, italics mine). It is important to note that the tears Achilles sheds in this passage are not the immediate consequence of any feelings that he has for Priam's fate. Achilles is crying because he is thinking of another old man, his own father, whom he has reason to believe will never see his son alive again.

The remainder of the passage that describes the effect of Priam's words confirms the distance between the two protagonists of the scene of comfort. Both men are crying together, sure, but they are not shedding tears of solidarity: their tears are not the outcome of a shared feeling, let alone a mutual one. *Eleos*, Aristotle writes in his famous discussion of the concept in the second book of his *Rhetoric*, '[is] a kind of pain excited by the sight of evil, deadly or painful, which befalls one who does not deserve it; an evil which one might expect to come upon himself or one of his friends, and when it seems near.'[18] As David Konstan has convincingly shown, *eleos* is not the exact same thing that in the modern Western world (since the start of the eighteenth century, say) came to be known as 'sympathy' or 'compassion', literally 'feeling something together'. The connotation of the Greek term is different, opposite even to a certain extent. '[T]o experience pity', Konstan writes, 'one has to recognize a resemblance with the sufferer, but at the same time not find oneself in precisely the same circumstances. Where complete identification occurs, one shares the emotion of the other, and that is not pity as the Greeks conceived it'.[19]

Konstan's description matches what we see in the following passage, where the distance between Achilles and Priam is made emphatically clear:

> he [Achilles] took the old man by the hand, gently pushed him away.
> Both had their memories: Priam of Hektor, killer of men,
> as, bitterly weeping, he crouched at Achilles' feet,
> while Achilles wept, now for his own father, now again
> for Patroklos: their joint mourning resounded throughout the hut.
>     (508–12)

At this moment in the text, it would be hard to see in the encounter between Achilles and Priam genuine compassion in the contemporary, modern sense of the word. Achilles, after all, pushes Priam away – 'gently', but still[20] – and the two mourn their dead separately, each struck by their own singular grief, without attention for the grief of the other. Still, the remainder of the passage makes clear that Priam's request for *eleos* does not remain unanswered. As soon as Achilles has dried his eyes, he lends his enemy a supportive hand:

> But as soon as noble Achilles had had his fill of weeping,
> and the urge for it had departed from his heart and limbs,
> he rose from his chair, took the old man by the hand,
> and raised him up, pitying his grey hair, his grey beard. (513–16)

We are given a good idea of Achilles' feelings in the text's subtle reference to the grey hair and beard that Priam no doubt shares with Achilles' own father. 'Priam's speech makes Achilles think of his own father and so enables him to feel pity for the Trojan father too', C. W. MacLeod writes in his insightful commentary to the *Iliad*'s closing book.[21] The causality that is implied in MacLeod's claim ('so') suggests that Achilles' pity derives from the recognition of the pain of the other in his own pain. He can only feel for Priam when he experiences the old man's grief as something that touches him personally, that is: as something that could easily happen to him.

To be clear, I am not so much concerned with the exact definition of 'eleos' as a concept in its own right. What interests me, here, is the relationship that we can see at work between this Greek notion of 'pity' and the practice of consolation. Achilles needs to become pitiful, the scene suggests at this point, in order to be able to offer words and gestures of consolation. The newly acquired insight in the pain of his enemy – '[pity] is not only an emotion, but an insight', MacLeod writes[22] – makes possible the words of comfort that Achilles begins to address to Priam at that very moment in the scene. The insight, as we will continue to see, is the result of a cognitive process of likeness and difference. Achilles is able to comfort Priam because he understands the old man's grief in relation (analogical and differential) to his own.

## Consolatory Discourse

Achilles' words prefigure a discourse that begins to consolidate several centuries after the formation of Homer's epic: the so-called *logos paramuthètikos*, the philosophical discourse of consolation that brings together a series of arguments that those who have been afflicted with considerable sadness can use in order to arrive at a new perspective that alleviates or even drives away that sadness. As we will soon see, Ancient Greek reflections on consolation are founded on an appeal to reason and with it on resistance to the destructive force of immoderate emotions. Those who are overpowered by grief need to be brought back to reason: that seems to be the guiding principle shared by the different philosophical 'schools' that will later be distinguished in what I am calling here the 'ancient regime of consolation'.

As I have said, Homer's text precedes the development of this philosophy of comfort by several centuries. Still, both the *Iliad* and the *Odyssey* offer telling examples of different ideas regarding the alleviation of suffering, several of which, in fact, return in various 'consolatory' writings of the classical period. To give just one example: the scene of comfort that we are discussing here feeds the claim by the author of the first-century 'Consolatio ad Apollonium' that Homer was 'extraordinarily successful in bestowing consolation'.[23] In the present scene, Achilles' words of comfort, as we will see, contain an admonition for Priam to return to a reasonable and therefore commonly accepted perspective. The central argument of Achilles' consolatory logic is that Priam should accept the tragic fate that the gods hold in store for him. Not only should he understand that his grief will not cause the gods to change their decision regarding his fate, he ought to see, moreover, that what happens to him is potentially the fate of every mortal being. Clearly, Achilles is also speaking for himself as he begins to rationalise the need to bring to an end feelings of grief. He is comforting himself as well as Priam, as we can sense from the plural possessive pronouns that dominate the first two of the following lines:

> Come then sit down on this chair, and let's allow our distress
> to lie at rest in our hearts, for all our grieving,
> for there's no profit accrues from numbing lamentation:
> that's how the gods spun life's thread for unhappy mortals –
> to live amid sorrow, while they themselves are uncaring.
> There are two great jars, sunk down in the floor of Zeus' abode,
> Full of gifts he hands out, one of ills, the other of blessings;
> (522–8)

Like most people, we should at least consider ourselves partly fortunate, Achilles argues, if only because Zeus does not continue to plague us with strokes of bad fortune. Priam and Achilles' father also belong to this category of the semi-fortunate. Even though the war between them inevitably brought them their share of grief, they were both blessed with the riches of material and spiritual possessions. Achilles' comparison between the two elderly fathers supports MacLeod's interpretation of the special form of solidarity that underlies the feeling of *eleos*. While Achilles is not explicit on this subject in this scene, it becomes clear at other places in the *Iliad* that, like Priam, Peleus will also lose his son to the god of war. The grief of Hector's father, then, enables Achilles to prefigure the sadness that will no doubt strike his own father at the trying time when he will hear of his son's death. The comforting reassurance that Achilles offers Priam, then, is grounded in his personal experience.

Moreover, he himself has learned from Patroklos' death – and from his own difficult dealing with that loss – that it makes no sense to continue the mourning of a loved one. The injunction to Priam that is central to his consoling words is also valid for Achilles himself:

> Bear up then, don't nurse unending grief in your heart:
> You'll gain nothing by mourning your son, you won't
> bring him back to life; before that you'll have other troubles.
> (549–51)

Priam's reaction does not immediately make clear whether or not Achilles' words of comfort actually result in the alleviation of his grief. His main concern seems to be the fast retrieval of his son's corpse, in exchange for 'the very great ransom' (556) that he has brought. Achilles, in turn, suddenly becomes upset by what he experiences as Priam's inappropriate impatience, which he takes as nothing less than a provocation (561). 'Stop working on my emotions amid my sorrows' (568), he exclaims, even threatening, against the will of the gods, to kill the old man ('lest I might not spare even you, while you're here in my hut' (569)). Achilles points out to Priam that he knows very well that the gods are behind his visit (how else would he have been able to enter his enemy's tent without being stopped?) and that the divine design is the reason why he agreed to return Hector's body in the first place. Together with Alkimos and Automedon he leaves his tent in order to unload from Priam's 'smooth-running wagon (. . .) the boundless ransom for Hektor's head' (578–9). Single-handedly he places Priam's washed and anointed body on a bier 'which he and his comrades lifted onto the polished wagon' (590). Upon this final gesture, he addresses the ghost of Patroklos:

> Don't be angry with me, Patroklos, if you chance to hear,
> even in Hades' realm, that I've given back noble Hektor
> to his dear father: the ransom he offered was not unfitting –
> and of this I'll allot to you all that's your proper due. (592–5)

In the meantime, though, we have not yet arrived at the end of our scene of comfort. As soon as he re-enters his tent, Achilles invites Priam, who has been waiting all along, to a meal of bread and roasted lamb. To describe that meal as comfort food is more than a mere *jeu de mot*, as it sets the stage for a second movement in the consolation speech that Achilles delivers in the *Iliad*'s closing book.

'[F]or now let's turn to supper' (601), the Greek warrior suggests to his enemy turned guest, calling to memory the story of Niobe. This mythological figure, inconsolable icon of parental grief, lost her twelve children to the revenge of the gods, as Achilles reminds Priam. Boasting a rich offspring of six sons and six daughters, Niobe considered herself better off than Leto, Zeus' wife, who was only mother of two, Apollo and Artemis. When after ten days the gods finally decide to bury her twelve children, Achilles says, 'Niobe's mind turned to food, since she'd tired of weeping' (613).[24] The analogy is more than clear: Hector's corpse has also remained unburied for some time and, as with Niobe's children, the burial of Priam's son will likewise be the result of interference of the gods. Still, the comparison also contains a warning that turns Achilles' classical consolatory rhetoric into the injunction that it is: Priam should be careful not to become like Niobe, inconsolable, an unquenchable source of tears, paragon of emotional and hence female behaviour. The time for more tears will come later, Achilles concludes, but first he and Priam must eat:

> So come, let the two of us likewise, noble old sir, take thought
> for food: after that you can mourn your dear son, when
> you've returned him to Ilion: much wept over he will be. (618–20)

In the second 'act' of this marvellous scene of comfort, the text does point out the effect that Achilles' consolatory speech has on Priam, leaving open the suggestion that the words' outcome may also be due to the food and wine to which the king of Troy is being treated. As the narrator puts it:

> but when they'd satisfied their desire for food and drink,
> then Priam, scion of Dardanos, gazed in wonder at Achilles,
> his stature and beauty, how like the gods he appeared;
> while at Priam, scion of Dardanos, Achilles gazed in wonder,
> observing his noble features, listening as he spoke. (628–32)

In this new and shared state of mind Achilles commits to a truce of twelve days, so as to allow Priam to honour his son with the usual burial rites. On the tenth day, Hector will be interred, and on the eleventh day a mound will be raised over his grave. The closing lines of the *Iliad* indicate that Achilles keeps to his promise. The Trojan ritual of mourning is described in great detail in the hundred or so closing lines of the *Iliad*'s Book 24, culminating in the very one on which the great epic ends: 'Such were the funeral rites for Hector, breaker of horses' (804).

## The Triumph of Comfort: The Classical Regime of Consolation

The two enemies are eating in silence, shared solitary sadness and mutual respect. '[T]hat exchange of admiring looks is the *Iliad*'s triumph', Adam Nicolson writes.[25] It is also the triumph of comfort, I would add, of literary comfort even. After all, Achilles' effort to console takes the shape of a story, the story of Niobe, an imaginary construct that calls upon Priam to reflect simultaneously on the ways in which it is his story and the ways in which it is not. As we will see later in this book, the consolatory force of literary writings is often related to the fictionality of their narratives. The two components of that conjunction (fictionality and narrativity) are equally important in that they create an imaginative space for the reader that leaves room for identification ('I am like Niobe') and distance ('I am not Niobe'), while at the same representing events that imply and involve change. The idea of consolation, whether in its classical, Christian or more contemporary guise, as we will see, rests upon the possibility that things can be or become different – in whatever direction: the idea that things will get better can be a source of comfort, as can the idea that things could be worse. Either way, the imaginary space that we require to be comforted owes some of its working potential to the awareness of development, that is, plot.

Having read, in class, the scene of comfort between Achilles and Priam, and having explained how it works within the context of what in the remainder of this chapter I will be calling the classical regime of consolation, my students confirmed my own intuition that even from a contemporary perspective on consolation we could easily take Achilles' rhetoric as comforting. A brief comparison of Homer's original scene with its heavily truncated counterpart in Wolfgang Petersen's *Troy* (2004) even heightened our response to the comforting potential of the touching encounter between Achilles and Priam in the grand finale of the *Iliad*. In Petersen's movie, the Greek hero (Brad Pitt) and the Trojan king (Peter O'Toole) remain enemies throughout: they continue to keep their guard in each other's presence. In *Troy*, the scene is not at all one of comfort: Achilles' consolatory speech has been cut, for the most part, and throughout the scene, the two characters keep their cool distance. There is no solidarity whatsoever between them; hence, there can be no comfort.[26]

What, then, can Homer's original scene teach us about the two phenomena that will continue to occupy us in the remainder of this book? And how can it help us to arrive at a deeper understanding of the historically determined conjunction between literature and consolation that is its central focus? Firstly, what does the conversation between Achilles and Priam tell us about how Homer's contemporaries regarded man's potential to console and be consoled, a human trait which we no doubt recognise intuitively in this touching scene, but whose pragmatics clearly cannot be straightforwardly interpreted in the conceptual framework of comfort that we are used to in the early twenty-first century? 'The human response to death and bereavement may well be a universally experienced emotion', Han Baltussen rightly claims, 'but it is always firmly embedded in a particular time and culture'[27]. Obviously, the same remark can be made with respect to our other central concept, literature. Yoking together our two concepts, the second question that confronts us is predictably clear: in what way does Homer's dramatisation of the encounter between the old Trojan king and the murderer of his son exemplify the idea that a literary text can have a healing, consolatory effect?

Let us begin with the former question. Consolation, in the Homeric scene, is clearly a matter of exhortation in the shape of rational arguments. It comes in the shape of a call to see things not emotionally (not through tears, that is), but in the revealing light of the *common sense* truth of human mortality, the fate that all mortal beings share and that distinguishes them from the gods. The occasion of your suffering, the comforting Achilles urges Priam to see, is something that *has* to happen: it is inevitable, it awaits us all. However unexpected death may be, its arrival is something we need to be (more) aware of, if only because that awareness will protect us, to some extent at least, against the pain that without it threatens to overpower us.

Without wanting to describe in great detail the history of classical thinking on consolation, I think it may be worthwhile to give a brief outline of how that thinking developed in the course of the Greek and Roman eras. After all, its development shaped our ideas of the conjunction between literature and consolation in decisive ways.[28] The starting point of my take on this first stage in the historical trajectory of the critical topos of literary comfort is the following: while the question of consolation (what it is and does and how it works) starts out as a literary theme – not only in Homer, as we will see later, but also in the poetic tradition centring on the figure of Orpheus – it does end up quite quickly as a philosophical issue, an issue, that is, most sensibly dealt with in philosophical writings proper. The move of 'consolation' from literature to philosophy, so to speak, coincides roughly with the rise of what Plato famously called 'the ancient quarrel between poetry and philosophy', a quarrel in which literature (poetry) and philosophy were pitched against each other. The outcome of the quarrel, for Plato at least, was that poetry should be treated with caution and suspicion. It could no longer be seen as a source of true knowledge – of true consolation, that is. I will deal with Plato's views shortly, but first we need to get a better grip on the philosophical treatment of consolation in Greece during the classical period.

In the centuries that follow Homer's literary treatment of it, the rhetoric of consolation gradually becomes part of what Paul Holloway labels the 'systematic' analysis of the philosophical reflection on death in Ancient Greece.[29] In the transition from the fifth to the fourth century BCE, a number of philosophical writings began to appear which focused centrally on the topic, while at the same time offering techniques and arguments to bring consolation to those in need. Even though it is difficult to define and delimit the 'genre' of classical consolatory writing as such,[30] the large majority of the texts at hand, as one useful definition has it, 'are writings of a philosophic bent, whose authors either try to dissuade individuals from grieving in the pace of misfortune, or proffer general counsel on overcoming adversity'.[31] The 'philosophical bent' of these consolatory writings is what concerns me here, and its character is diverse, as the definition goes on to show. Each of the different 'schools' that make up the heterogeneous landscape of Greek philosophy at the time introduces its own arguments, the same definition further makes clear:

> the Peripatos with the concept of 'moderate sorrow' or *metriopatheia*; the Academy with the reflection that death released the soul of earthly care and led it to a better life; Epicureanism with its methods of distraction (*avocatio*) and the recalling (*revocatio*) of pleasing aspects and activities (. . .); the Stoa particularly with the ideal of freedom from the affects (*apatheia*) and the scorning of *fortuita*, the workings of chance, as irrelevant to happiness; the Cyrenaics and others with the recommendation of *praemeditatio malorum*, the imagined anticipation of evil, to ward off unexpected blows of fate.[32]

Within the broad domain of (moral) philosophy, then, a separate genre began to develop, the so-called *logos paramuthètikos*[33] or *consolatio* in Cicero's Latin. The oldest representative text that we have (in fragmented form, at least) is a treatise written by Crantor of Soli (c. 335–c. 275 BCE): 'Peri penthous', 'On Mourning'.[34] The author was a pupil of Xenocrates, who in turn was a student of Plato, and the third *scholarch* of the Athenian Academy.[35] Judging by the discussion of Crantor in the *Lives* of Diogenes Laertius, the author of 'Peri penthous' can be situated in the same philosophical context.[36] His text was meant to console a certain Hippocles at the loss of his children. Crantor's letter of consolation owes its renown mainly to Cicero, who in his *Academica Priora* refers to it as a 'truly golden book'.[37]

The key contribution of Crantor's text lies in its response to the conviction of certain representatives of the Stoa (Cleanthes and Chrysippus are the most important names for us) that whenever we feel struck by sadness or pain we need above all to suppress the emotional expression of that pain. Against the Stoic ideal of *apatheia*, which calls for the rigorous suppression of our emotions, Crantor holds a plea for what he sees as a desirable moderation of them, a so-called *metriopatheia*. Obviously, Crantor does not want us to give in fully to our emotions (that would show little sense), but neither does he want us to suppress them altogether. To mourn is not a bad thing in itself, Crantor believes, but it needs to be done with moderation, for reasons which the scene between Achilles and Priam already shows in the example of Niobe: an excessive expression of one's feelings is counter-productive.

In the pages of the third book of his *Tusculanae Disputationes* that are devoted to the different schools in the Greek philosophy of comfort, Cicero quotes from Crantor's text in a way that shows his clear sympathy with the ideas of the author of the 'Peri penthous'. However eclectic Cicero's own ideas of consolation may be, the road of *apatheia* is clearly not the one he wants to follow:

> I do not in the least agree with those who are so loud in their praise of that sort of insensibility which neither can nor ought to exist. Let me escape illness: should I be ill, let me have the capacity for feeling I previously possessed, whether it be knife or forceps that be applied to my body. For this state of apathy is not attained except at the cost of brutishness in the soul and callousness in the body.[38]

Cicero himself played a central role in the tradition of the consolatory genre, not only on account of his survey of that tradition in the *Tusculanae Disputationes*, but also as the author of a *Consolatio* which he wrote in order to console himself at the loss of his daughter, Tullia. The text, now largely lost, was written in 45 BCE (Tullia's death occurred in February of the same year) and it gives us a better idea, as Han Baltussen argues, of the private aspects of Cicero's dealing with grief. Most classical *consolationes* are centrally marked by societal (i.e. public) concerns, which are clearly ethical: they show us how a person in grief is expected to behave, and they pay little or no attention to the difficulty that individual mourners may have to grieve successfully.[39] This is, indeed, as we will see, one of the big differences between our modern ideas of consolation and the classical and Christian traditions. In the former, consolation is primarily defined as a matter of the individual – singularly so, even – whereas in the latter traditions the task of the comforter is defined as a common cause, one in which the grieving individual needs to be reminded of a number of social and collective expectations.

After Cicero, the tradition of the Greek consolatory rhetoric was continued in the Roman period by Seneca (c. 4 BCE–CE 65), author of three surviving *consolationes* that are quoted time and again in writings on the topic,[40] and by the Greek philosopher Plutarchus (c. CE 46–120), who wrote a touching consolatory letter to his wife upon the death of their little daughter. For a long time, Plutarch was also considered to be the writer of the 'Consolatio ad Apollonium' to which I referred earlier. That text also borrows heavily from Crantor.[41] A somewhat particular position in the tradition is occupied by Lucian (c. CE 120–180), whose 'On Mourning' shares its (Greek) title with Crantor's treatise. Lucian's text is a smart parody of the genre, a 'half-serious, half-comic spoof on consolatory literature', as David Konstan puts it, in which a dead son rebukes his father for harassing him with his useless wails of grief.[42]

## Classical versus Modern Ideas of Consolation

If I have limited myself in this brief survey to the best known and most quoted names and titles (several of which will return later in this book), it is because most of these writings remain important at least until the early modern period. Also, for a good understanding of the historical background of our ideas on literary consolation, it is not so much the specific differences between various 'schools' in the classical regime that are of importance but what seems to be a common ground between them. However diverse the corpus of classical *consolationes* may be, in each of the texts belonging to it the practice of consolation involves, in the words of Holloway, 'the combating of grief through rational argument'.[43]

There lies another important difference between classical and current ideas of the practice and rhetoric of consolation. While nowadays we take it for granted that in order to console someone we need the right amount of emotional intelligence to arrive at a proper understanding of the pain of the person we are trying to comfort, in the classical period consolation is primarily seen as a matter of what Plato calls the rational part of our soul. The pain of the other does not have to be shared or felt; it has to be (largely) removed, on the basis of arguments that are tested on their logical value, not their emotional appeal.

This does not mean, as we have seen, that the emotions are entirely absent in the classical discourse of comfort. On the contrary, their role is a crucial point of discussion among the representatives of several philosophical schools. The most extreme position, from a modern perspective at least, is taken up by the members of the Stoa, for whom the final aim of philosophical reflection has to be a purely rational state of mind in which, as we have also seen, the emotions are to be fully eradicated. In this consolatory logic, a person who brings comfort has to try to drive away the pain of the one who is being comforted, by pointing out, for instance, that the pain is an evil that has to be avoided at all costs, or that it is not real, a mere illusion. Whenever we find ourselves in an emotional status (*pathos*), the Stoics argue, we threaten to become stuck in fear and that, according to them, is by definition a bad thing. To bring comfort, in this perspective, involves a prompt and firm call to reason and to the ideal of constancy that is allied to rational behaviour. To stand firm, and not allow oneself to be touched by the whims of Fortune, this is what the Stoics strive for.

However, if our sadness is caused by the death of a loved one, as Cicero's example also shows, it may be difficult if not impossible to keep to the hard Stoical approach.[44] In these circumstances, the more moderate approach of Crantor that allows for at least some degree of emotionality makes more sense, just like the ideas of the Peripatetics, whose reflections on comfort are equally targeted on *metriopatheia* but whose ideas Cicero seems less convinced by in this respect.[45] For our purposes, however, the common core of these classical reflections on consolation is of greater importance than the differences which Cicero singles in his discussion of the different groups in the third book of the *Tusculan Disputations*.

Apart from the strong rational appeal for which classical practices of comfort aim – 'Ancient consolers (...) understood their primary task to be not one of sharing in the grief of others, but one of removing that grief by rational argument and frank exhortation.'[46] – Greek and Roman consolations bear witness to a strong conviction of the self-evident success of these practices. The two ideas are clearly linked: the effectiveness of practices of comfort is the outcome of their rational foundation in the so-called *sensus communis*:

rational thoughts are thoughts that are shared by all rational beings, and those who don't share them cannot be seen (if only for the time being) as rational. Put differently: if the person in need of comfort manages to find the rational perspective on offer, they will find the right way (i.e. the wise way) to deal with (the causes of) their distress. Words of comfort are meant to bring us to that perspective; they guide us on the path to wisdom. Whoever fails to accept these words, for whatever reason, cannot be considered wise.

The thinking that underlies the classical reflections on consolation hardly leaves any room for the idea that the practice of comfort and the rhetoric that is coupled to it might turn out to be *not* successful. Obviously, this does not mean that every attempt to console was by definition successful in Antiquity. What it does mean is that in the numerous *consolationes* dating from that long period little to no attention is paid to the possibility that words of comfort could miss the desired effect. Related to this, it is striking that in these texts there is hardly any attention given to the perspective of the person in need of comfort. Again, this makes sense: in the end, the person being comforted needs to see things in the same comforting way as the person offering consolation. The one being comforted needs to adapt to the common-sensical perspective of the comforter. Consolatory writings, like Cicero's *Consolatio*, in which the comforter and the person being comforted are one and the same, confirm this structural pattern: classical consolations are in essence monologues of comforters in which a series of arguments are on offer that are ultimately taken to be proofs of conviction. The monological nature of these writings goes to show that it is taken for granted in them that the perspective on offer will be adopted by the listener or addressee who is in need of comfort. When authors like Cicero, Seneca, Plutarch and later Boethius write about consolation, their view on the matter presupposes that there is no need at all to actually doubt the success of the logic of comfort. After all, in their view, to offer consolation entails an appeal to reason, and reason is always self-evidently correct – if reason fails, it is not reason itself that is failing, but the person who fails to adopt a rational perspective.

The same goes for consolation, one could say: if one fails to be consoled, then the problem clearly lies with the one being consoled, or, as the case may be: the one *not* being consoled. The problem does not lie with the consoler or with the quality of the arguments being used. In most of our own experiences with the failure of consolation, I would expect us to think that the failure is caused by the person trying to bring comfort and the arguments that are being used in the process.

'Do you *really* think that by saying *this* you are *actually* offering me consolation?' is a thought that at one point in our lives most of us will have had and maybe even expressed. Yet it's the sort of response that appears to be discursively impossible in most ancient consolations. In the classical consolatory regime, the failure of consolation (if it is highlighted at all) is the failure to *be* comforted, not to bring comfort. If Priam, to return to the scene from which we started, had failed to be comforted in the closing book of the *Iliad*, the blame would have been on him, not Achilles.

## Literature and Consolation: 'the Therapeutic Word'

Before consolation became a topic of sustained philosophical reflection, it found a 'natural' home in literary writings, not only in the Homeric epics but also in the lyrical tradition that we associate with the cult of Orpheus. The mythical poet whose verse allegedly had the force to appease wild animals and move the gods presiding over the Underworld[47] became an icon of what Pedro Laín Entralgo in his magisterial survey of the earlier phase of Greek literary culture called 'the therapeutic word'.[48] The Orphic tradition shared the idea of the healing power of poetic language with Homer's epics, as Laín Entralgo shows. The textual characteristic of the Homeric epics that can be most easily related to our focus on consolatory 'therapeia' is what Laín Entralgo calls 'curing by speaking'.[49] The examples that he provides from the *Odyssey* and the *Iliad* warrant an inclusion of the scene between Achilles and Priam that we discussed earlier. In this scene, too, we witness 'a persuasive and strengthening conversation',[50] an instance of *terpnos logos*, 'cheering speech' as the English translators of Laín Entralgo's book call it.[51] It involves a use of words, the author suggests, that is marked by 'the regularity with which its acoustic effect upon the senses – the words and their intonation – reveals its latent property of working a favourable change in the minds of those in need'.[52] *Terpnos logos*, in other words, derives its effect not only from *what* is being said, but also from *how* it is said – its formal apparatus making an affective appeal on the recipient. 'The whole epic,' Laín Entralgo writes with reference to the *Odyssey*, 'is in a way an enthusiastic homage to superiority in the use of words and their power to touch men's hearts.'[53] The description is valid for the *Iliad* as well, I believe, and certainly for the scene in its closing book at which we have been looking.

One of the guiding ideas in Laín Entralgo's book concerns the conjunction between the Ancient Greeks' belief in the therapeutic potential of words and their understanding of what it meant to be ill. As Laín Entralgo shows, Homer's epics appear to conceive of disease mainly in terms of the psyche, not the body. People become ill when they are possessed by evil spirits or when they lose (either in part or entirely) their souls.[54] As Laín Entralgo sees it, the arrival on the scene of Hippocrates (c. 460–370 BCE) resulted in a decisive shift of medical attention from the mind (*psuchè*) to the body (*soma*), in such a way that the practice began to involve more centrally the diagnostic analysis of physical symptoms. Understandably, the ideal of verbal therapy began to lose its former monopoly in the medical treatment of disease. Interestingly, as Laín Entralgo's book makes clear, the Hippocratic 'revolution' in medicine was more or less contemporary with the rise of philosophy. While medicine gradually developed into a *technè* that involved the treatment of bodily ailments, philosophy began to take over the task of the curing of the mind.

In the course of this development, the notion of verbal therapy also underwent a significant change. Given its new philosophical impetus, the therapy of the word became more and more single-mindedly directed to what Plato, Hippocrates' near-contemporary, called the rational part of the psyche, the curing of which, in his view, involved the redress of man's appetitive and affective inclinations. The excessive presence of emotional energy, according to Plato, could not but result in thoughts and forms of behaviour that went against the goals of the philosopher. The emotions, in his view, stood in the way of the life of the pure mind that he was striving for. Plato's conception of the healing force of the philosophical *logos*, as Laín Entralgo shows, is best captured by the word 'katharsis' – 'the purification of the soul by means of the word'.[55] Whereas in Homer's time, illness was conceived mainly as a stain that needed to be washed away, Plato's conception is one of 'disorder': to be ill means to be subject to a mental imbalance, a 'disorder of the beliefs, knowledge, feelings, and appetites that give the *psyche* its content and structure'.[56] *Katharsis*, in Plato's view, involves the restoration of that perfect balance, by means of the therapeutic word – the word of the philosopher, the rational word. '[T]he essence of Platonic thought about verbal *katharsis*', Laín Entralgo writes, is the idea that '[t]he truth cleans and heals'.[57]

## Sophocles and the Failure of Consolation

The larger point that I'm trying to make here is that the classical regime of consolation – involving practices and words of comfort of the type that is central to the philosophical genre of the consolation that begins to develop in Hippocrates' and Plato's time – can be related to this larger medical, rhetorical and philosophical framework. Clearly, the scene of comfort that brings together Achilles and Priam can easily be read along the above lines: the therapeutic potential of Achilles' consolatory words enables Priam (but also the comforter himself, for that matter) to find the right, rational perspective on his grief, rather than succumb to the destructive force of an all too emotional response.

Similar examples can be found in the work of the great tragic writers of the fifth century BCE, especially Sophocles and Euripides. What is surprising, at first sight, as James H. Kim On Chong-Gossard puts it in a survey article, is that in those tragedies efforts to console are rejected rather than embraced.[58] The majority of these scenes show female characters who fail to be comforted because they reject the consolation on offer. As such, the tragedies confirm the gender bias of the classical consolatory regime: women find it more difficult to suppress the strong emotions and to arrive at the rational ideal that is presupposed by the successful act of comfort.

The most elaborate scene of comfort that Chang-Gossard discusses can be found in Sophocles' *Electra*.[59] In the second scene, the play's heroine refuses to be comforted by the chorus upon the death of her father Agamemnon. Years before the events portrayed in the play, Electra's father was killed upon his return from Troy by his wife Clytaemnestra and her lover Aegisthus. After all these years, Electra is still intent on revenge. Her desire for vengeance can be seen as the main reason behind her refusal to be consoled: possible feelings of genuine comfort would stand in the way of the anger that she needs in order to be able to take revenge on her mother.[60] When the chorus tries to talk reason into Electra (the reason that is at the heart of the classical regime of consolation), she ends up begging them to be left alone. Each of the topics that the chorus makes use of in its lengthy consolatory argument belongs to the appeal to reason on which this classical discourse is founded:

> CHORUS: [H]e has gone to the land to which we all must
> Go. Neither by tears nor by mourning can
> He be restored from the land of the dead.
> Yours is a grief beyond the common measure,
> A grief that knows no ending,
> Consuming your own life, and all in vain.
> For how can mourning end wrong?
> Cannot you part yourself from your long
> Sorrow and suffering? (137–45)[61]

Electra's unquenchable sadness will not bring back her father, the chorus argues. On the contrary, it will only result in her own downfall. The chorus's plea is clearly for *metriopatheia*, the moderation of sorrow. Later in the scene, Electra's unwillingness to be more moderate in her mourning is also seen by the chorus as an unwillingness to accept the will of the gods:

> CHORUS: Zeus is still King in the heavens.
> He sees all; he overrules all things.
> Leave this bitter grief and anger to him.
> Do not go too far in hatred with those you hate,
> Nor be forgetful of him. (173–7)[62]

No matter how unbearable the fate may be that the gods have in store for us, we need to bear it with dignity. This is the type of argument that can be found in numerous consolatory writings, in which the appeal to reasonable behaviour presupposes the existence of a *sensus communis*, a commonly accepted norm to which individual beings should conform. The collective ideal is visible in the argument with which the chorus confronts Electra just after the lines quoted above: surely, Electra is not the first to lose a parent? *Non tibi soli*, Chong-Gossard labels this topos ('Not upon you alone, my child / Has come the heavy burden of grief / That chafes you more than those with whom you live' (152–4)).[63] The person in need of comfort has to understand that they are not alone in their despair. As we know well, it is a comforting thought that is not limited to the classical regime of consolation.

'Greek tragedy is (. . .) a genre that engages with consolation with the express purpose of testing whether it can work at all', Chong-Gossard concludes.[64] The difference with the scene of comfort from the *Iliad* that we discussed earlier is immediately clear. The value of the comfort that Achilles offers Priam is beyond doubt. Homer's text shows us this value unambiguously: we only need to see what the text shows and accept it. Sophocles' tragedy expects more activity from its spectator. Here, the value of consolation is in a way shown *ex negativo*. Electra does not realise it herself, but we who are witnessing her tragic behaviour will understand more properly that comfort on offer is better embraced than rejected. 'Time and time again', Chang-Gossard writes, 'Greek tragedians penned characters who rejected consolation, partly because it was dramatically interesting and memorable, partly because they knew spectators would feel satisfaction that they were not as hard-hearted as an Electra or a Prometheus, and partly because they wanted to provoke sympathy from audiences who could recognize a bit of themselves in both the adamant rejection and the sincere offering of consolation.'[65]

## The Consolation of Literature: Plato versus Aristotle?

The different scenarios in the two scenes that we have been looking at should not blind us, however, to the fact that Homer and Sophocles share a similar idea of what comfort is and what it can do. In both cases, the comforter has noble purposes, which not only serve the individual being comforted, but also the collective within which that individual is being subsumed on the grounds of the logic of the *sensus communis*. The central message, as we have seen, is that we are never alone. The ideal of solidarity, which is still important in modern ideas of consolation, is in a way grounded in the classical ideal of consolation. In Homer and Sophocles' language the prefix in the verb that means 'to comfort' (*paramutheisthai*) already points unambiguously in that direction. The person who brings comfort aims 'to bring you back'. No matter how hard the message of the comforter may seem, they are the one who stands by you, 'in a spirit of intimacy', as Chang-Gossard puts it.[66] The encounter between Achilles and Priam makes clear that acts of comfort can even bring enemies together in that intimate spirit.

Still, *how* exactly do Homer and Sophocles bring comfort to readers, listeners or viewers of their scenes of consolation? What, exactly, is it in their texts that leads us to this idea? Put like this, the question seems to presuppose that their writings do exactly that: they comfort us by simply being there, in the former case (Homer) by showing us how wonderful it can be to give and receive comfort, in the latter (Sophocles) by showing us what we miss if we fail to see its beneficial force. In a book like the present one, such a presupposition makes sense, of course, but we do need to treat the issue with sufficient caution and scepticism. My aim in this book is not to prove (or disprove, for that matter) that literary writings can bring comfort, but to make an inquiry into the conceptual and historical nature of the arguments that we tend to use in making such assumptions.

Inasmuch, then, as writers like Homer and Sophocles aim for and indeed bring comfort, they do not simply do so by directly addressing and thematising the question of consolation, as is the case in philosophical treatises on the subject, or by giving practical advice to future comforters. Rather, they 'simply' stage scenes of comfort as a practice that is part of our daily life, that occurs and has specific effects – in the case of Homer's text Priam's acceptance of comfort seems to have an effect that is reassuring and positive, while in the case of Sophocles the refusal of consolation is at least in part responsible for Electra's tragedy. Had she but listened to the chorus and accepted the comfort on offer, things would have looked much better, would they not?

What, then, might be the effect of this 'staging of comfort' on those who are reading texts, listening to them or watching them performed in a theatrical setting? Opinions on this issue of the therapeutic value of literature diverged substantially in Antiquity, as we know. According to Plato, the impact of 'poetry' was potentially negative because the medium could provoke thoughts and feelings that went against man's natural rationality. Aristotle, by contrast, was convinced that the very texts that Plato warned against (they both take Homer and the great tragedians as their prime examples) could have a positive effect on man: poetry can guide us towards the insight that we need in order to think and act rightly. In the closing part of this chapter, I would like to relate the discussion between Plato and Aristotle to the topic of literary comfort.

Even though he does not address the topic of consolation explicitly or directly, it feels safe to presume that Plato would have treated the idea that literature is beneficial in bringing comfort with the right amount of scepticism. Towards the end of the second book of *The Republic* (in one of the passages in the dialogue in which Socrates voices his infamous critique of poetry), Plato refers, however shortly, to the scene of comfort with which I opened this chapter. The reference is, more specifically, to the allegory of the urns of good and evil that Achilles presents to Priam by way of consolation, the very passage that Alberto Manguel related to the readers of Homer's epic on the Colombian sierra.[67] For Socrates, the issue is not whether the allegory serves as a good (i.e. comforting) argument, but quite simply that it is plain wrong. The idea that Zeus holds in store bad things for man is but one example among many that poets (even Homer) have no real knowledge of what they talk about. Achilles tells a blasphemous lie, and Homer refrains from exposing the lie for what it is – the whole passage is a 'blunder', Socrates feels, 'a foolish mistake'.[68]

At the beginning of Book 3 of the same dialogue, Socrates returns to the encounter between Achilles and Priam in the closing book of the *Iliad*. They are both mentioned in a passage in which he complains about the bad habit of writers like Homer to portray 'men of good standing' in scenes in which we see them lament the loss of a loved one or child.⁶⁹ Even the gods themselves, Socrates adds with unmistakable disapproval, are portrayed in scenes in which they display immoderate and unreasonable behaviour. The basis of the criticism is clear: texts like Homer's that play such an important role in the education of young people should only show exemplary behaviour. To portray gods as if they are human beings (and vice versa) is beyond excuse.

So what if we allow ourselves to be comforted by texts like these? For Socrates, the answer seems to be clear: the comfort in that case has to be as illusory as the literary text in which it is offered to us. Plato returns to the issue of excessive grief in the tenth book of *The Republic*, where, again, it is related to the vexed issue of literary representation. '[T]hink about it,' Socrates says: 'you see the best of us, I imagine, listen to Homer and any of the other tragic poets representing the grief of one of the heroes as they pour forth a long speech in their lamentation, even singing and beating their breasts, and, you know, we enjoy it, we surrender ourselves to it and suffer along with the characters as we follow and eagerly applaud whoever thus affects us in this way the most as a good poet.'⁷⁰ But at the same time, Socrates goes on to say, we pride ourselves whenever we manage to behave moderately when we are touched by grief in our personal lives. In times of personal turmoil, 'we can stay calm and resolute as this is the manly thing to do, while what we approved of before is what women do'.⁷¹ In other words, we must be able to distinguish quite easily between literature and real life.

Still, it is this very thought that Socrates considers dangerous, more dangerous even than the possibility that we should model our behaviour on what we see in Homer's texts or in the tragedies of Sophocles and Euripides. If we think that we can distance ourselves from what we see represented, in the conviction that what we see is something that will never happen to us, we are making a serious mistake, Socrates argues. Homer's poetry and the plays of the tragedians have an effect on that part of the soul that in the fourth book of *The Republic* Socrates calls 'epithumètikon'. This is the part of our soul where, as Socrates puts it, 'desires such as love, hunger, and thirst are found and which is aroused over other passions too, the irrational and appetitive, related to certain gratifications and pleasures'.⁷² Our desires do not simply allow themselves to be guided by the rational principle that is located in the highest part of the soul (*logistikon*), Socrates believes, which is why we need proper training, by philosophers, not poets. The latter, after all, 'satisfy and gratify' the appetitive part of our soul:

That which is naturally the best part of us [the *logistikon*], because it has not been sufficiently educated by reason and habit, relaxes its restraint on the lamenting part, in that it is watching the suffering of other people, and there is nothing shameful for it in praising and pitying another person who claims to be good, but grieves inappropriately; but it thinks that the pleasure it gets is profit, and it wouldn't let itself be deprived of it by renouncing the whole poetical performance.[73]

The argument that we are inclined to call to our defence – that these representations do not really concern our own lives and that we remain fully aware of the distance between our own reality and the illusions that we see on stage – will not satisfy Socrates at all:

You see, I think only a few people have it in them to calculate that enjoyment from the suffering of others is bound to strike nearer home, since having fostered a strong sense of pity in viewing the former, it's not easy to control it in one's own emotions.[74]

## Aristotle: *Katharsis* and Consolation

According to Richard Sorabji and many others, the passage from *The Republic* that I just quoted is the direct occasion of the famous passage from the *Poetics* in which Aristotle discusses the cathartic potential of literary representations, tragedies most notably.[75] The discussion at hand revolves around the precise meaning of what is described in the sixth chapter of Aristotle's treatise as the effect of these tragic representations, an effect that Aristotle elsewhere in his text also relates to Homer's epics: 'through pity and fear accomplishing the catharsis of such emotions'.[76] More than any other sentence of the *Poetics* this one has caused long and numerous interpretive discussions. *Katharsis* is a notion that Aristotle does not define, Stephen Halliwell writes in his edition of the text and this is exactly why it has become 'the most controversial [term] in the work'.[77]

One thing is clear, however: according to the author of the *Poetics* the tragedy results in a *katharsis* ['purgation' or 'purification', see below] of the feelings the Greeks traditionally associated with the genre: 'fear' (*phobos*) and 'pity' (*eleos*). As we have seen, Aristotle deals with the two emotions extensively in the second book of his *Rhetoric* (Chapters 5 and 8, respectively). The question is, however, how exactly to interpret Aristotle's conception of this central notion of *katharsis*. The question is also which principle exactly determines its operations. Does the tragedy provoke feelings of fear and pity in the spectators and intensify them so as to make them disappear in the course of the theatrical experience – the original emotions are being 'purged away', as it were? Or should we understand the process as one of 'purification', moderation, a loss of excesses? Manfred Fuhrmann's German translation conceives of the sentence in that second way, as does Halliwell: 'purified' for Fuhrmann means 'rid of its excess'.[78] In the former case ('purgation') the original emotions disappear completely, while in the second ('purification') they change composition and assume, so to speak, an improved form. My own preference lies with the interpretation that Roselyne Dupont-Roc and Jean Lallot suggest in their edition of Aristotle's treatise and that ties in with that of Fuhrmann. For them, the purification involves the transition of a negative into a positive experience – from *peine* to *plaisir*, in the words of the French translators: in this way we manage in rising above the fear and the pity.[79]

Lest we misunderstand the latter suggestion: Aristotle obviously does not imply that we find pleasure in the suffering of other people (or comfort, for that matter, in the fact that some people are even worse off than we are). What he does imply is that our perception of suffering in a theatrical context results in a deeper and better insight into what Stephen Halliwell describes as a worldview in which the fragility of human existence is central, 'a vulnerability which is dramatically projected by events in which transformations of fortune, and thus great swings in the potential happiness of the central agents, are dominant.'[80] Tragedies show us the mishaps that strike other people to be the outcome of one or other fatal mistake (*hamartia*) that lies rooted in their personality. The lives of the 'other people' that we see on stage, undergo a tragic shift, which is neither expected nor deserved. We feel for these people from a distance, realising that similar things could well befall us too, but relieved, to a certain extent, that we are not the protagonists of the staged events that we witness. 'Tragedy', Halliwell writes, 'contains patterns of suffering which explore the experience of limitations upon human control of life. But it enlarges and heightens this experience by focusing it upon events that are typically "awesome" in scope and character, and by connecting it with characters who, while "like us" in their basic nature, are nonetheless "better than our normal level" (48a4) in the heroic scale and sweep of their lives.'[81]

The theatre, then, in Aristotle's view, does not remind us of something that *deep down* we already knew (that would be a Platonic thought), but it offers us a new perspective on life (our own and that of others), a perspective that we would be deprived of without this 'literary' experience. According to Dupont-Roc and Lallot[82] it is important to relate Aristotle's cryptic description of *katharsis* to the definition of 'mimesis' that we find in the fourth chapter of the *Poetics*. In his analysis of the 'pleasure' (*chairein*) that we derive from seeing mimetic representations, Aristotle stresses the distance or difference between the representation and that which it represents. In Halliwell's translation: 'we enjoy contemplating the most precise images of things whose actual sight is painful to us, such as the forms of the vilest animals and of corpses'.[83] That which repels us when we encounter it 'in real life' results in a different experience in the theatre, if only because we know that a staged corpse is never really dead. The cognitive effect of the mechanism of mimesis rests on the difference between the mimetic reality and the reality outside the theatre, not only to the extent that a different experience is involved (the 'pleasure' that we experience in seeing the representation is opposed to the 'pain' we would feel if we were witnessing the 'real' of which the representation is a mimesis), but also a different (and possibly more consoling) way of 'looking'. While we have our 'ordinary' way of looking at the real (*horan*), Aristotle seems to be suggesting, to look at representations of the real requires a more contemplative gaze (*theorein*), a gaze that also encourages us to relate what we see to our own situation, with an eye on difference as well as similarity. 'La *katharsis* tragique', Dupont-Roc and Lallot write, 'est le résultat d'un processus analogue: mis en présence d'une histoire (*muthos*) où il reconnaît les *formes*, savamment élaborées par le poète, qui définissent l'essence du pitoyable et de l'effrayant, le spectateur éprouve lui-même la pitié et la frayeur, mais sous une forme quintessenciée, et l'émotion épurée qui le saisit alors et que nous qualifierons d'esthétique s'accompagne de plaisir.'[84]

For Aristotle, Halliwell writes, a properly mimetic experience is 'psychologically rewarding and ethically beneficial'.[85] Put differently, (mimetic) literature helps us develop our personality in a valuable way and in doing so these texts and performances enable us to become better persons, better versions of ourselves. 'The tragic poet awakens us to the fact that there are certain emotional possibilities which we ignore in ordinary life,' Jonathan Lear writes in a fundamental contribution to the analysis of Aristotle's concept of *katharsis*.[86] In the closing section of his text, Lear relates the function of *katharsis* explicitly to the idea of consolation: 'For Aristotle', he writes,

> a good tragedy offers us this consolation: that even when the breakdown of the primordial bonds occurs, it does not occur in a world which is in itself ultimately chaotic and meaningless. (. . .) And there is further consolation in recognizing that even when they are responsible for their misfortunes, humans remain capable of conducting themselves with dignity and nobility.[87]

For sure, our need to be consoled is not limited to the sort of experiences that are central to Aristotle's definition of the tragedy (our mortality and that of our loved ones is generally not the result of any form of *hamartia*), but Lear's insight confirms my conviction that our current ideas regarding the consolatory potential of literary writings are somehow related to the mechanism that the author of the *Poetics* sees at work in the principle of *katharsis*. Like tragedies, literary texts that console have the capacity to provoke in readers a cognitive and affective response that is not only determined by what the text represents (its 'tearful' content, so to say) but also by its 'poetic' build-up, the construction of its narrative (*muthos*) and other formal characteristics that guide readers to the specific insight that we still associate with being comforted.

In my take on the relationship between *katharsis* and consolation, I would even go further than Lear and suggest that Aristotle's ideas about mimesis and *katharsis* not only underlie our ideas about the consolatory potential of literature, but also our ideas about what consolation is, in and of itself. In being consoled, we undergo a process that usually results in a new insight, a different way of seeing that enables us to look back on moments of suffering that are too painful to address in the rational way that Plato wants us to strive towards, and too self-destructive if we allow our emotions to dominate our response to them. In Aristotle's view, the ideal spectator of a tragedy experiences a similar process, of the sort that Achilles can be said to undergo in the scene from the *Iliad* with which I opened this chapter. While it would have come as no surprise had Achilles responded fiercely upon seeing Priam enter his tent, his encounter with the enemy leader is marked by uncharacteristic moderation. The meeting could have resulted (as it more or less does in the reshuffling of events in Wolfgang Petersen's *Troy)* in an outburst of warfare that would reduce the earlier bouts of violence in the *Iliad* to childish foreplay. In Homer's original, Achilles seems to have grown wiser – in contrast to Electra, he puts an end to his laments. His behaviour is all but overtly emotional; it is cautious, yet decided. He has clearly arrived at the insight of proper *eleos*, to which Priam's words have guided him: they came at the right moment and took the right shape. Also, Achilles was able to relate Priam's plea to his own life, and on the basis of that reflection he was in turn able to offer Priam what according to Aristotle we can only expect from friends – the gift of comfort, and with it the acceptance of what has happened and of what is no doubt bound to follow. In turn, Achilles was able to comfort Priam with the story of Niobe, whose tragedy enabled the Trojan king not only to understand his own tragic loss better but to live with it in the right way. The comfort, one might add, also lies in the fact that Niobe's experience comes in the form of a story. As Isak Dinesen puts it (her words are quoted by Hannah Arendt in *The Human Condition*): 'All sorrows can be borne if you put them into a story or tell a story about them.'[88]

## Nussbaum on Stoic Theories of Poetry

Clearly, Aristotle is more confident than Plato about our ability to allow ourselves to be guided in positive ways by our emotions, even though he shares with the author of *The Republic* the idea that the moderation of the 'passions' by our rational powers is necessary. As we have seen, Plato and Aristotle both make use of the concept of *katharsis*. For Plato, Robert Cushman writes, the 'purification' which the philosopher aims for involves the 'deliverance of the soul from the deceit of sense and from the attendant passions of the body'.[89] The ultimate moment of release, for Plato, is that of death, of which Socrates, as we know, shows no fear. For the author of *The Republic*, human life will always be marked by what James Kastely describes as an 'internal civil war', a conflict between the rational part of the mind and the passions.[90] This internal strife, Kastely goes on to write, manifests itself most clearly in Socrates' considerations on what he considers the proper response to grief. According to Socrates, Kastely writes, '[t]he good man is one who endures grief, responding with moderation to the pain he experiences'[91] – like Achilles and Priam in *Iliad* 24, one might say.

Even though Plato and Aristotle assume different positions with respect to the pragmatics of poetry and the role it can play in overcoming grief or other states of excessively emotional pain, I believe it would be a mistake to see their respective positions as fundamentally opposed. Even though it has been assumed that Aristotle's reflections on the positive potential of poetic mimesis on spectators of theatrical tragedy were first conceived in rebuttal of Plato's severe critique of poetry in *The Republic*, I follow Stephen Halliwell, who has shown that, in this dialogue, Plato's presumed banishment of the poets 'is dramatically *undercut* by Socratic expressions of hesitation and attraction towards poetry – in short, by indications of lingering if equivocal "love" of poetry'.[92] The issue for me is not so much whether or not Plato really wanted to banish the poets from his ideal city but rather, as Martha Nussbaum has shown, that Socrates' critique of poetry in *The Republic* helped inspire within the generations of Stoic philosophers that succeeded Plato two important positions with respect to the healing effect of literature upon spectators and listeners: the one Nussbaum associates with the work of Diogenes of Babylon and Posidonius, the other with Chrysippus.[93] The former view Nussbaum labels 'non-cognitive', because those who hold it are convinced that the passions are not rational, that is, they are not produced by our faculty of judgement; the latter she labels 'cognitive' because those who hold it are convinced that our 'passions' are related to the evaluative judgements that we make. The importance of the discussion for us lies in the fact that while both views allow for literature to play a (positive) role in the education of people, the difference between them lies in their conception of how (and where) literary writings affect those who are confronted with them. In the 'non-cognitive' camp (so to speak) the impact of literary writings is defined on the level of the rousing or soothing of one's emotions; in the other paradigm the effect of literature is defined cognitively: the potential impact of literary writings is such that it can help us change our views. In the non-cognitive view, the attention goes mainly to the acoustic (rhythm, melody, harmony) elements of the literary text,[94] while the cognitive view takes into account the fact that literary writings are more than just music: they express ideas and represent states of mind and affairs; they say *something* as well as produce sound of some sort.

Interestingly, Nussbaum also touches upon the issue of the consolatory potential of literary writings: in her discussion of Diogenes and Posidonius she argues that their view of consolation (like that of mourning, anger, love and reconciliation) is a 'very thin' one, one which passes by the fact that the experience of consolation is indeed a cognitive one.[95] The cognitive view of Chrysippus comes closes to Aristotle's definitions of mimesis and *katharsis*, but it also derives from a solid reading of Plato and takes into account the latter's critique of poetry. Here lies the central paradox, Nussbaum believes, of the Stoic view on poetry:

> on the one hand, the Stoics clearly took a very extreme position concerning the passions, holding that they should be not just moderated but completely extirpated from human life. (. . .) On the other hand, no other ancient school is more sympathetic to the poets, those notorious feeders of passion.[96]

The Stoics' solution to that seeming contradiction – 'The partisans of the cognitive view are also zealous defenders of poetry', Nussbaum writes[97] – involves a complex of arguments that she distils into three considerations. Each of these, in my view, can easily be related to the topos of literary comfort.

The first consideration starts from the given (also found in Plato) that while some literature is harmful, some clearly is not. Some texts will bring consolation, others will not. Consequently, the literary production that does result in the healing force of comfort will be said to have characteristics that bring them closer to the qualities that Plato singled out for the production of philosophers: they provide true knowledge and deep insight, they appeal to our rational part and – an argument that can be traced to Aristotle's *Poetics* – their formal make-up (their *plot*-structure) is such that they guide us to the right perspective.

The second consideration is that literary writings invite allegorical interpretation. Put differently: whereas they sometimes may be seen to promote the sort of message that no sane reader can tolerate – Nussbaum gives the example of Chrysippus' allegorical reading of a painting that shows Hera and Zeus in an unmistakable act of fellatio[98] – a less superficial, expert reading will manage to find an interpretation that stresses the truly curative meaning of this or that work of art. Similarly, as this book will show in later chapters, texts that appear to have an immediately disconsolate effect can be shown, if read in the 'proper' spirit, to be morally uplifting and, therefore, comforting.

The third consideration is related to the second one: the 'right' type of literature, in the Stoic view, is that which invites interpretations that move beyond the text's immediate surface and promotes what Nussbaum calls 'critical spectatorship'.[99] That ideal reading position involves 'a concerned but critical detachment', Nussbaum writes,[100] not a reading that simply hinges on identification and compassion with the characters. 'The good Stoic spectator is concerned with the characters', Nussbaum adds, 'with a friendly and humane concern that is perfectly compatible with detachment from their sickness of passion.'[101] For literature to be truly consoling, the reader (spectator) should be able not only to adopt this position of critical detachment with respect to the situations that the characters find themselves in, but do so also with respect to their own sorrowful state. The text will have its consoling effect if the reader is guided towards the novel insight that always comes with the mechanism of consolation.

\* \* \*

Those who argue, today, that literary writings have the power to console, generally found their claim on the conviction that these writings provide us with special insight in our suffering and in doing so make that suffering more bearable. Literature brings comfort, in the way that tragedy may result in *katharsis*. Others will oppose that idea by saying that it is a mistake to define literature in terms that bypass the aesthetic specificity of the medium. They will see comfort as a moral category, not a literary one. Still others will say that literature can also bring false comfort, as when it allows us to escape from our suffering in the shape of a fantasy – the alleviation of our pain can also boil down to escapism in our imagination. In those cases, literature may very well result in the very opposite of what consolation should really do: a confrontation with the painful reality. (But what is wrong, basically, with a view that sees consolation as a form of diversion?)

At the heart of each of these divergent views lie not only convictions about what literature is and should do, but also about what consolation is and should do. The present chapter will have made sufficiently clear, I hope, that Aristotle's foundational thinking on literature lies behind the first of the positions that I summed up in the previous paragraph: literature brings comfort when it leads us to a valuable insight in a state of sorrow because that insight enables us to bear that suffering more productively. However, as I also hope to have made clear, that does not mean that we should assign to Plato the role of the wicked messenger in the history that this book hopes to sketch. He is not merely the one who on the basis of a fundamental misconception of the possibilities of literature can only see her consolatory force as a form of fundamental deception. As we will continue to see in the following chapter, his critique of poetry played an important (and positive) role in the development of a poetical tradition that tries to define the philosophical and conceptual power of literary writings. Plato's philosophical critique of literature helped in this way to lay the foundations of an apology for a type of literature that, like philosophy, and even better according to some, can bring readers to the sort of insight that offers true consolation. In the second chapter, I will associate that development with the names of Boethius and Dante.

## Notes

1. Cicero, *Tusculan Disputations,* Book 3, 31, 76, 315–17.
2. Mendelsohn, *An Odyssey*.
3. Mendelsohn, *An Odyssey*, 6.
4. Mendelsohn, *An Odyssey*, 178–9.
5. Manguel, Homer's The Iliad *and* The Odyssey.
6. Manguel, Homer's The Iliad *and* The Odyssey, 5–6.
7. Manguel, Homer's The Iliad *and* The Odyssey, 6.
8. Manguel, Homer's The Iliad *and* The Odyssey, 6.
9. Manguel, Homer's The Iliad *and* The Odyssey, 7.
10. Quintilian, *The Institutio Oratoria*, Vol. 4, Book 10, 1, 47, 29.
11. Manguel, Homer's The Iliad *and* The Odyssey, 6.
12. Discussions of the scene are tantamount: see, for instance, Nicolson, *The Mighty Dead*, 206–7; White, *When Words Lose Their Meaning*, 53–8; Redfield, Nature and Culture in the Iliad, 215–18; Sels, '"A heart that can endure"'; Vidal-Naquet, *Le monde d'Homère*, 70; Weil and Rachel Bespaloff, War *and* The Iliad, 6–8 (Weil) and 79–85 (Bespaloff); Nussbaum, 'Tragedy and Self-sufficiency', 267; Perez-Bill, 'Priam ou la conscience endeuillée'.

    The scene is also referenced in works that deal with the tradition of the *consolatio*: see, for instance, Schaeben, *Trauer im humanistischen Dialog*, 6 and Scourfield, *Consoling Heliodorus*, 15–16. The place of Homer's literature within the cultural and social context of his time is the subject of (among others) Jaeger, *Paideia*, 63–88 ('Homer als Erzieher'). See also Latacz, *Homer*. In my analysis of the scene, I made use of Peter Green's recent translation: Homer, *The Iliad*, 452–8. All subsequent parenthetical line references are to this edition.
13. Quintilian, *The Institutio Oratoria*, Vol. 4, Book 10, 1, 50, 31.
14. Aristotle, *Nicomachean Ethics*, Book 9, 11 (1171b), 571.
15. They are the ones who serve Achilles his meals after Patroklos' death. See MacLeod (ed.), *Iliad: Book XXIV*, 125, note accompanying lines 472–6.
16. See MacLeod (ed.), *Iliad: Book XXIV*, 126, note accompanying lines 477–8. Illustration 20 in Vidal-Naquet, *Le monde d'Homère* shows a vase from the fifth century BCE that represents the scene.

17. An echo of lines 255–7: 'I sired sons who were the best / in the broad land of Troy, yet of them not one, I tell you, / is left.' The offspring that was spared by the God of war, Priam adds, (including Paris) are 'the no-goods - / the liars, the dancers only expert at matching the beat, / the lifters of lamb and kids from those in your own country!' (260–2).
18. Aristotle, *The 'Art' of Rhetoric*, Book Two, 8, 2 (1385b2), 225.
19. David Konstan, *The Emotions of the Ancient Greeks*, 201–2. See also the chapter 'Pity versus compassion' in Konstan, *Pity Transformed*, 49–74. 'To pity someone, then, we must recognize the possibility of suffering a like misfortune without actually being in that condition', Konstan writes (50).
20. In her analysis of the scene, Simone Weil seems to forget the presence of the adverb: see Benfey, 'Introduction', xv. Rachel Bespaloff's reading is more to the point in this respect. As she sees it, the line precedes 'one of the most beautiful silences in the *Iliad* – one of those absolute silences in which the din of the Trojan War, the vociferations of men and gods, and the rumblings of the Cosmos, are engulfed. The Becoming of the universe hangs suspended in this impalpable element whose duration is an instant and forever' (80).
21. MacLeod (ed.), *Iliad: Book XXIV*, 26.
22. MacLeod (ed.), *Iliad: Book XXIV*, 27.
23. (Ps-)Plutarch, 'Consolatio ad Apollonium', 7 (105b), 127.
24. 'Quelque chose dans ses entrailles se refuse au malheur' ['Something inside him (literally: in his innards) is resistant to unhappiness'], Michaël Fœssel writes in *Le temps de la consolation*, 99. I will come back to Fœssel's inspiring study more than once in the course of this book.
25. Nicolson, *The Mighty Dead*, 207.
26. In the movie, the scene does not come at the end of the narrated events, so that it cannot function as a peaceful culmination. On the contrary, in Petersen's *Troy*, the bitter encounter between Achilles and Priam precedes (and in a way prepares for) the actual sacking of Troy by the Greeks.
27. Baltussen (ed.), *Greek and Roman Consolations*, xiii.
28. I make use of several instructive sources on the Greco-Roman consolatory tradition. The classical surveys are Horst-Theodor, *Trauer und Trost*; Kassel, *Untersuchungen zur griechischen und römischen Konsolationsliteratur*; Constant Martha, 'Les Consolations dans l'Antiquité'. Convenient briefer surveys can be found in Holloway, *Consolation in Philippians*, 55–83; McClure, *Sorrow and Consolation in Italian Humanism*, 3–17; Schaeben, *Trauer im humanistischen Dialog*, 5–29; Scourfield, *Consoling Heliodorus*, 15–33 and Scourfield 'Towards a Genre of Consolation', 1–36.
29. Holloway, *Consolation in Philippians*, 56; see also Schaeben, *Trauer im humanistischen* Dialog, 7.
30. Scourfield, 'Towards a Genre of Consolation', 1–36.

31. Kierdorf, 'Consolatio as a Literary Genre', 704. The definition is inspired by the passage from Cicero's *Tusculan Disputations* which serves as a motto to this chapter.
32. Kierdorf, 'Consolatio as a Literary Genre', 704.
33. *Paramuthia* means 'exhortation', 'encouragement': see Scourfield, 'Towards a Genre of Consolation', 6 for the etymology of the word.
34. For an attempted reconstruction of Crantor's text, see Johann, *Trauer und Trost*, 127–36. See also Schaeben, *Trauer im humanistischen Dialog*, 14, Scourfield, 'Towards a Genre of Consolation', 3 and Sorabji, *Emotion and Peace of Mind*, 394.
35. See, for instance, McClure, *Sorrow and Consolation in Italian Humanism*, 6.
36. See Kassel, *Untersuchungen zur griechischen und römischen Konsolationsliteratur*, 35–6.
37. Cicero, *Academica Priora*, 2, 135, quoted in Holloway, *Consolation in Philippians*, 58.
38. Cicero, *Tusculan Disputations*, Book 3, 6, 12, 239–41.
39. See White, 'Cicero and the Therapists'. See also Baltussen, 'Cicero's Consolatio ad se', 67–92.
40. 'Ad Marciam', 'Ad Polybium' and 'Ad Helviam Matrem'. Some of the Letters to Lucilius can also be seen as consolatory. See, for instance, Wilson, 'Seneca the Consoler?, 93–121. See also Fantham et al., *Seneca: Hardship and Happiness* and Graver, 'The Weeping Wise', 235–52.
41. See Kassel, *Untersuchungen zur griechischen und römischen Konsolationsliteratur*, 49–98. See also Boys-Stones, 'The *Consolatio ad Apollonium*', 123–37. For a discussion of Plutarch's consolation to his wife, see: Schorn, 'Tears of the Bereaved'.
42. Konstan, 'The Grieving Self', 139–51.
43. Holloway, *Consolation in Philippians*, 56.
44. Graver, *Stoicism and Emotion*, 196.
45. Cicero, *Tusculan Disputations*, Book 3, 9, 22, 251; see also White, 'Cicero and the Therapists', 236.
46. Holloway, *Consolation in Philippians*, 1.
47. Orpheus will return in the next chapter, where I will integrate a discussion of the consolatory effects of the work of the mythical poet in my analysis of Boethius' *De consolatione philosophiae*.
48. Laín Entralgo, *The Therapy of the Word in Classical Antiquity*.
49. Laín Entralgo, *The Therapy of the Word*, 25.
50. Laín Entralgo, *The Therapy of the Word*, 23.
51. Laín Entralgo, *The Therapy of the Word*, 25.
52. Laín Entralgo, *The Therapy of the Word*, 30.
53. Laín Entralgo, *The Therapy of the Word*, 29.
54. Laín Entralgo, *The Therapy of the Word*, 8–10.
55. Laín Entralgo, *The Therapy of the Word*, 137.
56. Laín Entralgo, *The Therapy of the Word*, 132.

57. Laín Entralgo, *The Therapy of the* Word, 136. Referring to Plato's 'The Sophist', Entralgo writes: '*Katharsis* is the art of separating the good from the bad; it is in consequence *technè diakritikè*, the art of sifting or discernment' (131).
58. Chong-Gossard, 'Mourning and Consolation in Greek Tragedy', 37–66. See also Ciani, *La consolatio nei tragici greci*.
59. Chong-Gossard, 'Mourning and Consolation in Greek Tragedy, 46–9. Chong-Gossard deals with a similar rejection of comfort in Euripides' *Alcestis* and a preserved fragment of *Hypsipyle*. The latter (largely lost) play also contains a successful scene of consolation: see Chong-Gossard, 'Consolation in Euripides' *Hypsipyle*'.
60. See also Fœssel, *Le temps de la consolation*, 67: 'Dans cette mesure, la consolation ne serait pas apaisement, mais trahison.' ['In this way, consolation would not be seen as relief, but as betrayal'].
61. Sophocles, *Antigone, Oedipus the King, Electra*, 107. (Niobe is mentioned a few lines down.)
62. Sophocles, *Antigone, Oedipus the King, Electra*, 108.
63. Chong-Gossard, 'Mourning and Consolation in Greek Tragedy', 39.
64. Chong-Gossard, 'Mourning and Consolation in Greek Tragedy', 37.
65. Chong-Gossard, 'Mourning and Consolation in Greek Tragedy', 61.
66. Chong-Gossard, 'Mourning and Consolation in Greek Tragedy', 38.
67. Plato, *Republic*, Vol. 1, 203–5 (379e-d).
68. Plato, *Republic*, Vol. 1, 203 (379d).
69. Plato, *Republic*, Vol. 1, 229 (388a).
70. Plato, *Republic*, Vol. 2, 433 (605c-d).
71. Plato, *Republic*, Vol. 2, 433 (605d).
72. Plato, *Republic*, Vol. 1, 419 (439d).
73. Plato, *Republic*, Vol. 2, 435 (606a-b).
74. Plato, *Republic*, Vol. 2, 435 (606b).
75. Sorabji, *Emotion and Peace of Mind*, 291–2. See also Aristote, *La poétique*, ed. and trans. Roselyne Dupont-Roc and Jean Lallot, 188–93 ('La *katharsis*: essai d'interprétation').
76. Aristotle, *Poetics*, 47–9 (1449b27–8).
77. Aristotle, *Poetics*, 49na. Halliwell is the central voice in discussions on the *Poetics*. With respect to the issue that concerns us here, see, for instance Halliwell, 'Tragedy and the Emotions', and 'Tragic Pity'. See also Nussbaum, 'Tragedy and Self-Sufficiency', Nehamas, 'Pity and Fear in the *Rhetoric* and the *Poetics*' and Lear, 'Katharsis'. See also 'What is Catharsis in Aristotle', in Critchley, *The Greeks and Us*, 187–92.
78. Aristoteles, *Poetik*, translated and edited by Manfred Fuhrmann, 109n3. For Halliwell's considerations see his 'Introduction' to the Loeb edition; Aristotle, *Poetics*, 18–19.
79. Aristote, *La poétique*, 190.
80. Halliwell in the 'Introduction' to his Loeb edition of Aristotle, *Poetics*, 15–16.

81. Halliwell, 'Introduction' to Aristotle, *Poetics*, 16.
82. See also Halliwell, 'Tragic Pity', throughout.
83. Aristotle, *Poetics*, 37–9 (1448b9–12).
84. Dupont-Roc &-Lallot, *La poétique*, 190. 'Tragic *katharsis* is the outcome of an analogous process: when as spectators we find ourselves in the presence of a history (*muthos*) in which we recognize the *forms*, expertly handled by the poet, that define the essence of pity and fear, we experience pity and fear ourselves, but in a quintessential form, and the purified emotion that has a hold on us then and that we define as aesthetic is accompanied by pleasure'. My translation.
85. Halliwell, 'Introduction' to Aristotle, *Poetics*, 19.
86. Lear, 'Katharsis'.
87. Lear, 'Katharsis', 334–5.
88. Arendt, *The Human Condition*, 155.
89. Cushman, *Therapeia*, 56.
90. Kastely, *The Rhetoric of Plato's* Republic, 194.
91. Kastely, *The Rhetoric of Plato's* Republic, 194.
92. Halliwell, 'Antidotes and Incantations', quote on 242. See also Halliwell, *The Aesthetics of Mimesis*, 26 and Kastely, *The Rhetoric of Plato's* Republic, 199.
93. Nussbaum, 'Poetry and the Passions'.
94. We should keep in mind that the performance of these texts was generally accompanied by music.
95. Nussbaum, 'Poetry and the Passions', 121.
96. Nussbaum, 'Poetry and the Passions', 98–9.
97. Nussbaum, 'Poetry and the Passions', 123.
98. Nussbaum, 'Poetry and the Passions', 133.
99. Nussbaum, 'Poetry and the Passions', 136–45.
100. Nussbaum, 'Poetry and the Passions', 137.
101. Nussbaum, 'Poetry and the Passions', 143–4.

Chapter 2

# The Christian Regime of Literary Comfort: From Boethius to Dante

'I feel like I'm reading to save my life', I told her. 'I mean, I'm not going to die if I don't read Dante, but I have this feeling that there's something in this book that is going to make things different.'

'Careful with that', she warned. 'You know how you are.'

She didn't have to explain what she meant. Julie and I had long laughed at our shared faith in books to explain the world to us and solve our problems. For bibliophiles like us, books were a source not only of pleasure but also of wisdom about life and how to live it. 'Bibliotherapy' – using books to treat psychological disorders – may be a new trend, but for me, it came naturally.

Rod Dreher, *How Dante Can Save Your Life*[1]

## Joseph Luzzi on Dante: Teacher of Teachers

Rod Dreher's *How Dante Can Save Your Life*, one of the books that I singled out in the introduction as a telling example of the current bibliotherapeutic wave, is not the only recent addition to the output of this newly popular reading practice in which the author of the *Divine Comedy* features prominently. The same year in which Dreher's book came out (2015) also saw the publication of *In A Dark Wood*, the touching memoir Joseph Luzzi wrote in an attempt to overcome the tragic loss of his wife Katherine.[2] Late in November 2007, the young woman, heavily pregnant with baby girl Isabel, was the victim of a fatal car accident. The little girl was fortunate to survive, as a team of doctors from Poughkeepsie's Saint Francis Hospital hurriedly delivered her less than an hour before Katherine died from the massive injuries she incurred in the car crash. 'In one terrible instant', as we read on the inside cover of *In A Dark Wood*, 'Luzzi found himself both a widower and a father.'[3]

The memoir's subtitle – *What Dante Taught Me about Grief, Healing, and the Mysteries of Love* – does little to hide the bibliotherapeutic programme to which the book clearly subscribes. The central point of that programme is highlighted even before we begin reading. The author of the *Divine Comedy*, we are expected to presume on the sole basis of the book's title page, will be seen as a special teacher, one to whose work we feel drawn because we want to learn from him. Also, the lessons of this teacher concern the core of human existence – mortality, mourning and a superior form of love that enables us to go on and to find a way out of the 'selva oscura' life occasionally holds in store for us. Luzzi's subtitle also points to the long three-stage struggle (first you grieve, then you get better, and then you will understand what love is all about) for which he required the sort of assistance that his family and loved ones were not able to provide in the dramatic circumstances he had to face. 'I needed a guide,' Luzzi writes in the prologue of his memoir, 'someone who knew how to speak with the dead. Someone who had written about life in the dark wood.'[4]

A professor of Italian and Comparative Literature at Bard College in upstate New York, Luzzi clearly knew that Dante was indeed such a guide, one who could tell from personal experience how grief, healing and love might intersect in felicitous ways. His interest in the author of the *Divine Comedy* was not new. It dated back to 1987, as his memoir shows, from a student year abroad in Dante's native town. That memorable Italian stay not only allowed Luzzi to trace back the roots of his family in Calabria, it also enabled him to begin seeing the personal appeal that Dante's work had in store. Ever since his first Florentine reading of the *Divine Comedy*, Luzzi writes, 'I had turned to Dante with demanding questions'.[5] Clearly, this particular attraction did not wither away in the two decades that separated the student Luzzi of 1987 from the newly widowed father of 2007.

It makes every sense, then, that in this new and unexpected hour of personal trial, Luzzi would again turn to the author of the *Divine Comedy*. 'Nobody understands our need for the right kind of guidance better than Dante', he states in the Acknowledgements section of *In A Dark Wood*.[6] Having loved and lost his Beatrice early in life, and having found, in his writing, a way to continue and purify his exceptional love for her after her death, Dante provides Luzzi with the perfect example of the lesson embodied in the motto on which his book opens: 'Every grief story is a love story.'

The process of healing to which *In A Dark Wood*'s subtitle refers involves the slow transition from grief to love, and the awareness that the latter is at the heart of the former in ways that are unimaginable to us when misfortune first strikes. The parting of a loved one, as Luzzi learns, is followed by a feeling of immense loss that he just cannot believe he will ever be able to overcome. In the case of Dante, the loss was not just that of his beloved Beatrice, but twelve years later also that of his home in Florence, from which he was irreversibly exiled in 1302. In a famous passage of Canto 17 of the *Paradiso* (written more than a decade after the fact), Dante revisits the moment of that second loss in a scene in which his great-great-grandfather Cacciaguida prophesies the event that, in the end, proved so decisive for Dante's literary career:

> You will leave behind everything you love
> Most dearly, and this is the arrow
> The bow of exile first lets fly. (*Par.* 17, 55–7)[7]

'No other words could capture how I felt during the four years I struggled to find my way out of the dark wood of grief and mourning', Luzzi writes in his reading of these lines.[8] It is only one of several passages in his memoir in which it becomes clear that Dante's guiding force has to do not so much with the uniqueness of his life's central experiences as with the verbal and stylistic skills that enabled him to present them in a living and enduring voice. 'My reading of Dante had always been deep and personal', Luzzi admits, 'but when I found myself in the dark wood, his words became a matter of life and death.'[9] Stressing the importance of the poet's 'words', Luzzi makes clear that it is the specific way in which Dante writes – rather than just *what* he writes – that explains the lasting appeal of the *Divine Comedy* to him. In times of true need, Luzzi reads aloud Dante's lines, so as to allow the text's formal make-up its full effect, 'the poem's soothing sounds one of the few things that could calm me', as he puts it.[10]

To a large extent, the power of the poetic form for Luzzi is related to its musical force. Dante's poetry, he writes, is at times 'pure musical rapture meant to conjure an atmosphere of relief'.[11] The poem's music, we should note, is not enjoyed for its own sake, that is, for the sake of the sound itself, but for the effect that sound has on the person listening – it has a 'soothing' effect, Luzzi points out, an 'effect of relief'. The music of Dante's lines eases the pain; the poet's words bring comfort. 'Sounding Dante's rhyming tercets over and over, as if they were a charm to ward off evil spirits', as he writes elsewhere.[12] Again, the stress is on what one could call the work's therapeutics, which, admittedly, can never be taken for granted. There are moments, clearly, in which 'the soft (...) sounds of Dante's (...) words could not calm my racing heart', as Luzzi admits, 'no matter how many times I read aloud the passage about his exile'.[13]

## The Past is No Foreign Country

'My new guide may have lived in a distant time and a foreign land', Rod Dreher writes in his book on Dante, 'but to my great surprise and pleasure, I was no stranger to him.'[14] To Dreher, the author of the *Divine Comedy* was a new and sudden discovery in a Barnes & Noble bookshop in Baton Rouge, Louisiana, but Luzzi already knew well enough what he could expect when he turned to Dante for help and support. The crucial word in the 'bow of exile' lines above that Dante puts in Cacciaguida's mouth is definitely 'first'. Initially, the arrow of loss points away from the loved one that we have to leave behind (or away from Dante's native town, as the case may be). But as Luzzi finds out in the course of the bitter years that follow his wife's accident, the work of mourning enables one to slowly change the direction of the arrow and to return to the loved one, albeit with a difference: the one who was lost is now regained, provided that the work of mourning does its work the proper way. The loved one will then be loved anew, differently, as Dante found out, in a less life-threatening way, as Luzzi will.

The turning of the arrow of exile and loss, Luzzi is convinced, came to Dante as a consequence of his writing. It is this conviction that encourages Luzzi to write about his love for Katherine as well. It is not just his reading of Dante that helps him on his way out of the dark wood, but also, and maybe even more so, his writing about that reading. 'I cannot know what went through Dante's mind in those first bitter years of exile', Luzzi concludes, 'but I believe that it was only when he decided to write about the life he had lost that he was able to stop staring at it, just as I was only able to open myself again to love when I began to write about the pain of losing it.'[15]

Luzzi's identification with the author of the *Divine Comedy* is not absolute, as this passage already shows. The reading position which he adopts throughout is similar to the one that I pointed out in my discussion of Katharine Smyth's book on Virginia Woolf in the introduction to this book. Dante is like Luzzi in some respects (they share ideas and ideals about the importance of literature in life, for instance), but not in all. Obviously, the overtly Christian poet that

Dante is can never be a religious guide for the secular reader that Luzzi, in contrast to Rod Dreher, proclaims himself to be ('neither a natural believer nor a committed atheist', as Luzzi puts it).[16] 'I felt Dante's words on intellectual and emotional levels', Luzzi writes, 'but his absolute faith in Christian doctrine belonged to an order of experience far removed from my secular world. I could think and feel with Dante in hell and purgatory – but I didn't know if I could believe with him in heaven.'[17] Dante's understanding of the death of Beatrice rests on the belief – materialised in the third book of the *Divine Comedy* – that he will once be able to meet and converse with his loved one in the beyond of heaven. Luzzi's worldview precludes the possibility of such a future encounter because it lacks the foundation of that belief.

While for Dante the healing movement from grief to love involves the translation (transcendence even) of his erotic feelings for Beatrice into a form of spiritual love that shares in the love that God has for human beings, Luzzi's immediate struggle is with the fact that after Katherine's death he remains in love with her but can no longer experience this love physically. He is reminded, in this respect, of the eternal plight of Paolo and Francesca, the adulterous lovers that we meet in *Inferno*'s famous Canto 5: 'They float through the afterlife like two weeping doves,' Luzzi writes, 'condemned to a love that is not physical. Trying to love each other without a body.'[18] In this respect, the erotic poems of Guido Cavalcanti (Dante's first poetic mentor, whose impact is primarily present in the *Vita Nuova*) make more sense to Luzzi than Dante's. Indeed, the hard lesson he has to learn from the latter is that there are ways of loving that need not be physical.[19]

'I would never have told anyone this', he writes in the pages of his book that deal with the first phase of his grief, 'but I had not gotten over losing her body, the warmth of her touch, my desire to fuse with her. Her spirit was not enough – Dante's Beatrice could not help me with this one.'[20] Luzzi is with Freud rather than with the poet of the *Divine Comedy* on this one: 'Mourning can only end when you have detached your passion and physical desire from your beloved,' he concludes after having read Freud's central reflections on the topic. 'Freud believed that when you lose your beloved, you need to spend lots of time in the Underworld with her ghost, slowly letting her lose her body and fade into pure memory.'[21] This is clearly not what happens in Dante's *Paradiso*.

Luzzi's understanding of what his memoir's subtitle calls the 'mysteries of love' cannot but involve the arrival of a new woman, it would seem. And indeed, the book's final pages mark the beginning of what the author of *In A Dark Wood*, with yet another aptly Dantean reference, calls a 'new life' ('incipit vita nova'), a life with the British violinist Helena Baillie, whom he formally introduces to his daughter on 24 April 2011, 'the seven-hundred-and-eleventh anniversary of Dante's journey to the Underworld'.[22] Like the *Divine Comedy*, then, *In A Dark Wood* also has a happy ending, albeit one that could easily be misunderstood by the original audience of Dante's epic poem. To us, it makes sense that the arrival of Helena Baillie does not amount to the disappearance of Katherine in Luzzi's life (Katherine is Isabel's mother, after all), though we would find it strange (to say the least) if Dante were to include in his epic poem references to another significant other in his life.

That ultimate difference – if not crucial then at least telling – does not stand in the way of Dante's guiding force for Luzzi. On the contrary even: it may well be the difference between the thirteenth-century Christian poet and the twenty-first-century secular professor that enables the latter to assume the former as his teacher – a teacher of lessons that Dante would possibly be surprised to hear his work embodied. Luzzi writes in conclusion:

> He had taught me that you can love somebody without a body in a certain way but that you must reserve your truest love for somebody whose breath you can hear and feel – your child's, your wife's – and that you may visit the Underworld but you cannot live there. He also taught that self-pity is no substitute for free will, just as the electric air of grief is not the kind that can sustain your breathing in real life.[23]

## Literature and the Conversation with the Dead

In the end, life is life and literature, well, is just literature, as Luzzi keeps suggesting throughout his memoir. 'The *Divine Comedy* didn't rescue me after Katherine's death', he admits early on in the book. 'That fell to the support of family and friends, to my passion for teaching and writing, and above all to the gift of my daughter. Our daughter.'[24] Rather than serve as an argument against bibliotherapy ('it's *only* fiction, you know', 'books don't *really* cure you when you're sick'), expressions like these form the actual backbone of the reading practice. Of course, books don't work in the same way as real medicine does. Of course, they don't conquer bad cells and neither do they bring your blood count back to normal.

Or do they? As I have stressed earlier, the question of the actual effects of the reading of literature (positive or not, healing or sickening, direct or indirect) is not my concern here. What I'm interested in are the arguments that are being used in support of the claim that literary writings prove healthy or otherwise helpful for those reading them. What are the presuppositions with respect to books, reading and authors that we make use of in order to sustain the claims of professional and amateur bibliotherapists? What exactly do we mean when we say that a poet can teach us something? Teach us *what* and teach us *how*? Does the mystery of this teaching lie in the messages given, or (also) in the form these messages take? Why do we specifically look to literature for therapy and consolation? What are the specific and special characteristics of literary writings that warrant their supposedly unique therapeutic potential?

Like most of the examples of bibliotherapy that I have read in preparation of this book, Luzzi's memoir does not discuss these questions in any direct way, even though he clearly has answers to them, as my earlier references to his interest in the musical qualities of Dante's poem indicate. As several of the passages that I quoted from *In A Dark Wood* show, the claims that Luzzi makes with respect to the personal appeal of Dante's work on him rest on specific premises that also touch on the questions that are of interest to us here. Dante's work, we have seen, speaks to him personally, not despite the cultural distance that separates him from thirteenth-century Tuscany but on account of it. The underlying idea is clearly also that the work managed to survive and that even though the person who wrote it has been dead for over 700 years, his words are still a living presence, his voice still resounding. The questions that Luzzi turns to Dante for are questions that he clearly cannot ask the people who surround him: the grief counsellor that he visits on a regular basis[25] or the chaplain who presides over a memorial service for Katherine at Bard College,[26] let alone his mother and sisters, who take upon themselves the daily care of little Isabel as Luzzi tries to find comfort in his work, teaching and correcting the proofs of his first book. Only Dante can be asked and hopefully provide an answer to the question that, in a way, remains unspeakable among the living: 'Could I love Katherine now that her body was gone?'[27]

The idea that the voices of the dead continue to be heard is of course a literary topic that Dante knew well. Even if we subtract from the *Divine Comedy* the numerous Q-and-A passages between Dante *personaggio* and Virgil, nearly every one of the epic's hundred cantos offers a dramatisation of the topos: what Dante does throughout, after all, is have conversations with dead people. As I have argued elsewhere, the topical scenario of the conversation with the dead is underpinned in the literary history of the West by the rhetorical figure of *energeia*: the texts involved are marked by a vividness of language and a clarity of style that leave the reader (or listener, for that matter) with the impression of actual presence.[28] We can see before our eyes, so to speak, what the text's semiotic material is in fact only mediating. Readers of the *Divine Comedy* are familiar with the force of that impression: we don't really need Gustave Doré's wonderful illustrations in order to see (literally) what Dante's lines are all about: the text itself has plenty of visual force of its own.

Luzzi's conviction that Dante's text continues to speak to us is clearly related to this important tradition. However, more is at stake here. 'Dante's words gave me the language to understand my own profound sense of displacement', Luzzi writes in the prologue to his book. 'More important, they enabled me to connect my anguished state to a work of transcendent beauty.'[29] What these sentences make clear is that the texts' continued resonance depends not only on the rhetorical force of its language per se, but also on the 'connection' (Luzzi's word) that it makes possible with readers centuries later. 'I could feel him speaking to me directly', Luzzi writes as he recalls his early discovery of Dante's work in Florence.[30] While his impression of that immediate connection deserves further analysis, it is clear that Luzzi feels that Dante speaks to him on an idiosyncratically individual level, not as a member of a group of readers, yet not according to a logic of full identification either. As we have seen, Luzzi remains aware throughout of the difference between his own identity and that of Dante. The connection is found in a ratio of similarity *and* difference, in which the former is no less important than the latter, as numerous phrases that point out potential analogies between Luzzi and the author of the *Divine Comedy* show ('as Dante did', 'as Dante had', 'Dante too'[31]). Actually, this can also be related to the topical complex of the conversation with the dead. As Petrarch and Machiavelli (among others) have stressed: the selected dead are the sort of friends who don't simply tell you what you want to hear. (Also, as the Dutch seventeenth-century poet Constantijn Huygens pointed out, they never visit you without an invitation.[32])

The connection that Luzzi talks about does not work according to a straightforward logic of application. The idea is not that Dante simply gives advice of the sort that Luzzi can then go on to apply, as is the case in books that offer, for instance, culinary recipes or prescribe other sets of actions and regulations to be followed in specific what-to-do-situations. Texts like these are written with no regard whatsoever for the individuality of the reader: users of them are treated generically, as are the problems for which they require help. 'The *Divine Comedy*', Luzzi writes, 'was not a self-help manual, a means to a practical set of ends that I was able to negotiate based on Dante's advice. To say as much would do violence to the kind of poem that Dante tried to write.'[33]

But what kind of poem *did* Dante intend to write? Clearly not simply a didactic one, even though the adjective surely does cover part of the genre to which the *Comedy* belongs. The question will continue to occupy us in this chapter, but I do want to broach it here, because of the way in which Luzzi characterises Dante's epic poem in the remainder of the passage that I just quoted: the *Divine Comedy*, he writes, 'distracts us as much as it instructs us. But in that distraction – that pause on whatever purgatorial climb – we may find ourselves.'[34] Luzzi does not really explain what he means by 'distraction' (not that he needs to), but it is clearly related to what in an earlier passage that I quoted he calls the *Comedy*'s 'transcendent beauty of a work of art'. The poem's pragmatics of distraction, if I may call it that, is clearly related to its aesthetic qualities, to the fact that it is a work of art, not a religious treatise or manual, both of which, one might say, merely instruct. It is a pragmatics of distraction because the text's aesthetic (visual and aural) qualities enable Luzzi to see his own position differently by taking him away (literally: dis-tract) and opening his imagination, that is, by offering him alternative ways of seeing and thinking. 'Grief was choking my imagination,' Luzzi writes at one point, 'leaving me incapable of envisioning a different life.'[35] It is no wonder that it is a work of imagination that enables him to begin to see a different life, the possibility of a *vita nuova* on which the book ends.

The distraction on offer is visual as well as aural, as we have seen. It is surely no coincidence that Luzzi experiences the moment of epiphany that his memoir's narrative works up to (the moment he is really 'out of the dark wood') when he is attending a live performance of the Partita in D Minor that Bach (according to some scholars) composed shortly after he learned of the death of his wife Maria in 1720. Understanding that the piece's closing chaconne represents feelings that, in Luzzi's words, are '*both* a wail of grief and a celebration of [the woman's] life', he comes to the conclusion that 'Bach (had) achieved Dante's challenge, to love somebody without a body, while accepting that, like the beloved herself, the earthly love that was once shared is gone forever'.[36] It is this understanding – or better: the possibility of this understanding – that enables Luzzi to engage in his first serious romantic relationship after Katherine's death. His new love – the violinist performing Bach's chaconne '[o]n a blustery spring day in 2013',[37] as we read in the closing chapter of *In A Dark Wood* – came to his office late in 2010 to inquire about the possibilities of taking his Dante course. Surely, this was truly meant to be.

## The Christian Regime of Consolation

Towards the end of this chapter we will return to Luzzi's book, but first we need to have a closer look at Dante's own conception of the consolatory force of literature. My argument, in what follows, will be that the topos of literary comfort is central to the development of Dante's writing. In order to arrive at a proper understanding of that development, we need to have a preliminary look at Boethius' *De consolatione philosophiae*, a text whose discovery proved to be a decisive turning point in Dante's understanding of the consolatory potential of (his own) poetry. As might be expected, Dante's conception of the consolation of literature ties in with his Christian conception of consolation. The Christian regime of consolation, as we will see, differs from the classical regime, but is not entirely unlike it.

The iconic figure of the Christian regime of consolation is Job: no matter how great the hardship that befalls the Old Testament hero, no matter how inventive the lures of those who want to drive him away from his Creator, he keeps responding to whatever happens to him with the utmost conviction that what God wills is right for him. Even if God were to decide to abandon me, Job states, even '[t]hen should I yet have comfort; yea, I would harden myself in sorrow: let him not spare; for I have not concealed the words of the Holy One.'[38] 'Haec mihi sit consolatio', Job asserts, thereby relegating the many words of comfort spoken by his numerous consolers (some false, some well-meant) to their true stature. They are only words, spoken by humans, meaningless in comparison to the providential power of the Divine Logos.

The relationship between the classical and the Christian regime of comfort is one of continuity and discontinuity. The continuity lies in the fact that the central representatives of the Christian consolatory tradition – Jerome, Cyprian, Augustine, Ambrose and Boethius, to name the earliest ones – make use of arguments and topoi derived from classical *consolationes* (Cicero and Seneca are the most common sources) which they adapt and renew.[39] The discontinuity lies in what McClure describes as 'a fundamentally different spiritual perception of human misery, suffering, and death'.[40] In the classical regime, man's earthly sorrows are the result of an impersonal Fate that distributes both happy and painful moments, as in Achilles' allegory of the two urns of Zeus. In the Christian regime, McClure writes, '[d]eath and suffering are just punishment for Adam's Fall. Labor and sorrow are the wages of sin, the agents of divine retribution.'[41]

'[T]he central difference between pagan and Christian consolation', Ronald Rittgers adds, can be found in 'the centrality and certainty of the Resurrection (and the Last Judgement)' that early Christian thinkers stressed, in contrast with 'the ambivalence and ambiguity of their pagan counterparts on the afterlife'.[42] Both Rittgers and McClure refer to the figure of Job to illustrate the underpinnings of the Christian regime of comfort. 'The content and narrative drama of the Book of Job', McClure writes, 'is a compelling argument for the futility of mortal or rational solace; one cannot justly question or explain human suffering.'[43] The logic at hand could easily have resulted in the devaluation or even disappearance of a consolatory tradition in the course of the long Middle Ages. After all, the providential logic of the *quia vult* (whatever happens, happens because God wants it to happen) seems to rest on the idea that there is no real use in looking for human comfort.[44] Still, the extended period spawned a series of texts, practices and rituals which rest upon the same consolatory logic and concerns that we have found in Dante's work. After having surveyed in an exemplary manner a series of late Antique (Ambrose, Cyprian, Jerome), early medieval (Boethius, Pope Gregory I, Isidore of Seville) and late medieval (Dambach, Gerson, Petrarch) examples of Christian consolatory writings, Rittgers describes the core idea of what I have called the Christian regime of consolation as follows:

> suffering is an instrument that the sovereign and loving God uses to discipline his chosen ones so they may be fit to enter heaven. The appropriate response to this divine *ascesis* is to endure it patiently and thus, with the help of divine grace, to merit heaven by reducing *poena* and cultivating virtue, especially the love of God above all things. Time and again, these works urge patience on suffering Christians as the most important response to adversity and tribulation.[45]

## Boethius on the Consolation of Literature

The famous opening section of Boethius' treatise, one of the central texts of the West European Middle Ages, provides me with the second scene of comfort that I want to have a closer look at in this book. Written in the third decade of the sixth century by the Roman administrator Anicius Manlius Severinus Boethius (who at the time occupied the prominent position of 'Magister Officiorum' at the court of Theodoric, the Ostrogoth emperor who reigned over the remains of the Western Roman Empire in Ravenna), the work can be seen to epitomise the transition between the Late Antique period and the long Middle Ages, offering as it does a telling synthesis of Platonic philosophy and Christian religion. Earlier in his career, Boethius had planned, as he wrote, '[to] bring the thought of Aristotle and Plato somehow into harmony',[46] and his upbringing – typical of the class and generation to which he belonged – was marked by the conjunction of a formal education in classical rhetoric and a religious practice steeped in the Christian faith. In his *Convivio*, Dante singles out Boethius together with Cicero as one of his main sources of inspiration. In Canto 10 of the *Paradiso*, he counts Boethius among the twelve 'stars' that guide Beatrice and him, making Boethius part of an illustrious company that includes Thomas Aquinas, Albertus Magnus and Paulus Orosius, a famous pupil of Saint Augustine.

Together with the latter's late fourth-century *Confessiones*, Boethius' *Consolation of Philosophy* stands at the beginning of the important autobiographical tradition that helped define the literature of the West.[47] The treatise is said to have been written while its author was in prison in what is now Pavia (north of Milan), awaiting the execution he was sentenced to after having been accused (rightly or not) of treason by Theodoric. While we are not quite sure of the exact year of Boethius' death – it is usually dated to 524 though some sources point to 526; his grave can still be visited in Pavia's San Pietro in Ciel d'Oro – it is assumed that he finished the *De consolatione* not too long before he was executed.[48] It makes sense, then, that the writing of the text served its author as an exercise in the preparation of an imminent death, as it is said to have done on numerous occasions for readers coming after him, centuries later even. As Ernst Robert Curtius puts it in his magisterial survey of the medieval tradition in Latin literature, Boethius' treatise 'is a book which has refreshed innumerable minds, even down to our own day'.[49]

For the most part, the *Consolation of Philosophy* takes the shape of a series of dialogues between the text's I-narrator – the prisoner whose fate we are expected to identify with that of the text's creator – and Lady Philosophy, an allegorical figure whose wisdom in the course of the treatise's five books helps the prisoner to arrive at a better and deeper understanding of the situation he finds himself in. Whereas at the beginning of the text the imprisoned narrator complains bitterly of the bad fortune that he considers to have struck him unjustly, Lady Philosophy makes clear to him in a series of Socratic conversations that he should find faith in the providential love of God, who has meant his imprisonment not as a punishment but as the occasion of a necessary period of self-reflection on the path towards true knowledge and salvation. The end of that path can only be reached in the right mind-set, that is, by a mind schooled in the lessons that Lady Philosophy brings, lessons of reason and faith, indeed, of the necessary conjunction between those two capital qualities.

Formally speaking, Boethius' text is a prime example (possibly *the* prime example) of the mixed genre of *prosimetrum*: the prose-passages that dominate the work's five books of dialogue are interspersed with metrical passages, 39 in all.[50] The first book of the *Consolation* opens with the very first of these passages: a poem of 22 lines written in elegiac couplets (the first line of which is a dactylic hexameter, followed by a dactylic pentameter). Its main generic example may well be the *Tristia*, the poems of complaint written by Ovid after he was exiled from Rome by the Emperor August in CE 8.[51] In it, we hear the prisoner lament what he considers the simultaneous loss of his freedom, his professional stamina and his youth. 'My hair is prematurely white', he writes bitterly, 'and my skin hangs loose / on a poor, precarious frame' (Im1, 9–10).[52] In line with the rhetoric that characterises traditional consolations of exile (such as Seneca's *Consolatio ad Helviam Matrem* and the *Consolatio ad Polybium*, two sources Boethius will have known[53]), the poem begins by immediately contrasting the prisoner's current misfortune with the good days of yore, in which, as he puts it (in David Slavitt's enjoyably readable translation), he 'used to write cheerful poems, happy and life-affirming' (Im1, 1). The present situation clearly calls for another type of poetry altogether. In character, Boethius makes the point by echoing in the first two words of his poem's opening couplet ('carmina qui') the penultimate line of *The Georgics*, in which Virgil takes leave of bucolic poetry.[54]

For the prisoner, then, life as it is could not be more different from life as it used to be. In the sad state in which he finds himself, '[his] eyes are wet with tears' (Im1, 2), as he puts it, and the only work that he can produce are poems 'that only grieving Muses would prompt [him] to compose' (Im1, 3): 'heartbreaking verse from a suffering, heartbroken man' (Im1, 4). '[T]hese woeful songs turn out to be my consoling companions' (Im1, 5), the prisoner concludes. The suggestion is clear:

the production of poetic lament is meant to bring comfort and the present tense of the claim just quoted shows that the prisoner believes that it actually does. From the accompanying prose section (the first one of book one) it becomes further clear that the prisoner composes his elegy without uttering a word, 'in a silence', as he puts it, 'broken only by the scratchings of [his] quill' (Ip1, 2). The prisoner is not alone in his cell, though, as we can also see on several illustrations in the numerous manuscripts of (translations of) Boethius' text: gathered around his bed are 'the Muses of poetry' (Ip1, 3), who apparently dictate the 'gloomy thoughts' (Ip1, 2) that give shape and voice to the prisoner's lament.[55]

Before the reader of the *Consolation* is made aware of their physical presence, however, the text's narrator points to the sudden arrival of yet another female presence. At first, the woman is unknown to him – a sign of the sorry state he finds himself in, as we soon learn – but she immediately strikes him 'with awe' (Ip1, 2). The lengthy description of the strange figure that follows is organised around a set of contrasting qualities whose opposition the awe-inspiring woman with her 'burning gaze' somehow seems able to transcend. Holding in one hand (the right) a set of books and in the other a sceptre, she is said to be of a 'fresh and glowing [complexion] as that of a girl', while at the same time it is clear to the prisoner that she must be centuries old: 'nobody would mistake her for a creature of our time', he writes. Also, her dress, 'a miracle of fine cloth and meticulous workmanship' seems to be simultaneously torn and darkened, 'as if through neglect', even though that in itself clearly does not diminish the woman's force. The female figure is at once extremely tall ('I was certain that if she had a mind to stretch her neck just a little, her face would penetrate the skies') and yet at times obviously of normal stature. Describing in full the woman's dress, the narrator goes to say that he 'could see worked into the bottom border the Greek letters $\pi$ (*pi* – for practice) and slightly higher $\theta$ (*thèta* – for theory) with steps that were marked between them to form a ladder by which one might climb from the lower to the upper' (Ip1, 3). The detail of the letters (the one standing for practical philosophy and the other for theoretical philosophy) clearly does not help the prisoner to realise that he is in the presence of Lady Philosophy herself: it is only in the third prose section that he recognises his former teacher.

As soon as she enters the scene, Lady Philosophy focuses both her attention and her anger on the Muses of Poetry who surround the prisoner's bed. 'Eyes blazing', she dismisses them outright. Having detected from the outset that the prisoner's problem is not so much his material and physical imprisonment as the occluded mental state he finds himself in (she immediately refers to his bed as that of a 'sick' man), she claims with the strongest authority possible that the presence of these Muses runs counter to what this patient needs. Rather than provide him with a means of necessary healing, she believes, the words of complaint and the expressions of grief they help him produce only worsen his condition. The text's opening elegy to which the Muses of Poetry inspire the prisoner confirm him in his pitiful state instead of forcing him to see things differently. They continue and even strengthen the tearfulness that clearly clouds the prisoner's mind and vision. What he needs – the rational analysis that only Philosophy can bring – is something they cannot possibly secure. If we were to grant the prisoner that these Muses are indeed consoling companions, as he claims in the *Consolation*'s opening poem, the consolation which they have on offer is evidently false – their *pharmakon* is simply poisonous.

'"Who let these chorus girls in here to approach a sick man's bedside?"', Lady Philosophy wonders out loud: '"They have no cures for what ails him. Indeed, what they offer will only make his condition worse! What he wants is the fruits of reason, while all they have is the useless thorns of intemperate passion. If he listens to their nonsense, he will accustom himself to depression instead of trying to find a cure."' (Ip1, 4)[56] The dismissal continues with a direct address to the Muses, who are scolded even more because in this specific case they have tried to lure into their poetic trap 'an educated man', 'a student of Parmenides, Zeno, and Plato' no less: '"You are like the Sirens, and your blandishments will lead only to his destruction. Be gone! And leave him to my Muses to care for him and heal him."' Lady Philosophy's injunctions are immediately effective: 'My Muses blushed', the prisoner writes, 'hung their heads in shame, and withdrew from the room.' Their departure leaves him saddened ('my eyes filled with tears'), but also wondering about the exact identity of 'this woman of such commanding authority': 'Who was she? What did she have in mind for me?' he keeps asking himself (Ip1, 4).

## Poetry *and* Philosophy?

We hardly need the explicit reference to Plato in order to see that the opposition Lady Philosophy forges in the treatise's first prose section between the truly curative force of rational philosophy and the poisonous effects of emotional poetry is somehow related to Socrates' dismissal of literature in Book 10 of *The Republic*. But how, exactly, are the two related? With respect to the opening section of Boethius' treatise, the question is the same one that crops up from time to time in discussions of Plato's banishment of the poets in *The Republic*: does Socrates dismiss all forms of poetry or only a specific type? If we argue for the former position, how then does this absolute rejection square with other dialogues in which Plato seems to be more sympathetic to some types of literature? Also, how does the (literary) form of the text in which poetry is being criticised affect the message of the criticism? While some commentators have pointed out the irony that Plato is, basically, criticising the mechanics of dramatic representation in a form that is, itself, dramatic, the idea has not become central in the dialogue's reception.

If we accept John Ferrari's conclusion that 'for Plato there is no such thing as philosophic poetry, only (at closest) a poetic sort of philosophy',[57] then we ought to conclude that Boethius' position is different in at least this respect: for Boethius, there is definitely such a thing as philosophic poetry, the right sort of poetry. Given the more explicitly literary form of the *Consolation*, it makes sense that the question of the inter-relationship – as opposed to what Plato famously referred to as a 'quarrel'[58] – between philosophy and poetry is more pressing in discussions of Boethius' treatise than it is in discussions of *The Republic*. Not only is Boethius' treatise replete with literary references (some of which I have just identified[59]), it also takes the self-conscious form of poetry in the treatise's 39 metrical passages. What is more, the majority of these 'poems' are spoken by Lady Philosophy herself.

The first of these follows immediately after Lady Philosophy sends off the Muses of Poetry, exchanging the 'harlots' for her own muses ('leave him to my Muses to care for him and heal him', are her last words to the Muses of Poetry). To the attentive reader it becomes clear fairly soon, then, that the opposition between Philosophy and Poetry is one that Lady Philosophy may be trying to bridge as well. As Stephen Blackwood has recently argued, the metrical passages of the *De consolatione philosophiae* clearly show that Boethius tried to relate the text's formal elements (rhythmical and other aural patterns) to the treatise's thematic development of the consolatory theme.[60] Lady Philosophy brings comfort, then, not just because of what she says, but also because of the (poetic) ways in which she does so. Several decades ago, Seth Lerer pointed out that Boethius' entire treatise (not only the poems, but also the prose sections) is the result of a sustained attempt at 'literary method'.[61]

Lady Philosophy's muses, Antonio Donato argues on the basis of the opening passage of Boethius' second book (IIm1, 7–8 especially), are 'rhetoric and poetry'.[62] At the initial stage of his healing process, the prisoner is told that he should 'take some mild palliative that will, when you have absorbed it, prepare you for those stronger preparations that will be curative' (IIp1, 28). Lady Philosophy is aware of the difficulties involved and she comes with a plan that involves a gradual intensification of the remedial instruments. 'Let us begin', she argues, 'with the pleasant devices of rhetoric that are reliable only if they do not stray from our fundamental principles. We must be careful that it harmonizes properly with the modes of our preferred music' (IIp1, 28). Boethius' Latin defines the rhetoric as 'sweet' (*dulcedinis*), a qualification that is not at all unexpected, but which does call to mind the warning that Cicero voiced in his *Tusculanae Disputationes*: there is a distinct danger in writings – poetry above all – that are too *dulcis*.[63]

Be that as it may, the opening of Boethius' Book Three, in which the prisoner describes the effect of Lady Philosophy's sweet song, makes clear that her poetry brings that which the author's treatise strives for – for the time being at least. 'She finished singing', the prisoner states 'and the melody hung in the air, its sweetness still in my ears, which were eager for more. I waited a bit and then thanked her.'

> 'What wonderful comfort (*solamen*) you offer, with both your arguments and your poetry. You do revive me, so that I am no longer absolutely devastated by the blows of fortune but seem at least for the moment able to bear them. At any rate, I am no longer terrified by the prospect of your 'strong remedies', whatever they are, but eager for you to administer them.' (IIIp1, 59)

In his book on Boethius, Donato gives a good survey of the scholarly discussion regarding the relationship between philosophy and poetry in the treatise that I will not rehearse in full here. On the one hand, there are scholars who see a basic tension between the *Consolation*'s poems and the philosophical reflection that is central to the treatise.[64] Stressing (and possibly overstressing) the fact that Boethius' treatise shares its prosimetric form with the Menippean satire, some of these even go so far as to suggest that the poems are meant to undermine the text's serious philosophical message, or at least ironically expose its limits and self-contradictions.[65] On the other hand, there are those who believe that while the poems function as genuine and positive instruments in the healing process that

Lady Philosophy aims for, their role is not really central to Boethius' text. According to these scholars, Donato writes, the poems are only allowed to play 'a secondary and/or propaedeutic role'.[66]

However different these two critical positions may seem, they share the view that the difference between poetry and philosophy remains a basic and hierarchical one, in which the former is subservient to the latter. The conclusion of Anne Crabbe's influential essay on 'Literary Design in the *De Consolatione Philosophiae*' offers a good example: 'Boethius', Crabbe writes, 'makes his own plea in the *Consolatio* for a poetry that both serves and enriches philosophy'.[67] Donato's own reading of the treatise tries to make a basic difference in this respect, in that he aims for an integral and integrated reading of the poems in the philosophical exercise of the treatise. Focusing on a number of passages in the treatise that he takes as explicit comments on the positive force of poetry and rhetoric (such as the opening from Book Two that I referred to earlier, but also the reference in Book Four to the productive 'relief' by the 'charms of poetry' (IVp6, 139)), Donato wants to show that the poems are not merely ornamental but curative in their own way. A key element in poetry's positively therapeutic force, as we have seen, is its musical character,[68] an interest for which Donato traces back to Plato's *Timaeus* and to Boethius' own treatise on music (*De musica*).[69] Central to this tradition is the idea that music addresses the non-rational part of the soul, but more importantly, that its powers of harmony help to secure a successful integration of the soul's different parts. This, Donato argues, seems to be the main function of Lady Philosophy's poems in Boethius' *Consolation*. 'True music addresses the soul directly and brings it into harmony with the heavenly concord', Seth Lerer writes with reference to the closing poem of Book Three, the poem that takes as its subject Orpheus, the legendary poet-singer who managed to affect animals, rocks and trees, and even gods, but who, in the end, failed to console himself.[70] As we will shortly see, the figure of Orpheus, and Boethius' interpretation of his story, played an important role in Dante's reflections on the consolatory force of poetry.

## Dante's Discovery of Cicero and Boethius

The starting point for our discussion of Dante's own treatment of the topos of literary comfort is the famous passage in his *Convivio* – to be found in Chapter 12 of the treatise's second book – in which Dante points to the guiding force of Boethius' work. At the time, Dante was grieving for the death of his beloved Beatrice. Unable to find comfort in his own ruminations, he claims to have discovered a guide in the author of the *Consolation of Philosophy*. Here is the passage, which we will have a closer look at in what follows. It can be found at the beginning of Dante's explanation of the allegorical sense of the great *canzone* that is central to the second book of his *Convivio*, 'Voi che 'ntendendo il terzo ciel movete':[71]

> Nevertheless after some time my mind, which was endeavoring to heal itself, resolved (since neither my own consolation nor that of others availed) to resort to a method which a certain disconsolate individual had adopted to console himself; and I began to read that book of Boethius, not known to many, in which, while a prisoner and an exile, he had found consolation. And hearing further that Tully had written another book in which, while discussing Friendship, he had addressed words of consolation to Laelius, a man of the highest merit, upon the death of his friend Scipio, I set about reading it. (*Conv.* II, 12, 2)[72]

Boethius' *De consolatione philosophiae* is but one of two classical works of inspiration – indeed, of consolation – to which Dante refers explicitly in this passage. The other text that he mentions – I will return to the importance of Boethius for Dante shortly – is *De amicitia*, the dialogue on friendship that Cicero wrote in 44 BCE, the year after the death of his daughter Tullia.[73] *De amicitia* stages a conversation between Gaius Laelius and his two sons-in-law, Gaius Fannius and Quintus Mucius Scaevola (the latter was Cicero's mentor, and the presumed source of the materials that were used in this dialogue). The conversation between Laelius and his sons-in-law took place a few days after the death of Scipio Africanus the Younger (129 BCE) and it touched upon Laelius' exemplary friendship with the recently departed. The friendship that Cicero talks about is, as Laelius puts it in a central passage of the dialogue, 'that pure and faultless kind, such as was that of the few whose friendships are known to fame'.[74] Laelius was a general, who played an important role in Scipio's victories in Spain and northern Africa, but also a close personal friend of Scipio.

Dante's reference to *De amicitia* is more specifically to a passage in the opening pages of Cicero's treatise in which Laelius responds to the seemingly pressing query of his interlocutors as to why he had not turned up at the most recent commemoration of his dear friend. Surely, Fannius and Scaevola assume, the cause of Laelius' absence must have been 'ill health' rather than 'grief' (*maestitia*, 'dejection').[75]

Located at the very opening of Cicero's text, the importance of the issue becomes immediately clear: Laelius is being portrayed in *De amicitia* as a paragon of virtuous wisdom (*sapientia*): neither excessive mourning nor the neglect of one's official duties become a person of that status. Comparing Laelius to the likes of Cato, the wise man *par excellence* whom Dante chose as the guardian of Mount Purgatory in the second *cantica* of the *Divine Comedy*, Scaevola praises his father-in-law for the moderation of his mourning, stating that Laelius 'bear[s] with composure the pain occasioned by the death of one who was at once a most eminent man and your very dear friend'.[76] It obviously pains him having to defend his father-in-law against the criticism of some who must have spread the rumour that what kept Laelius away from the memorial service was not too much grief on account of Scipio's death but too little. The idea is simply preposterous, Scaevola concludes: such behaviour is not at all 'consistent with [Laelius'] refined and tender nature and [his] culture'.[77]

Laelius obviously confirms: only illness, indeed, could keep him from performing the mourning duties that his dear departed friend deserved. He does so by means of words that apparently struck a personal note with Dante:

> If I were to assert that I am unmoved by grief at Scipio's death, it would be for 'wise' men to judge how far I am right, yet, beyond a doubt, my assertion would be false. For I am indeed moved by the loss of a friend such, I believe, as I shall never have again, and – as I can assert on positive knowledge – a friend such as no other man ever was to me. But I am not devoid of a remedy, and I find very great consolation in the comforting fact that I am free from the delusion which causes most men anguish when their friends depart. I believe that no ill has befallen Scipio; it has befallen me, if it has befallen anyone; but great anguish for one's own inconveniences is the mark of the man who loves not his friend but himself.[78]

The wisdom of Laelius' words clearly lies in their exploration of the *via media* that involves the moderation of his emotions. More importantly, in his reply he also points out that those who mourn excessively should ask themselves for whose sake they are doing so. To feel overly dejected at the death of a friend, Laelius suggests, may ultimately be a very selfish thing to do. He does not find consolation in expressing or otherwise showing the pain that Scipio's death resulted in. Quite the contrary: his comfort, as he goes on to argue, lies in the fact that Scipio's death did not put an end to their friendship. In fact, as Cicero will make clear later in the dialogue, what actually defines friendship is the survival of the deep bond that exists between true friends beyond the line that divides the living from the dead. '[F]riends, though absent, are at hand', Cicero has Laelius say in a central passage of the dialogue: 'though in need, yet abound; though weak, are strong; and – harder saying still – though dead, are yet alive; so great is the esteem on the part of their friends, the tender recollection and the deep longing that still attends them.'[79] Commenting on this passage, Jacques Derrida concludes that for Cicero '[f]riendship provides numerous advantages (. . .) but none is comparable to this unequalled hope, to this ecstasy towards a future which will go beyond death.'[80]

Making use of an argument that in his survey of consolatory 'topoi' in the third book of his *Tusculan Disputations* Cicero relates to the philosophical school of the Cyrenaics – 'I judge the evil we speak of to lie in belief and not in nature'[81] – Laelius points out that we should not see the parting of a good friend as an occasion to think that death constitutes an evil that we should, consequently, fear. We may *think* death is a cause for fear (belief), but it is *not* (nature). It is not hard to imagine the great appeal that Laelius' words must have held for Dante. As he already seemed to realise in the *Vita Nuova*, there is something inherently selfish in the mourner's expression of grief, however heartfelt. Chief among the reasons why he had resolved not to deal with Beatrice's death was the idea that, as he puts it there, 'it isn't right for me to speak of this because I would have to praise myself, which is a reprehensible thing to do, no matter who does it'.[82] There is something self-centred in the complaints of the mourner, the possible danger of prioritising one's own feelings of loss over those of the person who passed away. In the *Convivio*, the example of Laelius' unwavering friendship for Scipio also provides Dante with a positive model for the continued love one can feel for a departed friend, beyond the divide that is taken to separate the living from the dead. They help him understand all the better that the continuation of his mourning over the death of Beatrice would count as neither wise nor honourable behaviour.

## Beatrice and Lady Philosophy

In his discussion of the significance of *De amicitia* for Dante, Filippa Modesto makes clear – taking her cue from Karl Vossler – that Cicero's analysis of friendship comes close to and indeed is fulfilled by the Christian concept of *caritas*.[83] The core values that found

Laelius' friendship for Scipio – virtue, goodwill, and the natural and mutual affection of like-minded noble creatures – are those that mark Dante's deeper understanding of his love for Beatrice. Her death, as the author of the *Convivio* comes to see more properly, should not be a cause for continued sorrow, but for gratitude, hope and humility – gratitude for the persistence of Beatrice's love, hope for being able to see her again, 'face to face', in due course, and humility on account of the greatness of her character. Cicero and Boethius appear to be Dante's joint guides on the path towards this new insight. 'Between the end of 1291 and 1295', Modesto writes, 'Dante had fully immersed himself in the study of philosophy taught by the Franciscans at Santa Croce and by the Dominicans at Santa Maria Novella.'[84] The years are those that follow Beatrice's death in 1290; they coincide with the final composition of the *Vita Nuova*.

This is what Dante further has to say about Cicero's and Boethius' texts in the passage from the second book of the *Convivio*, the opening sentences of which are quoted above (see page 80):

> Although it was difficult for me at first to penetrate their meaning, I finally penetrated it as deeply as my command of Latin and the small measure of my intellect enabled me to do, by which intellect I had perceived many things before, as in a dream, as may be seen in the *New Life*.
>
> And just as it often happens that a man goes looking for silver and apart from his intention finds gold, which some hidden cause presents, perhaps not without divine ordinance, so I who sought to console myself found not only a remedy for my tears but also the words of authors, sciences, and books. Pondering these, I quickly determined that Philosophy, who was the lady of these authors, sciences, and books, was a great thing. I imagined her fashioned as a gentle lady, and I could not imagine her in any attitude except one of compassion, so that the part of my mind that perceives truth gazed on her so willingly that I could barely turn it away from her. I began to go where she was truly revealed, namely to the schools of the religious orders and to the disputations held by the philosophers, so that in a short period of time, perhaps some thirty months, I began to feel her sweetness so much that the love of her dispelled and destroyed every other thought.
>
> Consequently, feeling myself raised from the thought of that first love to the virtue of this one, almost in amazement I opened my mouth to speak the words of the canzone before us, revealing my condition beneath the figure of other things, because no rhyme in any vernacular was worthy to treat openly of the lady of whom I was enamored; nor were the listeners so well prepared that they would have understood the fictive words so

easily; nor would they have given credence to their true meaning, as they did to the fictive, because in fact they fully believed that I was disposed toward this love, and not, as they believed, to the other. I began therefore to say *You whose intellect the third sphere moves* ['*Voi che 'ntendendo il terzo ciel movete*']. Since this lady, as has been said, was the daughter of God, queen of all things, most noble and beautiful Philosophy, we must consider who were these movers and this third heaven. And first I will speak of the heaven, according to the order already employed. Here it will not be necessary to proceed by dividing and explaining the text word by word; for, by turning the fictive words from what they say into what they mean, the meaning will be sufficiently clear from the exposition already given. (*Conv.* II, 12, 4–10)

After Beatrice's death, as he writes here, Dante continued to be 'pierced by such sorrow that no comfort availed [him]' (*Conv.* II, 12, 1). Unable to find consolation in himself or, for that matter, in the words of his living companions ('since neither my own consolation nor that of others availed'), he decides to look for it in what he calls 'that book of Boethius, not known to many, in which, while a prisoner and an exile, he had found consolation' (*Conv.* II, 12, 2). The suggestion that *De consolatione philosophiae* is a text 'not known to many' surely sounds strange to us. After all, we consider Boethius' treatise to be one of the central writings of the long Middle Ages, 'one of those books which no educated man left unread' as one commentator typically put it.[85] Irrespective of whether we should take Dante's description as further self-fashioning on his part or reconsider our own (over)estimation of the actual fame of the text in Dante's surroundings, the fact remains that his choice of Boethius as a possible bringer of solace definitely makes sense.

The choice definitely paid off. Reading Boethius' treatise together with Cicero's, Dante finds the gold of philosophy while he was looking for the silver of consolation – put differently, he finds the more valuable consolation that philosophy has to offer.[86] Reading Boethius not only enables Dante to put an end to his tears (an urge that is central, as we have seen, to the author of the *De consolatione philosophiae* from the very beginning), it also gives him the words of wisdom that he needs – the words of the philosophers that he encounters in the course of his study with the Florentine Dominicans and Franciscans, but also those of the *canzone* that is central to the second *trattato* of the *Convivio*. As he points out here, it is the inspiration of philosophy that, to his amazement, causes the words of the *canzone* to flow in the way that they do.

Clearly, the fact that Dante pictures for himself (*imaginava*) philosophy as a 'donna gentile' is due to the influence of Boethius – the allegorical image of Lady Philosophy opens up the possibility to fuse Beatrice with said Lady. Writing his text in the first years of his exile from Florence, it is little wonder that Dante continued to identify with the author of the *De consolatione philosophiae*.[87] Of the different references that the *Convivio* contains to Boethius' text, the longer passage that I just quoted is the one that is of most interest to us. In a way, one could say that in that passage, 'gentle' Lady Philosophy is actually dictating the 'sweet' words of the *canzone*. As such, the scene is reminiscent, albeit inversely, of the opening of Boethius' text in which, as we saw, Lady Philosophy sends off the Muses who are literally putting the words of the tearful elegy in the prisoner's mind. The 'analogy' becomes even clearer if we relate this passage from the *Convivio* to the chapter in the *Vita Nuova* (XXXI) in which, shortly after the moment in the narrative when we first hear of the death of Beatrice, Dante introduces the poem that begins with the line 'Li occhi dolenti per pietà del core'. This is the collection's first poem of mourning, in which, as Robert Pogue Harrison puts it in *The Body of Beatrice*, '[p]oetically [Dante's] grief bursts forth belatedly'.[88]

'Li occhi dolenti' is the very type of poem that Boethius' prisoner was writing on his sickbed as he was suddenly called to order by Lady Philosophy in the opening scene of the *De consolatione philosophiae* that we discussed earlier – 'heartbreaking verse from a suffering, heartbroken man' (Im1, 4). Like those of Boethius, Dante's eyes are also 'wet with tears' (Im1, 2 in Boethius' text; 'they are red and hurt as well' in Dante's line 2), but the tears prove anything but a remedy for the poet's sorrow. Neither, as a matter of fact, is the writing of these tearful, elegiac lines. The chapter in which Dante's poem occurs starts off with an expression of the poet's deep despair at the loss of his loved one ('After I had wept for so long that I was weary and still had not managed to relieve my sadness'), and it ends on pretty much the same note – the writing of these lines clearly does not have the positive effect that the poet was after. 'I decided to write a canzone in which I would speak of her for whom I was experiencing such grief as to destroy my soul', he writes in the opening sentence of the chapter, but no such solace is found. The topic of comfort is addressed no less than three times in the poem (lines 40, 56 and 76), but each instance seems to point out the poet's failure to find consolation.

In the second of these instances, at the end of the *canzone*'s fourth stanza – 'In mourning then, alone as my tears flow, / I call, "Beatrice, are you really dead?" / And calling out her name, I'm comforted' (54–6)[89] – the search for comfort might seem to be successful. However, from the remainder of the poem we can see quite clearly that the comfort in question is as illusory as the early conviction of Boethius' prisoner that the poems dictated by the Muses surrounding his sickbed are 'consoling companions' (Im1, 5). The closing stanza of 'Li occhi dolente' shows that, unlike Boethius' prisoner, the lyric persona of the *Vita Nuova* does not arrive – not yet, at least – at the insight that another type of poetry, and indeed another type of consolation, is called for. In it, Dante takes leave of the poem he is writing, in an apostrophe that does signal a farewell, though not the type of farewell that Boethius' prisoner is strongly encouraged to bid by Lady Philosophy in the opening scene of the *De consolatione philosophiae*. 'Figliola di tristizia' Dante calls his *canzone* and he urges her to go and spread the bad news that she is bringing (the news of Beatrice's death, that is) so that everyone who has ear to hear will be as 'disconsolate' as the poet and his poem:

> My sad canzone, go your way and weep:
> search out those women and those girls again
> to whom your sister-kin
> would once upon a time bring happiness:
> while you, who are the daughter of distress,
> go off disconsolate to be with them. (71–6)

## Towards a Truly Consolatory Poetry?

Reading Boethius in the years of sadness that followed Beatrice's death, Dante will have come to understand that his grief ultimately called for another type of consolation – and, indeed, for another type of poetry. The difference between 'Li occhi dolenti' and 'Voi che 'ntendendo il terzo ciel movete', the *canzone* that is discussed in the *Convivio*'s second book, and that apparently warranted Dante's Boethian excursion in it, becomes immediately clear, even from a superficial reading. While the former poem, as we have just seen, fails to move beyond the inconsolable sorrow of the bereaved poet, the first *canzone* in the *Convivio* marks a transition that is situated between the third and fourth stanzas. The movement is from the poet's 'weeping soul' ('l'anima piange' (30)) that feels abandoned by an unnamed being that used to bring comfort ('questo piatoso che m'ha consolata' (32)), to the realisation that Beatrice's comforting presence has not at all disappeared and that, therefore, the poet's soul is not dead but simply troubled ('tu non se' morta, ma se' ismaritta' (40)) and full of fear. Towards the end of the fourth stanza, the 'spiritel d'amor gentile' (42) that addresses the poet's soul points out the truly comforting truth of Beatrice's still living presence:

> See how compassionate she is, and humble,
> How courteous and wise in her magnificence:
> Resolve henceforth to call this one your lady.
> Unless you err through self-deceit you'll see
> The beauty of such lofty miracles
> That you will say: 'Love, my true lord,
> Behold your handmaid: Do as you please.' (46–52)

The difference between the two poems also shows in their closing stanzas. In both cases, the poem itself is addressed by the poet. But whereas in 'Li occhi dolenti', the poem's 'disconsolate' sadness is stressed, in 'Voi che 'ntendendo il terzo ciel movete' the *canzone* is being praised for its self-confident beauty. This quality, the suggestion seems to be, will be a new source of courage that enables those hearing it who are able to truly understand the poem's message to abandon all fear and thence find comfort.

> My song, I think they will be few indeed
> Who'll rightly understand your sense,
> So difficult and complex is your speech.
> So if by chance it comes to pass
> That you should find yourself with some
> Who do not grasp it well at all,
> I pray you then, dear newborn song,
> Take courage again and say to them:
> 'Consider at least how fair I am!' (53–61)

The three poems that are discussed at length in the *Convivio* make clear, in their distinct difference from the 'mere' love poems collected in the *Vita Nuova*, that Dante was looking for this new type of consolation in the direction pointed out by Boethius: the direction of philosophy and the 'donna gentile' who embodied that ideal. Unlike the poems of the *Vita Nuova*, which are only meant to be read as fairly direct and straightforward expressions of Dante's love for the particular woman that Beatrice was, the canzones in the *Convivio* are multi-layered, as the poet himself explains in the famous opening chapter of the book's second *trattato*. There, with specific reference to biblical and mythical writings, Dante distinguishes between four different senses that can be conveyed by one and the same text: the literal ('this is the sense that does not go beyond the surface of the letter, as in the fables of the poets' (*Conv.* II, 1, 3)), the allegorical ('this is the one that is hidden beneath the cloak of these fables' (*Conv.* II, 1, 3)), the moral ('this is the sense that teachers should intently seek to discover throughout the scriptures, for their own profit and that of their pupils' (*Conv.* II, 1, 5)) and the anagogical ('that is to say, beyond the senses; and this occurs when a scripture is expounded in a spiritual sense which, although it is true also in the literal sense, signifies by means of the things signified a part of the supernal things of eternal glory' (*Conv.* II, 1, 6)). Of these, apparently, Dante considers the former two of prime importance for the exposition of his own poems that he wants to present in the *Convivio*. As he points out in the opening chapter of his 'Banquet's' first book, it is his intention 'to explain these canzoni by means of an allegorical exposition, after having discussed the literal account' (*Conv.* I, 1, 18).[90]

Dante refers twice to the distinction between the literal and allegorical senses in this passage and on both occasions he is careful to stress what he sees as the implicated nature of their relationship: the one calls forth the other, in either direction. The allegorical meaning of a text is a 'truth' that is waiting to be discovered beneath the cloak of the text's first apparent meaning, that is, its literal sense, while, inversely, the allegorical truth also calls to mind its literal embodiment. The text's allegorical meaning is 'a truth hidden beneath a beautiful fiction' ('una veritade ascosa sotto bella menzogna') as Dante writes in one of the *Convivio*'s most quoted phrases. In a way, the relationship at hand resembles the dialectic that underlies Dante's concept of the 'figura', famously explained by Erich Auerbach in terms that refuse to make a hierarchical distinction between the actual, sensible reality of a given event or person (its literal meaning, say) and the larger (allegorical) meaning for which this event or person comes to stand.[91] In the case of Beatrice, one could say that the story that Dante first recounts in the *Vita Nuova* of his love for this woman and his sadness at her departure serves as the literal foundation for the later allegorisation (both of the woman and of the love that Dante continues to feel for her, and of his grief at her loss) in both the *Convivio* and the *Divine Comedy*.

We will return to the *Divine Comedy* in a moment, but first we need to get a clearer view of the way in which Dante himself conceives of the difference between the *Vita Nuova* and the *Convivio*. Looking back, in the latter text, on the earlier poems of the *Vita Nuova*, Dante stresses the youthful character of his former poetic production. The difference between the poems of the *Vita Nuova* and the later canzones is one of maturity or 'virility', as he puts it in the opening chapter of the *Convivio*'s first book ('piu virilmente si trattasse che ne la Vita Nuova' (*Conv.* I, 1, 16)). The reference to the poet's more mature approach clearly includes the way in which, in the respective works, he managed to deal with the loss of Beatrice, with the grief and sorrow that struck him after her sudden death. The suggestion is clear: in the *Vita Nuova*, Dante did not behave in as 'manly' a way as in the *Convivio*. 'I do not intend by this in any way to disparage that book [*the VN*] but rather more greatly to support it with this one [*the C*]', the poet goes on to explain, stressing that while the former book ('opera') was 'fervida e passionata', the latter one is 'temperata e virile' (*Conv.* I, 1, 16). In the *Vita Nuova*, in other words, Dante expressed his emotions openly and with fervour, while in the *Convivio* his approach was more moderate and more reasonable, less the work of a young man. The difference, indeed, is the result of the poet's having come of age. As Dante points out: 'I wrote the former work at the threshold of my youth, and this one after I had already passed through it' (*Conv.* I, 1, 17).

Describing the mature poems of the *Convivio* as more properly fitting the age of virility is more telling than might at first sight appear: the concept of 'virilitas' resonates with the Ciceronian ideal of *vir-tus*, virtue, and it is this theme that Dante makes central to the *Convivio* from the very beginning, in the paragraphs in which he sets out the treatise's (not fully realised) plan. The 'banquet' that Dante has in mind consists of meat served with accompanying bread; the poems are the former, the poet's own explanatory readings of them the latter: 'The meat of this banquet will be prepared in fourteen ways', Dante writes: 'that is, in fourteen canzoni, whose subject is both love as well as virtue' (*Conv.* I, 1, 14). The bread is there to make the meat more palatable, and more easily digested. 'By lacking the present bread', Dante continues to write, the poems 'possessed some degree of obscurity, so that to many their beauty was more pleasing than their goodness. But this bread (that is, the present explanation) will be the light that renders visible every shade of their meaning' (*Conv.* I, 1, 14–15).

The logic of the passage is similar to that of the final stanza of 'Voi che 'ntendendo il terzo ciel movete'. In the closing address to the poem, as we have seen, the difficulty and complexity of the *canzone* is also stressed, and with it the possibility that some readers will fall short of fully understanding the poem's intricate message. Those readers, Dante is suggesting there, can at least enjoy the poem's beauty ('Ponete mente almena com'io son bella!' (61)). Readers who want the poems' 'goodness' ('loro bontade') as well as their 'beauty' ('loro bellezza') will need the bread on offer in the fifteen chapters that make up the poet's own reading of the famous *canzone* in the second book of the *Convivio*.

The poems of the *Vita Nuova*, of course, also deal with love, but compared with the more mature canzones of the *Convivio* they are seen by Dante, in hindsight at least, to lack in virtue. In the transitional moment between the two works, the poet arrived at the discovery of an allegorical 'truth' that could be seen to reside within the story of Beatrice's love – the realisation, shared with Cicero's Laelius, that the death of a loved one does not have to result in the loss of that love, if only because that death is part of a divine plan, as the author of the *Convivio* learned, in turn, from Boethius. What Dante also came to realise in his reading of *De consolatione philosophiae* is that the story of Beatrice's love required the sort of analysis that would enable his readers to see the *vertade* behind (or better still, embodied in) its *bellezza*. The identification of Beatrice with Boethius' Lady Philosophy provided the perfect point of access to that truth.

## Orpheus, Iconic Consoler

It is interesting to note that Dante's explanation of the allegorical meaning of specific texts involves the example of Orpheus. As he puts it in the opening chapter of the second *trattato* of the *Convivio*:

> Thus Ovid says that with his lyre Orpheus tamed wild beasts and made trees and rocks move toward him, which is to say that the wise man with the instrument of his voice makes cruel hearts grow tender and humble and moves to his will those who do not devote their lives to knowledge and art; and those who have no rational life whatsoever are almost like stones. (*Conv.* II, 1, 3)

Hidden behind 'the cloak' of Orpheus' story, then, is the allegorical truth of the poet as a wise man, a source of comfort to those who need the sort of direction in their lives that they cannot provide for themselves. That direction – and the consolation to which it leads – involves an organic combination of knowledge and art, rationality and beauty, the *vertade* of the philosopher and the *bellezza* of the poet's song.

In itself, Dante's identification with Orpheus requires little further explanation, but it is interesting to point out that in *De consolatione philosophiae* the mythical poet features as well. Orpheus is the protagonist of the 12th *metrum* that rounds off the third book of Boethius' treatise. In that poem, spoken by Lady Philosophy at the end of a Socratic dialogue in which she reasoned with the prisoner about the essential goodness of God, Orpheus is portrayed as one who seems unable to find comfort for himself in the poems that have a distinct consolatory effect on all those who hear them. In this, Boethius' Orpheus is not unlike Dante himself, who, as we saw, found no comfort in the mournful elegies that he composed after Beatrice's death.

The fifth line of the poem contains a distinct echo of the opening line of the *De consolatione*'s very first poem, the tearful elegy dictated by the Muses to Boethius' prisoner – the verse that, as we saw, provoked the ire of Lady Philosophy:

Of old the Thracian poet mourned
His wife's sad death,
He who before had made the woods so nimbly run
And rivers stand
With his weeping measures,
And the hind's fearless flank
Lay beside savage lions,
Nor was the hare afraid to look upon
The hound, made peaceful by his song;
When grief burned yet more fierce and hot
His inmost heart,
And measures that subdued all else
Soothed not their master,
Complaining of inexorable gods above
He approached the halls below. (IIIm12, 5–19)

While most of the poem's remaining lines (20–51) develop Orpheus' story in line with Virgil's and Ovid's account of it[92] – Orpheus' descent into Hell; the immediate effect of his marvellous song on several inhabitants of the 'Tartarus' (Cerberus, Tantalus, Ixion, Tityus), including 'the King of the Underworld' (Hades), who grants the poet the unique permission to take Eurydice back to the world of the living; Orpheus' fatal transgression of Hades' single condition (not to look back upon Eurydice on their joint way out) – in the poem's seven closing lines, Lady Philosophy uncovers the fable's allegorical meaning. In the poem's finale, she addresses the prisoner and all those who, with him, continue to search for truthful meaning, but in doing so, are inevitably hampered by their all too human desires:

> To you this tale refers,
> Who seek to lead your mind
> Into the upper day;
> For he who overcome should turn back his gaze
> Towards the Tartarean cave,
> Whatever excellence he takes with him
> He loses when he looks on those below. (IIIm12, 52–8)

Commenting on the allegorical meaning of the poem's final lines, Antonio Donato rightly claims that '[Lady] Philosophy seems to use the story of Orpheus and Eurydice to capture the condition of the philosopher who is torn between attending to the needs of the body and fulfilling the soul's desire to ascend to the higher realms of reality'.[93] It is important to stress that whereas in the preceding prose section Lady Philosophy tries to convince the prisoner by means of a philosophical discourse that follows Plato's model of the Socratic dialogue, the poem that rounds off the treatise's third book offers a different exhortatory medium, the literary device of myth, one that may well be, as Donato puts it, 'more suitable to convey a spiritual truth than an abstract argument'.[94] The issue, for me, is not so much which of the two discursive 'genres' – philosophy or poetry – works best in the circumstances defined in Boethius' and Dante's respective texts. The point that I am trying to develop is that at the time of his writing of the *Convivio*, Dante found an important guide in Boethius in his search for a type of poetry that could be considered to have true consolatory force, a force which the poems of the *Vita Nuova* clearly lacked, in hindsight at least. The main lesson that Dante took from Boethius in this respect was that in order to bring consolation, poetry would need to be philosophical – more philosophical at least than the majority of the literary production of Dante's time, more attuned to truth and the cultivation of the wise and virtuous behaviour that the poet found embodied in Beatrice.[95]

What Dante may further have picked up from Boethius' reading of the Orpheus-myth – or, indeed, from the larger framework of the *De consolatione philosophiae* – is the principle of 'revision', not simply as a philosophical concept (derived from Plato, ultimately) but also as the centrepiece of a poetical practice. As Seth Lerer in particular has shown, Boethius' Orpheus-poem literally looks back to the treatise's opening poem: both the prisoner and the Thracian bard are shattered by an extreme form of grief that impedes their true poetical powers. The prisoner allows himself to be misled by the harlot Muses of Poetry; Orpheus clearly cannot help himself: he also needs proper guiding. The central difference between the two poems, Lerer argues, lies in the fact that the latter contains an invitation, offered to the prisoner by Lady Philosophy, to 'revise' his earlier behaviour and rise above it. Admittedly, that invitation is not immediately clear from the translated passage that I just quoted. 'To you this tale refers' in Boethius' original Latin is 'Vos haec fabula respicit'. That last word, Lerer claims, 'embodies one of the central metaphors of the *Consolation*'.[96] The act of revision, he goes on to write, 'signals the full exercise of rational abilities and the desire to review and interpret past events as guides for present behavior'.[97] In its capacity of 'fable' (the word is also used by Dante when he refers to the Orpheus-myth as we have seen), the story of Orpheus is an urge for the prisoner to look back on his former life and to look forward (differently from Orpheus' turning back to Eurydice) to a moment and a place (Heaven rather than the Underworld) where what Lerer calls 'the full exercise of rational abilities' can be attained. The story of Orpheus' behaviour (the dangers involved in *his* act of *re-spicere*) serves as an injunction to proper revision and interpretation, but it also involves, as Lerer has shown, a textual revision of one of Boethius' sources for the Orpheus-story: Seneca's *Hercules Furens*.[98] More importantly for our case, however, it provides an example which Dante will have taken to heart: to write means to revise, not just in terms of a moral imperative, but also in terms of a poetical one.

## The *Divine Comedy* and the Consolation of Religion

In the *Convivio*, Dante seems to opt for the Boethian position in the famous quarrel between philosophy and poetry. Not only does he found his poems on an allegorical 'truth', he also surrounds them with prose sections that both highlight and explain this truth. The prose sections of the *Vita Nuova* are quite different, in this respect: they are there, mainly, to create a narrative around the poems – a love story to accompany the love lyrics – and to highlight their structural division. The later development of Dante's poetic work, culminating in the grand finale of the *Divine Comedy*, marks the abandonment of the explanations in prose accompanying the author's poetic production.

Dante's verse no longer seems to need the author's explanatory comments; the poetry finally begins to speak for itself, one could say. But one could also say that after having finished the *Convivio* (and possibly even in the course of writing it), Dante became increasingly aware that in order to finally produce poems of true consolation his future writing would need an even more proper balance between philosophy and poetry than his 'Banquet' was able to serve.

Albert Ascoli has argued, convincingly in my opinion, that the fourth *trattato* of the *Convivio* already marks this future direction, in that the *canzone* that is central to it ('Le dolci rime d'amor') contains an explicit plea – in verse, that is – for a more philosophical diction that exchanges the 'tender rhymes of love' with 'more harsh and subtle rhymes', better suited to 'speak about the quality / Which makes a person truly noble'. As such, Ascoli writes, the *canzone* is a 'bald [sic] attempt to convert poetry directly into philosophy, or better, to absorb philosophy within poetic discourse'.[99] As it turns out from the ensuing chapters of *Convivio*'s Book Four, this *canzone* no longer needs the sort of explicit allegorical reading that the other two *canzones* get – in the *Convivio*'s final *trattato*, Ascoli writes, 'the poetic text [is freed] from utter dependence upon an explanatory philosophical prose',[100] a dependence which Ascoli traces back to Dante's definition of the allegorical nature of his poems as a 'verita ascosa sotto bella menzogna' ['a truth hidden beneath a beautiful lie']. 'Clearly,' Ascoli concludes, 'this is a definition that trivializes the poetic surface per se at the same time that it claims for its content the status of philosophy'.[101]

The lines from 'Le dolci rime d'amor' that I just quoted should not be taken at face value: Dante's point is not that the philosophical poems that he intends to aim for in the future can only be clad in 'harsh and subtle rhymes', as he puts it here, or that the quality of *dolcezza* is somehow anathema to this type of poetry. In the poem, he does state, after all, that he hopes 'to return anew' to 'the tender rhymes' that he once wrote – 'anew' being the crucial word: it implies the principle of 'revision' discussed above – and the verse of the *Divine Comedy* surely shows that he succeeded. Moreover, earlier in the *Convivio*, in the passage in the treatise's second book from which we started, Dante attributes the quality of 'sweetness' to the rhetorical style of the theologians and the philosophers that he was studying – it is the study of their work, Dante writes, that enabled him 'to feel [Lady Philosophy's] sweetness so much that the love of her dispelled and destroyed every other thought' (II, 12, 7).

A telling moment in the *Divine Comedy* of the hoped-for conjunction between the *dolcezza* of poetic discourse and the 'subtle' truthfulness of philosophical reflection can be found in Dante's account of his encounter with Casella in the second canto of the *Purgatorio*. Casella (about whose life very little is known)[102] was a singer and composer, a contemporary of Dante, who is presented here by the poet as a good friend ('Casella mio' (*Purg.* 2, 91)). Casella is among those who, at the beginning of the *Comedy*'s second 'cantica', find themselves in the 'Antipurgatorio', where they await the final possibility of the purgation of their souls – the beginning of that process being the ascent of Mount Purgatory. Upon seeing each other, Casella and Dante try to engage in a friendly embrace, but Dante soon finds out that to do so is impossible with a bodiless shade. 'Three times I clasped my hands behind him', the poet writes, 'only to find them clasped to my own chest' (*Purg.* 2, 80–1). After having listened to the account of the singer's prolonged stay in the 'Antipurgatorio', Dante asks Casella to perform for him 'the song / of love that used to soothe my every sorrow' ('l'amoroso canto / che mi solea quetar tutte mie doglie' (*Purg.* 2, 107–8)).[103] Casella seems to have a pretty clear idea of the exact canto Dante has in mind, possibly because of the poet's additional remark that he is convinced that hearing it sung, his soul will be 'somewhat comforted' ('di ciò ti piaccia consolare alquanto / l'anima mia') (*Purg.* 2, 109–10).

The song of consolation that Casella embarks upon is 'Amor che ne la mente mi ragiona', the *canzone* that Dante discusses in the third book of the *Convivio*. There, the poem is meant as a song of praise for Lady Philosophy, the 'donna gentile' whom Dante hopes will ease the pain that Beatrice's death has caused. The poem's opening lines focus on the very difficulty of finding the right words to convey the precise quality of the one being praised. In 'Amor che ne la mente mi ragiona', that difficulty and the stains that it leaves on the poet's verse are related to a conflict between Love's 'sweet' speech and the poet's 'intellect':

> Love, that speaks to me within my mind
> With fervent passion of my lady,
> Awakens often thoughts of her such that
> My intellect is led astray by them.
> His speech is filled with sounds so sweet
> That then my soul, which hears and feels him, says:
> 'Alas, I lack the power to speak
> Of what I hear about my lady!'
> And surely I must leave aside, if I
> Should wish to treat of what I hear of her,
> That which my intellect does not conceive,

As well as much of what it understands,
Because I know not how I should express it.
And so if fault is found to mar my verse
Which undertakes the praise of her,
Cast blame on my weak intellect
And on our speech, which lacks the power
To say in words the things that Love relates. (*Conv.* III, 1–18)

The effect of Casella's singing on Dante and his company (Virgil included) is immediate and absolute: the sweet sounds that the singer produces drive away whatever sorrow Casella's audience may have had. 'It seems reasonable to assume', John Freccero writes in his discussion of the scene, 'that Casella offers the same kind of consolation' that the 'donna gentile' brought Dante after Beatrice's death.[104] Having understood that the openly erotic love poetry of the *Vita Nuova* cannot bring the sort of consolation that he requires, Dante, as we saw, turned to the comfort embodied in Boethius' Lady Philosophy, whose Love, Freccero argues, is the topic of 'Amor che ne la mente mi ragiona'.[105] The immediate effect that the poem has in the second canto of *Purgatorio*, both on Dante and Virgil, and on the other shades attending the scene, seems indeed to be one of consolation. However, as the remainder of the scene makes clear, that immediate feeling warrants the sort of caution that Boethius' Lady Philosophy suggested the prisoner should feel with respect to the emotional outpourings of the Muses of Poetry. 'My master and I and all those standing / Near Casella seemed untroubled / As if we had no other care', Dante writes, stressing both the immediacy of the effect of Casella's song, and its potentially illusory nature ['seemed'/'parevan'] (*Purg.* 2, 115–17). 'We were spellbound, listening to his notes', Dante adds, after having pointed out, earlier, that even while writing down the scene he can still hear Casella's song (he sang 'so sweetly', Dante writes, 'that the sweetness sounds within me still' (*Purg.* 2, 113–4)). Still, the poet and his company's rapt attention is promptly broken by Cato, whom Dante had introduced in the previous canto as the guardian of Mount Purgatory and who now addresses the awe-inspired group as 'spiriti lenti', 'laggard spirits' (*Purg.* 2, 120), whom he urgently coerces to move on:

What carelessness, what delay is this?
Hurry to the mountain and there shed the slough
That lets not God be known to you. (*Purg.* 2, 121–3)

Cato's (and Dante's) point will be clear: the seductive sweetness of the love poem that Casella sings – and the temporary comfort that it has on offer – in the end may prove an obstacle for the purgatorial process that needs to be set in motion in the *Comedy*'s second *cantica*. 'Casella's song is a Siren's song', Robert Hollander argues in his exemplary analysis of the scene: the sweetness of its music is seductive, but dangerously so.[106] Taking her cue from Hollander, Teodolinda Barolini points out that the scene is 'paradigmatic' in that it captures perfectly the dialectical working of human desire in *Purgatorio*, 'as both the goad that keeps the souls moving upward and the source of the nostalgia that temporarily slows them down'.[107] Cato's rebuke is the former; the souls' wonder-struck attention for Casella's song the latter. As long as they stay rapt within the attraction of Casella's music, they will fail to know God in the proper way.

## Orphic Revisions

Interestingly, the Casella scene provides Barolini with an occasion to trace, in a brief excursion, the occurrence in Dante's work of the verb 'consolar'. Whereas in the *Vita Nuova*, as she shows, the practice and rhetoric of consolation still turn out to have pejorative connotations, references in the *Convivio* (Barolini counts six of them in the twelfth chapter of the treatise's Book Two) suggest that Dante begins to understand consolation in the Boethian, positive sense of the word: the comfort that Lady Philosophy brings is productive – 'consolation is ennobled by being presented on Boethian terms', Barolini concludes.[108] In the Casella scene – where, as we have seen, the verb also occurs – Barolini senses a more sceptical position with respect to the consolatory powers of philosophy. 'Dante went off the path (temporarily) when he allowed himself to be overly consoled by the sweetness of Philosophy in the *Convivio*', Barolini writes.[109] While she may be overstating the case when she further concludes that Lady Philosophy was indeed a 'mistake' for Dante, Barolini is right in suggesting that we should refrain from simply concluding – as we may have been tempted to do on the sole basis of the *Convivio* – that Boethius simply provided Dante with a positive concept of consolation. What the Casella scene makes clear, above all, is that earthly consolation should in no way be confused with the only real consolation that matters in the Christian regime: not the consolation of philosophy, but that of (the true) religion. What matters, as the wise Cato points out, is not the temporary alleviation of one's sorrow (through music, for instance, or philosophical reflection or any other form of earthly happiness), but the eternal supernatural truth of one's salvation.

As Ann Astell has shown, the Casella scene in *Purgatorio* 2 is the second in a series of three revisionary rewritings of the Orpheus myth that Dante included in the *Divine Comedy*.[110] The first one concerns the famous meeting between Dante and Paolo and Francesca in *Inferno* 6, where Dante is overpowered by the story of the two lovers who, like Orpheus and Eurydice, remain united in Hell. His fascination for this legendary story of earthly love is clearly anathema to the pursuit of true comfort, as he faints after having heard Francesca's story. The encounter with Casella, or rather the rebuke by Cato that follows it, is a step in the right direction, the direction that leads from Purgatory to Paradise. According to Astell, the third Orphic scene can be found in *Purgatorio* 30, where Dante takes leave of Virgil, the one whom he repeatedly called 'il mio conforto'. Obviously, the pagan poet Virgil cannot bring the sort of heavenly comfort that Dante aspires to. For that he will require the guidance of Beatrice, who comes to replace Virgil in this very canto. As Astell points out, Beatrice, in the cantos that immediately follow (*Purg.* 31–3), urges Dante to renounce 'both the false pleasures of *temporalia* (*Purg.* 31, 34–6) and the seductions of secular philosophy (*Purg.* 33, 85–7).'[111] While in the *Convivio* Beatrice is still clearly identified with Lady Philosophy, here, she moves beyond that 'questionable' status to become the messenger of religious comfort.

The outcome of the movement becomes ever so clear in Canto 18 of *Paradiso*, where Dante refers to Beatrice as 'il mio conforto', the very epithet he had earlier conferred on Virgil.[112] Interestingly, the passage contains a further revision of the mythical scene in which Orpheus breaks his vow to the gods of the Underworld and looks back on Eurydice against their will. In the poet's most telling rewriting, Beatrice ('that lady, who was leading me to God' (*Par.* 18, 4)) addresses Dante, urging him to revise his mental habits: 'Change your thoughts. Consider that I dwell / With him who lifts the weight of every wrong' (*Par.* 18, 5–6). This is what comfort is, after all: it is an invitation to see things differently. Dante accepts the invitation, in a move that reverses the Orphic scene of pagan transgression into one of Christian submission:

> At the loving sound of my comfort's voice
> I turned, and the great love I saw then,
> in her holy eyes, I have to leave untold,
>
> not just because I cannot trust my speech
> but because memory cannot retrace its path
> that far unless Another guide it.

> This much only of that moment can I tell again,
> that, when I fixed my gaze on her,
> my affections were released from any other longing
>
> as long as the eternal Beauty,
> shining its light on Beatrice, made me content
> with its reflected glow in her fair eyes. (*Par.* 18, 7–18)

The contrast with the Casella scene that we discussed earlier will be clear: the comfort that Beatrice's *amoroso suono* has on offer is a gift of the love of God. The heavenly comfort to which Dante is 'interpellated' – the scene anticipates Althusser's mechanism of *assujettissement* by some 650 years – differs from the blind and selfish wonder that marked Dante's earlier thrall. While Casella's singing served as an obstacle on Dante's purgatorial climb, the sound of Beatrice's voice points him in the right direction:

> Conquering me with her radiant smile
> she said: 'Turn now and listen:
> not in my eyes alone is Paradise.' (*Par.* 18, 19–21)

### Back to the Future: Dreher versus Luzzi on the *Consolatio Dantis*

It is time to round off this chapter and to return, as promised, to Rod Dreher and Joseph Luzzi's bibliotherapeutic readings of the *Divine Comedy*. Different though their backgrounds and reading attitudes are (more on that to follow), for both Dreher and Luzzi the goal of consolation requires some serious preliminary work – the work of reading attentively and interpreting actively. Dante may well be a willing guide, but that does not mean that he can do the work for them. The example that he sets for Dreher and Luzzi is not one that only requires the mere application of a given set of rules and techniques; the example requires contemplation and translation, not just from his native Italian into their native English, but also from textual theory into living practice, so to speak. Dreher and Luzzi – like Dante before them – have to make the words of the poet into their own.

The differences between these two readers of Dante are conspicuous. Dreher is an orthodox Christian, as he keeps reminding readers of *How Dante Can Save Your Life*. His fascination for the author of the *Divine Comedy* is the outcome of a true moment of conversion; his growing admiration for the poem ('the book of my life', he calls it[113]) the result of a set of beliefs shared with its author. '[A]mong the most beautiful passages in the entire *Commedia*' Dreher counts the lines spoken to Dante by Forese Donati in *Purgatorio* 23. In that canto, we read about Dante's meeting with his former friend on the terrace of gluttony. There, Forese describes how a group of weeping people who were used to 'follow[ing] their appetites beyond all measure' (*Purg.* 23, 65) are now starving themselves, in an attempt to 'regain, in thirst and hunger, holiness' (*Purg.* 23, 66). Realising they have lived a life of sin, the former gluttons now want to do things differently so as to be able to attain their heaven in the proper way. 'The fragrance coming from the fruit / and from the water sprinkled on green boughs / kindles our craving to eat and drink' (*Purg.* 23, 67–9), Forese admits to Dante, but he and his companions no longer allow themselves to be led astray. The continued attraction of the bounteous food is there, of course, and Forese at first describes it as the pain that results from a punishment (*pena*). But then he corrects himself, in a line that goes to the heart of the Christian idea of consolation: 'I speak of pain but should say solace' (*Purg.* 23, 72). That which is painful brings comfort; the comfort is found, not in an escape from what we consider, but in a confrontation with it, a confrontation that enables us to see the cause of our pain for what it really is, a ground for comfort.

The Forese passage clearly speaks to the glutton that Dreher considers himself to be: 'Here is a man who is starving – starving! – yet he and his fellow penitents take comfort in their sufferings, knowing that they hasten their union with God.'[114] Forese and his gluttonous companions seem to model themselves on Job during their time spent in Purgatory: what others would consider a painful punishment, they see as the outcome of divine consolation. For Dreher, Dante's text confirms and voices poignantly the truths of his religion: that is why the *Divine Comedy* brings him comfort. The text's aesthetic appeal appears to be relegated for him to the central given of his faith. He writes:

> As I first discovered thirty years ago in the nave of the Chartres cathedral, the shock of beauty catapults us out of the everydayness of our lives and gives us a new way to see ourselves and the possibilities before us. Though the encounter with beauty might make us suffer, in the end, it is through that pain that we are set free.[115]

As he explains earlier on in his book, it was during a visit to Chartres that Dreher first felt the force of his faith. He was seventeen at the time and visiting France on a trip that his mother had won in a lottery contest. Eager to get to Paris, he felt bored, as most teenagers would, at the prospect of having to stop over at Chartres. Of course, moments of conversion always come at times when they are least expected. 'I did not understand this at the time', Dreher writes, 'but God set the hook in me inside that cathedral. It was there that I began an ambivalent quest for him, not really wanting to find him, but also unable to deny the power of that revelation.'[116]

Reading Dante at a later stage of his life, Dreher came to a better understanding of the true meaning of faith, and of the guiding role that works of art can play in its gradual discovery. Dreher's description, in my earlier quotation, of what he calls 'the shock of beauty' seems to echo Forese's memorable line from *Purgatorio* 23: 'io dico pena, e dovria dir sollazzo' ('I speak of pain but should say solace' (*Purg.* 23, 72)). In Dreher's account of 'the shock of beauty', the experiences of pain and comfort become interchangeable, as it were. The pain incurred involves the consolation that awaits the erstwhile sinner: finally to be redeemed from one's sins and to be set free.

The central difference between Dreher's and Luzzi's 'curative' readings of Dante revolves around what in the passage from which I just quoted Dreher refers to as 'in the end'. In Dreher's (and Dante's) Christian conception, that end is the end of salvation in Paradise. For Luzzi, however, the end is, quite literally, the end of the story as it is told in his memoir. It is the happy ending, as we have seen, of a new love after an extended period of mourning. 'Every grief story is a love story', Luzzi concludes, in revision of Julian Barnes' contrary experience.[117] Dreher and Luzzi also seem to have a different take on the aesthetic function of Dante's text. For Dreher, the *Divine Comedy* functions as the final confirmation of the religious convictions that he shares with the poem's author, and as a perfect formulation of the experience of faith. Crucial in his reading is the full identification that the text forced upon him, so to speak:

> There is no lesson in the *Commedia* that I had not read or heard before, but Dante incarnated that wisdom in verses that pierced the rocky soil of my heart and planted seeds of truth there, seeds that neither my anxiety, nor my insecurity, nor my anger, nor my weakness could dislodge.
>
> At some point on this literary pilgrimage, a shift within me took place, one so subtle I had not noticed it. I ceased to be a reader observing a character called Dante and his adventures, and began to identify with the pilgrim in a way I never had before, nor had done with any literary character.[118]

As we have seen, Luzzi's reading position is more distanced, more aware of the differences between his own mind frame and that of the thirteenth-century Tuscan. As a professor of literature, Luzzi is also more attuned than Dreher to the formal aspects of Dante's poetry and to the musical qualities of the poet's verse – possibly also because he masters the Italian language better. But there is a further issue in this respect, a more telling one, I think. While for Dreher, Dante's epic poem is essentially didactic (not only for its original audience, but also for the twentieth-century reader that is Dreher), Luzzi, in a crucial passage that I quoted earlier, points out that we fail to see the true potential of Dante's poem if we see it as merely didactic. 'The *Divine Comedy*', as he already knew from his initial encounter with the text,

> was not a self-help manual, a means to a practical set of ends that I was able to negotiate based on Dante's advice. To say as much would do violence to the kind of poem that Dante tried to write. In my grief his words cast a spell, just as Dante himself was entranced by Casella's song. Reading the *Divine Comedy*, we pause on the journey we're supposed to be taking. We linger by poetry's beautiful sea-girls wreathed in red and brown. The poem distracts us as much as it instructs us. But in that distraction – that pause on whatever purgatorial climb – we may find ourselves.[119]

It is interesting to see that Luzzi comes to this conclusion with specific reference to the Casella passage that we focused on earlier. In his reading of the scene, his sympathy is clearly with Dante and Virgil in being spellbound by the beauty of Casella's singing. It will come as no surprise that Dreher in his reading of the same passage focuses on Cato's stern admonition: the penitents' wonder is useless if not counter-productive, since it serves as an obstacle in the purgatorial process. Referring to Cato's words of wisdom, Dreher concludes: 'It's not that music and poetry are bad; it's that they are bad at this moment, because they distract the people from their mission.'[120]

For Dreher, the distraction of the aesthetic experience (of this one, at least) is bad since it threatens to advocate a perspective that goes against the grain of the poem's didactic purpose. For Luzzi, the aesthetic experience provoked by the text – even as it undermines or threatens to subvert the 'lesson' which the text is meant to provide – is a central part of the poem's consolatory force. The idea that an effect of 'distraction' (whether or not caused by a work of art) can be consoling clearly does not fit the Christian regime of comfort. That regime is centrally oriented towards the *telos* of salvation, the ultimate reward given by God, our single source of comfort, as the example of Job keeps reminding us. Little surprise, therefore, that Luzzi finds it much harder to follow that example. 'I tried to identify with Job', he writes, 'but he was too old, his suffering impossibly extravagant.'[121]

Anything that threatens to divert the believer from the path of salvation is suspect, in the Christian logic of comfort, unless the 'diversion' at hand results, ultimately, in the revision of sinful behaviour. For Dreher, comfort lies in whatever confirms the single truth of God's decree, no matter how painful that truth may look. In the end, what befalls us is the result of the benevolent but just will of God's providence. In this respect, Dreher's reading of Dante's work subscribes to the very logic that Lady Philosophy intended to instil in the prisoner of Boethius' treatise. Christian believers find comfort in the unwavering certainty that what God wants is good. For Luzzi, to be consoled boils down to finding peace in and coming to terms with the fickleness and often painful duality of a reality that can neither be controlled nor fully understood.

While it is not clear whether Dante himself would ever be able to find comfort in Luzzi's God-forsaken world, he would no doubt appreciate the ironical reversal at hand: in Dante's work, the heathen Virgil is given pride of place in a world where he does not really belong; in Luzzi's book, the same thing happens to the Christian poet. In the course of their joint climb of Mount Purgatory, Dante addresses Virgil twice as 'il mio conforto', as we have seen. The apostrophe is synonymous with the other ones that the author of the *Divine Comedy* uses to refer to the poet of the *Aeneid*: Virgil is also Dante's *maestro* and his *guida* – he is the masterful guide because he brings comfort and he brings comfort because he paves the way from which Dante is now and then allowed to stray. Something similar can be said about the role the Italian poet fulfils for his pupil Joseph Luzzi.

As we will see in what follows, Luzzi's conception of consolation – secular to the bone – begins to come to the fore in the early modern period. The grounding ideas of this modern regime of consolation will be discussed in the following three chapters. In the next chapter, I begin by illustrating the development of that regime – and its basic difference from the classical and Christian ones – by means of a number of scenes of comfort in several plays by Shakespeare.

## Notes

1. Dreher, *How Dante Can Save Your Life*, 96.
2. Joseph Luzzi, *In A Dark Wood*.
3. Luzzi, *In A Dark Wood*, inside cover, also on page 3.
4. Luzzi, *In A Dark Wood*, 9.
5. Luzzi, *In A Dark Wood*, 29.
6. Luzzi, *In A Dark Wood*, 295.
7. All references to Dante's *Divine Comedy* in this chapter will be to Jean and Robert Hollander's verse translation.
8. Luzzi, *In A Dark Wood*, 5.
9. Luzzi, *In A Dark Wood*, 287.
10. Luzzi, *In A Dark Wood*, 37.
11. Luzzi, *In A Dark Wood*, 124.
12. Luzzi, *In A Dark Wood*, 45.
13. Luzzi, *In A Dark Wood*, 39–40. The reference is to the opening lines of *Paradiso* 25, where Dante describes his exile as 'the cruelty that locks me out / of the fair sheepfold where I slept as a lamb, / foe of the wolves at war with it'. (4–6)
14. Dreher, *How Dante Can Save Your Life*, 83.
15. Luzzi, *In A Dark Wood*, 201.
16. Dreher, *How Dante Can Save Your Life*, 28.
17. Luzzi, *In A Dark Wood*, 183.
18. Luzzi, *In A Dark Wood*, 34.
19. Luzzi, *In A Dark Wood*, 108.
20. Luzzi, *In A Dark Wood*, 112.
21. Luzzi, *In A Dark Wood*, 126.
22. Luzzi, *In A Dark Wood*, 270.
23. Luzzi, *In A Dark Wood*, 288.
24. Luzzi, *In A Dark Wood*, 9.
25. Luzzi, *In A Dark Wood*, 72–4.
26. Luzzi, *In A Dark Wood*, 4.
27. Luzzi, *In A Dark Wood*, 29.
28. Pieters, *Speaking with the Dead*, 8–9, 31–2.
29. Luzzi, *In A Dark Wood*, 10.
30. Luzzi, *In A Dark Wood*, 16.
31. Luzzi, *In A Dark Wood*, 108, 109, 47.
32. Pieters, *Speaking with the Dead*, 38–9.
33. Luzzi, *In A Dark Wood*, 131.
34. Luzzi, *In A Dark Wood*, 131.
35. Luzzi, *In A Dark Wood*, 70.
36. Luzzi, *In A Dark Wood*, 258–9, his italics.
37. Luzzi, *In A Dark Wood*, 257.
38. *Job*, 6, 10 – King James Version.

39. See Rittgers, *The Reformation of Suffering*, 41–3, for examples from Ambrose, Cyprian and Jerome. Chapters 2 and 3 of Rittgers provide an excellent survey of the late Antique and Medieval consolatory tradition. The remainder of his book is devoted to early modern German consolatory writings.
40. McClure, *Sorrow and Consolation in Italian Humanism*, 9.
41. McClure, *Sorrow and Consolation in Italian Humanism*, 9.
42. Rittgers, *The Reformation of Suffering*, 43.
43. McClure, *Sorrow and Consolation in Italian Humanism*, 11.
44. 'If suffering is but the result of Adam's Fall, worldly sorrow but an unworthy emotion, tribulation but the test of piety, death but a welcome deliverance from this ephemeral earthly state, then the tenor and parameters of Christian solace must necessarily differ from those of classical consolation.' McClure, *Sorrow and Consolation in Italian Humanism*, 10.
45. Rittgers, *The Reformation of Suffering*, 61.
46. Quoted by Lerer in his 'Introduction' to David R. Slavitt's translation of Boethius' text: Boethius, *The Consolation of Philosophy*, xiii. The quotation is from Boethius' early Commentary on Aristotle's *Perihermeneias*. See also Ebbesen, 'The Aristotelian Commentator', 34–55.
47. For the impact of Augustine see, for instance, Abrams, *Natural Supernaturalism*, 83–7. The Augustinian echoes in Boethius' treatise are discussed in Crabbe, 'Literary Design in the *De Consolatione Philosophiae*', 254–63.
48. The exact year is uncertain. See also Moorhead, 'Boethius' Life and Late Antique Philosophy, 19. For a succinct biographical sketch see Matthews, 'Anicius Manlius Severinus Boethius'; see also Chadwick, *Boethius*, 1–68. The 'Introduction' to Gruber, *Kommentar zu Boethius* (second expanded edition) is also very useful.
49. Curtius, *European Literature and the Latin Middle Ages*, 22.
50. All 39 poems are discussed in detail in Scheible, *Die Gedichte in der Consolatio Philosophiae des Boethius* and O'Daly, *The Poetry of Boethius*. For a good definition of the prosimetric genre (and the term's close relationship with the Menippean satire, see Greene (ed.), *The Princeton Encyclopedia of Poetry and Poetics*, 1115–16.
51. For the Ovidian parallels see, apart from Gruber, *Kommentar*, also Crabbe, 'Literary Design in the *De Consolatione Philosophiae*', 244–8; Scheible, *Die Gedichte in der Consolatio Philosophiae des Boethius*, 12 and Seth Lerer, *Boethius and Dialogue*, 96.
52. All (parenthetical) references are to David R. Slavitt's translation of Boethius' treatise. References to the metrical passages (Im) are followed by a specification of the cited lines; references to the prose passages (Ip) are followed by the corresponding page number.

53. See Crabbe, 'Literary Design in the *De Consolatione Philosophiae*', 243. For a discussion of Boethius' treatise within the consolatory tradition see Chapter 4 ('*Consolation* and the Genre of Consolation') in Relihan, *The Prisoner's Philosophy*, 47–58.
54. Scheible, *Die Gedichte in der Consolatio Philosophiae des Boethius*, 12. There is also an echo of the opening of the *Aeneid*.
55. A representative selection of illustrations is given in Courcelle, *La consolation de philosophie dans la tradition littéraire*.
56. Crabbe traces the 'harlots' back to one of Propertius' elegies in 'Literary Design in the *De Consolatione Philosophiae*', 249–50.
57. Ferrari, 'Plato and Poetry', 142.
58. Plato, *Republic*, Vol. 2, 437 (607b5).
59. O'Daly (*The Poetry of Boethius*, 69–70) also sees several references to Homer, including one to the consolatory scene from *Iliad* 24 in the second prose chapter of Book Two. Lady Philosophy's reference is to the allegory of Zeus' (here Jupiter's) two jars. In Slavitt's translation: 'Did you not learn as a young man that Jupiter has on his threshold 'two jars, with evils in one and blessings in the other?' You have had more than an average share of the good things I can give, but even now I have not deserted you entirely' (IIp2, 33).
60. Blackwood, *The* Consolation *of Boethius as Poetic Liturgy*.
61. Lerer, *Boethius and Dialogue*.
62. Donato, *Boethius'* Consolation of Philosophy *as a Product of Late Antiquity*, 103.
63. See Crabbe, 'Literary Design in the *De Consolatione Philosophiae*', 250. Crabbe's reference is to *Tusculanae* II, xi, 27, page 175 in the Loeb edition of which I made use.
64. Donato, *Boethius'* Consolation of Philosophy *as a Product of Late Antiquity*, 105.
65. Relihan's *The Prisoner's Philosophy* would be a case in point.
66. Donato, *Boethius'* Consolation of Philosophy *as a Product of Late Antiquity*, 105.
67. Crabbe, 'Literary Design in the *De Consolatione Philosophiae*', 255–6.
68. See also Blackwood, *The* Consolation *of Boethius as Poetic Liturgy*.
69. Donato, *Boethius'* Consolation of Philosophy *as a Product of Late Antiquity*, 111–19. More on Boethius' reflections on music can be found in Caldwell, 'The *De Institutione Arithmetica* and the *De Institutione Musica*'. Boethius' familiarity with *Timaeus* becomes clear from the so-called 'Timaean Hymn', metrum 9 in Book Three of the *Consolation*.
70. Lerer, *Boethius and Dialogue*, 157.
71. For a succinct overview of Boethian references in Dante's writings see the entry for Tateo, 'Boezio', in Bosco, *Enciclopedia Dantesca*, Vol. 1, 654–8. See also Murari, *Dante e Boezio* and Alfonsi, *Dante e la Consolatio Philosophiae di Boezio*.

72. My reference is to the translation by Richard Lansing, available through Columbia University's Digital Dante-project: <https://digitaldante.columbia.edu/text/library/the convivio>. The Italian annotated edition (including comments) that I made use of is Dante, *Convivio*, ed. Piero Cudini. The parenthetic reference reads as: *Convivio* (Book) II, (chapter) 12, (paragraph) 2.
73. Treggiari, *Terentia, Tullia and Publilia*, 136–8.
74. Cicero, *De amicitia*, vi, 22, 133.
75. Cicero, *De amicitia*, ii, 8, 117.
76. Cicero, *De amicitia*, ii, 8, 117.
77. Cicero, *De amicitia*, ii, 8, 117.
78. Cicero, *De amicitia*, ii, 10, 119.
79. Cicero, *De amicitia*, vii, 23, 133.
80. Derrida, *Politics of Friendship*, 3–4.
81. Cicero, *Tusculan Disputations*, Book 3, xv, 31–2, 265.
82. Dante, *La Vita Nuova*, trans. David R. Slavitt, 109–10.
83. Modesto, *Dante's Idea of Friendship*, 53.
84. Modesto, *Dante's Idea of Friendship*, 53.
85. Rand quoted in Means, *The Consolation Genre in Medieval English Literature*, 1.
86. See also Modesto, *Dante's Idea of Friendship*, 54.
87. The exile began in 1302, whereas the *Convivio* was written, according to Cudini, 'tra il 1304 e I 1307' (*Convivio*, 'Preface', x). According to Albert Ascoli, Dante knew Boethius' text 'well before his exile' (Ascoli, *Dante and the Making of a Modern Author*, 69).
88. Harrison, *The Body of Beatrice*, 99. In what follows I made use of David R. Slavitt's translation and of the Italian edition in Garzanti's 'I grandi libri' series.
89. For the translation of 'Li occhi dolente' I made use of Andrew Frisardi's version, available through Columbia's Digital Dante-website (<https://digitaldante.columbia.edu/text/library/la-vita-nuova-frisardi>). Slavitt's translation does not contain the 'consolatory' references to which I allude here ('me conforta' (56), 'sconsolata' (76)).
90. See also *Conv.* II, 1, 15: 'I shall on each occasion discuss first the literal meaning concerning each canzone, and afterwards I shall discuss its allegory (that is, the hidden truth), at times touching on the other senses, when opportune, as time and place deem proper.'
91. Auerbach, 'Figura'. Auerbach's ideas about Dante's 'figural realism' can be traced back to his earlier *Dante: Poet of the Secular World* (originally 1929).
92. They appear to be Boethius' main sources, but Scheible points out further possible allusions in *Die Gedichte in der Consolatio Philosophiae des Boethius*, 118–25.

93. Donato, *Boethius' Consolation of Philosophy as a Product of Late Antiquity*, 141.
94. Donato, *Boethius' Consolation of Philosophy as a Product of Late Antiquity*, 141
95. In the poems of the *Convivio*, Auerbach writes, 'a fusion of philosophy and poetry was achieved for the first time; each of the two had attained a s stage of perfection, where it was prepared to accept help from the other and was indeed needful of such help'. Auerbach, *Poet of the Secular World*, 72–3.
96. Lerer, *Boethius and Dialogue*, 158.
97. Lerer, *Boethius and Dialogue*, 158.
98. Lerer, *Boethius and Dialogue*, 160.
99. Ascoli, *Dante and the Making of a Modern Author*, 116.
100. Ascoli, *Dante and the Making of a Modern Author*, 116.
101. Ascoli, *Dante and the Making of a Modern Author*, 110. Here, Ascoli concludes, 'the secondariness of poetry and its dependence on philosophical commentary is reinforced' (111).
102. Peirone, 'Casella', in Bosco (ed.), *Enciclopedia dantesca*, 856–8.
103. Translation slightly adapted: I exchanged the translators' plural 'songs' for the singular 'song': the original has 'canto'.
104. Freccero, *The Poetics of Conversion*, 189.
105. Freccero, *The Poetics of Conversion*, 188.
106. Hollander, '*Purgatorio* II, in *Studies in Dante*, 91–105, quote on 91.
107. Barolini, *Dante's Poets*, 33.
108. Barolini, *Dante's Poets*, 37.
109. Barolini, *Dante's Poets*, 39.
110. Astell, *Job, Boethius, and Epic Truth*, 136–40. In her book, Astell also traces the intertextual relationships between Boethius' treatise and the Book of Job in ways that have been useful for the development of my argument. However, a full exposition of that excursion would go beyond my concerns here.
111. Astell, *Job, Boethius, and Epic Truth*, 139–40.
112. The apostrophe can be found in *Purg.* 3, 22 and *Purg.* 9, 43.
113. Dreher, *How Dante Can Save Your Life*, 219. 'The *Commedia* was speaking to me more powerfully than Scripture, and in so doing was leading me closer to the God of the Bible than anything I had ever read', Dreher adds.
114. Dreher, *How Dante Can Save Your Life*, 248. 'On this terrace', Dreher adds, 'I grasped the nature of my hunger, my craving, for approval and acceptance by my family' (249).
115. Dreher, *How Dante Can Save Your Life*, 218.
116. Dreher, *How Dante Can Save Your Life*, 16.
117. Luzzi, *In A Dark Wood*, 281: 'Every love story is potentially a grief story, Julian Barnes once wrote. But by the time Dante got to Paradiso he understood it was actually the other way around.' The reference is

to Barnes' *Levels of Life*, the memoir in which he pays tribute to his departed wife, Pat Kavanagh. (Barnes' book returns in my fifth chapter, alongside the author's *Flaubert's Parrot*.)
118. Dreher, *How Dante Can Save Your Life*, 218–19.
119. Luzzi, *In A Dark Wood*, 130–1.
120. Dreher, *How Dante Can Save Your Life*, 189.
121. Luzzi, *In A Dark Wood*, 27.

Chapter 3

# Towards a Modern Regime of Literary Comfort: Shakespeare and the Failure to Console

> My father was dying; I read *Hamlet*. No, not that play about assassination but the one about a young man who can't get over his father's death. That's what *Hamlet* is about. I had a tempestuous Latin boyfriend so I studied Shakespeare's bad boys: Petruchio, Troilus, Diomedes. I was approaching forty; I read *Antony and Cleopatra* for examples of midlife career and romance. Everything I needed to know in life I learned from Shakespeare.
>
> Laurie Maguire, *Where There's A Will There's A Way*[1]

## Bibliotherapy Behind Bars: Laura Bates and Larry Newton

In the broad sense in which I have been using the word in the previous chapters of this book, bibliotherapy can also be taken to encompass the therapeutic use of literary writings – prescribed as well as self-chosen – in the corrective context of penal institutions. In cases like these, the situation at hand resembles that in Boethius' *De consolatione philosophiae*: prisoners find help, counsel or guidance in their encounter with fictional voices that come to represent reason to them – or at least are supposed to do so. While it may be less obvious in such cases to describe the outcome of the therapeutic process as 'comfort' or 'consolation', the effect of the act of reading is clearly similar to the one that Boethius' prisoner undergoes: it offers new insight, instilling the idea that one can see things differently – in the case of actual inmates: the insight that there are other ways of looking (back) at one's life and one's actions, ways that refuse to take as inevitable the outcome of criminal behaviour and which call for victim empathy.

Take, for instance, some of the stories that Amy Scott-Douglass presents in her exhilarating book *Shakespeare Inside: The Bard Behind Bars*. In that book, as we can read on its back cover,

> [w]e hear ex-offender Mike Smith detail how playing Desdemona was vital to his rehabilitation; we sit in the audience of women inmates as they respond to the all-male *Shakespeare Behind Bars* touring production of *Julius Caesar*; and we listen to a chorus of unnamed voices explain how rewriting *Hamlet* helps them to survive solitary confinement.[2]

Scott-Douglass' book is an account of her own experiences with what is now informally called 'Prison Shakespeare'. As a scholar – she is currently Associate Professor of English at Marymount University (Arlington, Virginia) – Scott-Douglass specialised in Shakespeare programmes that have been running, for several decades now, in penal institutions across the United States. Artistic Director Curt Tofteland's 'Shakespeare Behind Bars' is probably the most representative and inspiring venture in the field.[3] Founded in 1995, Tofteland's programme involves the staging of Shakespeare plays inside prisons (Luther Luckett Correctional Complex in LaGrange, Kentucky, in this case) and performed by inmates. In Scott-Douglass' words, Tofteland's programme

> is meant to function as a safe forum in which violent offenders are able to come to terms with their pasts – a process which frequently involves the inmates acknowledging crimes and abuses they themselves suffered in childhood as well as taking responsibility for their own violent acts as teenagers and adults through the experiences of identification, role-playing and catharsis.[4]

The numerous witness statements by participating inmates that Scott-Douglass lists in her book show that Tofteland's aims – idealistic as they may sound – are quite often realised. 'Shakespeare has changed my entire outlook on everything that is everything', Big G, an inmate who performed Caliban and Hamlet in SBB-productions, is quoted as saying.[5] Like other prisoners that she interviewed for her book, Big G makes use of what Scott-Douglass describes as a distinct 'discourse of conversion' whenever he tries to explain what Shakespeare did to him, the sort of discourse, as we saw, that Lady Philosophy encourages Boethius to engage in.[6] Other prisoners, too, stress the spiritual nature of their new encounter with Shakespeare's plays. Most of them came across the Bard's work in class, but at the time the texts clearly did not leave a lasting impression ('I *read* it. Didn't *understand* it.'[7]). What they mostly stress is the fact that their renewed, more direct encounter with the plays – the fact that they were now performing the characters' words as if they were their own – taught them new and valuable things about themselves. '[W]hat Shakespeare has allowed me to do by inhabiting characters like Othello, Aaron, and even Proteus', a convicted murderer states, 'is to see myself and to see how destructive I have been, the effect I have had on people'.[8] 'When you play a character, you're able to see through the character's eyes', another inmate adds. 'And I was able, even when I played Tamora, to find myself saying, "If I were in that person's shoes, would I respond that way?" And it also made me think about the hurt that throughout my life I have brought other people when you look through other people's eyes.'[9]

'[E]ach of us are resolving issues through Shakespeare', a further convict sums up.[10] The plays, and the characters' speeches making up those plays, allow for deeply personal reflection and as such provide the occasion for the prisoners to come to terms with the complexity of real-life situations and of their own emotions.[11] A second memorable Prison Shakespeare project that Scott-Douglass refers to is Laura Bates' 'Shakespeare in Shackles', a programme that was begun in 2003 at Indiana's Wabash Valley Correctional Facility.[12] The specificity of this programme lies in the fact that it is targeted (and limited) to inmates of the Security Housing Unit (SHU), a 'supermax' wing reserved for prisoners who are kept in solitary confinement – for years on end. One of the inmates who is centrally involved in Wabash's Shakespeare programme is the subject of a remarkable book that Bates wrote about her experiences as a teacher in the SHU: *Shakespeare Saved My Life: Ten Years in Solitary with the Bard*.[13] The book owes its title to the answer the book's protagonist – the convicted murderer Larry Newton, who spent more than a decade in the isolation of his SHU cell – gave to the question that Bates asked each participant at the end of the programme: 'What has Shakespeare done for you?'[14] Shakespeare saved his life both literally and figuratively, Newton added in a conversation that Bates records in her book. 'Literally, Shakespeare saved my life', Newton is quoted as saying:

> For so many years, I had been really self-destructive, on the razor's edge every day. I'm confident that I would've done something drastic and ended up on death row. Or I would've found the courage to take my own life. So literally, he saved my life. (. . .) And I meant it figuratively (. . .). Shakespeare offered me the opportunity to develop new ways of thinking through these plays. I was trying to figure out what motivated Macbeth,

why his wife was able to make him do a deed that he said he didn't want to do just by attacking his ego: 'What, are you soft? Ain't you man enough to do it?' As a consequence of that, I had to ask myself what was motivating me in my deeds, and I came face-to-face with the realization that I was fake, that I was motivated by this need to impress those around me, that none of my choices were truly my own.[15]

In a very touching TedX-lecture that Laura Bates gave at UCLA ('Shakespeare in Shackles: The Transformative Power of Literature'), we see video-footage of Larry explaining the meaning of the life-saving qualities of Shakespeare.[16] The video was shot shortly after Larry's release from the SHU, where he spent, as he puts it, every single day of his twenties ('I went in as a 19-year-old kid and I didn't get out until I was a 30-year-old man') in the isolation of his windowless concrete cell. The shackles in the title of Laura Bates' book are the shackles – on their hands as well as their feet – that the prisoners participating in the programme had to wear as they were escorted from their cells to the specially designated area in the SHU where Laura's Shakespeare classes took place. During these classes, each prisoner sat in an individual holding cell. The only contact they had with their teacher and with one another was through the cuff ports in the doors.

*Shakespeare Saved My Life* shows a picture of Bates sitting in the hallway between two rows of individual holding cells, listening to her students who are debating a scene in one of Shakespeare's plays, discussing their interpretations of the text on which they had prepared a written assignment.[17] The picture calls to mind some of the illustrations that accompany manuscripts in Boethius' *Consolation of Philosophy*, but it comes with a difference. Laura Bates is definitely no Lady Philosophy: she is not trying to correct her students (neither in matters Shakespearean nor in moral ones), and she is listening most of the time, instead of instructing and finding fault. Also, she is not allowed inside the prisoners' cells. But the central lesson that she manages to instil in the prisoners' minds is quite similar to the one that Lady Philosophy teaches Boethius' prisoner in the first book of the *De consolatione philosophiae*. In the course of his instruction, as we have seen, Boethius comes to see that his true problem is not his actual imprisonment, but rather the depressive state of mind in which he finds himself. 'You have forgotten what you are' (Ip2, 6), Lady Philosophy points out to the prisoner in the opening book of the *Consolation of Philosophy*, and that mental exile is much more problematic than the prisoner's physical isolation.[18] Similarly, Larry Newton comes to see, as he puts it in Laura Bates' book, that 'prison isn't the great prison. Prison is being entrapped by those self-destructive ways of thinking' that determined the thoughts and behaviour that put him behind bars in the first place. As he goes on to say:

> That's one of the problems I think a lot of people have (. . .) They associate their misery to the fact that they're in prison, and it's not that. I think a lot of my misery was me hating me, and hating me made me hate everyone else. I felt like such a punk, I felt so weak. I really was a coward. I never stood up for myself. I mean, I stood up for myself as we associate standing up for yourself – fighting and violence. But that's not standing up for yourself. I mean standing up for myself like thinking for myself. Now, I feel more okay with myself. I'm feeling stronger in my abilities every day, and the world just opens up. You really can do anything, you can shape your life any way you want it to be.[19]

### Self-Help Shakespeare: Laurie Maguire on 'Character'

Larry Newton's engagement in the Shakespeare programme that Laura Bates set up, resulted, in the end, in a workbook (designed by Larry) that could help guide his fellow prisoners in their future encounters with Shakespeare's texts. The reading method that Larry promoted did not require much sophistication: in Bates' words, it simply 'invited prisoners to look deeply into the text, and into themselves'.[20] Like the other recent bibliotherapeutic endeavours that I referred to both in the introduction to this book and in the chapters on Homer and Dante, the Prison Shakespeare programmes mentioned above rest on the idea that texts written centuries ago remain relevant (and, actually, retain their relevance) because they never stop speaking to us in ways that continue to surprise. Shakespeare's texts, Laura Bates writes, are 'beautifully crafted works of literature written hundred years ago that can connect with us here and now'.[21]

Part of the answer to the question why that is, in Bates' analysis, lies in the concept of character. Even though Shakespeare's dramatis personae do not really speak the way that we do, they are like us in so many ways. They may have different ideas about honour, respect for one's elders and the love of one's country, but they do seem to share with us a conception of what it means to have a personal identity and to be(come) aware of that identity. 'As readers engage in an analysis of Shakespeare's characters, they cannot help but engage in an analysis of their own character, motivations, and objectives', Bates writes, stressing the inescapable nature of the process.[22] Her point is corroborated by Larry Newton:

> The hope is that the more insight you get into these characters, the more insight you get into yourself (. . .). That's what happened to me: I'm questioning why Macbeth does what he does, and I start to question why I do what I do.[23]

For sure, the reading practice that underlies most Prison Shakespeare projects (diverse though they may be) will differ in some specifics from other, more medically and/or psychologically oriented bibliotherapeutic endeavours. But there is a common ground, as the near identity of the titles of Laura Bates' book on Larry Newton and Rod Dreher's account of his own life-saving experience with Dante's *Divine Comedy* make clear. *Shakespeare Saved My Life* and *How Dante Saved My Life*: in both cases, authors writing centuries ago are granted the status that we usually reserve for either heroes or medicinal substances. The life-saving success of Dante and Shakespeare seems to be founded on the force of their texts to open their readers' eyes to possibilities undreamed of before. Speaking about Larry Newton's fellow prisoners in Wabash, Laura Bates claims that '[n]o one had ever asked them to question such fundamental concepts that drive their lives and motivated their criminal choices. No one, that is, until Shakespeare'.[24] Likewise, at different moments in his book Dreher wonders at the fact that it took a fourteenth-century poet to make him see what no one else apparently could.[25]

Shakespeare is given a similar status in Laurie Maguire's *Where There's A Will There's A Way: Or, All I Really Need to Know I Learned from Shakespeare*. The Dutch translation of Maguire's book (*Shakespeare als therapeut* – 'Shakespeare as Therapist'[26]) already makes clear that the book fits within the broader bibliotherapy scheme. Like Bates and other bibliotherapists, Maguire has an instrumental take on Shakespeare's texts: for her, these writings are tools for living, 'strategies for survival and success'.[27] '[Shakespeare] should also be in the self-help section' of bookstores, she claims.[28] While this may come as a provocation for more traditional Shakespeare scholars (those of a historicist bent as well as those of a more formalist leaning), it is clearly not meant as such. As Maguire suggests:

> The sixteenth century thought and wrote about what it means to be human and how to improve one's behaviour and change one's attitudes. There is thus nothing anachronistic about us reading Shakespeare today as self-help literature, for advice about humanity and identity and personal relations.[29]

As with Bates and Larry Newton, the emphasis in Maguire's book is on character analysis: Shakespeare's plays are mainly seen as explorations of human situational behaviour and it is there that their therapeutic value is seen. Not in the sense that his plays provide us with paragons of moral behaviour (or monsters of immorality, for that matter), but in their systematic analysis of what it means to be an individual, and to have an identity of one's own. 'Shakespeare continually explores identity', Maguire argues, 'but he does not tell us how to be ourselves. No one can tell us how to be ourselves. Therapists do not prescribe; they unlock.'[30]

Like Harold Bloom and Stephen Greenblatt, Maguire is convinced that Shakespeare's plays are clearly related to our time in their conception of character. Our ideas of what it means to have a personality and to behave in ways that we consider typical of ourselves began to develop in the early modern period, which was traditionally seen, as of Burckhardt's *Kultur der Renaissance in Italien*, as the harbinger of Western individual consciousness. 'Shakespeare's plays', Maguire writes, 'show us our own situations writ large, our own character writ large. It is this understanding of the interaction between character and situation that makes Shakespeare a psychologist before the field of psychology existed as a profession.'[31] The reference – made explicit later in the book – is to *Shakespeare: The Invention of the Human*, in which Harold Bloom argues that Shakespeare was already practising psychoanalysis several centuries before Freud was born.[32] But one could also refer to Stephen Greenblatt's work on the early modern idea of self-fashioning, which, Greenblatt believes, Shakespeare brought to perfection in his work, providing us with plenty of memorable human beings who came to understand, by trial and error, that their individual destinies, albeit shaped and determined by external forces, were also things they could take into their own hands. As Greenblatt sees it, '[the] sense that one is not forever fixed in a single, divinely sanctioned identity' is one that begins to arise in the early modern period, and it still dominates our late-modern times.[33]

Even though Maguire's focus lies primarily on Shakespeare's plays and not on the personally trying circumstances from which she has been reading them, her book does contain a number of characteristic bibliotherapeutic reflections. In the passage that serves as the motto to this chapter, for instance, she mentions how reading *Hamlet* helped her to cope with the death of her father,[34] while at another decisive moment in her life Shakespeare's insights into the seductive nature of manipulative men enabled her to break with an impossibly narcissistic boyfriend.[35] 'Everything I needed to know in life I learned from Shakespeare', Maguire writes in the opening pages of her book.[36]

## Shakespeare and the Modern Regime of Consolation

In the remainder of this chapter, I want to return to the central topic of this book and look at a number of scenes in Shakespeare's plays in which both the practice and the rhetoric of consolation are placed centre-stage. Hardly unexpectedly, the c-word soon crops up in Maguire's description of the therapeutic effects that Shakespeare's work had on her. Interestingly, it does so in the very passages where she points out the self-help qualities of Shakespeare's work. 'We read self-help books', Maguire writes, 'for the same reason we read literature. To find solace and inspiration. To find guidance and advice. To find comfort: comfort that we are not alone, that others have shared our experience. Shakespeare and self-help will always overlap.'[37] Still, like several of the other bibliotherapeutic works that I have been referring to, Maguire does not seem to wonder what it is, exactly, that causes the effects that she claims these plays can have. How, to rephrase the question in line with my own concerns here, do Shakespeare's plays offer solace? The question is all the more urgent since these are plays, as we will see, that show a distinct interest in staging scenes where attempts to bring comfort fail and where, in some cases, those who manifest themselves as offering consolation are exposed as frauds – if not by the person being comforted, then at least by the audience.

In reading these scenes together, I want to offer a more systematic analysis of Shakespeare's treatment of what in the title of this chapter I refer to as 'the failure of consolation'. The different implications of that phrase – and its conjunction with what I see as a modern regime of consolation – will become clearer in the course of this chapter, I hope, but I want to single out its central point from the beginning.

That point is related to the history of the inter-relationships between literature and consolation that I started to explore in the previous two chapters. In Homer and Dante, as we have seen, scenes of consolation stress the moral importance of the practice and focus, therefore, on its successful outcome. The literary representations of it are in line with the central idea underlying most consolatory writings that have come down to us from Antiquity. When authors like Cicero, Seneca, Plutarch, and later Augustine or Boethius write about consolation, their view of the phenomenon leaves little room for doubt about the effectiveness of words of comfort. The practice of consolation is basically an appeal to reason, as we have seen in the previous chapters: the person in need of comfort needs to be released from the temporary emotional turmoil caused by their sadness. The best way to success is the way guided by *ratio* (considerations of comfort are first and foremost rational arguments), which presupposes the existence of a *sensus communis* or a shared faith: rational thoughts are thoughts shared by every sensible person and on which a shared perspective (the 'right' perspective) is available. If we manage to find a rational perspective on (the causes of) our grief – the comforter's words are directed towards the opening up of that perspective – the practice of consolation cannot but be successful. From this it follows that in the classical and Christian regimes of consolation the very opposite of the phenomenon ('desolation') has no place, except as that which has to be overcome and driven out. True, that is, successful, consolation involves the final disappearance of desolation – for the Christian believer this happens in the ultimate restoration of happiness, with God, in the climactic moment of salvation. The undeniable truth of that promise is what turns God into the only possible source of genuine consolation, as the story of Job makes clear.

In what I want to call the modern regime of consolation, the possibility of a permanent and lasting state of desolation is implied in all acts of consolation. My analysis of this modern regime of consolation is to a large extent inspired by Michaël Fœssel's *Le temps de la consolation*. Fœssel, a French philosopher who, in turn, takes his inspiration from Michel Foucault's genealogical analysis of antique and early Christian 'technologies of the self', holds a plea in his book for what he sees as a properly philosophical analysis of consolation. His starting point is that in Western modernity the topic of consolation has been exiled to the domains of religion and psychology.[38] Whereas in Antiquity consolation was primarily a distinct form of rationality, Fœssel argues, the Christian Middle Ages resulted in a 'divorce' between philosophy and consolation.[39]

The gradual rise, beginning in the early modern period, of new ideals of scientific rationality (Descartes and Spinoza, and later Kant) further increased that divide: the 'reason' that underpinned what I have called the classical regime of consolation clearly could no longer serve as a foundation for modern consolatory writings. Add to this Nietzsche's proclamation of the 'death of God' and it becomes clear why modern man (the non-religious part of that breed, at least) required a new conception of consolation. That new conception, as I pointed out in the introduction, is formulated and analysed quite aptly by Hans Blumenberg, the German philosopher whom Fœssel rightly calls 'one of the rare contemporary thinkers to take consolation seriously'.[40]

In one of the most interesting analyses that I know of the experiential phenomenon of comfort, Blumenberg argues that human existence is marked by two mutually incompatible force-fields: the necessity of being comforted on the one hand and the impossibly of being comforted on the other – 'Trostbedürfnis und Untröstlichkeit', in Blumenberg's German.[41] Consolation, for Blumenberg, is the central anthropological marker: in contrast to other living beings, man is a creature of comfort. Blumenberg agrees with Georg Simmel in this. 'Man', Simmel writes in a fragment of his *Nachlass* that Blumenberg quotes, 'is a creature on the outlook for consolation',[42] and this is what distinguishes mankind from other animals. Animals require help, Simmel argues, and help is categorically different from comfort.[43] According to Simmel, man 'invented' the notion of comfort because our earthly existence confronts us with certain aspects of our condition that would otherwise leave us completely helpless: our awareness of our mortality, mainly. 'By and large, man cannot really be helped', Simmel writes. 'That is why he has come up with the wonderful category of 'consolation' – which he does not only derive from words which other human beings address to him with that specific goal in mind, but also from numerous things in the world.'[44]

For Blumenberg, much as for Simmel, the experience of comfort is related to the awareness of our finality and of the fundamental absence of a 'solution' for that existential problem. Hence Blumenberg's analysis of the fundamental paradox of what I see as typically modern ideas of consolation: we are essentially inconsolable (death brings an end to life, inevitably), but we need comfort in order to live with that awareness. 'It is not the task of comforters to do away with grief or to bring joy', the Dutch philosopher Cornelis Verhoeven writes in an intelligent essay on the modern conception of consolation. 'The duty of comfort involves the return of the person afflicted to the world.'[45]

Like Blumenberg, Verhoeven focuses on the paradoxes of modern ideas of consolation. For him, the central paradox seems to be the fact that practices of comfort 'mobilise' and therefore also provoke the sadness they are simultaneously meant to alleviate.[46] While the success of the practice of bringing comfort is beyond reasonable doubt in the classical and Christian regimes of consolation, modern texts dealing with the subject tend to focus on its difficulty if not impossibility. As Paul Rabinow puts it, for modern man to be consoled 'consists in *imagining* being consoled while remaining aware that whatever consolations are currently available will never be definitive as there is no ultimate restoration of a prior state of well-being or wholeness'.[47] Indeed, the modern regime of comfort lacks the convictions that serve as the keystones of both the classical and the Christian regimes: a belief in the absolute rightness of rational thinking, of common-sense values (i.e. values that are self-evident for everybody) and of the divine order. Its iconic figure, Fœssel writes, is the inconsoled one, 'l'inconsolé'.[48] The term does not refer to the refusal or rejection of consolation, Fœssel hastens to add, but to an attitude that tries to accept (and even welcome) gestures and words of consolation while being aware that these will never really resolve the problem for which they are meant.

To bring comfort in the logic of classical consolatory writings requires a sharp and rational confrontation of the person being comforted with the events in the real that caused distress and grief. Out of that confrontation comes recovery in the form of insight – the insight that things are not as bad as they seem, that what happened was in one way or another inevitable. In the Christian regime of consolation, that in many ways involves the appropriation of classical consolatory topoi, comfort comes in the awareness that what we considered painful or grievous is in the end the outcome of a larger divine plan, or maybe even the occasion of a test of faith. In order for that insight to appear, the consolatory practice has to be successful and the rhetoric in which it is embodied truly convincing. In the modern regime of consolation the success of practices of comfort is thoroughly problematised and at best very temporary. A good example is provided by the brief essay that the Swedish author Stig Dagerman finished just before he committed suicide on 5 November 1954.[49] In his final text, Dagerman labels man's need for consolation literally insatiable. From the very beginning of his essay, the author presents himself as an unbeliever, who cannot, in consequence, find comfort in religious convictions. Consolation for him is by definition temporary – '[t]he breath of consolation is as fleeting as a breeze sifting through the treetops', as Steven Hartman's translation of the essay has it[50] – and is presented throughout the text as a flash of significant freedom in an absurd, oppressive world. Dagerman finds comfort in the momentary realisation that life ought not to lead to permanent despair: 'This then is my sole consolation', he writes in the final paragraph of what became his last text ever:

> I realize that lapses into hopelessness may come often and run deep. And yet my memory of the miracle of liberation is enough to carry me, as on a wing, to dizzying new heights and to my ultimate goal: a consolation that is so much more than a consolation and also greater than a philosophy – a reason to live.[51]

The fact that the author decided to end his life a mere two days after writing down this consoling thought points out the very temporary nature of the comfort that it brought. His suicide confirmed the image with which his essay opens: those who desperately seek consolation will soon be frustrated, like hunters who shoot at anything that even remotely suggests the impression of movement.[52]

The examples from Homer and Dante show that in the classical and Christian regimes comfort works because it is the result of a shared experience by the person offering comfort and the one receiving it. Priam is comforted by the murderer of his son because he feels that despite their antagonism the pain they feel is a common one; Dante is comforted by Virgil because he shares with the pagan writer a number of central convictions regarding the ideals of morally upright human behaviour (not to mention regarding the role that literature plays in the transfer of those ideals). Shakespeare's scenes of comfort, as we will see, follow an entirely different scenario, one in which the practice of consolation turns out to be a problem and fails – and in those cases where it doesn't fail, it is no less a problem, as we will see. My analysis of a number of consolatory encounters in *Hamlet*, *Richard II*, *Measure for Measure*, *Romeo and Juliet* and *The Tempest* indicates that there are several possible causes for this failure. In some of the scenes that I want to discuss, the rhetoric of comfort is experienced by the person to whom it is addressed as inauthentic, produced by flatterers or downright liars. In the ears of the audience, too, the words of comfort sound hollow and empty, in no way fulfilling the promise they are expected to hold. More than once in Shakespeare's plays, characters who are being comforted simply fail to connect their inner experience with the consolation on offer. Their sorrow resists, so to speak – it is continued rather than alleviated. The singularity of these characters' pain fails to become embedded in the narrative of solidarity and communal experience that in classical consolations is traditionally opened up by the promise of comfort. In order to be comforted, we have to accept that we are not alone in feeling what we feel.

Written in an age in which core arguments that made up the classical discourse of consolation became appropriated within a Christian framework, Shakespeare's scenes of consolation go strikingly against the grain. As we will see, Shakespeare had a sound knowledge of the classical consolatory tradition. He makes use of many of its founding topoi, but he does so in a way that undercuts the conventional mechanism underlying the classical logic of comfort. His scenes show the failure of consolation rather than its self-evident success. The scenes that I have in mind display the failure of comforting arguments to convince truly and deeply – somehow, in Shakespeare, these arguments seem to have lost at least some of their rhetorical power and self-evidence. In the scenes that I want to discuss, the problem of consolation is not solved by religious arguments either. Most (if not all) early modern consolations (Catholic as well as Reformed) urge their readers to find ultimate comfort in the idea that human suffering is a necessary part of the divine plan. The biblical character of Job is the iconic figure of religious consolation, as I pointed out in the previous chapter: no matter how extreme the hardship that God allows to be inflicted upon him, Job never loses faith. In the scenes discussed in which Shakespeare explicitly addresses the comfort of religion, that form of consolation is equally treated as a problem: priests who offer comfort are on at least two occasions (*Romeo and Juliet* and *Measure for Measure*) exposed as frauds, while in both *Hamlet* and *Richard II* no positive mention is made of heavenly comfort.

## 'Words, Words, Words' – but No Real Comfort

I want to begin with *Hamlet*. How is the tragedy of the prince of Denmark a play about consolation? How, as a play, moreover, does Shakespeare's text invite us to think about the shifting nature of that cultural practice? There is a fairly direct way of answering at least the former question. In 1934, the American Shakespeare scholar Hardin Craig published an article in *The Huntington Library Bulletin* in which he tried to corroborate the idea, suggested by more than one nineteenth-century critic, that the book Hamlet is reading in the second scene of the play's Act Two is Girolamo Cardano's

*De Consolatione Libri Tres*. Cardano's text is a fairly typical humanist treatise on the nature of consolation and on its most effective discursive forms.[53] Cardano is best known as the author of *De Vita Propria*, the famous autobiography that he wrote in the last year of his life (1576), and of a number of astronomical and mathematical writings, among which a pioneering study on algebra.[54] His treatise on consolation was first published in Venice in 1542 and translated into English by Thomas Bedingfield under the title of *Cardanus Comforte*.[55] We have editions of the translation dating from 1573 and 1576 (the year of Cardano's death), dedicated by the translator to Edward de Vere, the 17th earl of Oxford, of whom we know that he was instrumental in the development of Shakespeare's career.

The textual relationship between Shakespeare's *Hamlet* and *Cardanus Comforte* has been convincingly documented by Craig and others before him. As early as 1845, Joseph Hunter, in a monograph that deals with several of Shakespeare's plays, decidedly claimed that 'the book which Shakespeare placed in the hands of Hamlet' could be none other than the English translation of Cardano's *De Consolatione Libri Tres*.[56] Hunter relied for his conclusion on the work of the 'antiquarian' Francis Douce, who had already asserted in a book from 1807 that Shakespeare had to be well acquainted with Cardano's treatise.[57] But while Douce argued that Cardano's reflections on consolation served as the basis for a number of passages in *Macbeth*, Hunter was convinced that Bedingfield's translation of Cardano's treatise inspired Shakespeare directly in writing Hamlet's famous 'to be or not to be' monologue.[58] Hardin Craig elaborated on Hunter's findings and found that the textual parallels between *Hamlet* and *Cardanus Comforte* were more numerous than Hunter thought and not limited, moreover, to the prince's many monologues. Craig also found echoes from Cardano in the conversations that Hamlet has with Horatio and Ophelia. '[I]t may be said', he concluded, 'without great exaggeration and irrespective of whether or not Shakespeare presented his hero as reading in this particular book just before he spoke his soliloquy [*'to be or not to be'*], that Cardan's *De Consolatione* is pre-eminently "Hamlet's book", since the philosophy of Hamlet agrees to a remarkable degree with that of Cardan'.[59]

Craig's findings have led some critics and theatre directors to suggest that in 3.1 Hamlet can be seen to deliver the play's most famous monologue carrying in his hand the same book that he is reading in the opening scene of the play's second act. The latter is the scene where Polonius tries to convince Claudius and Gertrude that he has finally discovered why Hamlet is behaving so strangely of late. The prince's mad behaviour is due, Polonius believes, to 'ecstasy of love' (2.1.103) and to the lovesickness that resulted from the fact that he was denied access to Ophelia by Polonius, the girl's father. In the passage from the scene that I am interested in, Polonius intends to 'unmask' Hamlet before the eyes of his mother and his stepfather, who both withdraw the moment Hamlet comes onstage, 'madly attired, reading on a book', as the stage-text of my Oxford edition has it. Immediately, Polonius embarks upon a conversation with the prince that leads to the question that occupies us here (what indeed is Hamlet reading?) and to his infamous answer to that question: 'Words, words, words' (2.2.195).

Whether or not we can identify Hamlet's book with Cardano's treatise on consolation will not affect the immediate meaning of Hamlet's reply. 'Words, words, words' means as much as: 'go away, man', 'leave me alone', 'do not bother me with your questions'. Still, if we assume that the 'matter' Hamlet is reading about is the matter of consolation, then his tri-syllabic reply may well gain new meaning. What Hamlet is reading in *Cardanus Comforte* are to him in fact mere words, words that are of no use whatsoever to him since they do not give him what he wants. The book is about something that will not help him at all in his search for revenge, since they deal with quite the opposite of revenge: they deal with consolation. The book is quite simply the wrong book for Hamlet and we may well wonder why he is reading it in the first place.

To be clear: I'm not trying to prove what in the end can never be proven: that *Cardanus Comforte* is indeed the book that Hamlet is reading.[60] However, I do think it is worthwhile to try to imagine Hamlet as actually in the process of reading a book on consolation. Hamlet is, after all, struggling to come to terms with the sudden death of his father and with the overwhelming grief that was triggered by this unexpected event. Hamlet's grief is mentioned at one point in Sigmund Freud's classical analysis of mourning, 'Trauer und Melancholie'.[61] Freud mentions Hamlet's name only once in his text, but it is clear that the essay has a number of interesting things to say about the prince.[62] The question is not so much whether Hamlet's strange behaviour is that of a person undergoing a 'normal' process of mourning or, rather, that of the victim of the 'pathological condition' of 'melancholia' that, according to Freud, ultimately results in the destructive loss of self and the desire to disappear.[63] What Freud's analysis of the intersections between mourning and melancholy makes clear is that Hamlet's thoughts and actions are marked by what the Flemish philosopher Patricia de Martelaere, in a discussion of 'Trauer und Melancholie', has labelled 'the desire not to be consoled'.[64]

At one point in her essay, De Martelaere deals with Shakespeare's Juliet, but what she writes about the young Veronese heroine applies no less to the Danish prince, who is supposedly twice her age.[65] Neither of them *can* be consoled in the immediacy of the grief of their loved one (Romeo in the case of Juliet, Hamlet's father in the case of the Danish prince) because they don't *want* to be: the success of any attempt at consolation would mean that they are willing to give up their beloved here and now. Why, then, did Hamlet pick up this particular book by Cardano from what will no doubt have been Elsinore's rich library? Consolation is definitely not what the eponymous hero of Shakespeare's most famous play is after. What he is after – as soon as he has spoken to the ghost of his dead father in the final scene of the play's first act – is justice and revenge, revenge based on the specific idea of justice that his society (rotten Denmark) is built upon. Revenge is in many ways the exact opposite of consolation: revenge aims for the righting of a wrong that is considered unjust and not rightful. Revenge is payback time, nothing more, nothing less. Consolation is quite the inverse: it is about coming to accept that which is unjust and not rightful as somehow inevitable – as the way things have to go, even if we don't want them to go that way. Consolation is about coming to terms with a real that is considered unacceptable but that has to be accepted.

While consolation only works on the basis of acceptance, revenge begins from and ends with the unwillingness to accept. The person seeking revenge wants to change things and has to secure this change by means of an act. Consolation is not about executing an act. While it may be about the desire for change, the change involved is a change in perspective, the sort of change that for the person in need of consolation mere acts will never produce. The change that is needed in the successful process of consolation is a change in thinking and only in thinking. There can only be consolation, Blumenberg writes in his text on consolation to which I referred earlier, if the person to be consoled has managed to embrace the idea that nothing can be changed about the state of affairs that provokes our need of consolation.[66] That which causes us to hurt is not going to change; it is our perspective on it that has to change in order for us to be able to accommodate the hurt.

## The Prince Fails to Be Comforted

Hamlet, clearly, is not asking for a change of perspective; he simply refuses to see things differently. But while he wants to be able to do something, his tragedy remains that he cannot act, as most readings of the play have come to stress. It is interesting to note that before we come to understand Hamlet's fundamental impossibility to really take revenge, it is his unwillingness to be consoled that is being highlighted. Even before he is put into the clear as to how his father (supposedly) died, the play points out that Hamlet is not at all responding to what appear to be well-meant attempts at consolation. In the first scene in which he is introduced to us (1.2), both Gertrude and Claudius try to point out to him that the time may have come for Hamlet to stop his mourning. They urge and ultimately command him to stop grieving over the loss of his father. They do so by trying to convince him that it is wise, more common-sensical and more fitting for a man to give up the sort of behaviour that could still be tolerated from a bereaved son in the immediate aftermath of his father's death but which now, after two months,[67] verges on the inappropriate.

In consoling Hamlet (i.e. in trying to convince him to behave reasonably), Gertrude and Claudius make use of a series of arguments that Shakespeare could have found in any of the classical consolatory writings that probably belonged to the early modern humanist curriculum. While there are different strands and schools in the art of consolation in Antiquity, as we have seen, all share the idea that those who are in need of comfort must be driven away from the temporary confusion in which the emotional turmoil that resulted from their distress has placed them. The way to success lies on the path of rationalisation: classical considerations of consolation are exercises in the regaining of one's reason. The appeal to reason presupposes in Antiquity the existence of a *sensus communis*, as I have stressed: rational thoughts are thoughts that are shared by everybody, provided that one succeeds in attaining the perspective of the wise. Put differently, if we manage to find the right way (the wise way) of looking at our distress and the things that cause it (the words of comfort are meant to direct us on that path), the art of consolation will always be successful.

This is more or less what Gertrude and Claudius urge Hamlet to do in the scene that I want to have a closer look at. Even though to modern ears they may sound less consoling than we would care for, all of Gertrude and Claudius' exhortations come straight out of an early modern manual for consolation. To exaggerate in mourning is to allow oneself to be exclusively driven by one's emotions and this leads to a lack of stability. To mourn in the proper way is what Claudius upon his first entry onstage describes as follows: 'with wisest sorrow [to] think on him / Together with remembrance of ourselves' (1.2.6–7). In mourning we should neither forget nor lose ourselves, Claudius argues. The unwise mourner threatens to lose himself in mourning, then, and Hamlet is in serious danger of doing just that.

The wisdom that Claudius refers to (the wisdom of 'wisest sorrow') is reminiscent of the ideal of *sapientia* that he may have known from the Stoic perspective that greatly determined classical writings of consolation and that was mediated in the European West through Cicero's work.[68] To give one example that I referred to in my discussion of Dante's search for a poetics of comfort: in *De amicitia*, Cicero has Laelius say (with respect to the great loss that he suffered after his good friend Scipio died) that the only consolation that he needs is the idea that his friend's death was not an evil that was inflicted upon Scipio. Those who are inconsolable at the loss of loved ones, Laelius adds, suffer from a despicable form of self-love. In them, the love of self is far greater than the love of the person they have lost. In later, Christian conceptions of consolation to which both Gertrude and Claudius also seem to refer, the idea that the loved ones that we lose go to a better place is also a source of comfort and consolation. However, this is also a perspective that Hamlet, for several reasons, cannot begin to adopt. It is, nevertheless, the perspective that *Cardanus Comforte* puts forward: the point of Cardano's book (especially of the passages from which Shakespeare seems to have borrowed) is that death is not only something inevitable that we need to accept, but something that can even bring us peace and quiet, the sort of peace that Hamlet's father seems to be deprived of as long as he wanders about in his capacity of purgatorial ghost.

Hamlet should simply take a rational perspective on the cause of his distress and come to understand that it lies in the natural course of things that fathers die. 'Do not for ever with thy vailèd lids / Seek for thy noble father in the dust', Gertrude implores him. 'Thou know'st 'tis common – all that lives must die, / Passing through nature to eternity' (1.2.70–3). Variants of Gertrude's argument can be found in most classical consolations. The same logic is used by Cicero, Seneca and Plutarch, each of whom are sources that Cardano made use of: death is an essential part of human life and for that reason we need to deal with it properly – all things come to an end. Claudius continues in the same vein:

> 'Tis sweet and commendable in your nature, Hamlet,
> To give these mourning duties to your father;
> But you must know your father lost a father;
> That father lost, lost his; and the survivor bound
> In filial obligation for some term
> To do obsequious sorrow. (1.2.87–92)

At first, the comforting logic of these words comes across as fairly encouraging, but in what follows Claudius raises the stakes. He continues the argument by confronting Hamlet with a number of assertions that are part and parcel of the classical discourse of consolation, but which Hamlet can only take as reproaches targeted towards the core of his personality: Hamlet is behaving stubbornly, Claudius claims, unlike anything that can be expected of a man. Also, he is downright foolish in resisting that which God in his eternal wisdom has predetermined. References to the will of the gods can be found in classical consolations as well, as we have seen, but in Christian ones they move centre-stage. Christian consolations are founded centrally by the idea that we need to realise that whatever causes us pain has been willed by God. Continued complaints against states of affairs that trouble us (and the refusal to be consoled can only be taken as such) come down, in the end, to complaints against God. In other words: in stubbornly and foolishly clinging to his mourning, Hamlet is a sinner. (The fact that we are expected to believe that these words are spoken by a man who single-handedly murdered his own brother, makes them all the more questionable, of course.)

> But to persever
> In obstinate condolement is a course
> Of impious stubbornness, 'tis unmanly grief,
> It shows a will most incorrect to heaven,
> A heart unfortified, a mind impatient,
> An understanding simple and unschooled;
> For what we know must be, and is as common
> As any the most vulgar thing to sense,
> Why should we in our peevish opposition
> Take it to heart? Fie, 'tis a fault to heaven,
> A fault against the dead, a fault to nature,
> To reason most absurd, whose common theme

Is death of fathers, and who still hath cried
From the first corpse till he that died today,
'This must be so.' (1.2.92–106)

The arguments that together make up Claudius' long exhortation seem to come straight out of Cicero's discussion of comfort in Book Three of the *Tusculanae Disputationes*. The book has also been named as one of the possible sources of the famous 'to be or not to be' monologue that comes later in the play,[69] but I would argue that specific passages of it also underlie Claudius' consolatory speech in the scene that we are looking at. The passages that I am thinking of follow upon Cicero's reference in paragraph 25 of the third book of the *Tusculanae* to a discussion between Carneades and Chrysippus, the latter being the authority in matters of consolation with whom Cicero feels most affiliation.[70] The idea 'that the lot of man must be endured', Cicero writes, 'prevents us from contending as it were against God (*quasi cum deo pugnare*) and also warns us that we are human'. 'This reflection (*cogitatio*) is a great relief to sorrow', he continues, encouraging 'the mourner to think that he must bear the burdens which he sees many men have borne in a spirit of quiet restraint (*moderate et tranquille tulisse*).'[71] When we are overcome with distress, Cicero argues, we are prey to a false belief (*opinio*), which we can only overcome by serious thinking: 'by reflection (*cogitatio*) men gradually realize the extreme falsity of their belief'.[72] Comfort comes from deep thinking, then, from rational thought.

In describing Hamlet's attitude as that of 'a heart unfortified, or mind impatient', Claudius seems to be referring to the Ciceronian ideals of *fortitudo* and *patientia*, the strength of mind that bears the whims of fortune with endurance. '[I]t is in one's power to throw grief aside when one will', Cicero writes, 'in obedience to the call of the hour'.[73] Whoever continues to mourn beyond the required term does it out of his own will, a will, as Claudius puts it, 'most incorrect to heaven'.[74] 'Indulgence in [grief] is useless', Cicero concludes,[75] and he goes on to write – yet another echo that can be found in Claudius' speech – 'that sorrow and mourning [are] unbefitting in a man', 'degrading' even.[76] 'Who is so mad as to mourn of his own free choice?', Cicero asks rhetorically, invoking the counter-examples of Quintus Maximus, Lucius Paullus and Cato the Censor, who showed no signs of distress when they buried their children.[77]

However, we should be careful not to identify Claudius' perspective completely with that of Cicero. The idea that we have a certain obligation to express what Claudius calls 'mourning duties' in public is also an instance of what Cicero considers false belief. 'In consequence of this idea', the author of the *Tusculanae* writes, 'come the different odious forms of mourning',[78] of which he gives several examples. The inconsolable Niobe, to whom Hamlet later compares his hypocritical mother ('all tears' (1.2.149)) is one of them.

The big difference between Cicero's treatise and Shakespeare's tragedy is that in the former the text's premise is that good practices of the art of consolation will always be effective, whereas in the latter the rhetoric of consolation doesn't work at all: Hamlet is not convinced by Claudius' Ciceronian arguments because he simply doesn't want to be convinced. Maybe it's safer to say that he doesn't allow himself to be convinced, because there is something inside him that prevents him from following the logic that Claudius displays to him. One might say, as Cicero did, that it's a matter of simple will, but there seems to be more at stake here: Hamlet doesn't see the reason behind Claudius and Gertrude's words, not because he is mad (Hamlet is a very rational human being, after all) but because he doesn't share the common sense with which they try to convince him. In fact, he opposes it with another common sense of his own: 'a beast that wants reason / Would have mourned longer!' he says about his mother (1.2.150–1), who from Hamlet's perspective immediately gave up all thoughts about her late husband, by rushing into a new marriage with that husband's brother, 'within a month, / Ere yet the salt of most unrighteous tears / Had left the flushing of her gallèd eyes' (1.2.153–5), as Hamlet puts it in the soliloquy that follows on from Claudius and Gertrude's failed attempts at consoling him.

Gertrude, like Niobe, expressed her grief abundantly, Hamlet suggests here, but were those tears genuine expressions of actual pain?[79] He doubts sincerely that they were, playing upon the distinction that he had introduced earlier in the scene, when he explained to his mother that there is no telling that his outer expression of pain adheres fully to any feeling within. Even if I were to give up the external signs of my grieving, he told Gertrude, there would still be something inside me that remains inconsolably sad, 'that within which passeth show' (1.2.85), as he famously puts it, and it is that 'within' that fails to be addressed by what he experiences as the empty rhetoric of his mother's and his stepfather's meagre attempts at consolation – 'words, words, words', as he will say in the later scene that we discussed earlier.

## Hamlet and the Problem of Consolation

The words of comfort that Claudius and Gertrude express in the scene that we have been looking at 'ring empty though nonetheless true', Simon Critchley and Jamieson Webster write in *The Hamlet Doctrine*.[80] Even though Critchley and Webster don't deal with the topic that interests me here, theirs is an accurate description of consolatory words that do not result in consolation – true words that ring empty. Whenever we try to comfort someone, Michaël Fœssel writes, we need to make sure that our words are not taken as an 'illegitimate intrusion' in the experience of suffering to which we are, by definition, alien.[81] It is clear from his response to Claudius and Gertrude's attempts at consolation that Hamlet indeed considers their words as such. Throughout the scene his suggestion is that their words of comfort have nothing whatsoever to do with him.

However, the irony involved in Hamlet's 'words, words, words' is that consolation is indeed often what he is saying: it generally comes in 'words, words, words'. Consolation is a matter of rhetoric, but not, obviously, in the negative sense which that term no doubt has for Hamlet. If we allow ourselves to be comforted or consoled, we will allow ourselves to be convinced by the words, words, words that are offered to us and by the arguments that are couched in those words, words, words. Hamlet simply does not want to be convinced or consoled: most of the time when he is conversing with other characters in the play he expresses suspicion with respect to the power of words and to the people making use of these objects of duplicity. Whether he is being addressed by Gertrude, Claudius, Ophelia, Rosencrantz and Guildenstern or Polonius, he keeps resorting to a way of speaking that is aware of and exploits an essential rift between 'signifiers' and 'signifieds', between 'les mots et les choses', to borrow Foucault's phrase.

Every word, for Hamlet, is inherently duplicitous and therefore it is impossible for him to consider words as being intrinsically and essentially related to the real or to some or other shared meaning. What Hamlet tells us about the phenomenon of consolation is *ex negativo*: if we want to be comforted we should in no way doubt the force and the authenticity of the words that are meant to bring comfort. Consolation is only effective if the one being consoled not only believes in the sincerity of the consoler but is also willing to open up to the comfort on offer. That is definitely not the case for Hamlet: he seriously doubts the sincerity of Gertrude and Claudius' words – not so much because he is convinced that they are schemers and liars (he will come to see them that way later in the play) but because he experiences some existential rift between the words that they are using in order to talk sense into him, and the actual pain that he feels. There is also a rift, he suggests, between the man that he is (or, seems) outwardly and the person within: the dark clothing that he wears, the grief that others see in his gestures and on his face, none of this 'denote[s] me truly', Hamlet says (1.2.83). There is something inside him – 'that within which passeth show' – that cannot be reduced to the *sensus communis* that Gertrude and Claudius invoke in their efforts to bring Hamlet to the reason of comfort. This core of singular individuality resists the logic of human solidarity that warrants the success of the classical practice of consolation. Hamlet cannot and will not be comforted because he is convinced that the appropriation of his sorrow by a narrative of common sense would not do justice to what he feels and to the person that he is. To allow himself to be comforted would involve the betrayal of his inner self, of his grief and of the love for his father that lies at the heart of this grief.

The main obstacle, in this case, to the success of the classical consolatory logic seems to be Hamlet's conviction that he is somehow different from all those who lost a father before him. The idea that what he experiences is part of 'the course of things' and therefore simply has to be accepted, in no way encourages him to change either his thoughts or his behaviour. On the contrary, it would appear that the idea adds to his inconsolability. Throughout the play, Hamlet continues to manifest a single-minded 'self' that refuses to behave in the way that is expected by the common sense of those who surround him. The inner self to which Hamlet is referring seems to be a new force of resistance against the self-evidence of classical ideas on consolation. The claim that the early modern period saw the rise of new conceptions of human identity and individuality is a commonplace of cultural history, and it would seem, as I have argued earlier in this chapter, that it also impacted the development of our modern ideas of consolation.

Shakespeare's play is marked by the conspicuous absence of markers pointing to Christian ideas of consolation, to the extent even that it becomes difficult to align the text's ideas on consolation either to the tradition that predates what Ronald Rittgers has called the 'Reformation of suffering' or to Luther's new ideas on suffering as a test of faith rather than as penance.[82] In his discussion of *Hamlet* in *A Will to Believe: Shakespeare and Religion*, David Scott Kastan does not relate Claudius and Gertrude's consolatory arguments to either the tradition of classical *consolationes* or its humanist revival in the early modern period, but to the sixteenth-century Protestant critique of expressions of excessive mourning. As Kastan claims, Claudius' scolding of Hamlet could by some contemporary spectators be taken as a sign that the latter's grief should be seen as 'somehow Catholic'.[83] But all in all, he concludes, 'Hamlet's grief is merely grief – not evidence of religious commitments, however doctrinally imagined, but of emotional ones.'[84]

In line with this conclusion, the staging of consolation in *Hamlet* contains no trace whatsoever of the possibility of religious comfort. The calm realisation that death's final relief can bring peace in our earthly life – a source of clear comfort to the prisoner in Boethius' treatise and to Dante in the *Divine Comedy* – is quite alien to Hamlet's consciousness. Death will relieve and release us finally of all the blows that life on earth can deal – at least, it does so if we manage to conceive of the relationship between life and death in a reasonable framework, which is the perspective of the man who accepts what happens either with the magnanimity, wisdom and courage that Roman Stoic philosophers aimed for, or on the basis of the religious perspective of Job, the iconic figure of Christian consolation who in the direst of circumstances keeps confirming that whatever God does is a source of consolation in itself. God doesn't offer or provide consolation, to Job: he *is* consolation.

The fact that Hamlet does not manage to adopt either of those two perspectives becomes very clear in the central passage of the 'To be or not to be' monologue in which he famously puts the dilemma that faces him as follows:

> To be, or not to be; that is the question:
> Whether 'tis nobler in the mind to suffer
> The slings and arrows of outrageous fortune,
> Or to take arms against a sea of troubles,
> And, by opposing, end them. To die, to sleep –
> No more, and by a sleep to say we end
> The heartache and the thousand natural shocks
> That flesh is heir to – 'tis a consummation
> Devoutly to be wished. To die, to sleep.
> To sleep, perchance to dream. Ay, there's the rub,
> For in that sleep of death what dreams may come
> When we have shuffled off this mortal coil
> Must give us pause. (3.1.58–70)

The choice in Hamlet's view is clear: either he must suffer the blows of a *mala fortuna* or he must voluntarily leave this world and go to what later in this monologue is aptly described as '[t]he undiscovered country from whose bourn / No traveller returns' (3.1.81–2) – yet another possible echo of Cardano's *De consolatione*.[85] For Hamlet, the second option (to leave this life voluntarily) seems to be the only possible way to avoid the blows of fortune. Death is seen as a sleep that can free him from the nightmare of his existence.

In the cruel conversation with Ophelia that directly follows on from this monologue (the famous nunnery scene), Hamlet at one point says 'that it were better my mother had not borne me' (3.1.125–6). In his recent close reading of *Hamlet*, Gabriel Josipovici relates this line to a passage from the Book of Job in which the eponymous hero of the Old Testament text rants in a similar way: 'Why died I not from the womb? Why did I not give up the ghost when I came out of the belly? Why did the knees prevent me? or why the breasts that I should suck? For now should I have lain still and been quiet, I should have slept: then had I been at rest.'[86] 'Hamlet does not have Job's eloquence', Josipovici writes, but neither does he have his patience, I would add.[87] In the end, Job comes to see that whatever God has in store for him is part of a divine plan that supersedes his own powers of reason. Even when God strikes me, Job asserts, I am comforted and strengthened by His presence. 'Even that it would please God to destroy me; that he would let loose his hand, and cut me off! Then should I yet have comfort; yea, I would harden myself in sorrow: let him not spare; for I have not concealed the words of the Holy One.'[88]

## Towards a Modern Regime of Comfort?

The Book of Job is one of Shakespeare's more conspicuous biblical intertexts, as Julia Reinhard Lupton and others have recently shown.[89] However, *Hamlet* is definitely not one of the plays in which its presence shows. True, the prince does share with Job an interest in what Lupton calls 'the worm-eaten destiny of corpses',[90] but it obviously makes sense that, in a play that centres around an inconsolable protagonist, the biblical character that more than any other embodies the patience that seems to be a prerequisite of consolation (religious or not) is markedly absent. Shakespeare's more clearly recognisable Job-like figures are, on average, older men (Lear, Timon, Shylock), who have been dealt more serious blows by Fate and whose advance in life may well make them more inclined to be patient and attain the wisdom required by that classical and Christian quality.

'All-in all', Frans-Willem Korsten writes, 'one could call Job the paradigm of Christian subjection, as he subjected himself to the one and only world possible: a world ruled by God.'[91] The same thing that makes Job the Christian subject *par excellence* makes him an icon of religious consolation: in order to find comfort even in God's 'decretum horribile' one needs to allow oneself to be fully subjected to the omnipotent and apparently indifferent will of the divine order. To become a true Christian subject, one needs to be fully subjected. It is quite ironical that Shakespeare decided that his inconsolable Danish prince should be a student at Wittenberg, the university from which Luther began the Reform of the Christian church. The idea that comfort can be derived from submission to God's will is fairly absent in Hamlet's considerations, or those of his comforters for that matter. On the contrary, even: one could say that Shakespeare's tragedy gives us an idea of what is bound to happen once man stops submitting his own experience to God's plan because he no longer finds comfort in the idea that whatever happens is what God willed. It is a further irony of the play that what prevents Hamlet from being comforted – the prince's feeling that his inner experience (that which denotes him truly) does not cohere with what is expected of him – is generally seen as the product of the movement of Reform that Luther and Calvin, among others, began to advocate in the century leading up to the emergence of Shakespeare's major works.

There were plenty of consolatory treatises available in the age of Shakespeare. The period's great humanists were obviously familiar with the prime classical texts on consolation (Plutarch, Seneca, Cicero, Boethius) and some of them (Petrarch, Erasmus, Luther, Calvin) added to that rich library new additions of their own, in which the classical regime of comfort was 'translated', without much difficulty, into a Christian framework.[92] Cardano's *De Consolatione Libri Tres* is but one example of that category. The scene of comfort in *Hamlet* that I just discussed seems to indicate that Shakespeare's treatment of the issue is altogether different. In what follows, I want to have a look at a number of other scenes from his plays that confirm this hypothesis. The point that I will be making – or rather, the further hypothesis that I will be developing – is that Shakespeare's treatment of the 'problem' of comfort points to a new, modern regime of consolation. In that new regime, we no longer find comfort in the final salvation that God's plan ultimately held for Job. In this modern, secular regime, the self-evidence of the effectiveness of practices of comfort, and the rhetoric in which these are usually couched, becomes problematised. The new scenario becomes one in which the 'solidarity' between comforter and comforted that was taken as a given in the classical and Christian regimes of consolation is put under a strain. Related to that, the idea that there is such a thing as a *sensus communis* (a shared set of ideals and expectations to which everybody can conform, 'the one and only possible world' that Korsten refers to) is no longer available. There are two sides to the practice of consolation and two parties involved – rare is the occasion, in the modern regime, that the twain actually and fully meet.

### 'The Inward Soul': *Richard II* and the Failure of Consolation

Hamlet fails to be comforted by his mother and his uncle because there is something inside him that refuses to be convinced by their efforts at consolation. In the scene of *Richard II* that I now want to have a closer look at, Shakespeare labels this 'something' the 'inward soul'. Interestingly, the phrase occurs in yet another scene of failed consolation. As in *Hamlet*, we are confronted in this history play with a character that somehow does not manage to be consoled by the sort of arguments that used to serve as the foundation of the classical rhetoric of consolation. In both plays, the failure of consolation seems to be due to a similar cause, even though the scenario of the scenes (and the typology of their participants) is somewhat different: both in *Hamlet* and in *Richard II* the one being consoled cannot simply accept the comfort on offer – not because those who try to bring comfort say or do the wrong things. On the contrary, in both cases, the consolers express ideas that in the given circumstances are perfectly apt. Still, the practice of consolation fails to work and to lead to the connection that is necessary for its success – a form of solidarity between consoler and consoled, where the latter one, as Hans Blumenberg puts in his fascinating analysis of the mechanism and the experience of comfort, feels that he can 'delegate' his sorrow (however virtually and momentarily) to the person bringing comfort.[93]

The one being comforted in the scene in *Richard II* that I now want to have a closer look at (2.2) is Isabel, Richard's queen, whose sadness is caused by the absence of her husband, who suddenly had to leave on a military mission to Ireland. For some reason or other, Isabel is convinced that the unexpected separation from her spouse is a premonition of greater distress to come. She fears that she may never see Richard again. Isabel's main comforter is one of the king's courtiers, Bushy, who warns her about the obvious dangers of too great an amount of distress. His arguments against the possible threat of Isabel's immeasurable sadness entails yet another plea for *metriopatheia* and the counterbalancing of emotional responses to distress with a necessary degree of reason:

> Madam, your majesty is too much sad.
> You promised when you parted with the King
> To lay aside life-harming heaviness
> And entertain a cheerful disposition. (2.2.1–4)

As in *Hamlet*, extreme distress is portrayed as a potential source of self-loss in *Richard II*. The threat that is involved in excessive mourning is 'life-harming' according to Bushy and that is why his attempts to console the queen need to be directed at the aversion of that threat. The arguments that he makes use of are typical of the ones used in classical consolations. We have also seen them at work in Gertrude and Claudius' speeches of comfort: in the remainder of the scene, Bushy continues to appeal to Queen Isabel's powers of reason. The brief passage that I just quoted points out a tension or conflict that is also present in the scene in *Hamlet* that we discussed: the tension or conflict between the outer expression or appearance of how people behave and how they feel 'within' (the dark clothes and the dejected facial expression of which Hamlet said that it cannot make clear how he feels; in Isabel's case the 'cheerful disposition' that she upholds towards her husband).

Isabel's character is different from that of Hamlet, whose sadness results in a fairly aggressive form of resistance against the demands or wishes of others. The difference between them is that between the figures Fœssel calls 'l'inconsolable' and 'l'inconsolé', 'the inconsolable one', and the 'inconsoled'. The former (Fœssel's examples are Niobe and Electra) refuse to be consoled; they actively resist reasonable attempts at consolation by their well-meaning surroundings. As such, they belong to the classical regime of comfort, in which they serve as *exempla ex negativo*. Hamlet, obviously is different from them: like Electra, he fails to move beyond his grief, but Shakespeare's play does not stage him as a negative example. His active resistance to being consoled, however, makes him different from Queen Isabel too, as I hope to show in what follows. Her inability to be consoled offers a better illustration of what Fœssel calls the modern 'inconsoled': she no doubt craves comfort, as Blumenberg would say, but she soon comes to realise that what her comforters have on offer will never fully do.

Still, there is an important parallel between the two Shakespearean characters: like Hamlet, Isabel does not know what it is precisely that causes her to be as sad as she is. The indistinctness of her sorrow is central in Isabel's first reply to Bushy. She has no idea how to interpret her sadness, she says, she only knows that it is there.

> To please the King I did; to please myself
> I cannot do it. Yet I know no cause
> Why I should welcome such a guest as grief,
> Save bidding farewell to so sweet a guest
> As my sweet Richard. Yet again, methinks
> Some unborn sorrow, ripe in fortune's womb,
> Is coming towards me; and my inward soul
> At nothing trembles. With something it grieves
> More than with parting from my lord the King. (2.2.5–13)

What Hamlet describes as 'that within which passeth show' is here described as the 'inward soul', a concept to which Isabel will refer a second time later in the scene. Like Hamlet's phrase, Isabel's notion can be related to what Katharine Eisaman Maus (with a reference to *Hamlet*) has identified as Shakespeare's preoccupation with ideas of 'inwardness'.[94] Maus relates the notion of inwardness to Shakespeare's exploration of theatrical metaphors: once a structural difference is experienced between what a character feels and how they behave, the possibilities of role-playing and feigning become legion. Several of Shakespeare's major characters are the result of that principle (next to Hamlet, we immediately think of Iago, of Duke Vincentio in *Measure for Measure* and of Richard III in the play that bears his name). The scene at hand, however, goes to show that the potential difference between outward behaviour and 'inward soul' offers more possibilities than the mere foundation of 'Machiavellian' characters who pretend to be what they decisively are not. Isabel, after all, is in many ways honest and authentic. She does not hide what she feels for reasons of deviousness; on the contrary, she makes clear who she is by pointing out the indecisiveness of her inner core. She has the outspoken feeling that it is not the temporary separation from Richard that makes her sad, but something else, a something that gives her the feeling that Fate has something in store for her that will cause her pain and grief – something that is not there yet, but is waiting to happen, 'some unborn sorrow, ripe in fortune's womb', as she calls it. The as yet unidentified cause of Isabel's feeling

Shakespeare refers to as 'nothing', rather than 'something', a word whose existential polysemy will be later developed in *King Lear*. Isabel does not exclude the possibility that she is worried about 'nothing', but the 'nothing' that causes her deep concern may well turn out to be the major Nothing (capital N – *le néant* of twentieth-century existentialist philosophy), the moment in which everything threatens to lose its meaning. That moment, as the play's spectators will have been able to fathom long before Isabel, will be the moment when Richard loses his crown and with it his privileged position in the social order. (It is significant, obviously, that after the climactic deposition, Richard systematically makes use of the same vocabulary: 'for I must nothing be', he says during the actual 'deposition' scene (4.1.191)).

Bushy wants Isabel to get a grip on what causes her distress by making a rational analysis of it. Again, his response is quite predictable in the ancient logic of consolation: by means of a rational argument he will try to convince her that there is no real cause for her sadness, that it is grounded in illusion, that she imagines something that is not real, because she allows herself to be led by her emotions. If you think that the cause of your tears is something larger than the king's departure (which you see as the foreshadowing of something worse), Bushy argues, then you are seeing things the wrong way:

> Each substance of a grief hath twenty shadows
> Which shows like grief itself but is not so.
> For sorrow's eye, glazèd with blinding tears,
> Divides one thing entire to many objects –
> Like perspectives, which, rightly gazed upon,
> Show nothing but confusion; eyed awry,
> Distinguish form. So your sweet majesty,
> Looking awry upon your lord's departure,
> Find shapes of grief more than himself to wail,
> Which, looked on as it is, is naught but shadows
> Of what it is not. Then, thrice-gracious Queen,
> More than your lord's departure weep not: more is not seen,
> Or if it be, 'tis with false sorrow's eye,
> Which for things true weeps things imaginary. (2.2.14–27)

The logic of comfort that Bushy develops in these lines fits perfectly in a classical consolatory discourse, since it concerns the absolute distinction that is made in the writings belonging to that regime between the correct, rational view of sadness and despair (a view that subordinates one's subjective experience to the *sensus communis*, thus allowing us to 'work through' our pain) and the wrong emotional view that turns our pain into something that can never be overcome. The latter view is caused in Bushy's logic by the 'blinding tears' which enable 'false sorrow's eye' to transform things into something that they are not. In order to see things the way they really are, we would need in the classical consolatory logic the one and only possible perspective of the *sensus communis*.

## Consolation and the Art of Perspectives

Of course, Bushy's words are *not* part of classical *consolatio*; they are the product of an era in which perspectives begin to function differently, as becomes clear from the comparison that Shakespeare develops in Bushy's reply. The 'perspectives' to which he refers in the fifth line of the above passage are those of the 'anamorphotic' paintings that became popular in the early modern period and of which Holbein's 'The Ambassadors' probably provides the best known example.[95] When we look at representations like Holbein's anamorphotic skull from a conventional, common-sensical perspective ('rightly gazed upon') it is hard to see what it represents; if we look at it from a different, in this case oblique, perspective ('looking awry'), the image suddenly and unexpectedly takes on a more recognisable shape. Isabel's view of her own sadness, Bushy suggests, is that sort of perspective. By looking at it from an angle that to her seems sound but is basically not right, she does not see her sadness for what it 'really' is. This is the implication of Bushy's first comparison: 'sorrow's eye' is seen as a glass that is cut in such a way that it turns that which it represents into different things ('many objects'), all of which relate to the real that they represent as the twenty different shades that are contained within 'each substance of a grief' – they are not the thing in itself, but an opaque transformation of it.

In his commentary on this specific passage in his edition of *Richard II* in the Arden series, Charles Forker stresses the 'puzzling ambiguity' produced by Bushy's comparisons, because in Forker's reading, the passage yields two mutually contradictory meanings.[96] In the first instance, the message seems to be that Isabel should not rely too much on her own subjective experience, since that experience starts from the wrong perspective – her perspective threatens to render her sadness larger than it actually is. Bushy's second comparison invites Isabel not to face her sadness directly and straightforwardly, but to look at it from an oblique perspective. Slavoj Žižek, who derives the main title of his *Introduction to Jacques Lacan through Popular Culture* from Bushy's 'looking awry' also sees a fundamental contradiction between the two comparisons: 'What we have here', Žižek concludes in his brief reflection on Bushy's words,

> are thus two realities, two 'substances'. On the level of the first metaphor, we have common-sense reality seen as 'substance with twenty shadows', as a thing split into twenty reflections by our subjective view, in short, as a substantial 'reality' distorted by our subjective experience. If we look at a thing straight on, matter-of-factly, we see it 'as it really is', while the gaze puzzled by our desires and anxieties ('looking awry') gives us a distorted, blurred image. On the level of the second metaphor, however, the relation is exactly the opposite: if we look at a thing straight on, i.e., matter-of-factly, disinterestedly, objectively, we see nothing but a formless spot; the object assumes clear and distinctive features only if we look at it 'at an angle', i.e., with an 'interested' view, supported, permeated, and 'distorted' by desire.[97]

Bushy's second metaphor points Žižek in the direction of Lacan, more specifically in the direction of the way in which the French psychoanalyst conceives of the relationship between the subject and the symbolic order. In *Les quatre concepts fondamentaux de la psychanalyse*, Lacan himself makes use of the idea of 'anamorphosis' (and of Holbein's 'The Ambassadors') in order to found and explain his theory of the formation of the subject.[98] What the anamorphotic stain/skull on Holbein's painting shows us, Lacan believes, is who we are and how we are. We may be convinced that there is a right and proper perspective on the real, a perspective that yields a certain fullness of true meaning (the metaphysical perspective that both in the classical and in the Christian discourse of comfort functioned as the very grounds of consolation), but that to Lacan is an illusion. Holbein's painting makes clear to him that no such perspective 'really' exists, but also that the real ('le réel') is always looking back at us. It is in the tensional interplay between our own (limited) view and our awareness that while looking we are looked at (by an order that escapes our view and that renders the pretensions of our subjective perspective futile) that for Lacan the modern subject is produced, 'le sujet comme néantisé' as he calls it in his discussion of Holbein's painting.[99]

In her response to Bushy's reply, Queen Isabel turns out, like Hamlet, to be such a modern subject, to the extent that Žižek – in a characteristic moment of hyperbolic inversion – comes to the conclusion that Shakespeare understood Lacan very well. Isabel is not convinced by Bushy's argument. Deep inside her, there is something that is more convincing, her 'inward soul', that functions as an insurmountable obstacle against the consolation that Bushy offers her:

> It may be so, but yet my inward soul
> Persuades me it is otherwise. Howe'er it be,
> I cannot but be sad: so heavy-sad
> As thought – on thinking on no thought I think –
> Makes me with heavy nothing faint and shrink. (2.2.28–32)

'A difficult line', the editors of the Norton Shakespeare rightly conclude,[100] even though it is clear that Isabel is once more referring to the great Nothing to which she alluded before. While her thoughts may boil down to nothing (she is 'thinking on no thought', thinking thoughts she shouldn't) this 'nothing' has a clear destructive impact: the thoughts weigh heavily on her, to the extent that she weakens and shrinks. Bushy continues his efforts to convince Isabel that she should see things differently (''Tis nothing but conceit, my gracious lady' (2.2.33)), but obviously his consolatory attempts continue to fail. I'm not imagining anything, Isabel replies (''Tis nothing less' (2.2.34)) and even if I do, there is a real reason for that, a cause that is beyond me:

> 'Tis nothing less: conceit is still derived
> From some forefather grief; mine is not so;
> For nothing hath begot my something grief –
> Or something hath the nothing that I grieve –
> 'Tis in reversion that I do possess –
> But what it is that is not yet known what,
> I cannot name; 'tis nameless woe, I wot. (2.2.34–40)

Shakespeare's masterful rhetorical play with the 'nothingness' of Isabel's sorrow enables Žižek to relate Isabel's words to Lacan's concept of the *objet petit a*, the object that founds the subject's desire in Lacan's theory. In Lacan, that object is a product of the desiring subject's phantasy, Žižek explains with reference to this passage from *Richard II*, and that is why it is like the 'nothing' of Isabel's sadness. Objectively speaking, it may not be there, but that doesn't make it any less real. On the contrary, as Lacan sees it, the reality of our desire is always a product of the imaginary order. As Žižek puts it:

> The paradox of desire is that it posits retroactively its own cause, i.e., the object a is an object that can be perceived only by a gaze 'distorted'

by desire, an object that does not exist for an 'objective' gaze. In other words, the object a is always, by definition, perceived in a distorted way, because outside this distortion, 'in itself', it does not exist, since it is nothing but the embodiment, the materialization of this very distortion, of this surplus of confusion and perturbation introduced by desire into so-called 'objective reality'. The object a is 'objectively' nothing, though, viewed from a certain perspective, it assumes the shape of 'something'.[101]

The chiasmus that Shakespeare uses in the third and fourth lines of the passage that I quoted earlier functions like Holbein's anamorphosis, in a way: it opens up a space in which on the one hand it turns out to be impossible to reduce phenomena in the real to singular meanings (since there is no longer a single perspective that unifies their meanings) while on the other hand the words that we use in order to refer to them will no longer be seen to coincide fully with the phenomena. Isabel's description of her unidentifiable sadness as 'nameless woe' fits the Lacanian interpretation perfectly, as does the fact that in the immediate remainder of the scene her imagined sorrow suddenly seems to become terribly real. Just after the last line quoted above, another courtier arrives (Green) who tells Isabel that the banished Bolingbroke made use of the absence of the king to assemble a group of supporting noblemen. Bolingbroke has just set foot in England in what Shakespeare's text refers to as Ravenspurgh (and what is now known as Spurn Head, south of Hull). Isabel understands that her premonition – the 'nothing' that she labelled the 'forefather' of her grief and that she referred to earlier as an 'unborn sorrow, ripe in fortune's womb' – has suddenly become, in the moment of Green's announcement, a living something. In her reply to Green's messages she resumes the maternal metaphor, again referring to the 'soul' within:

So, Green, thou art the midwife to my woe,
And Bolingbroke my sorrow's dismal heir.
Now hath my soul brought forth her prodigy,
And I, a gasping new-delivered mother,
Have woe to woe, sorrow to sorrow joined. (2.2.62–6)

After these lines, Bushy once more takes up the role of consoler – again, he encourages Isabel to behave more reasonably ('Despair not, madam' (2.2.67a)), and again, the queen fails to find comfort in what he says. Who will stop me from despairing, Isabel retorts ('Who shall hinder me?' (2.2.67b)), and in the remainder of her reply she refers to the opposite of despair as 'cozening hope' (hope that misleads), giving it a name that is also applicable to the courtier Bushy: hope is a 'flatterer', much like the one pretending to bring comfort – the consoler turns out to be someone who misleads, who may be saying things that are nice to hear, but whose words fall short of presenting the harshness of the real as it really is. Bushy belongs to the same crowd that surrounds Hamlet: his words of comfort definitely paint a nice picture, but they are just 'words, words, words':

> Who shall hinder me?
> I will despair, and be at enmity
> With cozening hope. He is a flatterer,
> A parasite, a keeper-back of death,
> Who gently would dissolve the bonds of life,
> Which false hope lingers in extremity. (2.2.67–72)

At the very moment of Isabel's sharp analysis of the flatterer hope, the duke of York arrives onstage. He is one of Richard's uncles and he is 'wearing a gorget', my Oxford edition tells me, 'a sign of war', as Isabel understands. His grave concern is immediately noticed by the young queen ('full of careful business are his looks!' (2.2.75), Isabel exclaims) and she begs him to comfort her: 'speak comfortable words' (2.2.76). In a scene that is dominated by the failure of consolation – by the failure of classical ideas of consolation, at least – York's reply makes perfect sense. The usual words of comfort that Isabel is now urging him to profess would be false words, he says, words that, moreover, would fail to take into proper account the dire situation at hand:

> Should I do so, I should belie my thoughts.
> Comfort's in heaven, and we are on the earth,
> Where nothing lives but crosses, cares and grief. (2.2.77–80)

York's reply will hardly come as a surprise in my reading of this scene of failed comfort, but we should not forget that the text in which it occurs is the product of a culture in which the idea that 'comfort is in heaven' is not usually coupled to the idea that human attempts at (self-)consolation are futile or void. York's words can easily be read in that way, though, as the prefiguration of a modern, secularised regime of consolation, in which the heavens no longer provide the steady basis of mental comfort. In a more clearly Christian text the idea that life on earth is nothing more than 'crosses, cares and grief' would no doubt be immediately coupled to the comforting thought that our suffering is not only temporary, but in the end a prefiguration of better times to come in the life beyond. Neither Hamlet nor Isabel take comfort from that idea, nor are they offered any council in its direction.

## Comfort is Comfort is Comfort is Comfort

The rhetoric of Hamlet's and Isabel's comforters would fit perfectly in a classical text of consolation, as we have seen, founded as it is on the undisputable distinction between the correct, rational perspective on things (the *sensus communis* that enables one to overcome one's sadness) and the wrong, emotional one that presents that same sadness as something that can never be overcome. However, their words are not part of an ancient *consolatio*; they are part of a play that dates from a different period in time, one which begins to develop the idea that different perspectives can produce different truths, the one no less real than the other. In a manner of thinking in which the traditionally stable distinction between truth and illusion becomes blurred, any practice of comfort that prides itself on pointing the person comforted to the actual truth of their problem becomes more and more difficult to realise.

As I have indicated, the passage in which Bushy talks about different ways of looking at sorrow has often been related to Hans Holbein's famous anamorphotic experiment of 'The Ambassadors', a painting that has been invoked more than once to capture the budding modernity of Shakespeare's era.[102] The painting has references to the early modern wars of religion, the discovery of the New World and new cultures, the development of scientific rationalism, all resulting in an increasing awareness of the perspectival nature of truth and hence of the fundamental ambivalence of all practices of signification – even natural perspectives, as Shakespeare suggests in *Twelfth Night* can show something (or someone) simultaneously as it 'is and is not' (5.1.214). Words of comfort can indeed continue to bring comfort, but the same words can result in comfort's very opposite. While this insight is definitely not an early modern invention, this central ambivalence of the rhetoric of consolation is striking in Shakespeare's dealings with the phenomenon, which exchanges the monological view of consolation that we find in most consolatory writings from Antiquity (and in Dante) with a dialogical conception of it. Shakespeare's dialogical construction of consolation stresses that there are two different, and not necessarily compatible, perspectives to the phenomenon (that of the consoler and that of the consoled), and very rarely are the two in complete agreement. In this way, Shakespeare's scenes of failing comfort show the intractability and mutability of distress, the something that can be nothing but even in its nothingness cannot be denied.

Shakespeare's philosophical guide in that respect (as in many others) may well have been Montaigne, whose work he could read both in the original French and in the English translation of Florio which appeared in 1603. Montaigne is the philosopher *par excellence* of what Shakespeare called 'the inward soul', of what in his book on Shakespeare and Montaigne Robert Ellrodt labels 'a simultaneous awareness of experience and the experiencing self'.[103] It is the possibility (and indeed the slipperiness) of the distinction between an experience and the self experiencing it that underlies Shakespeare's sceptical treatment of consolatory practices in both *Hamlet* and *Richard II*. How can we know the pain of the other (Susan Sontag's question does not seem to be asked in classical consolations[104]), especially if we begin to doubt, as Hamlet urges us to do, the traditional premise that one's outer expressions are mere mirrors of the soul? How can we even know this soul, our pain ourselves, if like Queen Isabel we grieve without apparent cause? How can we be consoled by people who clearly misunderstand what we ourselves have so much difficulty understanding?

Isabel is not the only one who fails to be comforted in *Richard II*. There are several other scenes in the play which also deal with spoken practices of consolation and in which those practices are yet again shown to be fundamentally problematical – comfort goes not without saying, it would seem, and if it is taken to do so, Shakespeare's play makes clear that its supposed self-evidence cautions a good amount of distrust. 'This must my comfort be', Bolingbroke states, just after he has been banished by Richard for a period of ten years, in the third scene of the play's first act:

That sun that warms you here shall shine on me,
And those his golden beams to you here lent
Shall point on me and gild my banishment. (1.3.138–42)

It is a fact, Bolingbroke reasons in rhyme, that the same sun that shines on him in England will shine on him abroad. In itself, the idea could serve as a form of comfort (as it does in Seneca's *Consolatio ad Helviam Matrem*, written at the occasion of the philosopher's banishment to Corsica), but it clearly does not for Bolingbroke. The idea 'must' be a source of comfort, he says, but he doesn't want it to be. To accept this comfort would require Bolingbroke to accept the punishment which the comfort is meant to remedy. The remainder of the play makes clear that this is not what Bolingbroke has in mind. Even after Richard reduced the initial penalty of ten years to six, he is no less determined to start a rebellion against his king. On the contrary, the very banishment is what he needs in order to finally take action. The failure of this specific consolatory topos is also stressed in the remainder of the scene, when John of Gaunt (Bolingbroke's father, who is also uncle to Richard) makes use of it in a way that according to the editor of the most recent Arden edition of the play can be related, via John Lyly's *Euphues*, to a passage from Plutarch's *De Exilio* and to the *Tusculanae Disputationes*.[105]

> All places that the eye of heaven visits
> Are to a wise man ports and happy havens.
> Teach thy necessity to reason thus:
> There is no virtue like necessity.
> Think not the King did banish thee,
> But thou the King. Woe doth the heavier sit
> Where it perceives it is but faintly borne.
> Go, say I sent thee forth to purchase honour,
> And not the King exiled thee; or suppose
> Devouring pestilence hangs in our air
> And thou art flying to a fresher clime.
> Look what thy soul holds dear, imagine it
> To lie that way thou goest, not whence thou com'st.
> Suppose the singing birds musicians,
> The grass whereon thou tread'st the presence strewed,
> The flowers fair ladies, and thy steps no more
> Than a delightful measure or a dance;
> For gnarling Sorrow hath less power to bite
> The man that mocks at it and sets it light. (1.3.275–93)[106]

Gaunt's message is clear. If Bolingbroke behaves reasonably ('wise'), he will understand that happiness is something that we take to the places where we live. Seen from that perspective, to be banished can never result in unhappiness. Again, the mechanism of comfort is clear: it involves the willingness to take a different perspective, a rational one. You need to tell yourself ('suppose', 'imagine'), Gaunt stresses, that it is not the king who is banishing you, but the other way around. Also, if England is struck by pestilence, you will be safely away. To be comforted also involves seeing what happens as something that needed to happen ('Teach thy necessity to reason thus'). But again, Bolingbroke *won't* and he *can't*, for the same reason that

Isabel could not allow herself to be comforted. There is something inside him that resists the urges of those who try to convince him to see things differently. Inversely, what his father wants him to do goes against the wishes of his deeper drive. To imagine what his father wants him to imagine would be an act of self-delusion. Trying to imagine how good things are would only make him realise even more how bad his situation is.

> O, who can hold a fire in his hand
> By thinking on the frosty Caucasus?
> Or cloy the hungry edge of appetite
> By bare imagination of a feast?
> Or wallow naked in December snow
> By thinking on fantastic summer's heat?
> O no, the apprehension of the good
> Gives but the greater feeling to the worse:
> Fell Sorrow's tooth doth never rankle more
> Than when he bites but lanceth not the sore. (1.3.294–303)

## Comfort, though not for this Prisoner

There is a third character in *Richard II* whose fate confirms what I have written so far about the play's failure to represent successful consolatory encounters: King Richard himself, who remains disconsolate in a series of scenes. Charles Forker is right: the word 'comfort' is a true *leitmotif* in the first of those, the second scene of the play's third act.[107] In that scene, the king returns from his visit to Ireland at Barkloughly Castle (today's Harlech Castle in Wales). He is immediately notified that the banished Bolingbroke has managed to attract a growing number of soldiers in his rising against the king. Richard also finds out that his uncle, the duke of York, is now supporting the rebels and that some of his more prominent courtiers – Bushy and Green, among others – have been killed by Bolingbroke. One of his remaining supporters, the duke of Aumerle, twice tries to take away Richard's worries by means of the same phrase ('comfort, my liege', 3.2. 71 and 78), but the king wants to hear no more. Words of comfort are nothing more than flattery, he knows ('He does me double wrong / That wounds me with the flatteries of his tongue' (3.2.211–12), and the words in which comfort is couched cannot make him forget how different things are in reality. '[O]f comfort no man speak', Richard demands: we need to face the truth and that truth is one of graves, of dead bodies that worms feed on and of phrases that can be put on tombstones. His reality is that of a king who, like so many others before him, threatens to lose his crown:

> Let's talk of graves, of worms and epitaphs,
> Make dust our paper, and with rainy eyes
> Write sorrow on the bosom of the earth.
> Let's choose executors and talk of wills –
> And yet not so, for what can we bequeath
> Save our deposèd bodies to the ground?
> Our lands, our lives, and all are Bolingbroke's;
> And nothing can we call our own but death,
> And that small model of the barren earth
> Which serves as paste and cover to our bones.
> For God's sake, let us sit upon the ground,
> And tell sad stories of the death of kings –
> How some have been deposed, some slain in war,
> Some haunted by the ghosts they have deposed,
> Some poisoned by their wives, some sleeping killed,
> All murdered. For within the hollow crown
> That rounds the mortal temples of a king
> Keeps Death his court; and there the antic sits,
> Scoffing his state and grinning at his pomp,
> Allowing him a breath, a little scene,
> To monarchize, be feared and kill with looks,
> Infusing him with self and vain conceit,
> As if this flesh which walls about our life,
> Were brass impregnable; and humoured thus,
> Comes at the last, and with a little pin
> Bores through his castle wall; and farewell, king!
> Cover your heads, and mock not flesh and blood
> With solemn reverence. Throw away respect,
> Tradition, form, and ceremonious duty,
> For you have but mistook me all this while.
> I live with bread, like you; feel want,
> Taste grief, need friends. Subjected thus,
> How can you say to me I am a king? (3.2.140–73)

Things move fast in this scene: while initially Richard is still convinced that his God-ordained kingship is untouchable, by the end of the scene he already seems to be beyond the despair that he might lose his crown – he is sure that Bolingbroke will become king quite soon. At the end of the scene, he addresses Aumerle once more, the bringer of bad news that he described earlier as his 'discomfortable cousin' (3.2.32). His words round off the motif of comfort in this scene, in a way that by now will be predictable. Let no one try to comfort me, Richard exclaims: I will hate those who try to forever:

> Beshrew thee, cousin, which didst lead me forth
> Of that sweet way I was in to despair.
> What say you now? What comfort have we now?
> By heaven, I'll hate him everlastingly
> That bids me be of comfort any more. (3.2.200–4)

The play's famous deposition scene – the first scene of Act Four – stages what Richard in the lines that I just discussed considered an imminent threat. The passage that interests me most in this scene follows on from the actual moment of deposition, Richard's handing over to Bolingbroke of the crown and sceptre, the outward signs of his regal office. Richard is given by the earl of Northumberland papers to be signed which contain the confession of 'grievous crimes' committed by him '[a]gainst the state and profit of this land' (4.1.215). Richard protests that the tears in his eyes prevent him from reading the papers ('Mine eyes are full of tears; I cannot see' (4.1.244)), but not from identifying the traitors that surround him onstage. The passage is reminiscent of the earlier scene in which Bushy tried to comfort Isabel by pointing out that she should try to see beyond her 'blinding tears' and avoid the perspective of 'false sorrow's eye'. The verbal connection between the two scenes becomes even clearer when Richards asks the new king to have a mirror fetched: he wants to see with his own eyes, as it were, whether his outlook has changed, now that he is no longer king ('That it may show me what a face I have, / Since it is bankrupt of his majesty' (4.1.256–7)). Looking at himself in the mirror, Richard continues the play's reflection on the commensurability between outwardly visible signs and the immediate unseen that they stand for, in whichever capacity and from whichever perspective.

> No deeper wrinkles yet? Hath Sorrow struck
> So many blows upon this face of mine
> And made no deeper wounds? O flatt'ring glass,
> Like to my followers in prosperity,
> Thou dost beguile me! Was this face the face
> That every day under his household roof
> Did keep ten thousand men? Was this the face
> That like the sun did make beholders wink?
> Is this the face which faced so many follies,
> That was at last outfaced by Bolingbroke?

A brittle glory shineth in this face.
As brittle as the glory is the face,
For there it is, cracked in an hundred shivers. (4.1.267–79)

And with that last exclamation, Richard shatters the mirror, reducing it to smithereens of glass that no doubt have the same anamorphotic effect that the queen's tears had, '[d]ivid[ing] one thing entire to many objects'. It is significant, of course, that Richard labels the mirror a flatterer: any comfort that he could possibly consider from finding the 'right' perspective on his fallen situation would turn out to be idle.

Mark, silent King, the moral of this sport:
How soon my sorrow hath destroyed my face. (4.1.280–1)

It is ironic that Bolingbroke responds to this last line as a traditional comforter would – not by remaining silent, but by producing words that are meant to bring an alleviation of pain: 'The shadow of your sorrow hath destroyed / The shadow of your face' (4.1.282–3), Bolingbroke retorts, whether in jest or earnestness, pointing out that Richard should be able to find comfort in the rational knowledge that his presumed sorrow is actually not real, but a mere shadow of sorrow – the fact that this presumed sorrow left no real traces on his face is the best possible proof of its illusory nature, Bolingbroke's words imply. Richard's reply is in line with what Isabel told her comforter and Hamlet his: it is not because you don't see my pain that I don't feel it inside. My face does not denote me truly, Richard is basically saying, and what you think you see on it are nothing but 'external trappings' of what I feel within. Richard's lines predate Hamlet's by some five years, but it is clear that the two passages echo one another:

'Tis very true: my grief lies all within,
And these external manner of laments
Are merely shadows to the unseen grief
That swells with silence in the tortured soul.
There lies the substance (. . .). (4.1.285–9)

There is a third and final scene in the play where Richard fails to find comfort: the fifth scene of the final Act, where we find the former king in the prison cell in which by the end of the scene he will be cruelly murdered at Bolingbroke's treacherous request. Interestingly, it is through his astute reading of this scene that Laura Bates, as she writes, first got to know Larry Newton better.[108] The failure of comfort in this scene is a failure of self-comfort, in this case. At the beginning of the scene, Richard is holding forth a monologue in which he tries but fails to compare the cell in which he finds himself to the world at large in which he used to live. 'I have been studying how I may compare / This prison where I live unto the world' (5.5.1–2), Richard says, but the conclusion must be that his attempts have not been successful ('I cannot do it' (5.5.5)). The will to analogise is apparently the result of studious exercise, possibly of the type that Lady Philosophy famously advocated upon her visit to Boethius in his prison cell. Shakespeare must have been familiar with the sixth-century treatise, if only because of Queen Elizabeth's translation of it.[109] Lady Philosophy's efforts at consolation were aimed at bringing the imprisoned author of the *De consolatione philosophiae* back to his reason: sound logic would make him see that things weren't really as bad as he thought they were. He would come to understand, after thinking the right thoughts, that he was safe in the hands of God's providential will. Richard, by contrast, is alone in his cell, unvisited by Philosophy's saving grace and apparently indifferent to the possibility of religious comfort. True, he does philosophise, but in the process he produces, as he puts it, '[a] generation of still-breeding thoughts' (5.5.8), thoughts that keep producing new and other thoughts, not in the dialectical march towards consolatory insight that structures Boethius' encounter with Lady Philosophy, but in the form of an ever-growing jumble of sceptical and contradictory ideas. Whereas Boethius gradually becomes convinced that true freedom resides in submission to God's justice[110] – and in the fact that Lady Philosophy is the best possible guide on the path that leads to that wisdom – Richard's mind fails to free itself altogether. Each time he manages to find some relief or comfort in thinking a specific thought that sounds right and feels satisfactory, the former king is immediately reminded of the fact that the thought must be as illusory as its very opposite. In the following passage, he is especially critical of the consolatory topos that aims to find reason in the fact that one is never alone in one's pain. Others have been there before us, and will thereafter:

> Thoughts tending to content flatter themselves
> That they are not the first of fortune's slaves,
> Nor shall not be the last – like seely beggars,
> Who, sitting in the stocks, refuge their shame
> That many have, and others must, set there;
> And in this thought they find a kind of ease,

Bearing their own misfortunes on the back
Of such as have before endured the like.
Thus play I in one person many people,
And none contented. (5.5.23–32)

Comfort is indeed 'a kind of ease', but in Richard's relativistic use of the phrase, it is the ultimate shortcoming of consolation that seems to be stressed, its flattery that cannot lead to real contentment, rather than the fact that sometimes it may be successful in bringing what it does. Any comforting thought, in Richard's mind, is ultimately countered by another thought that undermines it. The fundamental failure of consolation – the idea that it will always fall short of delivering the good that it promises – is again emphasised in the second half of Richard's final monologue, as the prisoner is suddenly confronted with music. Traditionally, music is a bringer of soothing comfort, but here the opposite seems to be the case. Given the listener's dire situation and the player's clumsy performance, the music does not bring comfort at all ('How sour sweet music is / When time is broke and no proportion kept. / So is it in the music of men's lives' (5.5.42–4)). Richard's ultimate response is the demand that the music be stopped: 'This music mads me. Let it sound no more, / For though it have holp madmen to their wits, / In me it seems it will make wise men mad' (5.5.61–3).

In considering himself wise, Richard would seem to open up the possibility that in the end he may well find comfort. In order to be truly consoled, the author of the *De consolatione philosophiae* shows, one needs the sort of wisdom that is proclaimed in most classical consolatory writings. However, as I have remarked earlier, Shakespeare's play clearly does not belong to that tradition. Neither, as we have seen, does *Richard II* hint at the possibility of religious consolation. Nowhere do Isabel, Bolingbroke or Richard express the conviction that whatever happens is willed by God. In the case of Richard, this is all the more strange since as king he does consider himself to be divinely ordained. Also, in the monologue of failed self-comfort that makes up the larger part of this scene, he does exhibit sufficient scriptural knowledge (5.5.16–17), but that knowledge in no way helps Richard to achieve the sort of comfort that his imminent execution would require.

## *Measure for Measure*: Comfort in Disguise

There is another play of Shakespeare's in which a character facing death fails to find religious comfort. The play is *Measure for Measure*, the character Claudio, a convicted felon awaiting his execution. Claudio's comforter (in the first scene of the play's Act Three) is a philosophising monk, Vienna's Duke Vincentio in disguise, as the audience knows. The consolation he has to offer is intended as a relief for Claudio's anxiety in the face of an imminent death. The young man is in prison because of a pre-marital (and therefore extra-marital) sexual relationship with a young woman, Juliet, whom he intended to marry, but the two had intercourse before the banns were announced. The offence appears to be a capital one according to the strict Viennese rules. In the play, these rules are embodied in the inflexible character of the Puritan Angelo, whom Duke Vincentio, in an attempt to morally purify his city without himself being held accountable for it, has appointed as his deputy. The appointment was supposedly due to the duke's temporary absence, but in contrast to what he announced in public, Vincentio does not travel abroad. He stays in Vienna, incognito. As such, he is able to watch over Angelo's stern governing and to intervene, if necessary. While Angelo's government is that of the inflexible letter of the Law, the duke's approach stands for a more merciful approach that can interpret the Law according to its spirit, whenever the circumstances demand such a reading.

The scene of failed comfort that I want to have a further look at is structured around three encounters, each of which will give us a more concrete idea of how Shakespeare's staging of scenes of failed consolation relates to what I have called the Christian regime of comfort. The first encounter involves a consolatory conversation between Claudio and the monk (Duke Vincentio in disguise). Claudio seems to be aware that the only thing that can truly save him is for Angelo to suspend or annul his sentence, but since this is unlikely to happen he wants to prepare mentally for the execution that will soon follow ('I've hope to live, and am prepared to die' (3.1.4)). The logic of comfort that the monk develops in his encounter with Claudio involves a clear appeal to rational behaviour: 'Reason thus with life', he says (3.1.6): Claudio should not allow himself to be overcome by fear. The main argument that the monk uses (life is not really worth valuing) comes straight out of a classical *consolatio*, while it would make more sense for this servant of God to point out that what God has willed cannot be considered an evil in itself. God's plan, in the Christian logic of comfort, cannot be but just. But God is nowhere to be seen in the monk's discourse, which only refers to heavenly powers in a phrase ('skyey influences') that sounds pagan rather than Christian:

> Be absolute for death. Either death or life
> Shall thereby be the sweeter. Reason thus with life.
> If I do lose thee, I do lose a thing
> That none but fools would keep. A breath thou art,
> Servile to all the skyey influences
> That dost this habitation where thou keep'st
> Hourly afflict. Merely thou art Death's fool,
> For him thou labour'st by thy flight to shun,
> And yet runn'st toward him still. Thou art not noble,
> For all th'accommodations that thou bear'st
> Are nursed by baseness. Thou'rt by no means valiant,
> For thou dost fear the soft and tender fork
> Of a poor worm. Thy best of rest is sleep,
> And that thou oft provok'st, yet grossly fear'st
> Thy death, which is no more. (3.1.5–19)

The monk's point will be clear: Claudio needs to be prepared for death, not so much because God decided to call him, but because man is powerless in the face of Death's inevitability. The explicit presence in this passage of references to the classical discourse of consolation (the lines in which death is compared to sleep derive, according to the editor of the play's Arden edition, from the first book of Cicero's *Tusculanae Disputationes*[111]) confirms the pattern that we began to see in our reading of *Hamlet* and *Richard II*. Shakespeare's reflections on the nature and function of consolation are more clearly related to classical ideas (which in their new use are turned inside out) and this is quite exceptional. As J. W. Lever puts it in the accompanying note in his Arden edition: 'The analogy to sleep was a commonplace of the "consolation" but usually Christianised by making death the sleep from which one woke to eternity.'[112] As in Hamlet's 'To be or not to be' monologue, death is not invoked here in terms of a possible transition to a new life that brings eternal betterment, but as the welcome end to all the toil that our earthly existence brings. Monk Vincentio does not offer Claudio the comforting prospect of a future awakening. Still, if we judge by Claudio's response, the monk's pagan rhetoric seems to have some effect: 'I humbly thank you', he replies and joins in with an epigram that sounds like a paraphrase of Matthew 16, 25: 'To sue to live, I find I seek to die, / And seeking death, find life. Let it come on' (3.1.41–3).

The second encounter that we are witness to in this lengthy scene is between Claudio and his sister Isabella, a true icon of moral righteousness, who has come to visit her brother. She has decided to become a member of the order of Saint Clare. The audience is expected to understand that Isabella is of the same inflexible bent as the Puritan deputy. However, in two earlier encounters (in 2.2 and 2.4 to be precise), in which Isabella came to plea with Angelo for her brother's life, the young nun-to-be provoked in the deputy lustful feelings that are so strong that he becomes other than himself: he is willing to allow Claudio to go unpunished provided that Isabella breaks the vow of chastity that she promised to God and spends the night with him. The test that Shakespeare has in store for Isabella is clear: will she be able to put the love that she feels for her brother before her love of God?

Isabella has come to visit Claudio in order to tell him the outcome of her plea with Angelo. The audience can easily guess that for reasons that are crystal-clear to her, she cannot accept Angelo's diabolical offer even though she is aware of the consequences. Her life is devoted to God and therefore she cannot offer her body to a man, not even to save her brother's life. At the beginning of her conversation with Claudio – 'Now sister, what's the comfort?' (3.1.54), he asks, as Duke Vincentio listens in on them, unseen – she does not as yet mention Angelo's dishonourable proposal. Instead, she delivers the final news to which Claudio, after his earlier talk with the monk, had apparently already resigned himself: he has to die. Her answer to her brother's question picks up on the motif of comfort and is indeed couched in the traditional consolatory rhetoric which Shakespeare's characteristic punning unmasks:

> Why, as all comforts are: most good, most good indeed.
> Lord Angelo, having affairs to heaven,
> Intends you for his swift ambassador,
> Where you shall be an everlasting leiger.
> Therefore your best appointment make with speed;
> Tomorrow you set on. (3.1.53–8)

Isabella makes use of the consolatory topos that likens death to the journey to a foreign land, not Hamlet's 'undiscovered country from whose bourn / No traveler returns', but a place that she as a devout believer in God's justice knows to be good. 'Is there no remedy?' (3.1.60), Claudio wants to know. His choice of word makes clear that 'remedy' and 'comfort' are altogether different notions – whether or not Isabella's reply brings comfort seems to be no issue for him; the fact remains that her words do not really change his situation. Claudio's new question prompts Isabella to hint at the possibility that her brother could indeed continue to live, but as far as she is concerned the remedy at hand is not a real option, since it would force her brother to live in eternal remorse. In this specific case, 'to save a head' (to save Claudio from being executed, that is) would be nothing less than 'to cleave a heart in twain' (3.1.59–60). The so-called remedy, Isabella adds, 'will free your life / But fetter you till death' (3.1.64–5).

Claudio obviously has no clue what his sister is talking about, and with a series of further questions, he tries to come closer to finding out what her message might be ('Let me know the point' (3.1.71)). Isabella continues in the same vague consolatory vein, suggesting that her brother has less reason to fear death than to continue living in a state of sin. From the perspective of her faith, the prospect of a saved future (a future in salvation, that is) is definitely worth more than a life in permanent sin:

> O, I do fear thee, Claudio, and I quake
> Lest thou a feverish life shouldst entertain,
> And six or seven winters more respect
> Than a perpetual honour. Dar'st thou die?
> The sense of death is most in apprehension,
> And the poor beetle that we tread upon
> In corporal sufferance finds a pang as great
> As when a giant dies. (3.1.72–9)

Claudio's response to Isabella's words of Christian consolation is interesting because it makes clear the basic difference between the classical and the Christian regimes. Claudio is not at all helped by what he calls the 'flowery tenderness' (3.1.81) of Isabella's words: her vision of heavenly comfort is a false prospect, as far as he is concerned. He has a different conception of death, a distinctly pagan one that is central in at least some of the schools of thought that determined the classical tradition of consolatory writing: 'If I must die / I will encounter darkness as a bride / And hug it in mine arms' (3.1.81–3), he says. The image also hints at a more modern conception of the death-drive, but it ties in with other passages in the scene in which Claudio – and the monk before him – tried to imagine what it feels like to be dead. In Isabella's Christian conception, the light of the afterlife would without doubt be the more central image in any such attempt; in that of Claudio, death is dark and black.

It is only at this point that Isabella begins to speak of the condition that Angelo has set for Claudio's life to be spared. The question that she asks her brother is obviously a rhetorical one:

> Dost thou think, Claudio:
> If I would yield him my virginity
> Thou might'st be freed?
> (...)
> This night's the time
> That I should do what I abhor to name,
> Or else thou diest tomorrow. (3.1.95–101)

Since Isabella cannot even name the shameless deed that is expected of her, Claudio immediately understands that her mind is set. 'Thou shalt not do it', he replies, and his words can be expressed by actors in several different ways – with some degree of resolution (he does not want to force a choice on his sister that she doesn't want to make) but also, as Allan Bloom suggests, with some degree of resignation.[113] Whichever reading we prefer, the line seems to introduce Claudio's final attempt, against his better knowledge no doubt, to convince Isabella to have his life spared. He begins by wondering out loud whether the specific vice that is expected of her can be so sinful if even Angelo is prepared to commit it: 'Sure it is no sin', he says, and if it is, then definitely 'of the deadly seven it is the least' (3.1.109–10). And then he confronts his sister one last time with a very dark image of the 'fearful thing' that death must be – 'based upon classical descriptions of Hades tinged with a Lucretian scepticism', as J. W. Lever puts it.[114] Claudio's description of how it feels to be dead echoes the consolatory message that the monk gave him earlier in the scene: there is not in the least any sign of Christian hope of a brighter life in what lies beyond, only a dark and cold state of eternal hopelessness:

> Ay, but to die, and go we know not where;
> To lie in cold obstruction, and to rot;
> This sensible warm motion to become
> A kneaded clod, and the dilated spirit
> To bathe in fiery floods, or to reside
> In thrilling region of thick-ribbèd ice;
> To be imprisoned in the viewless winds,
> And blown with restless violence round about
> The pendent world; or to be worse than worst
> Of those that lawless and incertain thought
> Imagine howling – 'tis too horrible!

The weariest and most loathèd worldly life
That age, ache, penury, and imprisonment
Can lay on nature is a paradise
To what we fear of death. (3.1.118–32)

Claudio begs Isabella to save his life one more time ('Sweet sister, let me live' (3.1.134)) by arguing that the sin that she would commit in saving him can easily be seen as a virtue ('What sin you do to save a brother's life, / Nature dispenses with the deed so far / That it becomes a virtue' (3.1.135–7)), but again his turn of phrase ('Nature', not 'God') betrays a worldview that is decidedly not of the religious type his sister embraces. Understandably, Isabella's reply is unwavering, even though some of Shakespeare's contemporaries may have considered it heartless. Calling her brother a 'beast', 'a faithless coward' and a 'dishonest wretch' (3.1.137–8), she compares his logic to committing incest: 'Is 't not a kind of incest to take life / From thine own sister's shame?' (3.1.140–1). Before she leaves his cell, she even goes so far as to suggest that the sin that put him in prison was 'not accidental, but a trade' (3.1.151).

## Comfort and the Manipulation of Anxiety

With Isabella's exit, the third and final part of the scene begins. First, Duke Vincentio, still in his monk's disguise, briefly talks to Claudio, encouraging him once more to prepare for the inevitable outcome of his execution ('Go to your knees, and make ready' (3.1.172)). Having excused himself, he asks for a separate conversation with Isabella, in which he explains to her that he has come up with a plan that will allow him to save Claudio's life without her having to yield her body to the deputy. He explains to her that Angelo was once engaged to be married to a woman called Mariana, but that the marriage never happened because of issues surrounding the dowry. The duke suggests that Isabella pretends to accept Angelo's offer but just before entering his bedroom swaps places with Angelo's original betrothed. In that way, Claudio's life can be saved without Isabella's vow of chastity being broken and Mariana will get the marriage that was once promised to her. If it all works out, the deputy's mischief will be exposed as well, Vincentio claims in the more informally conversational prose style that he has suddenly began to adopt: 'by this your brother saved, your honour untainted, the poor Mariana advantaged, and the corrupt deputy scaled' (3.1.255–6).

The dramatic logic of Shakespeare's play requires that it makes perfect sense for Isabella to fully trust this man of God, and with his blessing she agrees on a scenario that does include some betrayal. After all, she will have to lie to Angelo about accepting his offer. Still, she takes leave of the 'good father', thanking him 'for this comfort' – the very word that runs as a motif through this scene. But how are we to take this 'comfort'? In contrast to the scenes in *Hamlet* and *Richard II* that we had a look at earlier, here the practice of comfort does appear to work. Yet, given that the comforter pretends to be someone that he is not, and given that his words of consolation hide what is undeniably a manipulative character, can this really be called comfort? Does not the practice of comfort require that the one providing it *be* honest as well as be *considered* to be honest?

Isabella's trust in the monk is blind, because he is a man of God. The audience knows very well, of course, that he is just pretending to be a monk: he is a fixer behind the scenes, a schemer who refuses to show his true face and who pulls the strings of everybody that he deals with in the play.[115] Since that play is a comedy, things need to end happily, preferably with a series of marriages, including that of Isabella and the 'good' duke. Their marriage is the ultimate perversion in a society in which perversities were meant to be erased: now that Isabella has managed to avoid Angelo's test, she has to give up her vow of chastity in order to marry the duke.

Vincentio's manipulative behaviour is already in evidence at the very beginning of the third part of the scene that we have been looking at. Even though he is already determined to make his plan work and thus to save Claudio's life, he does nevertheless keep the young man in the dark. While it is in his power to give Claudio hope, the final comfort that he brings ('Do not falsify your resolution with hopes that are fallible. Tomorrow you must die. Go to your knees and make ready' (3.1.170–2)) involves yet another straightforward lie: he pretends to be Angelo's confessor and to know, in that capacity, that the deputy will never keep the promise that he made to Isabella. Angelo is merely testing Isabella, the monk says, so Claudio should definitely not get his hopes up. The duke's most despicable act of manipulation, however, concerns his decision to keep Isabella, the woman he has obviously been planning to marry all along, in the dark about the actual rescue of her brother. The cruel logic behind that decision is expressed very aptly by Laurie Maguire who in her reading of the play in *Where There's A Will There's A Way* describes Claudio's 'arrogantly pious' logic as follows: 'despair in the present will lead to greater comfort for Isabella in the future when she finds out the truth'.[116]

Maguire's interpretation offers a concrete instance of what Stephen Greenblatt in his reading of *Measure for Measure* in *Shakespearean Negotiations* has labelled 'the manipulation of salutary anxiety', an ideological (in this case religious) mechanism that Greenblatt considers prototypical of early modern conceptions of subject-formation.[117] What Maguire's conclusion makes clear is that Christian ideas of consolation are in fact embedded in this larger cultural framework: it is not just that for the comfort to work we first need to despair, but also that those who bring comfort will be all the more successful if they first enhance the despair that the practice of comfort is meant to alleviate. In the classical regime, consolation is ultimately defined along the same lines as the Platonic mechanism of *anamnesis*: to be consoled is to recover something that one had lost along the way; it is to refind a position or state of mind that one had abandoned because of this or that painful experience. To be consoled is to regain one's rational stamina. As Lady Philosophy puts it in one of her first addresses to the imprisoned Boethius:

> He is in no real danger. He merely suffers from a lethargy, a sickness that is common among the depressed. He has forgotten who he really is, but he will recover, for he used to know me and all I have to do is clear the mist that beclouds his vision.[118]

Ideas such as this one proved to be easily compatible with a Christian worldview, as indeed the case of Boethius shows. His text is, after all, a Christianised classical consolation. The Platonic conception of *anamnesis* began to function, via Boethius and Augustine before him, as the mechanism underlying Christian ideas of conversion, as many early modern humanistic consolations also show. Petrarch's numerous consolatory writings (treatises like *De remediis utriusque fortunae* and the *Secretum*, but also many of his letters) are examples of this, as George McClure pointed out.[119] But Shakespeare's staging of scenes of comfort is different, as we have witnessed. That difference is best seen, I think, if we understand this 'staging' in the literal sense of the word: Shakespeare's scenes of consolation show us acts and practices of comfort as ritualised, theatrical events that involve a form of role-playing that is guided by specific conventions and presuppose the development of a given scenario that is either acted out or not. Classical and Christian consolation writings are structured 'monologically', as I have already suggested, both in the sense that in them comforters and comforted act in solidarity (sharing a common concern and aiming for a common goal) and in the sense that their consolatory efforts are always presented as effective. Shakespeare's conception of practices of comfort, by contrast, is a dialogical one: the possibility of failure is not the state of exception, here, on the contrary even. Also, Shakespeare seems to start from the awareness that any practice of consolation presupposes the existence of two separate participants (the one bringing comfort and the one receiving it) whose interests rarely, if ever, fully coincide. Shakespeare's staging of practices of comfort shows an acute awareness of the underlying conventions (the felicity conditions, one could say) that define what comfort is and how it works – or, rather, as the case may be, what it is not and why it often does not work.

### Comfortable Liar: Friar Laurence in *Romeo and Juliet*

Ultimately, the question is what will happen to our ideas of comfort in a secularised world in which God is no longer seen to be at the foundation of all things. As soon as bringers of religious comfort are exposed as frauds and manipulators, we enter a new phase of consolatory thinking, one that Michaël Fœssel in *Le temps de la consolation* calls the modern paradigm and which Shakespeare's plays seem to announce. In Western modernity, religion is no longer available as a foundation of consolatory practices, and neither is the principle of reason that served as the keystone of the classical regime.

Shakespeare wrote at least one other scene in which a priest who brings comfort is exposed as a fraud – not because the priest is not a real priest, as was the case in *Measure for Measure*, but because the comfort that he brings is consistently shown to be a lie. The name of that priest is Friar Laurence and the play in which he himself stages a scene of comfort is *Romeo and Juliet*. In the play's final scene, Juliet addresses him as 'comfortable friar' (5.3.148), one who on the basis of his profession should be doing exactly that: bringing comfort. In Shakespeare's play, Laurence is a member of the Franciscan Order. In the smart and entertaining Baz Luhrmann movie of 1996, he is played memorably by the late Pete Postlethwaite, in a way that heightens the original character's moral ambivalence. The interest in herbal medicine that Laurence has in Shakespeare is here turned into an obvious fascination with drug-related substances – he appears to have his own laboratory. In the first scene in which we see him he is wearing a Hawaiian flower-shirt and later we find out that he has a huge tattoo of a cross on his back. But at the same time, Postlethwaite's Laurence represents, as in the original play, the wise and common-sensical voice of moderation that tries to rein in the emotional excesses of several of the other characters.

In Shakespeare's play, the friar is also an ambivalent character. He is always on the outlook for what is good, but at the same time he is very cunning. He generally opts for the *via media*, but he has clear sympathy for the exceptional love between the young heroes after whom the play is named. Like Vincentio in *Measure for Measure*, he tries to influence the course of the play's events, but in contrast to the duke he does not really succeed in doing so. That is why *Measure for Measure* is a comedy and *Romeo and Juliet* a tragedy. Like Vincentio, Friar Laurence clearly does not refrain from scheming, or from lying if necessary. At least one scholar believes that Shakespeare himself played the part in the play's first ever production, which some put in the summer of 1595 and others in 1596.[120] If that is the case, we may be sure that he will have enjoyed playing the priest as rather more than the stock character of plain good morality, whom Harold Bloom apparently finds so uninteresting that he devotes no more than half a sentence to him in *Shakespeare: The Invention of the Human*.[121]

The scene that I want to have a closer look at is, depending on the edition used, either the fourth or the fifth one of Act Four:[122] it is the scene in which, on the morning of their daughter's marriage to Paris, father and mother Capulet find out that Juliet has died the night before – at least, so they think. In a way, the scene mirrors the one from *Measure for Measure* that we looked at above. Here again, words of comfort are clearly being spoken, but the audience knows that the one speaking them (in the former case a false priest, in this case a real one) is not at all sincere. In both scenes, the pseudo-comfort on offer is destined for the presumed death of a loved one (that of a brother in *Measure for Measure*, that of a daughter and a future wife in *Romeo and Juliet*), while the comforter knows very well that there is no real cause for the grieving of the parting of the loved one. The comforter is a cheat, in other words, and if only for that reason his comfort cannot be real. One of the felicity conditions that determine the speech act of comfort seems to be that comforters must mean from the bottom of their hearts the words of consolation that they speak. Since comfort is a transactional phenomenon, it does not suffice that the one bringing comfort means what they say – both parties have to accept the authenticity of the consolation at hand. Comforters may pretend that their intentions to console are sincere, but as soon as they know that the pain their consolatory efforts are meant to alleviate has no actual reason of existence, the comfort that they provide is at least dubious. This is clearly the case in the two scenes at hand. Both in *Measure for Measure* and in *Romeo and Juliet*, the comfortable friars are comfortable liars: with their words of comfort they try to reconcile those whom they console with an unbearable truth ('he or she may be dead, but you must realise that your loved one has gone to a better place'), while the comforter knows full well that the loved one is not dead at all. It would be much more humane on the part of the priest to bring relief rather than 'comfort' and reassure Juliet's parents that there is no cause for grief whatsoever.

Friar Laurence does more than merely hide from the Capulets and Paris that their beloved daughter and bride-to-be is actually still alive. In addressing them, he adopts a fairly aggressive rhetoric of admonition, of which one could say that it is not entirely untypical of the hortatory approach of classical consolatory thinking. In that mind-set, as we have seen, to bring comfort is to correct, instruct and coerce those who are in need of consolation into moving beyond the temporary delusion of their emotional state. Laurence literally calls those whom he comforts to order: they need to exchange their emotional responses to what grieves them for the rational understanding that what happened is actually better for the person who just passed away. Juliet's immediate future is in heaven, and how could that be a painful thing?

> Peace, ho, for shame! Confusion's cure lives not
> In these confusions. Heaven and yourself
> Had part in this fair maid. Now heaven hath all,
> And all the better is it for the maid.
> Your part in her you could not keep from death,
> But heaven keeps his part in eternal life.
> The most you sought was her promotion,
> For 'twas your heaven she should be advanced,
> And weep ye now, seeing she is advanced
> Above the clouds as high as heaven itself?
> O, in this love you love your child so ill
> That you run mad, seeing that she is well.
> She's not well married that lives married long,
> But she's best married that dies married young.
> Dry up your tears, and stick your rosemary
> On this fair corpse, and, as the custom is,
> All in her best array bear her to church;
> For though fond nature bids us all lament,
> Yet nature's tears are reason's merriment. (4.4.92–110)

For us moderns, Friar Laurence's rhetoric will come across almost as cold and hard as that adopted in most classical consolations. For us to be consoled requires that our emotional distress sufficiently be taken into account and treated with respect, not as a sign of silly and overly emotional behaviour. The immediate emotional response of those who mourn Juliet's death, the priest suggests, should be a cause of embarrassment and shame ('for shame!') to them, since it is clearly a sign of collective 'confusions'. Those who wail in despair should know that the solution to their problem ('cure') lies in the very opposite of 'confusion': not in the troubled vision of tears but in the clarity of true understanding, in seeing things the way they really are. That is the sensible and rational perspective to which the 'comfortable friar' wants to bring his audience, by instilling in them the rational logic that is central to the remainder of his speech and grounded in the conviction that a heavenly life is by definition to be preferred over a mortal existence. Now that Juliet's role on earth has come to an end, she has gone to the choicest place possible ('all the better is it for the maid'). Laurence refers to the Capulets' wish that their daughter would be 'advanced' in life: her marriage to the promising Paris, 'a noble young kinsman to the Prince' (as the list of 'dramatis personae' in the Arden edition tells us[123]), was no doubt an example of that sought-for 'promotion'. Why then cry and complain when clearly Juliet has obtained the highest possible form of promotion in being sent to heaven? Father and mother Capulet's bitter tears obviously do not render their daughter a service: they are the wrong sort of sign of the wrong sort of parental love, Laurence concludes: they must be either parents ('in this love you love your child so ill') or out of their minds ('mad'). The friar's last two lines also target the contrast between the emotional and the rational mind-set that is often encountered in classical and early modern consolations: our emotional inclinations ('fond nature') cause us to cry in despair ('lament'), but judged from the rational perspective of spiritual man ('reason'), our earthly tears are actually a source of 'merriment'.

Laurence's logic is strict and hard, but it is above all deceitful. There is more to the friar's lies than the basic fact that he knows very well that Juliet is still alive. Twice in the above speech he refers to the young woman as a virgin ('maid'), while he knows very well that Juliet's marriage to Romeo that he blessed at the end of Act Two will by then have been consummated. The fact that the nearly fourteen-year-old is by now already a married woman[124] is left unspoken in the priest's ambiguous claim that 'she's best married that dies married young' – the suggestion is also that the younger one dies the longer one's life in heaven will be and therefore the longer Juliet's marriage to God. The epigram also identifies Juliet's marriage to her funeral and in the structural logic of the play that is indeed an apt comparison: Juliet was supposed to get married, but now she will have to be buried, preferably in the very clothes that were chosen for the initial service. Laurence's reference to rosemary underlines the conjunction between marriage and funeral, since the herb was traditionally used in both rituals: it is associated with love as well as memory.[125] Earlier in the play Romeo was also associated with rosemary: 'Doth not rosemary and Romeo begin / both with a letter?', Juliet's nurse asks Romeo at the end of the scene in which she tries to figure out what the young man's intentions are (2.4.197–8). The association of his name and person with the herb that represents the steadfastness of love is a good sign for the nurse.

In a play that relates love to death in such a systematic way (Romeo and Juliet are precursors to the *Liebestod* of Wagner's Tristan und Isolde), it is of course no coincidence that Friar Laurence can so easily turn a marriage service into a funeral service. This is all the more the case since from the friar's perspective the marriage in question was not wanted and the funeral nothing more than a charade. Still, we should not forget that no matter how logical the build-up of the play's narrative seems, Juliet's death (both her pseudo-death in the scene that we had a look at and her actual death later in the play, when she commits suicide after she finds out that Romeo has poisoned himself) is not at all the outcome of a tragedy if we look at the play from the perspective of comfort that Friar Laurence offers to her parents. On the basis of that logic, her premature death, like that of Romeo, would have to be welcomed rather than mourned, since it allows the young lovers to be together in heaven for ever and always. Their earthly love is just a prelude to the transcendent happiness that awaits them in the life beyond. However, as Ramie Targoff has shown, the perspective that Shakespeare's play offers for a while is altogether different. In contrast to the sources that he used in his adaptation of the story of the young 'star-crossed' lovers,[126] Shakespeare's text contains no suggestion whatsoever that Romeo and Juliet's death will transcend the borders that separate death from life. 'In Shakespeare's play', Targoff writes, 'this interest in the lovers' spiritual afterlife finds no place whatsoever. Instead, he gives us a relentlessly materialist view of both love and death.'[127] Within that materialist framework the comforting perspective that Friar Laurence upholds (or rather, pretends to uphold) has no serious function at all. That also becomes clear in the full title that the play was given in its second Quarto of 1599: 'The Most Excellent and Lamentable Tragedy of Romeo and Juliet.'[128] The play is not just a tragedy, it's a 'lamentable' one, the occasion of authentic sadness and complaints. The very adjective runs through the scene that we have been looking at: Juliet's nurse labels the day of the young woman's presumed death 'lamentable' no less than three times (4.4.43b, 57a and 81a), while father Capulet calls the moment an 'uncomfortable time' (4.5.87a), disconsolate one could say. The consolatory perspective that Laurence has on offer for those who mourn Juliet's death is a challenge that Shakespeare's play cannot force on its audience: Romeo and Juliet's tragedy cannot be seen as other than a tragedy.

## The Desire *not* to be Consoled

It will probably be clear by now that Friar Laurence plays a role in *Romeo and Juliet* that is in more than one respect similar to that of Duke Vincentio in *Measure for Measure*: he directs parts of the action while most of the other characters are not in the know. But whereas Vincentio manipulates his subjects, forcing them into a scenario that is primarily to his own advantage, Friar Laurence has a more kind-hearted nature: he is primarily interested in the well-being of others. Allan Bloom calls him 'the nicest character in the play'[129] in his discussion of *Romeo and Juliet*, and many of the play's viewers and readers will agree. He is, after all, the one who blesses the love between Romeo and Juliet and who keeps supporting them in their love, not only because he has a specific affection for the youngsters, but also because he hopes that their marriage can bring an end to the feud between the Montagues and the Capulets. In the first scene in which we see him (the third one of Act Two) he is quick to be coerced by Romeo into marrying him to Juliet the following day. In Baz Luhrmann's movie he has a vision when Romeo tells him about the new love of his life. At first, he teases Romeo with the fickleness of his love – at the beginning of the play Romeo is said to be in love with a certain Rosaline, who treats him with the sort of indifference that is typical of the idealised lady in the Petrarchan sonnet tradition – but he soon begins to understand that the marriage between a Montague and a Capulet could bring to an end the devastating war between the two families. He already sees the headlines ('Montague and Capulet reconcile') and the photographs of the families' patriarchs who shake each other's hands. He decides that he cannot let go of this historic opportunity:

> But come, young waverer, come, go with me.
> In one respect I'll thy assistant be;
> For this alliance may so happy prove
> To turn your households' rancour to pure love (2.2.89–92)

The big difference between Friar Laurence and Duke Vincentio in *Measure for Measure* is that the outcome of the former's attempts at directing the course of events in the play do not result in a happy ending at all. Not that we should have expected that. The very opening lines of *Romeo and Juliet* already point out that things will end badly for the two 'star-cross'd lovers' (Prologue, 6). The priest whom Laurence planned to send to Mantua in order to bring Romeo in on the friar's plans to reunite the young lovers never manages to reach Romeo. Because of suspicions that the house in which he stayed was a source of pestilence, the priest had to remain in quarantine and did not meet with Romeo. In the meantime, Romeo had been alerted by his own servant of Juliet's funeral. The devastating news causes him to buy poison from a Mantuan 'apothecary': now that Juliet is dead (or so he thinks) he still wants to be united with her. He goes back to Verona to visit the Capulet family grave, where he encounters Paris, mourning the young girl whom he thought would be his wife. A struggle follows in which Romeo kills Paris (his second victim in the play) and takes the poison that must unite him with Juliet.

At that same moment, Friar Laurence arrives at the grave, too late to stop Romeo but just in time to see Juliet awaken. This is actually the moment when she addresses him as 'comfortable friar', a role that Laurence will clearly no longer be able to play. The friar cannot but conclude that his plan has failed spectacularly. In principle, he could resort to saying that whatever happened, happened because it was willed by God, but even that comforting thought is apparently no longer viable. The friar also lacks words of comfort for Juliet. The only thing that seems to be on his mind is to get away from the grave, together with the young bereaved woman. It is important for him that nobody finds out that she is not really buried. Again, Laurence comes up with an immediate plan: he will make sure Juliet is placed in a nunnery.

> I hear some noise. Lady, come from that nest
> Of death, contagion, and unnatural sleep.
> A greater power than we can contradict

Hath thwarted our intents. Come, come away.
Thy husband in thy bosom there lies dead,
And Paris, too. Come, I'll dispose of thee
Among a sisterhood of holy nuns.
Stay not to question, for the watch is coming.
Come, go, good Juliet. I dare no longer stay. (5.3.151–9)

It goes without saying that Juliet has no intention whatsoever to follow the friar. She is more determined than ever to be with her husband, in death as well as in life. As soon as she discovers the cause of Romeo's death ('What's here? A cup closed in my true love's hand? / Poison, I see, hath been his timeless end' (5.3.161–2)), she kisses him one last time, hoping to taste some of the poison that is still on his lips. Seeing that even this wish is not granted, and hearing the footsteps of a servant, she stabs herself with the same dagger that Romeo used to kill both Tybalt and Paris: 'O happy dagger' (5.3.168) is the apostrophe that introduces her final words.

In Luhrmann's movie, all the daggers are replaced by impressively shining pistols. In his version of the play's tragic outcome, Juliet shoots herself in a scene that follows on immediately from Romeo's suicide. The two lovers' deaths are brought as closely together as possible in the movie. As we first see Romeo addressing Juliet's presumably dead body – 'Ah, dear Juliet, / Why art thou yet so fair? Shall I believe / That unsubstantial death is amorous, / And that the lean abhorrèd monster keeps / Thee here in dark to be his paramour? (5.3.101–5) – her fingers and eyelids begin to twitch, but Romeo inevitably remains blind to these barely visible movements. Having drunk from the poison that he brought from Mantua, he kisses his beloved one last time ('Thus with a kiss I die' (5.3.120)). That final kiss of death is in Luhrmann's movie the kiss that brings Juliet back to life: with a joyous smile on her lips she opens her eyes, only to discover that the kiss that Romeo gave her was the last thing he did on earth.

In order to be able to bring the deaths of the lovers together in one scene, Luhrmann needed to cut Friar Laurence out of the grave scene. In the movie, we don't get to hear or see him, and that is to some extent unfortunate, because the final scene in which he is present in Shakespeare's play is the one in which the friar moves beyond the caricature of the wise and well-meaning priest. This becomes clear at the moment when, just before Juliet awakens, Laurence discovers the bodies of Paris and Romeo and begins to understand the broader ramifications of the tragic development that he has played a role in. 'Ah, what an unkind hour / Is guilty of this lamentable chance!' (5.3.145–6): the words that Friar Laurence uses are rather surprising. In principle, one would expect a priest to see the course of events as the result of God's providential design rather than as the outcome of an indifferent coincidence ('chance'). It is time that is to be blamed, Laurence argues, time that decided that Romeo could not be warned in time. The fact that Laurence labels chance 'lamentable' is reminiscent of the play's subtitle and of the scene in which he tried to convince those who were of the same mind to see things differently. In the consolatory rhetoric of admonition that Laurence adopted a couple of scenes earlier, God's will was still central. Here, the comforter no longer seems to have any thoughts of comfort ready; that is how impressed he is by the course of events.

This also seems to be the case in the remainder of the scene, where Laurence clearly no longer manages to adopt the rational perspective that by now we should be allowed to expect of him. Clearly, fear has taken hold of him: he wants to leave the Capulet family grave as soon as possible. While the text does not make clear why, it soon become obvious that the friar behaves in ways that earlier in the play he himself marked as feminine. When he is caught at the end of the play by the prince's guards, he is clearly overcome by emotion ('Here is a friar that trembles, sighs, and weeps', the third guard says (5.3.183)). It is only when he testifies to what happened to the prince, Juliet's parents and Romeo's father[130] that he seems to regain his bearings. What before he considered to be the 'fault' of 'lamentable chance' he now sees as the work of heaven that he apparently asked Juliet to accept in a dignified manner ('and I entreated her come forth / And bear this work of heaven with patience' (5.3.259–60)). This is not the first lie to come out of his mouth. His version of what happened, as he puts it himself, involves an attempt to tell what he knows and to excuse himself by emphasising his good intentions ('And here I stand, both to impeach and purge / Myself condemnèd and myself excused' (5.3.225–6)). If he has done something wrong, he concludes in his last reply in the play, he is willing to undergo the punishment he deserves. The prince of Verona decides that that will not be necessary. ('We still have known thee for a holy man' (5.3.269)).

How we are to judge Friar Laurence in the end is hard to say. W. H. Auden was quite hard on him: 'He wants to play God behind the scenes. But he is a coward, afraid of anything happening to him, and he runs away from Juliet at the end out of self-conceit and fear.'[131] That may be overstretching things a bit, but then again, Laurence is hardly the unfortunate victim of his good intentions. At times, he is a pragmatist and a liar, who in the end is mainly interested in saving his own skin. The question that interests me more is what this character teaches us about Shakespeare's staging of practices of consolation, in this specific case about the relationship between comfort and the absolute nature of love that the play takes as its central theme. Part of the answer to that question is provided by the essay of Patricia de Martelaere to which I referred in my analysis of *Hamlet*: absolute love presupposes the opposite of comfort, what De Martelaere calls the desire to remain inconsolable. The example that De Martelaere gives in her essay is not Hamlet but Juliet, who does not manage to be consoled because to do so would require that she is able to relativise the importance of her love and loved one. 'What if Juliet, the inconsolable Juliet, had allowed herself, after a fitting period of mourning, to find consolation and after some years to have taken a new partner (maybe even another Montague, if she really wanted to aim for the unthinkable or harass her father)?', De Martelaere wonders. Her answer to the question leaves little room for discussion: 'That could only have meant that what she felt for Romeo was actually not Absolute Love, but merely, as is wont to happen in life, a young girl's case of puppy love. I don't want to be comforted, the real Juliet says, I just want him back.'[132]

Juliet's inconsolability is the subject of the second scene of Act Three, in which the young woman reflects on her feelings as she finds out that Romeo has killed her cousin Tybalt. She begins by wondering how it is possible that the person to whom she gave her love could have the cruel heart of a murderer. But when the nurse decides that no man is to be truly trusted ('There's no trust, no faith, no honesty in men' (3.2.86)), Juliet protests emphatically: her man does definitely not belong to that category. Generalisations cannot apply to him, since there is only one Romeo. Juliet even becomes angry at herself for having scolded her lover and it is in this passage that Shakespeare presents love and comfort as the opposing forces that they have to be in Romeo and Juliet's story. Juliet is wondering why she is so caught up in sadness, when she should find comfort in the fact that Romeo is still alive. Things could have been very different indeed:

Back, foolish tears, back to your native spring!
Your tributary drops belong to woe,
Which you, mistaking, offer up to joy.
My husband lives, that Tybalt would have slain;
And Tybalt's dead, that would have slain my husband.
All this is comfort. Wherefore weep I then? (3.2.102–7)

The answer to that final question is obvious: Juliet is crying because Romeo is no longer with her. He has been banished for having killed Tybalt and it is the meaning of that banishment that is beginning to dawn on her in the course of this scene. Juliet simply cannot be comforted by the deceitful thought that she should be happy because Romeo is still alive. As long as Romeo is not with her, Juliet will remain inconsolable. After all, his banishment feels like his death to her:

> 'Romeo is banishèd!' –
> There is no end, no limit, measure, bound,
> In that word's death. No words can that woe sound. (3.2.124–6)

## Romeo and the Discomfort of Banishment

That Romeo is caught in the same inconsolability as Juliet will be self-evident. But it is worthwhile to have a closer look at the moment in the play at which this becomes crystal-clear. That moment occurs in the play's last scene of comfort that I want to address here. It is the scene that follows on from the one from which I just quoted. In the third scene of Act Three, Romeo finds out from Friar Laurence the punishment that awaits him for having killed Tybalt. According to the friar, Romeo should be satisfied with simply being banished, because the prince could as easily have sentenced him to death: 'A gentler judgment vanished from his lips / Not body's death, but body's banishment' (3.3.10–11). Romeo does not agree, because like Juliet he does not see the difference that Laurence points out to him: to be banished feels like an execution in itself. Since he will be separated from Juliet, he might as well be dead, he replies:

> There is no world without Verona walls
> But purgatory, torture, hell itself.
> Hence banishèd is banished from the world,
> And world's exile is death. Then 'banishèd'
> Is death mistermed. Calling death 'banishèd'
> Thou cutt'st my head off with a golden axe,
> And smil'st upon the stroke that murders me. (3.3.17–23)

Friar Laurence tries to make Romeo see reason – which is what early modern comforters are expected to do, as we have seen. He makes use of the same type of arguments that we have come across in the scenes of comfort from *Hamlet* and *Richard II*: Romeo should be 'patient' (3.3.16) and come to see things the way they truly are; not to see reason is a form of stubborn madness, of sinful denial (3.3.24) even. He should come to understand that what he sees as injustice is in fact a deed of mercy on behalf of the prince ('This is dear mercy, and thou seest it not' (3.3.28)). But obviously, Romeo does not allow himself to be convinced by these arguments. If he did, he would admit that he can imagine a life without Juliet – and this he just cannot do. On the contrary, the very thought that other human beings will be able to witness Juliet's beauty from nearby is unbearable to him, a constant torture. How, then, can the friar speak of mercy?

> 'Tis torture, and not mercy. Heaven is here
> Where Juliet lives, and every cat and dog
> And little mouse, every unworthy thing,
> Live here in heaven and may look on her,
> But Romeo may not. More validity,
> More honourable state, more courtship lives
> In carrion flies than Romeo. They may seize
> On the white wonder of dear Juliet's hand
> And steal immortal blessing from her lips,
> Who, even in pure and vestal modesty,
> Still blush, as thinking their own kisses sin.
> But Romeo may not, he is banishèd.
> Flies may do this, but I from this must fly.
> They are free men, but I am banishèd.
> And sayst thou yet that exile is not death?
> Hadst thou no poison mixed, no sharp-ground knife,
> No sudden mean of death, though ne'er so mean,
> But 'banishèd' to kill me—'banishèd'?
> O friar, the damnèd use that word in hell.
> Howling attends it. How hast thou the heart,
> Being a divine, a ghostly confessor,
> A sin-absolver and my friend professed,
> To mangle me with that word 'banishèd'? (3.3.29–51)

Friar Laurence fears that Romeo must really have turned mad. Whether or not that is the case, by literally designing heaven as the place on earth where Juliet resides, he does take away the foundation of Christian comfort. In a final attempt to bring light into Romeo's dark mind, Friar Laurence tries to convince the young man that the word 'banishment' means something different altogether. Philosophy, comforter *par excellence*, must lead Romeo to the right insight and guard him against his thoughts of impending disaster:

> I'll give thee armour to keep off that word –
> Adversity's sweet milk, philosophy,
> To comfort thee, though thou art banishèd. (3.3.54–6)

But Romeo has no need for philosophy, which, after all, cannot change reality as such. In the same way that a rose will smell the same if we give her a different name (2.1.85–6) and in the same way that Romeo would remain the same person if his name were not Montague, Mantua, the city of his banishment, will forever remain Mantua. Juliet will remain absent and his fate will be that of an exiled one:

> Hang up philosophy!
> Unless philosophy can make a Juliet,
> Displant a town, reverse a prince's doom,
> It helps not, it prevails not. Talk no more. (3.3.57–60)

Romeo no longer wants to hear about comfort ('Words, words, words', ... ) and when Friar Laurence tries one more time ('Let me dispute with thee of thy estate' (3.3.63)) he retorts with a claim that renders the priest's consolatory attempts meaningless. You cannot give me comfort, he says, because you don't know how I feel and therefore you cannot put yourself in my place:

> Thou canst not speak of that thou dost not feel.
> Wert thou as young as I, Juliet thy love,
> An hour but married, Tybalt murderèd,
> Doting like me, and like me banishèd,
> Then mightst thou speak, then mightst thou tear thy hair,
> And fall upon the ground, as I do now,
> Taking the measure of an unmade grave. (3.3.64–70)

Romeo's words prefigure Hamlet's response to the consolatory efforts of Gertrude (''Tis not alone my inky cloak ... '). They also beg the more principal question of whether it is really necessary that the one who brings comfort actually feels that which the person in need of comfort feels. His rejoinder is effective, though. Not only does Friar Laurence stop his attempts at convincing Romeo to be patient, as soon as it becomes clear – Juliet's nurse has come onstage – that Romeo's beloved needs the presence of her young husband, the priest becomes the man with the plan whose outcome in the meantime we know. Romeo should act like a real man, Friar Laurence concludes, rather than 'like a mishavèd and sullen wench' (3.3.142) to despair about his unfortunate fate. He should realise above all that he has at least three reasons to be happy:

> What, rouse thee, man! Thy Juliet is alive,
> For whose dear sake thou wast but lately dead:
> There art thou happy. Tybalt would kill thee,
> But thou slewest Tybalt: there are thou happy too.
> The law that threatened death becomes thy friend
> And turns it to exile: there art thou happy. (3.3.134–9)

It is ironic that Friar Laurence basically makes use of the same arguments that he tried out on Romeo in the first part of the scene. Why do the arguments work this time while they failed before? The answer is quite simple: Juliet, Juliet, Juliet. The very thought that he will see her again has become the only possible impulse that can move Romeo to act. Inversely, Romeo is the only one who will be truly able to comfort Juliet, as Friar Laurence seems to have understood: 'Go, get thee to thy love, as was decreed, / Ascend her chamber; hence and comfort her' (3.3.145–6).[133]

Love and consolation only go together when it is the loved ones themselves who bring comfort. If that is not the case, there can only be what Patricia de Martelaere in her reflections on Freud's 'Trauer und Melancholie' has called 'the inconsolability of desire'. Hamlet is a true melancholic in Freud's analysis because he does not manage to begin the *Trauerarbeit* that should enable him to accept the final goodbye to this father. As Freud sees it, the process of mourning has to lead to a symbolic killing of the person that we lost, Darian Leader claims in his discussion of Freud's essay. Leader quotes from a letter to Ernest Jones, in which Freud indicates that the death of a loved one places us before a cruel dilemma: 'one then has the choice of dying oneself or of acknowledging the death of the loved one, which again comes very close to your expression that one kills this person . . .'.[134] Both Romeo and Juliet choose the former option. On the basis of Freud's logic, their death may be tragic, but it clearly makes sense. The idea that one of them would remain and continue to mourn the absence of the other is a possibility that Shakespeare's version of their love story excludes from their first encounter. It is one of the unforgettable scenes in Baz Luhrmann's movie: Leonardo DiCaprio and Claire Danes approach each other from two different sides of a blue-lit aquarium in a room adjacent to the ballroom in the Capulets'

176 *Literature and Consolation*

mansion. The light in their eyes presupposes and demands the lasting presence of the other: they will have to be together, forever. The scene's background is provided by the performance of Des'ree, who sings the movie's theme song ('Kissing you'), that announces both the beginning of the love between Romeo and Juliet – the first kiss that follows soon after the meeting by the aquarium ('You kiss by th' book' (1.5.109)) – but also its ending, the kiss in the family grave ('Thus with a kiss I die' (5.3.120)). In Luhrmann's movie, Romeo and Juliet end their lives together on a funeral bier, in the romantic image of a last(ing) embrace that suggests a joint future beyond the moment of death. In Ramie Targoff's reading of the play, Shakespeare's text does not contain that promise, since it conceives of the love between the young people as earthly, mortal, a matter of the here and now. For these lovers, comfort simply cannot be in heaven, as *Richard II*'s Queen Isabel was expected to believe.

### *The Tempest*: Montaigne and the Comfort of Diversion

I want to have a look at one final scene of Shakespeare's in which consolation fails. The scene is the first one of the Second Act of *The Tempest*, the last play that Shakespeare wrote single-handedly. The words of comfort that start off the scene are spoken by the good-natured Gonzalo, 'an honest old councillor' as he is labelled in the play's list of characters. Gonzalo's words are addressed to the king of Naples, Alonso. Together with the other men present in the scene (there are several of them), Gonzalo and Alonso have been the victims of a shipwreck, the result of a sudden storm that washed them up on the shores of the quasi-deserted island that is the scene of the play. The words of comfort that Gonzalo utters urge Alonso not to forget, despite his evident distress, how fortunate he has been. Other victims of similar natural disasters, he argues, have been much worse off. While there is sufficient cause for sadness, the good councillor admits, there is also cause for joy, since lives have been saved. Therefore, Gonzalo invites his master to 'wisely, good sir, weigh / Our sorrow with our comfort' (2.1.8–9).

Gonzalo's plea offers a variant of the argument that (pseudo-)Plutarch introduces in the opening paragraphs of the famous letter of condolence that he wrote to Apollonius sometime after the death of the latter's son.[135] The opening section of the letter unambiguously argues against 'those who extol that harsh and callous indifference, which is both impossible and unprofitable', the author claims. The negative reference must be understood as a criticism of the Stoic perspective of *apatheia*. It is followed by an endorsement of Crantor, the fourth-century author of what is sometimes seen as the arch-*consolatio*, 'Peri penthous' ('On Mourning').[136] Opposing the Stoic perspective, Crantor, as we have seen, supports the idea that 'moderate indulgence [in grief] is not to be disapproved'. On the contrary even, it is taken as a sign of wisdom and hence to be commended:

> Reason therefore requires that men of understanding should be neither indifferent in such calamities nor extravagantly affected; for the one course is unfeeling and brutal, the other lax and effeminate. Sensible is he who keeps within appropriate bounds and is able to bear judiciously both the agreeable and the grievous in his lot, and who has made up his mind beforehand to conform uncomplainingly and obediently to the dispensation of things.[137]

Such, it would seem, is also the advice of Gonzalo: Alonso needs to bear in mind that bad luck is part of life's deal, but that there will always be people who are worse off. '[H]e who tries to console a person in grief', as we can read in the 'Consolatio ad Apollonium', 'and demonstrates that the calamity is one which is common to many, and less than the calamities which have befallen others, changes the opinion of the one in grief and gives him a similar conviction – that his calamity is really less than he supposed it to be.'[138] In *The Tempest*, however, Gonzalo's attempts at consolation are decidedly less successful than the previous quotation would have us believe. Alonso does not appear to respond at all positively to Gonzalo's words. While at first he does not say anything at all, it is clear from the response of others that he is neither convinced nor enthused by the wisdom of the good councillor. 'He receives comfort like cold porridge' (2.1.10), Sebastian, who is witness to the scene, comments to Antonio (the former is brother to Alonso, the latter brother and successor to Prospero, the banished duke of Milan whose art of sorcery is responsible for much of the action of the play, including the storm that caused those present to be both shipwrecked and saved).

Sebastian's remark opens a series of mocking comments in which Gonzalo's honest consolatory attempts are further being derided. First, his rhetoric is compared to a series of mere witticisms ('Look, he's winding up the watch of his wit. / By and by it will strike' (2.1.13–14)), delivered by one who is more concerned to produce words than to actually bring comfort ('What a spendthrift is he of his tongue!' (2.1.26)). Also, Sebastian and Antonio suggest, Gonzalo is obviously more interested in his performance as comforter than in the actual effect of his words. 'He will be talking' (2.1.29), Sebastian says, implying that the necessity of this comforter's talk is not defined by the distress of some or other person in need of consolation, but by the desire of the consoler to produce words, words, words. Gonzalo's messages of comfort, it is further suggested, are not statements of truth; on the contrary, they are lies that embellish and transform what is blatantly and painfully real. 'If but one of his pockets could speak, would it not say he lies?', Antonio wonders out loud (2.1.70).

The latter comment is meant to mock the second part of Gonzalo's consolatory speech, in which the old councillor is trying to argue how fortunate the survivors of the shipwreck have been in having landed, of all places, on such a beautiful island. 'Here is everything advantageous to life', Gonzalo exclaims: 'How lush and lusty the grass looks! How green!' (2.1.54, 57)). It takes quite a while before Alonso responds, but when he finally intervenes, it is immediately clear that he is not at all receptive to Gonzalo's well-meant arguments. The councillor's words of consolation go against Alonso's inner feelings. 'You cram these words into mine ears against / The stomach of my sense', he retorts (2.1.112–13). What he hears does not at all connect with how he feels. While Gonzalo is talking about the good fortune of having landed where they are, the only thing Alonso can think about, obviously, is that he lost both his children on this lethal journey. 'Would I had never / Married my daughter there! for, coming thence, / My son is lost and, in my rate, she too, / Who is so far from Italy removed / I ne'er again shall see her. O thou mine heir / Of Naples and of Milan, what strange fish / Hath made his meal on thee?' (2.1.113–19).

Alonso's outcry of despair is countered by what may well be the scene's single unproblematic attempt at consolation. One of the lords attending, Francisco, tries to convince Alonso that his son could still be alive. Describing in detail how he saw Ferdinand fight the waves he concludes: 'I not doubt / He came alive to land.' At that point, however, Sebastian rebukes his brother, in a gesture that is both cruel and politically pragmatic. There is no real cause for Alonso to complain, he says. After all, he has only himself to blame for the loss of his two children, having gone against the advice of many (including Sebastian, no doubt) not to marry his daughter outside of Europe:

> Sir, you may thank yourself for this great loss,
> That would not bless our Europe with your daughter,
> But rather loose her to an African,
> Where she at least is banished from your eye,
> Who hath cause to wet the grief on't. (2.1.129–33)

The only comfort that remains, in other words, is that Alonso cannot permanently see the cause of his distress and, hence, will not continuously be reminded of the absent daughter. As to Ferdinand, Sebastian continues, with a clear eye on his own political profit: 'We have lost your son, / I fear, for ever. Milan and Naples have / More widows in them of this business' making / Than we bring men to comfort them: / The fault's your own' (2.1.137–40).

The cynical undertone of these lines will not have been lost on Alonso, whose need for comfort is literally made subservient by Sebastian to the political outcome of the loss of this son who was seen by Alonso as the future king of the joint houses of Milan and Naples. Had he continued to live, Alonso would have married Ferdinand to the queen of Milan, but with his presumed death Sebastian himself becomes heir to the Neapolitan house. Gonzalo is understandably shocked by the frank brutality of Sebastian, but, ever the perfect diplomat, he rejoins with kindness, a gesture which obviously fails to impress Alonso's scheming brother: 'My lord Sebastian', Gonzalo says, 'The truth you speak doth lack some gentleness / And time to speak it in. You rub the sore, / When you should bring the plaster' (2.1.142–4). While there may be truth in what Sebastian says, Gonzalo feels that he is not only too direct but certainly also lacks the good sense of timing that is of the utmost importance for a successful consolation. Again, the honest councillor seems to be taking to heart suggestions made in the 'Consolatio ad Apollonium'. Comforters should not arrive on the scene too soon after a calamity has taken place, the author of that treatise writes:

> For even the best of physicians do not at once apply the remedy of medicines against acute attacks of suppurating humours, but allow the painfulness of the inflammation, without the application of external medicaments, to attain some assuagement of itself.[139]

As Gail Kern Paster has shown, it is not unlikely that Shakespeare derived Gonzalo's idea from one of the essays by Montaigne that he read in Florio's translation as he was preparing the text of *The Tempest*.[140] Critics have indicated that Montaigne's essay 'On Cannibals' is a notable intertext for Shakespeare's play, but Paster also points in the direction of the essay 'Of Diverting or Diversion', in which Montaigne talks about consolation (not to mention shipwreck), stressing from the beginning that 'a physician's first entertainment of his patient should be gracious, cheerful, and pleasing'.[141] Gonzalo's medical analogy supports the consolatory approach that he has been taking from the beginning of the scene. As far as he is concerned, there is no use in confronting a person in distress directly with the painful reality from which he is suffering; words of comfort should be gentle and, like plasters, cover up a wound rather than expose it.

Montaigne would seem to agree. In his essay 'Of Diverting or Diversion', he presents his argument as a matter of personal experience, derived from the comfort he was once expected to bring to a woman in distress: 'a truly afflicted lady'.[142] The essay contains an explicit refutation of each of the traditional approaches of the Ancient art of consolation – Montaigne alludes to the Stoic approach of Cleanthes, to the Peripatetics, to Chrysippus, to Epicurus and even to Cicero[143] – and he proposes instead a new one of his own, the method of 'diversion'. In his brief description of it, the approach seems simply to boil down to distracting the mind of the person suffering from the actual cause of distress. In Montaigne's own words: 'I unperceivably removed those doleful humours from her so that, as long as I was with her, so long I kept her in cheerful countenance and untroubled fashion.'[144] The approach is one also favoured by real doctors, Montaigne adds,[145] and founded on the premise that very few people (Socrates being prime among them, if not the only one) can deal directly – and 'with an undaunted ordinary visage' – with the harshness of a harsh truth. While Montaigne readily admits that the method of 'diversion' does not manage to root out distress,[146] he does believe that the approach has a remedial effect in the alleviation of one's misery, in that it complies with both the given of human psychology ('we ever think on somewhat else'[147]) and with the inconstancy of nature.[148]

Obviously, Gonzalo does not really succeed in distracting Alonso 'unperceivably', as Montaigne would have it. Clearly, Sebastian and Antonio's jokes attract too much attention to his stratagem of comfort. Still, the approach of 'diversion' is the one he continues to favour throughout the scene that we are looking at. Interestingly, Gonzalo's words beg a question that turns out to be important in the modern history of (literary) consolation. If, as Gonzalo's metaphor seems to suggest, 'rubbing the sore' equals telling the truth, does this mean that the opposite act of 'bringing the plaster' entails the opposite of truth? Are words of comfort actually lies of the sort to which Sebastian was referring earlier in the scene, creations of a pleasing illusion meant to distract our attention from a painful reality? That indeed seems to be the suggestion made by Antonio when he scathingly compares Gonzalo's words of comfort to the practices of the legendary singer Amphion, who, accompanied by his harp, managed to raise the walls of Thebes: 'His word is more than the miraculous harp', Antonio exclaims (2.1.91). The ironical suggestion is clear: Gonzalo may think that his words have great effect, but to both Sebastian and Antonio, they are empty rhetoric. 'What impossible matter will he make easy next?', Antonio wonders out loud. 'I think he will carry this island home in his pocket and give it his son for an apple', Sebastian replies (2.1.94–6).

Antonio's reference to Amphion is meant as further mockery of Gonzalo, but the musical analogy will remind readers or viewers of *The Tempest* of a previous moment in the play, when words sung actually do have a consolatory effect. Four-fifths into the long second scene of the opening act, the shipwrecked Ferdinand (washed on a different shore of the island) is being sung to by Ariel, Prospero's magical aid. Ferdinand is convinced that his father fell victim to the storm and the distress over the calamity causes him to continue weeping bitter tears. But the 'sweet air' of the music that he suddenly hears (and that he associates with 'Some god o'th' island' (1.2. 392)) somehow soothes both his soul and the waves of the sea:

Sitting on a bank,
Weeping again the King my father's wreck,
This music crept by me upon the waters,
Allaying both their fury and my passion
With its sweet air. Thence I have followed it –
Or it hath drawn me rather. But 'tis gone.
No, it begins again. (1.2.392–8)

Ariel's music attracts and distracts, but the specific force of 'diversion' that it exerts illustrates nicely the paradox at the heart of Montaigne's special consolatory strategy. Diversion does not simply mean looking away or ignoring the cause of one's distress. Contrary to what Dorothea Heitsch writes, it is not a 'cannily naïve act of transference',[149] nor the simple exchange of one affection (distress) for another (pleasure). After all, the words of Ariel's song do confront Ferdinand with the painful reality of his father's death ('Full fathom five thy father lies; / Of his bones are coral made; / Those are pearls that were his eyes' (1.2.397–9)). Alonso's son clearly understands that the song refers to his father ('The ditty does remember my drown'd father', he says (1.2.406)), but the potential painfulness of that experience seems to be somehow mitigated by the sweetness of the musical form in which the message is brought.

This is, in a nutshell, the diversion of artistic consolation and it seems to me to be the idea that lies behind several of the bibliotherapeutic books to which I referred in the introduction, most notably Ella Berthoud and Susan Elderkin's *The Novel Cure*. In the brief introduction to their book, Berthoud and Elderkin suggest that the consolation brought by literary texts is related to those texts' specific powers of 'transport' (a form of 'diversion', one could say). By reading a novel, the reader is temporarily taken away from their problem, to a fictional universe, but that detour through fiction involves a mechanism of indirect confrontation ('By indirection find directions out', Polonius says in Hamlet). By seeing our own pain, and the causes of that pain, through the eyes of another person, a fictional character at that, we are offered a new perspective on our own situation, and judging from actual responses by actual readers, that perspective appears to bring comfort in some cases – not in spite of the fictionality of the medicine at hand, but thanks to it.

To be clear, my suggestion throughout has not been that Shakespeare simply anticipates the critical commonplace that underlies the programme of contemporary bibliotherapy. As always, his work is extremely sensitive to the ambiguities, ambivalences and limits of common-sense ideas and experiences that are thought to be generically human (he is a true follower of Montaigne in that respect). With respect to the ways in which the phenomenon of consolation is represented in both *Hamlet* and *The Tempest*, there is the distinct irony that the scenes of consolation turn out to be staged events. Claudius, as we find out later in the play, is merely acting out his role as consoler. He is not at all sincere in his efforts to comfort his nephew-turned-stepson, since he killed the father whose unexpected death Hamlet continues to mourn. In the last scene of consolation from *The Tempest* that we have been looking at, Ariel knows very well that Ferdinand's father is not dead; that fact in itself throws a different light on the musical comfort that he supposedly brings – it would have been more comforting to say 'hey, your father is still alive, don't despair'. So here, as well, somebody is playing at consoling.

## Shakespeare and Consolation's Theatre of the Absurd

Shakespeare, we have seen, is quite sceptical about some of the premises that underlie classical theories of consolation, but that doesn't mean that he gives up on the phenomenon. He was also sceptical about love, but he didn't give up on that either. What the scenes we have been looking at show is that consolation fails to go without saying – both literally and figuratively speaking. Shakespeare's scenes of failed comfort urge us to think more deeply about the rules and expectations that govern the practice of consolation, as well as about some of the felicity conditions of the speech-act that make it work. 'Shakespeare's most recurrent metaphor is of life as theatre', Laurie Maguire writes in the epilogue to her reflections on the (biblio)therapeutic values of Shakespeare in *Where There's A Will*: 'He knew that theatre parallels life. Understanding theatre can therefore help us understand life. And the process is reciprocal: understanding life can help us understand Shakespeare.'[150] It is precisely there, I would argue, that Shakespeare's staging of the difficulties of comfort – both its giving and its finding – manages to be effective. The scenes remind us that the practice of consolation involves a form of role-playing, a cultural 'game' that is premised upon specific conventions which Shakespeare, in his astute sensitivity to social and cultural norms and expectations, brings to the fore.

The Christian regime of consolation, one could argue, ideally follows a dramatic pattern that is 'comic', in the sense that it ends happily, with the divine warrant of heavenly salvation. The modern regime, as we have seen, lacks the foundation of this happy ending. While it would be an exaggeration to say that in the modern regime practices or rituals of consolation display a tragic development, it is clear that in Blumenberg's and Fœssel's analysis of the phenomenon there is no actual ending to speak of, at least not in the sense of a 'solution'. The drama that it enacts is that of absurd plays like Beckett's *Waiting for Godot* – what we await (the return of a state of happiness prior to our grief) will never return as such. 'Comfort' in the modern sense of the word, Cornelis Verhoeven writes, 'is indeed an absurdity'. Taking his cue from Goethe ('Trost ist ein absurdes Wort / Wer nicht verzweifeln kann, der muss nicht leben'), Verhoeven comes to a conclusion that Blumenberg and Fœssel would no doubt agree with: 'The phenomenon makes sense, independently of the success of its attempts'.[151]

What Shakespeare's scenes of failed comfort show, I have argued in this chapter, are some of the conventions that underlie modern consolatory attempts and that define the interplay between the two participants in those interactions, the person being comforted and the comforter. A prime prerequisite in these encounters is that comforters acknowledge the authenticity of the pain of the person in need of comfort – at least, that they see it for what the person in need of comfort takes it to be. All of us will, at one time or another, have ended up in a situation where we want to bring comfort but

184   *Literature and Consolation*

fail to do so because the person whom we are frantically trying to console responds by saying that we have no clue what they are going through. 'It is impossible to comfort without the confirmation of the authenticity of the pain of the other', Cornelis Verhoeven writes:

> We can only bring comfort if we believe in the suffering of the other to the same extent that we feel urged to give comfort. Comfort is powerless in the face of feigned suffering, that is, of suffering that is being experienced as feigned. At the same time, we find it impossible to find comfort if we flee from suffering. There is no comfort in forgetting, because forgetting involves the negation of suffering.[152]

The second half of this quotation sounds like an apt description of what we saw happen in the consolatory scene from *Hamlet*. Gertrude's well-meant attempt at consolation cannot but fail as long as her son refuses to make his mother privy to what he truly feels. But the scene also shows that comfort is equally powerless in the face of a feigned rhetoric of comfort, that is, of a rhetoric that is experienced by the person to whom it is addressed as nothing but 'words, words, words'. The scenes from *Measure for Measure* and *Romeo and Juliet* that featured in this chapter confirm this, if not from the perspective of the person being comforted, then at least from the perspective of the audience who know full well that they are watching false priests providing false comfort.

The scene from *Richard II* in which Queen Isabel failed to be comforted shows the problem of modern inconsolability in an exemplary way. However willing she may be to listen to her comforters, there is something inside her that resists. In the classical and Christian regimes of consolation, there is a relationship of authority between comforter and comforted: the former speaks from a position of presumed mastery. The practice of comfort only works if the person being comforted accepts that authority and responds accordingly, with openness and the willingness to be comforted. In the modern regime, it is the comforter who acts from a position of subservience. Whether or not the words and gestures of comfort work seems to be up to the person being comforted. As the examples of Hamlet and, especially, Queen Isabel show, comforters can use any argument they want: as long as the person being comforted refuses to accept what is on offer (for whatever reason), any consolatory effort will fail.

Blumenberg's analysis of the phenomenon lies bare another fascinating paradox. In the modern regime, as we have seen, it is crucial that the authenticity of suffering be acknowledged by the person bringing comfort, while inversely the person in need of comfort needs to be convinced of the authenticity of the comforter's consolatory intentions and means. This double authenticity condition, however, does not change the fact that there is something 'illusive' at the core of the modern conception of consolation. As Blumenberg writes,

> It would appear that our suffering can be truly influenced by others, not only when they provide us with their help, but also by means of an authentic act of fictive diffusion, in which they participate in something to which they don't have any actual access. To the extent that the others pretend that they suffer, a kind of delegation of suffering takes place. It is not irrelevant how many of them are there and to which degree they appear trustworthy in wanting to take up their part or in actually taking it up. The person who suffers hands over part of his pain; he delegates the function, which, as the one who is truly burdened, he will have later to carry on himself, alone.[153]

In this quotation, Blumenberg recalls the crucial distinction that Georg Simmel made between 'consolation' and 'help'. I referred to Simmel's logic earlier in this chapter. 'Help' is 'real', Simmel argues, as it makes an actual (material) difference in the solving of a problem. 'Consolation', by contrast, is not real: it is a fiction, in the sense that the people who offer comfort pretend (*simulieren*) to take over the pain of the person in need of comfort. The simulation on the part of the comforter is complemented by a simulation on the part of the person awaiting comfort: the latter 'delegates' their pain to the comforter, in a reciprocal act of pretence. In the end (*zunächst*), Blumenberg's closing words imply, the people in need of comfort will have to carry that pain all by themselves. We may feel that we are not alone when we are being comforted, Blumenberg seems to suggest, but in the actual dealing with our pain we are, of course. In order to be comforted, then, we need to be able to imagine that we are not alone, without at the same time feeling as if in this act of imagination we are simply kidding ourselves. The modern attitude, Fœssel writes, 'consists in imagining consolation, in the full knowledge that it will never offer a final solution, since a return to the moment beyond (i.e. before) the loss, can never be realized'.[154]

To be clear, the 'fictional' nature of practices of consolation does not mean, for Blumenberg, that we ought to see the words that accompany or make up these practices as downright lies. It may be instructive to recall at this point John Searle's speech-act analysis of fictional utterances. Fiction, Searle writes in his famous essay on 'The

Logical Status of Fictional Discourse', involves the production of 'non-deceptive pseudo-statements'.[155] Rather than take expressions of comfort as 'mere' statements, I would venture that we see them as 'non-deceptive pseudo-promises' – non-deceptive because in order to be 'felicitous' (Searle's term) expressions of comfort cannot work if they are taken as 'lies'; 'pseudo-promises' because they are directed towards a future moment of improvement which, however, can never become really true ('everything will be okay'). Words of comfort are promises that cannot be kept, literally speaking. Of course, in the modern regime of consolation expressions of comfort should never be taken literally. It is a further irony of Shakespeare's great tragedy that Hamlet, who is so obstinately convinced of the fundamental figurativeness of language, does not manage to grasp this essential albeit plain fact.

\* \* \*

In the next three chapters, we will pursue our analysis of how literature functions in the modern regime of consolation. In the chapter that follows, we move from the early seventeenth to the second half of the nineteenth century, and from there, in Chapters 5 and 6, to the literature of the twentieth and twenty-first centuries. The question that will occupy us is framed, in the next chapter, by an epistolary discussion between novelists George Sand and Gustave Flaubert: if we conceive of the task of literature in the autonomous terms that Flaubert proposes – literary production ought to be measured exclusively by literary standards – what happens to the old idea that literature is meant to bring moral comfort? In his discussion with Sand, Flaubert clearly wants to get rid of that idea. However, as the remaining chapters of this book will show, no matter how important his example was for the development of modern(ist) literature, his decree against literary comfort did not hold sway. While Flaubert's literary ideals decisively impacted the debate on the consolation of literature, they definitely did not put an end to it.

## Notes

1. Maguire, *Where There's A Will There's A Way*, 2.
2. Douglass, *Shakespeare Inside*, back cover.
3. See <https://www.shakespearebehindbars.org>. For other examples see Pensalfini, *Prison Shakespeare*. Pensalfini, who himself is involved

in Australia's Shakespeare Prison Project (Queensland), discusses Curt Tofteland's work at length in his book (22–31). For other, non-Shakespeare-related examples of the use of literature in bibliotherapeutic projects in penal facilities see Sweeney, *Reading Is My Window*; Sweeney (ed.), *The Story Within Us*; Walmsley, *The Prison Book Club* and 'Reading in Prisons', Chapter 7 in Josie Billington (ed.), *Reading and Mental Health*.

4. Scott-Douglass, *Shakespeare Inside*, 1.
5. Scott-Douglass, *Shakespeare Inside*, 14.
6. Scott-Douglass, *Shakespeare Inside*, 20.
7. Scott-Douglass, *Shakespeare Inside*, 29, emphasis in the original.
8. Scott-Douglass, *Shakespeare Inside*, 29.
9. Scott-Douglass, *Shakespeare Inside*, 37.
10. Scott-Douglass, *Shakespeare Inside*, 12.
11. In *Prison Shakespeare*, 90–106, Rob Pensalfini gives an interesting survey of what participants in the Queensland Shakespeare Prison Project listed as personal outcomes of their intense involvement in the programme.
12. See also Pensalfini, *Prison Shakespeare*, 41–3.
13. Bates, *Shakespeare Saved My Life*.
14. Bates, *Shakespeare Saved My Life*, 152.
15. Bates, *Shakespeare Saved My Life*, 173–4.
16. See <https://tedx.ucla.edu/talks/laura_bates_shakespeare_in_shackles>
17. Bates, *Shakespeare Saved My Life*, 35.
18. Boethius, *The Consolation of Philosophy*, Ip6, 24. Earlier still (Ip2, 6), she says: 'He has forgotten who he really is'.
19. Bates, *Shakespeare Saved My Life*, 140.
20. Bates, *Shakespeare Saved My Life*, 170.
21. Bates, *Shakespeare Saved My Life*, 12.
22. Bates, *Shakespeare Saved My Life*, 252.
23. Bates, *Shakespeare Saved My Life*, 107.
24. Bates, *Shakespeare Saved My Life*, 108.
25. Dreher, *How Dante Can Save Your Life*, 125, for instance: 'Once Dante unmasked this within me, I saw that I too had made false idols of family and place.'
26. Maguire, *Shakespeare als therapeut*.
27. Maguire, *Where There's A Will*, 1.
28. Maguire, *Where There's A Will*, 3.
29. Maguire, *Where There's A Will*, 7.
30. Maguire, *Where There's A Will*, 29.
31. Maguire, *Where There's A Will*, 3–4.
32. Harold Bloom, *Shakespeare: The Invention of the Human*. Shakespeare's heroes, Bloom writes, and Hamlet and Falstaff especially, represent 'the inauguration of personality as we have come to recognize it' (4).
33. Greenblatt, *Renaissance Self-Fashioning from More to Shakespeare*, 235.
34. Maguire, *Where There's A Will*, 2, 197.

35. Maguire, *Where There's A Will*, 97.
36. Maguire, *Where There's A Will*, 2.
37. Maguire, *Where There's A Will*, 8.
38. Fœssel, *Le temps de la consolation*, 11.
39. Fœssel, *Le temps de la consolation*, 14.
40. Fœssel, *Le temps de la consolation*, 10, my translation. For a good account of how Blumenberg's analysis of consolation relates to his earlier work, see also Pavesich, 'Hans Blumenberg: Philosophical Anthropology and the Ethics of Consolation' and Sels, '"A Heart That Can Endure"'.
41. Blumenberg, 'Trostbedürfnis und Untröstlichkeit des Menschen'.
42. Simmel, *Fragmente und Aufsätze*, 17, my translation.
43. Simmel's conviction that animals cannot experience 'comfort' seems to be confirmed by Frans de Waal, who, in his bestselling *The Age of Empathy*, claims that chimpanzees, in contrast to 'ordinary' apes, do develop specific strategies of consoling. De Waal relates this to the fact that the behaviour of most apes is marked by 'an inability to adopt another's point of view'. De Waal's claim is also relevant to modern ideas of consolation: one of its conditions of possibility is the talent of the consoler to empathise with the feelings of the consoled (De Waal, *The Age of Empathy*, 141). The consolatory prowess of chimpanzees is also mentioned on pages 90 and 139.
44. Simmel, *Fragmente und Aufsätze*, 17. 'Dem Menschen ist im grossen und ganzen nicht zu helfen', Simmel writes: 'Darum hat er die wundervolle Kategorie des Trostes ausgebildet – der ihm nicht nur aus den Worten kommt, wie Menschen sie zu diesem Zwecke sprechen, sondern den er aus hunderterlei Gegebenheiten der Welt zieht.'
45. Verhoeven, *Het leedwezen*, 23, my translation.
46. Verhoeven, *Het leedwezen*, 23.
47. Rabinow, *Unconsolable* Contemporary, 135, italics mine. Rabinow also takes his cue from Fœssel's book (131–3).
48. Fœssel, *Le temps de la consolation*, 20.
49. Dagerman, 'Our Need for Consolation'. See also Montserrat-Cals, *Consolation à Dagerman* and Fœssel, *Le temps de la consolation*, 15.
50. Dagerman, 'Our Need for Consolation', 301.
51. Dagerman, 'Our Need for Consolation', 307.
52. 'I seek out consolation like a hunter dogging his prey. Wherever I catch a sudden glint of it in the woods, I shoot. Seldom do I hit anything but the empty air. And yet once in a while my quarry will drop at my feet.' Dagerman, 'Our Need for Consolation', 301.
53. McClure, *Sorrow and Consolation in Italian Humanism*, 161–2.
54. Grafton, 'Introduction' to Girolamo Cardano, *The Book of My Life*, xi.
55. Cardanus, *De Consolatione Libri Tres*.
56. Hunter, *New Illustrations*, 243.
57. 'Whoever will take the trouble of reading over the whole of Cardanus's second book as translated by Bedingfield, and printed by T. Marshe, 1576,

4to, will soon be convinced that it had been perused by Shakespeare.' Douce, *Illustrations of Shakespeare*, 377.
58. Hunter, *New Illustrations*, 244.
59. Craig, 'Hamlet's Book', 18. See also Campbell, *Shakespeare's Tragic Heroes*, 17–18.
60. See also Calvino, 'Gerolamo Cardano', esp. 77.
61. I made use of the English translation: Sigmund Freud, 'Mourning and Melancholia'.
62. See also Critchley and Webster, *The Hamlet Doctrine*, 119–25.
63. Freud, 'Mourning and Melancholia', 243.
64. De Martelaere, *Een verlangen naar ontroostbaarheid*, 63–76, my translation.
65. De Martelaere, *Een verlangen naar ontroostbaarheid*, 76. In his conversation with the gravediggers in 5.1 we learn that Hamlet is thirty years old, while Juliet, according to her nurse, is not yet fourteen. Hamlet's Wikipedia page has much to say about the prince's age: <https://en.wikipedia.org/wiki/Prince_Hamlet>. See also De Grazia, *Hamlet without Hamlet*, 82–3.
66. Blumenberg, 'Trostbedürfnis und Untröstlichkeit des Menschen', 627.
67. Not even two months, Hamlet claims: 'But two months' (1.2.138).
68. See also Boyce, 'The Stoic Consolatio and Shakespeare', esp. 775–7.
69. Soellner, *Shakespeare's Patterns of Self-Knowledge*, 187.
70. Graver, *Cicero on the Emotions*, 121.
71. Cicero, *Tusculan Disputations*, Book 3, 25, 297.
72. Cicero, *Tusculan Disputations*, Book 3, 24, 295.
73. Cicero, *Tusculan Disputations*, Book 3, 27, 303.
74. Claudius' reference to 'heaven' should not necessarily be taken as a sign of the Christian nature of his attempt consolation, as Cicero's 'quasi cum deo pugnare' shows. Classical consolations contain numerous references to the will of the gods: see Holloway, *Consolation in Philippians*, 65.
75. Cicero, *Tusculan Disputations*, Book 3, 28, 305.
76. Cicero, *Tusculan Disputations*, Book 3, 28, 309.
77. Cicero, *Tusculan Disputations*, Book 3, 28, 309.
78. Cicero, *Tusculan Disputations*, Book 3, 26, 299.
79. In the consolatory encounter between Achilles and Priam in *Iliad* 24, Niobe, as we have seen, is an icon of unquenchable grief, not of false tears. On Niobe's inconsolability in Antiquity, see also Fœssel, *Le temps de la consolation*, 68–70.
80. Critchley and Webster, *The Hamlet Doctrine*, 80.
81. Fœssel, *Le temps de la consolation*, 35.
82. Rittgers, *The Reformation of Suffering*.
83. Kastan, *A Will to Believe*, 125.
84. Kastan, *A Will to Believe*, 126.
85. Craig, 'Hamlet's Book', 22.

86. Job 3: 11–13, quoted in Josipovici, *Hamlet Fold on Fold*, 128.
87. Josipovici, *Hamlet Fold on Fold*, 128. See also Pieters, 'Coornhert en Calvijn over Job' and Korsten, *A Dutch Republican Baroque*, 58: 'Whereas in the Catholic Middle Ages, Job was first and foremost an icon of Stoic fortitude, patience and humility, the *exempla patientiae*, and an icon of purification through suffering, in the Reformation he also became the paradigmatic human figure accepting God's incomprehensibility and sovereign power.'
88. Job 6: 9–10.
89. Lupton, 'Job of Athens, Timon of Uz', 131–59, further references on 131.
90. Lupton, 'Job of Athens, Timon of Uz', 138.
91. Korsten, *A Dutch Republican Baroque*, 58.
92. See, for instance, McClure, *Sorrow and Consolation in Italian Humanism* and Schaeben, *Trauer im humanistischen Dialog*. The impact of Boethius' *De consolatione philosophiae* in early modern thinking on consolation is the topic of Nauta, 'A Humanist Reading of Boethius's Consolatio Philosophiae'.
93. Blumenberg, 'Trostbedürfnis und Untröstlichkeit des Menschen', 625. I will come back to this idea at the end of this chapter.
94. Maus, *Inwardness and Theater in the English Renaissance*. In her book, which starts from Hamlet's reference to 'that within which passes show', Maus does not deal with the scene from *Richard II* that is central to my concern here.
95. The tradition of this type of visual representation is the subject of Baltrušaitis, *Anamorphoses ou perspectives curieuses* and *Les perspectives dépravées*. For further analyses of the relationship between the phenomenon and this particular scene of *Richard II* see also Gilman, '*Richard II* and the Perspectives of History'; Moore, 'Queen of Sorrow, King of Grief'; McMillin, 'Shakespeare's Richard II'.
96. Forker (ed.), *King Richard II: The Arden Shakespeare*, 490.
97. Žižek, *Looking Awry*, 11–12.
98. Lacan, *Les quatre concepts*, 93–104 ('L'anamorphose').
99. Lacan, *Les quatre concepts*, 102.
100. Greenblatt et al. (eds), *The Norton Shakespeare*, 973n3. Not all editors construe the line in this way, apparently: some read 'as though' instead of 'as thought'.
101. Žižek, *Looking Awry*, 12.
102. The fullest historical analysis of the painting that I know is North, *The Ambassador's Secret*. For further references see also Pieters, 'Facing History, or the Anxiety of Reading'.
103. Cited in Kirsch, 'Virtue, Vice, and Compassion in Montaigne and *The Tempest*', 337. The reference is to the French original of the book that was later published as: Ellrodt, *Montaigne and Shakespeare*.
104. Sontag, *Regarding the Pain of Others*.

105. Forker (ed.), *King Richard II*, 230. Forker also points to a similar passage in Marlowe's *Edward II* (5.1.2–4).
106. The passage is not in the Oxford edition; in the Norton it is, but the editors say that it comes from the *First Quarto* (1597), which is the text that the Arden edition used, complete with the 'deposition' scene that was censured from the *First Quarto* by Elizabeth. I made use of the Arden edition (by Forker) in this case.
107. Forker (ed.), *King Richard II*, 316.
108. Bates, *Shakespeare Saved My Life*, 18–20.
109. The Queen's translation (1593) can be found in Mueller and Scodel (eds), *Elizabeth I: Translations 1592–1598*, 72–367. See also Riddehough, 'Queen Elizabeth's Translation of Boethius'.
110. Boethius, *The Consolation of Philosophy*, Ip5, 20.
111. Lever (ed.), *Measure for Measure*, 67. The reference is to Book 1, par. 92 of Cicero's text.
112. Lever (ed.), *Measure for Measure*, 67.
113. Allan Bloom, *Shakespeare on Love and Friendship*, 68.
114. Lever (ed.), *Measure for Measure*, 74.
115. Several scholars have seen in the Vienna of *Measure for Measure* a premonition of the modern disciplinary society that Foucault sketches in *Surveiller et punir*, a society in which individuals are unwittingly but permanently subjected to an instance of power that is present everywhere but nowhere to be seen. For examples see Ryan, *Shakespeare*, 133–8; see also Pieters, 'Normality, deviancy, critique'.
116. Maguire, *Where There's A Will*, 70.
117. Greenblatt, *Shakespearean Negotiations*, 129–42.
118. Boethius, *The Consolation of Philosophy*, Ip2, 6.
119. McClure, *Sorrow and Consolation in Italian Humanism*, 18–72.
120. Southworth, *Shakespeare the Player*, 100. The 'problem' of the play's date of composition is dealt with in Brain Gibbons' introduction to the Arden edition of the play: Gibbons (ed.), *Romeo and Juliet*, 26–31.
121. Allan Bloom, *Shakespeare on Love and Friendship*, 103. Of the less central characters Bloom is mostly interested in Mercutio and Juliet's nurse.
122. The former is the case in the Oxford edition, the latter in the Arden.
123. In the Oxford edition he is merely 'County Paris'.
124. Juliet's age is referred to in 1.3, in a conversation between Juliet's mother and the nurse: she will turn fourteen at 'Lammas-tide', 1 August, about a fortnight after the moment of the play's events.
125. Gibbons (ed.), *Romeo and Juliet*, 212n79. In *Hamlet*, Ophelia tells Laertes that 'Rosemary is for remembrance' (4.5.175).
126. For a survey of the sources, see Targoff, *Posthumous Love*, 98–105; see also Gibbons' introduction to the Arden edition, 32–7.

127. Targoff, *Posthumous Love*, 105. See also 98: 'In Shakespeare's sources, the tragedy of Romeo and Juliet's deaths was softened by the idea, articulated by the lovers themselves, that their souls would share some form of meaningful, sentient afterlife. Shakespeare removed any such transcendent vision of posthumous love from his play. In doing so he created his most potent expression of what it meant for love to be mortal.'
128. There is a first printed version of 1597, but it is generally assumed that that edition is a corrupt, memorial reconstruction by actors: see Brian Gibbons' introduction to the Arden edition, 1–26.
129. Allan Bloom, *Shakespeare on Love and Friendship*, 24.
130. Romeo's mother seems to have succumbed under the pain that the banishment of her son inflicted upon her. (5.3.210)
131. W. H. Auden, *Lectures on Shakespeare*, 49. Harold Bloom calls him 'the wretched Friar Laurence, who fearfully abandoned Juliet'. Bloom, *Shakespeare: The Invention of the Human*, 103.
132. De Martelaere, *Een verlangen naar ontroostbaarheid*, 76, italics in the original; my translation.
133. Juliet's nurse had already understood this in the previous scene, where she assures her: 'I'll find Romeo / To comfort you' (3.2.138–9).
134. Freud in a letter to Ernest Jones, quoted in Leader, *The New Black*, 114.
135. (Ps-)Plutarch, 'Consolatio ad Apollonium', 108–211.
136. For further references to Crantor's text see Chapter 1, notes 34–6.
137. (Ps-)Plutarch, 'Consolatio ad Apollonium', 4, 113.
138. (Ps-)Plutarch, 'Consolatio ad Apollonium', 9, 131.
139. (Ps-)Plutarch, 'Consolatio ad Apollonium', 1, 109.
140. Paster, 'Montaigne, Dido, and *The Tempest*'.
141. Montaigne, 'Of Diverting or Diversion', 226.
142. Montaigne, 'Of Diverting or Diversion', 226.
143. Montaigne, 'Of Diverting or Diversion', 227.
144. Montaigne, 'Of Diverting or Diversion', 227.
145. Montaigne, 'Of Diverting or Diversion', 229 (with a reference to *Tusculanae*, Book 4, 35, 74–5, 414–15).
146. Montaigne, 'Of Diverting or Diversion', 227.
147. Montaigne, 'Of Diverting or Diversion', 231.
148. Montaigne, 'Of Diverting or Diversion', 233.
149. Heitsch, 'Approaching Death by Writing', 102.
150. Maguire, *Where There's A Will*, 199.
151. Verhoeven, *Het leedwezen*, 26, my translation.
152. Verhoeven, *Het leedwezen*, 24, my translation.
153. Blumenberg, 'Trostbedürfnis und Untröstlichkeit des Menschen', 625, my translation.
154. Fœssel, *Le temps de la consolation*, 21, my translation.
155. Searle, 'The Logical Status of Fictional Discourse'.

# Chapter 4

# The Religion of Despair: George Sand and Gustave Flaubert on Reading and Writing

> Ellen. My wife: someone I feel I understand less well than a foreign writer dead for a hundred years. Is this an aberration, or is it normal? Books say: she did this because. Life says: she did this. Books are where things are explained to you; life is where things aren't. I'm not surprised some people prefer books. Books make sense of life. The only problem is that the lives they make sense of are other people's lives, never your own.
>
> Julian Barnes, *Flaubert's Parrot*[1]

## Modern Literature / Modern Comfort?

Why is it that we keep saying that we seek and find comfort in some of the plays that we see and some of the poems and novels that we read? What is it, precisely, that we mean when we make such a claim? Is the comfort that we claim to derive from books and other literary works of art any different from the comfort that we get from the people around us? If not, where does the advantage of literary comfort lie? Also, which qualities do we ascribe to the texts that sustain our consolatory convictions? Are these convictions triggered by the ideas that these texts grapple with, by certain actions that the characters in them perform or words they express? Or is literary comfort primarily a matter of form, of that which some critics claim distinguishes literary writings from non-literary ones?

As we have seen in the previous chapters, some of our ideas and intuitions with respect to literature's powers of comfort find support in the joint conceptual histories of the two notions that are central in my enquiry: 'literature' and 'consolation'. If we contend that our encounter with literary writings helps us to transform specific emotions that affect us negatively into positively productive forces (leading to a new refreshing insight, say, or the ability to reconcile ourselves with a state of affairs previously held unbearable), we are pursuing a line of reasoning that supports Aristotle's analysis of mimetic *katharsis*; if we say that the comfort of literature is at least in part due to the aesthetic appeal of its formal build-up (a suggestion that Aristotle would no doubt applaud, given his distinct appreciation of the organisation of a well-made plot), then we apply the sort of lesson Dante took from Boethius' analysis of the consolatory force of philosophical poems; if we allege that literary fiction enables us to distinguish real comforters from their fake counterparts who merely play at bringing comfort, then Shakespeare is our man.

The present chapter moves into what is generally seen as the 'modern' phase of Western literature. It works towards a central focus on the famous epistolary discussion in which Gustave Flaubert, the godfather of the contemporary novel, felt coerced into defending himself against the accusation of his writer-friend George Sand, who tried to convince him – unsuccessfully, of course – to stop writing what she called 'literature of desolation'. Sand was hoping that Flaubert would consider producing the sort of literature that she did: 'literature of consolation'. As in the previous chapters, I will relate the materials that are part of the larger history of literary comfort to a contemporary instance of bibliotherapy. This time, I did not opt for a reading memoir, but for a novel. As I hope to show, Julian Barnes' *Flaubert's Parrot* offers an apt reflection on the values and limitations of what bibliotherapists Ella Berthoud and Susan Elderkin have labelled 'the novel cure', the use of literary fiction for purposes of mental healing. In the novel, Barnes' first-person narrator refers directly to the letters in which Flaubert and Sand quarrelled over the question of literary comfort. His failed attempt to find help in Flaubert's life and letters, as I want to argue, helps us understand a central prerequisite of the usefulness of bibliotherapy, even as it enables us to reflect on its limits.

### Geoffrey B., the Parrot Man

Geoffrey must be in his early sixties. He is a fairly tall man, six foot one; he has brown eyes and grey hair. He likes to describe himself as 'cheerful if inclined to melancholy'.[2] He lives in Essex, but likes to travel to the north of France on a regular basis. He used to be a doctor, but he is retired now, a widower for seven years. He and his wife married in 1940. They have two adult children, one of whom was born in 1942, the other four years later. Geoffrey sees or hears from his offspring rarely, nowadays. 'They write whenever guilt impels', as he puts it – without much regret, it would seem ('They have their own lives, naturally.'[3]). Geoffrey doesn't mention any grandchildren, but that should not cause us to assume that he has none. Geoffrey likes to keep himself to himself, in matters of family business at least. His wife, Ellen, died in 1975. She took her own life. Geoffrey is still at a loss to understand why. For all that we know, he may be suffering from a serious case of protracted grief. He obviously loved his wife very much. He still does.

Ellen was fifty-four when she died. While it is unclear whether her final suicide attempt was also her first, Geoffrey feels quite certain that what caused the calamity (not Geoffrey's word, mind you) is what he calls his wife's 'despair'.[4] The term seems to refer to a general state of depression, caused by an equally unspecified feeling of worthlessness and, quite probably, loneliness. Geoffrey seems inclined to think that his wife's dark mood set in around her fiftieth birthday.[5] However, from what little he divulges about her earlier life, it is fair to assume that Ellen's depression was chronic. Geoffrey doesn't hide the fact that his wife had several lovers, not necessarily consecutively. The few details that he provides – he is not very specific about any of Ellen's relationships – show that what he refers to as his wife's 'secret life' started well before the birth of their first child and was resumed after both children left their parents' house. It is clearly not a subject that husband and wife ever discussed. Geoffrey claims to have been faithful himself. There is no reason not to believe him.

Ellen committed suicide by taking pills. It was, as Geoffrey puts it, 'the only occasion when being a doctor's wife seemed to help her'.[6] While entirely in character, Geoffrey's irony covers up an understandable amount of guilt. 'Perhaps I made her worse,' he admits in one of his more openly confessional moments, 'perhaps those who forgive and dote are more irritating than they ever suspect.'[7] If the question were put to him, he would probably say that as far as he was concerned, his marriage was a happy one. Ellen would undoubtedly say otherwise. In 1965, the spouses had the opportunity to celebrate their twenty-fifth anniversary, but from what Geoffrey lets on, there probably was no party. As Geoffrey puts it – again, entirely in character – no photographs remain that could serve as documentary evidence of the event.[8] Around a decade later, an overdose landed Ellen in hospital, in a state of what medical procedures refer to as non-resuscitation. Geoffrey granted his wife her last wish and allowed the doctors to switch off the machine. To be precise, he switched it off himself: 'I think she would have preferred me to', he concludes by saying.[9] It is hard to ascertain whether or not the thinking may be rightly characterised as wishful.

Julian Barnes' *Flaubert's Parrot* – the 1984 novel in which Geoffrey Braithwaite, the book's first-person narrator, ends up telling the story of his failed marriage – has a number of interesting things to say about bibliotherapy, both of the phenomenon and of its limits, as we will see. In what follows, I want to use the novel as a point of entry into the epistolary discussion between Flaubert and George Sand that will be central to this chapter. In this famous exchange of letters, Sand asked Flaubert why he so adamantly refused to write the sort of 'literature of consolation' that she felt her duty to produce. Why, Sand wondered, did Flaubert always end up writing 'literature of desolation' instead? Braithwaite refers to the correspondence on several occasions in *Flaubert's Parrot*, and his inventor later wrote an essay on it.[10] The discussion between Sand and Flaubert, as we will shortly see, is not only about whether or not literature can or should actually bring comfort, but also about how we should define that most elusive of phenomena.

My earlier synopsis of Barnes' novel (presented as a case history of Geoffrey B., so to speak) does not point out, yet, how and to what extent *Flaubert's Parrot* could be read as the sort of work with which I begin every chapter of this book: as a further illustration, that is, of how readers make use of literary writings in order to find mental comfort. From the novel's opening chapter, it quickly becomes clear that we are dealing with a narrator who has a strong if not obsessive interest in the imposing figure of Gustave Flaubert. Still, we have to wait until the final few chapters of the novel to understand where Geoffrey's interest actually comes from and what it is meant to cover up. By the end of *Flaubert's Parrot*, the reader has come to see more properly that the narrator's obsession with the author of *Madame Bovary* is directly related to his desire to understand his wife's decision to end both her life and her marriage.

Geoffrey Braithwaite, then, is practising bibliotherapy. He is reading Flaubert's work and letters in order to understand his late wife's state of mind better, but at the same time to ease his own mind and, quite possibly, to decrease his sense of guilt at not having been a better husband.

The choice of Flaubert, in that respect, makes double sense. As his most famous novel shows, Flaubert excelled at dissecting the mind of adulterous doctors' wives (Emma Bovary shares more than just her initials with Ellen Braithwaite). Moreover, Flaubert is no less an expert in the analysis of what Geoffrey, in a central passage of the novel calls 'the religion of despair'. As the author's impressive correspondence shows, Flaubert was a master of just that which Geoffrey feels his wife fatally lacked: the power of being able to 'gaz[e] down into the black pit at one's feet'.[11] 'Perhaps this was Ellen's weakness', Geoffrey comes to think: 'She could only squint at it, repeatedly. One glance would make her despair, and despair would make her seek distraction.'[12]

The expression 'roosts in my head', Geoffrey acknowledges in the novel's final chapter.[13] It is borrowed from a letter of condolence that Flaubert wrote to his friend Georges Feydeau.[14] The ideal to which it refers is one which Geoffrey's wife clearly failed to appreciate. After having finally come to confide in us about his wife's suicide, Geoffrey ends up adamantly disputing Edmond Ledoux's 'slanderous assertion' that Flaubert also committed suicide, hanging himself in his bath in his house in Croisset.[15] This cannot but be 'pure crankery', Geoffrey rages. The mad idea clearly 'runs counter to the writer's deepest beliefs': despair is not something from which Flaubert would ever have wanted to escape.[16] Quite the contrary: it is precisely what kept him going his entire life. (Ironically, Geoffrey's rant against Ledoux seems to be directly inspired by the discussion of Flaubert's final moments in *Flaubert the Master*, the biography by Enid Starkie, the Cambridge scholar whom Geoffrey takes to task (and puts to ridicule) in the novel's sixth chapter, 'Emma Bovary's Eyes'.)[17]

Barnes' novel has been read, predominantly, as an exemplary experiment in what Linda Hutcheon famously called 'historiographic metafiction'.[18] While there is no denying that it is also that, there is more to the novel than meets the postmodernist eye. '[O]bviously', as Barnes himself put it in an interview with Vanessa Guignery, 'it's a book about the shiftingness of the past, and the uncertainty and unverifiability of fact'. But, as he immediately added, 'beyond all that it's a novel about grief', a topic which Barnes went on to develop, masterfully, in such works as *Nothing To Be Frightened Of* (2008), *The Sense of an Ending* (2011) and *Levels of Life* (2013). In the author's own words, *Flaubert's Parrot* is basically

> a novel about a man whose inability to express his grief and his love is shifted (I'm sure there's a psychiatric term for it – displacement activity might be the one), is transposed into an obsessive desire to recount to

you the reader everything he knows and has found out about Gustave Flaubert, love for whom is a more reliable constant in his life than has been love for Ellen.[19]

The contrast with Barnes' later analysis, in the third section of *Levels of Life*, of the grief that struck him after the death of his own partner, Pat Kavanagh, may be instructive, here. Referring to his own grief and that of others like Ivy-Compton Burnett, Ford Madox Ford and H. L. Mencken, Barnes comes to understand the need to continue the conversation with the deceased spouse in a quite literal way. 'So I talk to her constantly', he writes: 'This feels as normal as it is necessary. I comment on what I am doing (or have done in the course of the day); I point out things to her while driving; I articulate her responses. I keep alive our lost private language. I tease her and she teases me back; we know the lines by heart.'[20] The difference with Geoffrey Braithwaite's struggle with grief will be clear:[21] since Ellen and he seem to have had no real 'private language' to begin with, and no actual conversations in the years before her suicide,[22] it makes sense that in order to work through his grief Geoffrey needs another dead person to converse and at times banter with. Flaubert seems to be perfectly equipped to serve as the 'dead foreigner to sustain [him]'.[23]

## The Ambulance Flaubert

In the course of the novel, it takes quite a while before we get to know Geoffrey's name, longer still before we hear that of his wife. Describing (doctor) Charles Bovary to Louise Colet, in a letter of 15 January 1853, Flaubert discloses the quintessence of the male protagonist of his new novel-to-be in terms that fit Geoffrey Braithwaite perfectly: 'my gentleman is of a sober temperament'.[24] In Barnes' entire novel, there are only two scenes in which Geoffrey comes near to losing his temper. The first of those rounds off the novel's third chapter.[25] In an unidentified London restaurant, Geoffrey has a dinner meeting with Ed Winterton, an American scholar he had met a year before at a bookseller's fair where they were both aiming for the same copy of Turgenev's *Literary Reminiscences*.[26] Doing research for a biography of Edmund Gosse, Winterton claims to have secured a long-lost collection of some seventy-five letters between Flaubert and Juliet Herbert, the English governess to Flaubert's niece Caroline who at one point was working on an English translation of *Madame Bovary* and with whom Flaubert may or may not have had a sexual relationship.[27] In the absence of epistolary evidence, biographers continue to disagree on the matter. Convinced that Ed will hand him over the letters, Geoffrey is already dreaming of publishing a piece in the *Times Literary Supplement* about this lost moment in the author's published lives ('Juliet Herbert; A Mystery Solved – by Geoffrey Braithwaite'[28]). After having told him about their precious content – yes, there was something serious going on between Gustave and Juliet, and, yes, the Master came to visit her in London – Ed tells him that he destroyed the letters, complying with Flaubert's wishes that Juliet would burn their correspondence after her lover's death.[29] It is upon hearing this that Geoffrey loses his temper for the first time in the novel, internally at least, thinking of calling Ed all sorts of names ('maniac', 'smug, moralising bastard'[30]) – but even then he remains the perfect gentleman, paying for the American's meal.[31]

At the moment of this grand 'explosion', we still know little about Geoffrey Braithwaite's personal (and marital) past. In the novel's first chapter, we learn that he is a veteran of World War Two. Not only did he participate in the Anglo-Canadian part of the Normandy Landing (6 June 1944), he was also present at the subsequent liberation of Rouen (30 August 1944).[32] However, the visit to the region and the city with which his story opens is not so much in commemoration of 'the sudden friends those years produced'[33] but to indulge in what appears to be, at first sight, mere literary tourism. It is clear from the beginning that Geoffrey's interest goes out more to Flaubert's life than to the author's works. The irony is certainly not beyond him: Geoffrey knows full well that Flaubert systematically appealed for an interest in the writer's work apart from its maker, but, as we can gather from his scathing remarks about Roland Barthes, he is simply not a believer in theories that proclaim the death of the author.[34]

In hindsight, however, the first chapter of *Flaubert's Parrot* already gives away to some extent the bibliotherapeutic need that hides behind Geoffrey Braithwaite's tourist-like interest in the life and works of Gustave Flaubert. On the third day of the first stay in Rouen that he mentions in his story, Geoffrey is walking towards the Hôtel-Dieu, the old city hospital where Flaubert's father was appointed 'chirurgien-chef' (chief surgeon) in 1818[35] and where Gustave was born 'at 4AM on December 12 1821' as one biographer puts it.[36] The author's birthplace now houses the 'Musée Flaubert et de l'Histoire de la Médecine', where Geoffrey first spots the stuffed parrot that is said to have stood on Flaubert's desk as he was writing 'Un cœur simple'. On his way to the Musée, as he puts it, '[a]long the avenue Gustave Flaubert, past the Imprimerie Flaubert and a snack-bar called Le Flaubert' ('you certainly feel you're going in the right direction'[37]), Geoffrey spots a car that cannot fail to attract his monomaniacal attention:

> Parked near the hospital was a large white Peugeot hatchback: it was painted with blue stars, a telephone number and the words AMBU-LANCE FLAUBERT. The writer as healer? Unlikely. I remembered George Sand's matronly rebuke to her younger colleague. 'You produce desolation', she wrote, 'and I produce consolation.' The Peugeot should have read AMBULANCE GEORGE SAND.[38]

The reference to both the ambulance and the letters returns at the end of Chapter 10, in which Geoffrey takes up Flaubert's defence against a number of recurrent critical charges. It crops up in Geoffrey's reply to charge 15 ('That he didn't believe Art had a social purpose'[39]). 'No he didn't', Geoffrey admits. 'This is wearying', he adds:

> 'You provide desolation', wrote George Sand, 'and I provide consolation.' To which Flaubert replied, 'I cannot change my eyes.' The work of art is a pyramid which stands in the desert, uselessly: jackals piss at the base of it, and bourgeois clamber to the top of it; continue this comparison. Do you want art to be healer? Send for the AMBULANCE GEORGE SAND. Do you want art to tell the truth? Send for the AMBULANCE FLAUBERT: though don't be surprised, when it arrives, if it runs over your leg.[40]

Geoffrey's reference, in both cases, is to a series of letters that Flaubert and Sand exchanged between mid-November 1875 and mid-February 1876. At the time, Flaubert was finishing 'La légende de Saint-Julien l'Hospitalier', the first of three stories that would later, in April 1877, be published together as *Trois contes*. The collection was to open with the more famous 'Un cœur simple', which Flaubert was sure his old friend would appreciate, as he puts it in what ended up being his last letter to her: 'I believe you will like the moral tendency, or rather the underlying humanity, of this little work.'[41] Unfortunately, Sand was never able to read Flaubert's letter of 29 May 1876: she died little over a week later, on 8 June. Fourteen months after Sand's death, Flaubert assures her son Maurice that he wrote the story especially for her. 'I began *Un cœur simple* exclusively for her,' Flaubert writes in his letter of 9 August 1877, 'solely to please her. She died while I was in the middle of my work. Thus it is with all our dreams.'[42] As Barnes rightly says in his review of the Sand-Flaubert *Correspondence*: we should be careful to believe that this is more than 'innate gallantry' on Flaubert's behalf.[43] It is a conclusion, of course, which Geoffrey Braithwaite is less willing to draw.[44]

## Friends in Letters

At the time of the correspondence that we will now have a closer look at, Flaubert and Sand had already been writing to each other for several years.[45] Their first exchange of letters dates from the beginning of 1863, just after the publication of *Salammbô*.[46] Sand had reviewed Flaubert's new novel with much approval (more than most other critics, at least) and the grateful author got in touch with her. Sand invited him to pay her a visit at her estate in Nohant and he, in turn, asked her to send him a portrait, to be hung in his writer's retreat.[47] In the course of the dozen years that separate the beginning of their remarkable friendship from the epistolary discussion to which Geoffrey Braithwaite twice refers, Sand and Flaubert had numerous encounters, both in real life and in their incessant letter-writing. Sand was the only woman ever to be invited to the famous bi-weekly Magny dinners that Flaubert attended (apparently, he was the one who secured her an invitation, which she was able to accept for the first time in February 1866[48]). Later in the same year, she came to visit Flaubert and his mother in Croisset, twice in fact. On both occasions, Flaubert read to her from his work in progress. In August, he shared with her the second version of *La Tentation de Saint Antoine* and in November he read to her from *L'Éducation sentimentale*, the novel he was then working on.

Towards the end of 1869, Flaubert was, in turn, invited to Nohant, to spend Christmas with Sand. It was a difficult time in his life. He had just published *L'Éducation sentimentale*, but remained saddened by the loss of good friends. '[I]nconsolable after the death of Bouilhet, saddened by that of Sainte-Beuve', as one biographer puts it, the company of George Sand provided 'true consolation'.[49] Sand was also the true friend Flaubert could turn to when his beloved mother died (6 April 1872). 'It would be sweet to see you here', he writes in a letter of April 29, 'in her house, now, while her presence still lingers.'[50] 'Now more than ever', he confides to her in a later letter, 'I'd like to have you here at Croisset, to have you sleeping near to me, in my mother's room.'[51] To be clear, when Sand was in need of consolation herself, Flaubert was there to provide it equally successfully. When Sand's secretary (and lover) Alexander Manceau died in August 1865, Flaubert hurried to

Palaiseau, a village to the south of Paris, where Sand had bought a little house for Manceau.[52]

Without fail, Flaubert's biographers point out the exceptional nature of the writer's warm friendship with Sand. 'When Sand died', Michel Winock writes,

> [a] great friendship had come to an end, a friendship that was paradoxical in its very existence as well as in its intensity. She celebrated life; he loathed it. She was optimistic and idealistic, while remaining grounded in life's practical matters. He was an old bear without a grasp on material realities. She was a progressive; he was a conservative. Their political, philosophical, and aesthetic notions led to insurmountable disagreements. Yet they still appreciated each other and loved each other with a tender, faithful friendship.[53]

'In many ways it would be difficult to imagine a more unlikely conjunction', Geoffrey Wall concurs. 'On all questions political, sexual and literary, they held quite contrary views.'[54] As far as the former two topics are concerned, Wall opposes Sand's libertarianism and utopian socialism to Flaubert's fundamentally anti-democratic scepticism, and her emancipatory feminism to his 'emphatically conservative' view of women, typical of most men of Flaubert's time.[55] With respect to the third topic – their differences in literary matters – the overview that Barnes provides in his review of the *Correspondence* is both concise and apt:

> Flaubert, lordly and inflexible, always takes the high aesthetic line: the making of art necessarily entails the partial renunciation of life; the artist can only know humanity, but cannot change it; truth is a sufficient good in itself. Sand's position, to which she is just as committed, is pragmatic and involving: life, and especially love, are more important than art; artists cannot negotiate a detachment from the rest of human species, since art springs precisely from their intimate, messy commingling with it; art must be useful and moral.[56]

The passage confirms the opposition that Geoffrey Braithwaite forges in his second reference to the *Flaubert-Sand Correspondence*: Sand's profile is that of the 'artist as healer' whereas Flaubert profiles himself as the teller of hurtful truths, 'the writer as butcher, the writer as sensitive brute', as Geoffrey puts it with a reference to the famous cartoon in which we see Flaubert holding up Emma Bovary's dissected heart.[57] The letter that starts off the discussion of the winter of 1875 is the one that Sand writes on December 18–19 of that year. Referring to her recently finished novel *Flamarande* (1875) and to Flaubert's own indication (in his letter of 16 December to which Sand is here responding) that he started writing 'a little medieval trifle, which won't take up more than 30 pages',[58] she wonders out loud how their new works will relate to each other:

> So what shall we be doing? You'll go in for desolation, I'll wager, while I go in for consolation. I don't know what our destinies stem from. You watch them go by, analyze them, but abstain, literarily, from judging them. You confine yourself to describing them, carefully and systematically concealing your own feelings. And yet those feelings can be seen through what you write, with the result that you make your readers sadder than they were before. I'd like to make them less unhappy. I can't forget that my own conquest of despair was due to my will, and to a new way of seeing things that is completely opposite to the view I once had.[59]

If anything, the letter makes quite clear how Sand conceives of comfort, apart from the artistic shapes it can and should take. In her view, to console people is to reassure them in times of distress and to remind them that they have it in them to rise above the painful circumstances that caused their distress in the first place. To bring comfort is to reassure readers that things will turn out for the better, in the end. This message of hope is one that Sand as a writer wants to share, without at the same time giving the impression that life will never be painful. Sand considers herself too much of a realist to simply colour over the less pleasant aspects of reality. However, against what she sees as Flaubert's poetics of despair – a poetics that results, without fail, in stories that end up bad – she proposes a poetics of hope, the heartfelt outcome of an experience that, judging from the last sentence of the passage just quoted, proved vital to her.

The key characteristic of humanity, in Sand's view, is man's resilience. Picking up on Flaubert's remark that he is reading Shakespeare, Sand is happy to stress that a proper reading of the Bard's work will show him people actively – and successfully – trying to make something of their lives. 'He makes men do battle with facts', Sand writes, urging Flaubert to 'please note that his men always topple the facts, for better or worse, crushing them or being crushed by them.'[60]

The same idea seems to underlie Sand's criticism of Flaubert's previous novel, *L'Éducation sentimentale*. How is it possible, she wonders, 'why a book so weighty and well written should have aroused so much rancour'? Having thought through the question that she confesses kept bugging her, Sand claims to have finally found the answer: 'The fault lay in the fact that the characters do not *act* upon themselves. They are influenced by facts, but never grapple with them.'[61] Flaubert's novel is without any doubt well written, Sand grants, but at the same time it is too single-mindedly focused on the display of the author's unique style. It misses, therefore, what Sand refers to as 'the depths' of human reality;[62] it fails to present to its readers 'a broad and definite view of life'.[63] The latter adjective is clearly meant to suggest that in Sand's view, Flaubert limits himself to the representation of negative, desolate aspects of reality, thereby painting a picture of mankind that is both meagre and unfair. 'Criticism and satire depict but one aspect of truth', Sand points out.[64] They limit themselves to man's shortcomings; they consider his potential to fail as something that is sure to happen. Sand adds that her own ideal is 'to see man as he is. Not good or bad, but good *and* bad.'[65]

## Consolation vs. Desolation: Hope vs. Despair

Sand's critique of Flaubert's work starts from the pragmatic premise that underlies her prior description of her own work as literature of consolation. That premise (and the subsequent weighing off of Flaubert's work against that criterion as its inevitable opposite) requires, first, that the literary work be defined in terms of the effect it has on its readers and, secondly, that the author's activity be seen as the hoped-for fulfilment of that intention. If Sand's work is truly consoling, then Flaubert's work cannot but be its opposite on both accounts – it cannot but lead the reader to despair and it can only be seen as the logical outcome of the wrong sort of artistic intention.

For Flaubert, the comfort that Sand pretends to provide is not truly consoling; if it is, then the presumption that the phenomenon for which the word stands is unambiguously positive should be fiercely disputed. It may be instructive, at this point, to insert a brief excursion into the letter in which Flaubert writes about what he calls 'the religion of Despair' (alluding to it, Geoffrey Braithwaite seems to forget to capitalise the central word). In this letter, Flaubert tries to talk sense into his writer-friend Ernest Feydeau, who has just lost his wife after a protracted illness. Feydeau's wife died on 18 October 1859, and Flaubert got in touch with his friend just over a week later, on the evening of 26 October. Given that short time-span, the letter sounds inappropriately direct, to the point of rudeness even, like classical letters of consolation sometimes do to modern ears. Flaubert's message is not, as he says emphatically, one of consolation ('I would like you to understand that I am in no way offering consolation'[66]). To send words of comfort, he goes on to write, would be nothing short of offensive. Words of comfort, the suggestion seems to be, do not take way or even alleviate the grief, but continue and even heighten it. Ironically, Flaubert's critique of contemporary forms of consolation seems to be sustained by the central argument that underlies what I called the classical regime of consolation, the idea that we need to fight the emotional turmoil that accompanies our grief as fiercely as we possibly can. 'Have you been able to get rid of all your pain', Flaubert asks Feydeau. 'Did you manage to "roam the bitter pasture of your memories"? Did you manage to have a big orgy with all the sadness that you could put on display?'[67]

Interestingly, in advocating that his friend leave behind his sadness as quickly as possible, Flaubert appeals to Feydeau to serve the cause of Art and return to work. Only Art – not Life – is worthy of one's respect, Flaubert believes, and it is to that ideal that Feydeau needs to aspire:

> Still, in the name of the only respectable thing on earth, in the name of Beauty, hold on tight, with both your hands, jump furiously on your heels and get away from there! I know very well that we can find pleasure in pain and that we are able to enjoy crying. But it dissolves our soul as our tears melt away our spirit. Suffering becomes a habit and a way of looking at life that renders life unbearable.[68]

However tempting it may be to wallow in sadness, Flaubert seems to be suggesting, there is a real danger that one becomes used to seeing life as a source of suffering. He therefore urges Feydeau to forget his distress and to aspire to a state of forgetfulness ('do not resist the idea of forgetting'[69]). It is here, in this very paragraph of his letter of non-consolation, that Flaubert refers to the religious conviction that Geoffrey Braithwaite considered his wife to be lacking in: 'People like us need the religion of Despair', Flaubert reminds Feydeau. Despair, here, is the opposite of hope, the ideal that lies behind ideas of consolation such as those of George Sand, the hope that things will get better at one point. The problem, for Flaubert, is double: not only is man's belief in that ideal frustrated on a near-daily basis, but also, and more importantly, it teases us out of the state of indifference that Flaubert considers essential in order to survive. Geoffrey Braithwaite is definitely right in one thing about Flaubert: he is 'a man whose stoicism runs as deep as his pessimism'.[70] Fate behaves in a way that is fundamentally indifferent to us, Flaubert claims in his letter to Feydeau, therefore we should act accordingly and return the favour: 'Mankind needs to keep pace with Destiny, that is, it has to become equally indifferent.'[71]

The ideal of indifference (*impassibilité, apatheia*) is also that which presides over Flaubert's poetics, as we know well: 'An author in his book', as he put it in one his earliest and most famous expressions of this ideal, 'must be like God in the universe, present everywhere and visible nowhere'.[72] In life, Flaubert often found it very hard to arrive at that state of indifference, but in his writing – which served as an instrument in his struggle with Life – all his stylistic efforts were directed at making himself unheard and unseen in the text at hand, as we can also see in his correspondence with Sand of winter 1875. In his reply to what he describes as Sand's 'good letter of the 18th, so affectionate and maternal',[73] Flaubert begins by writing that he is not sure that he understood her denunciation of his desolate writing well enough. He asks for further clarification, but retorts at the same time:

> I don't 'go in for desolation' wantonly: please believe me! But I can't change my eyes! As for my 'lack of conviction', alas! I'm only too full of convictions. I'm constantly bursting with suppressed anger and indignation. But my ideal of Art demands that the artist reveal none of this, and that he appear in his work no more than God in nature. The man is nothing, the work is everything! This discipline, which may be based on a false premise, is not easy to observe. And for me, at least, it's a kind of perpetual sacrifice that I make to good taste. It would be very agreeable for me to say what I think, and relieve M. Gustave Flaubert's feelings by means of such utterances; but of what importance is the aforesaid gentleman?[74]

In producing literature, Flaubert is, as he puts it, above all trying to write well: 'I try to think well *in order* to write well. But my aim is to write well – I don't conceal that.'[75] Unlike that of Sand, his goal is not, so we are expected to surmise, to convince readers to adopt this or that viewpoint. He wants his readers to decide for themselves which conclusions they want to draw from what they read, and he wants them, above all, to adopt an aesthetic stance in judging his work. In order to write well, Flaubert is convinced that the author should 'appear in his work no more than God in nature', a distinct echo of what he wrote almost a quarter of a century earlier in one of his oft-quoted letters to Louise Colet.

Sand, of course, disagrees. In her lengthy response of 12 January 1876, she claims that she just cannot understand how a man like Flaubert, who in real life proves to be blessed with a 'graceful and simple kindness', feels the need to become a different person when he is writing: '[A]s soon as you're dealing with literature', she writes,

> you insist for some reason or other on being a different person, one who has to disappear or even annihilate himself – one who doesn't exist! What a strange obsession! What misguided 'good taste'! Our work can never be better than we are ourselves. (. . .) If a writer conceals his opinion of his characters, and so leaves the reader uncertain what *he*'s to make of them, then that writer is asking to be misunderstood, and the reader is bound to abandon him. For if your reader is to want to understand the story you're telling him, he must be shown clearly which of the characters are supposed to be strong and which are supposed to be weak.[76]

In the remainder of the letter she points out what to her is the inevitable consequence of Flaubert's indifferent authorial stance – that his work is misunderstood. Once more, she refers to Flaubert's latest novel:

> *L'Éducation sentimentale* was misunderstood. I kept telling you, but you wouldn't listen. It needed either a short preface, or some expression of disapproval, if only a significant word here or there, to condemn evil, call weakness by its right name, and draw attention to endeavour. All the characters in the book are weak and come to nothing except those whose instincts are evil: that's the criticism people make, because they haven't understood that your intention was precisely to depict a deplorable society which encourages bad instincts and ruins noble efforts. But when we are misunderstood it is always our own fault. What the reader wants most of all is to be able to grasp what we think; but you loftily refuse to comply.[77]

As Sand sees it, Flaubert's unmistakable presence as an author would not only have prevented him from being misunderstood, it would also have enabled him to do what she considers her moral duty: not to limit the writer's sketch of society to manifestations of what she calls the human 'sewer',[78] but 'to perceive how everything, tangible or intangible, constantly gravitates towards the necessity of goodness, kindness, truth and beauty'.[79] She rounds off with a final appeal to her friend: 'return to true reality, which is made up of a mixture of good and evil, bright and dull; but in which the desire for good nevertheless has a place and a use'.[80]

In his reply of 6 February, Flaubert makes clear – once more! – that he is not interested in writing for the sort of reader that Sand portrays in her letter. The right kind of reader, so he thinks, does not require any pointers in this or that direction from the author. 'If the reader doesn't draw from a book the moral it implies, either the reader is an imbecile or the book a sham, in that it lacks authenticity', Flaubert claims somewhat haughtily.[81] At this point in their correspondence, Flaubert and Sand appear to be engaged in a dialogue of the deaf, in which each participant seems increasingly reluctant to concede a point. Flaubert cannot but come to the inevitable conclusion, he writes:

> here, I think, is the essential difference between us. You, always, in whatever you do, begin with a great leap towards heaven, and then you return to earth. You start from the *a priori*, from theory, from the ideal. Hence your forbearing attitude towards life, your serenity, your – to use the only word for it – your greatness. I, poor wretch, remain glued to the earth, as though the soles of my shoes were made of lead: everything disturbs me, everything lacerates and ravages me, though I make every effort to soar. If I tried to assume your way of looking at the world I'd become a mere laughing-stock. For no matter what you preach to me, I can have no temperament other than my own. Nor any aesthetic other than the one that proceeds from it.[82]

However, as Wendy Deutelbaum has argued, while in their correspondence Sand and Flaubert continue to occupy 'opposite poles', in the literary works they produce 'they sometimes inhabit some more complex middle ground'.[83] Deutelbaum's point is corroborated, I feel, by 'Un cœur simple', the story that Flaubert announces in his letter of 6 February and at which I now want to take a closer look. The story, as we will see, is also central in Geoffrey Braithwaite's narrative, having provided Julian Barnes with the title of the novel that centres around Geoffrey's struggle with the imposing figure of the hermit of Croisset.

### 'Un Cœur Simple'

'You will see from my *Histoire d'un cœur simple* (in which you will recognize your own direct influence) that I am not as obstinate as you think', Flaubert wrote to Sand in what ended up being his last letter to her. 'I believe you will like the moral tendency, or rather the underlying humanity, of this little work.'[84] Whether or not Sand ever received the message is unclear, as she was in the painful process of losing her final battle with life at the time. She definitely never got to read 'Un cœur simple', which Flaubert finished at one o'clock in the morning of 16 August 1876.[85] Although he was still struggling with the story's opening page around the middle of March,[86] Flaubert was finally able to round off his 'Histoire d'un cœur simple' some five months later. 'I will probably have finished it in two months' time', as he told his actress-friend Edma Roger des Genettes in a letter of 19 June, in which he also gives an account of George Sand's funeral. There was a huge crowd, Flaubert writes from his home in Croisset: 'A crowd of good country folk muttered its prayers, fidgeting with their rosaries. It resembled a chapter of one of her books.'[87] The funeral service seems to have been a catholic one, contrary to Sand's wishes, but Flaubert is happy to say that there was no priest around when Sand died, 'perfectly impenitent', as he puts it. It rained heavily, as the author of 'Un cœur simple' recalls. He cried excessively, embracing 'la petite Aurore', Sand's beloved granddaughter, as he was looking at his old friend's coffin.

In the same letter to Edma Roger des Genettes, Flaubert offers a good account of what, according to him, 'Un cœur simple' is about and what his goal in writing the story has been all along:

> *L'histoire d'un cœur simple* is quite simply the story of an obscure life, the life of a poor country girl, devout but not in any mystical way, devoted without being exalted and tender as a fresh loaf of bread. Her love goes out, successively, to a man, the children of the woman she works for, a nephew, an old man whom she takes care of, and then her parrot. When the parrot dies, she has the animal stuffed. As she is dying herself, she confounds the parrot with the Holy Ghost. In no way have I meant this to be ironical, as you might think; on the contrary, it is very serious and very sad. I want to provoke pity and make sensitive souls cry, being one myself.[88]

In another letter, written over a month later, to yet another female friend, Flaubert mentions that while he is writing the story his writing desk is adorned with a stuffed parrot, 'obtained', as Enid Starkie tells us, 'from the Museum in Rouen'.[89] The author needed the animal, Starkie adds, so 'that he could describe its appearance at any hour of the day'.[90] As Flaubert puts it himself, he had borrowed the stuffed animal 'to fill my brain with the idea of a parrot'.[91] But after three weeks, the sight of 'the Amazone' was getting on his nerves. The dead bird kept looking at him, as he told his niece Caroline (22 July), 'with his glassy eyes'.[92]

This is how Julian Barnes, in the first chapter of *Flaubert's Parrot*, has Geoffrey Braithwaite give an outline of 'Un cœur simple'. Geoffrey has just seen Flaubert's parrot in the Musée Flaubert at Rouen's former Hôtel-Dieu – at least, that is how the animal is presented: 'Parrot borrowed by G. Flaubert from the Museum of Rouen and placed on his work-table during the writing of Un cœur simple, where it is called Loulou, the parrot of Félicité, the principal character in the tale'[93] – and he is on his way back to his hotel. Having just bought a copy of the book, Geoffrey provides us with a synopsis of the story, the specific phrasing of which already suggests that he feels for the heroine. 'Un cœur simple' is basically the story of a series of losses, Geoffrey feels, and of increasing isolation. It is a story with which, as a reader, he can easily identify:

> Perhaps you know the story. It's about a poor, uneducated servant-woman called Félicité, who serves the same mistress for half a century, unresentfully sacrificing her own life to those of others. She becomes attached, in turn, to a rough fiancé, to her mistress's children, to her nephew, and to an old man with a cancerous arm. All of them are casually taken from her: they die, or depart, or simply forget her. It is an existence in which, not surprisingly, the consolations of religion come to make up for the desolations of life.[94]

Like Félicité, Geoffrey seems to have led a life in the service of others. On top of that, he is also forgotten by some (his children) and left alone, if not by many, then at least by his wife. While he does not seem to share Félicité's religious devoutness, it soon becomes clear that he is on a pilgrimage of a different kind. In his first discussion of the story, however, Geoffrey does not seem to be aware of the similarity between his own situation and that of Félicité. The analogy, to him, is between the heroine of 'Un cœur simple' and the author who invented her. 'Both of them were solitary,' Geoffrey says, 'both of them had lived lives stained with loss; both of them, though full of grief, were persevering.'[95] As the reader of *Flaubert's Parrot* soon comes to see, though, the description also fits Geoffrey like a glove.

In the second of three 'chronologies' of Flaubert that make up the novel's second chapter, Barnes has Braithwaite focus on the countless deaths that marked the author's later life. The selection of the biographical materials tells us as much about the amateur biographer as about the person whose life is being written. As Flaubert confessed to Princesse Mathilde Bonaparte, the death of George Sand hurt him more than words could possibly say. 'My heart is becoming a necropolis', Flaubert wrote, 'that has some place left for a few people who are still living. How the void gets larger and larger! It seems to me that the earth is in the process of depopulating!'[96] Geoffrey also refers to the letter, but in quoting it, he significantly leaves out the passage in which Flaubert mentions the place that he continues to keep in his heart for the living. One of the sharp ironies of Geoffrey's story is that, unlike Flaubert, he seems to be unable (possibly unwilling, even) to relate to the living. 'Perhaps this is the advantage of making friends with those already dead', as he puts it just before his discovery, in Croisset, of the second parrot that, allegedly, also stood on Flaubert's writing desk in the spring and summer of 1876: 'Your feelings towards them never cool.'[97]

## Reader of Parrots

'Although Flaubert had intended "Un cœur simple" to be consoling', Enid Starkie writes in her discussion of the story in *Flaubert the Master*, 'it turns out to be basically as pessimistic as his other work. Its message is that all we are left with at the end, in spite of all our goodness and effort, is a moth-eaten stuffed parrot to act as the Holy Ghost.'[98] Given the strong feelings that he displays elsewhere against the late 'Reader Emeritus in French Literature at the University of Oxford',[99] it comes as quite a surprise that Geoffrey Braithwaite does not take Starkie to task for this apodictic conclusion. Where on earth does Dr Starkie get the idea that a Flaubert text can be reduced to a message (let alone that, in that case, *this* would be its message)? On which grounds, exactly, does she found her conviction that Flaubert wanted this story to be 'consoling'? And why does she preclude the possibility that a blatantly pessimistic story could have a consolatory effect on the reader? (Is 'Un cœur simple' *that* pessimistic?, one might add.)

Whether or not we are right in concluding that Starkie failed to understand Flaubert's story properly, Geoffrey's own appreciation of 'Un cœur simple' is decidedly more to the point. What the story shows above all, according to him, is the stylistic virtuosity of which it is the outcome. 'The control of tone is vital', as Geoffrey puts it admiringly:

> Imagine the technical difficulty of writing a story in which a badly-stuffed bird with a ridiculous name ends up standing in for one third of the Trinity, and in which the intention is neither satirical, sentimental, nor blasphemous.[100]

The latter part of the quotation echoes Flaubert's injunction that the story should definitely not be mistaken for an exercise in irony. His life of Félicité, the author stated emphatically in his letter of 19 June to Edma Roger des Genettes, was 'very serious and very sad'.[101]

Interestingly, when Geoffrey tries to describe what Loulou means to Félicité, he makes use of terminology that comes close to Winnicott's understanding of the effect of transitional objects.[102] Given his broad cultural and intellectual frame of reference (he mentions Nabokov and Anthony Powell, among others), Braithwaite may well be familiar with the work of the famous British psychoanalyst, to which I will return more properly in the next chapter. 'The final object in Félicité's ever-diminishing chain of attachments', he calls the parrot. Several details in Flaubert's story underline the analogy that is of interest here. As soon as Félicité lays eyes on it, the animal begins to occupy her imagination.[103] Coming from America, the parrot reminds her of her favourite nephew, who had left as a sailor and died there ('it came from America, a word which always reminded her of Victor').[104] Loulou is also a reminder of Félicité's attachment to Madame Aubain, the mistress she served for the majority of her life. While the narrator of Flaubert's story makes clear more than once that the servant has every reason to dislike her mistress, Félicité remains loyal to her in every sense of that word. The parrot was given to Madame Aubain as a souvenir by one of her upper-class friends, but as soon as it began to annoy her, she gave it to her servant, 'pour toujours', as the narrator adds in the original.[105] Félicité takes care of the parrot, lovingly, as if it were the child or the lover that she never had ('In her isolation, Loulou was almost a son to her; she simply doted on him').[106]

Towards the end of the story – somehow inevitably, given that the narrative of 'Un cœur simple' is driven by a succession of deaths – Loulou also dies. Having followed Madame Aubain's advice to have the animal stuffed, Félicité puts Loulou in a central position in her room, which the narrator describes as follows: 'This room, which few were allowed into, was filled with a mixture of religious knick-knacks and other miscellaneous bits and pieces and resembled something between a chapel and a bazaar.'[107] There, the animal functions as a reminder of past times, both happy and sad: 'Every morning, as she woke, she would catch sight of him in the early morning light and would recall the days gone by, trivial incidents, right down to the tiniest detail, remembered not in sadness but in perfect tranquility.'[108]

Understandably, since Félicité is a very devout woman, Loulou also quite soon becomes a comforter in the religious sense of the word. On one of her daily visits to church, she notices a similarity between her parrot and the representation of the Holy Ghost in one of the church windows. In Félicité's mind, the similarity soon develops into a distinct sense of identity. After she has bought an 'Epinal colour print' of the Holy Ghost to adorn her room, the image and the animal become one. The process is self-evident from the perspective of Félicité, as the narrator suggests, 'the parrot becoming sanctified by connection with the Holy Spirit and the Holy Spirit in turn acquiring added life and meaning.'[109] It makes sense, Félicité feels, that God opted for 'one of Loulou's ancestors' to symbolise the Holy Spirit rather than 'a dove'.[110] 'Logic is certainly on her side', Geoffrey Braithwaite adds: 'parrots and Holy Ghosts can speak, whereas doves cannot.'[111] There is further logic, I would add, in the fact that the Holy Ghost is traditionally seen as a comforter (*paraklètos*), as we can see, for instance, in Dr Johnson's *Dictionary*.[112]

When Madame Aubain dies, there is the threatening possibility that Félicité has to leave the house she has served in for almost her entire life. The prospect of having to abandon her room – 'it was the perfect place for poor Loulou'[113] – saddens her so that she begs the Holy Spirit for help, kneeling down before the stuffed parrot in what the narrator cannot but refer to as '[an] idolatrous habit'.[114] Living alone in the empty and abandoned house that fails to be sold, she finally catches pneumonia. Almost in tandem with Félicité's own deteriorating health, the stuffed Loulou's material shape also wears down. 'One of his wings was broken and the stuffing was coming out of his stomach', as the narrator puts it.[115] The description is reminiscent of Winnicott's occasional reference to teddy bears and other cuddly toys that retain their function even after they have lost a limb or an eye. Even in this dilapidated form the parrot retains its original force for the ailing Félicité, and it continues to do so to the very end. When that final moment comes, Félicité has the vision on which the story ends – the Holy Spirit, in the inevitable shape of a giant parrot, comes to welcome her heavenwards: 'With her dying breath she imagined she saw a huge parrot hovering above her head as the heavens parted to receive her.'[116]

Of course, the parrot – Flaubert's, not Félicité's, in this case – is a transitional object for Geoffrey too. Whereas in the mind of Félicité Loulou represents the religious powers of the Holy Ghost, Geoffrey Braithwaite takes the parrot for what at the occasion of his first encounter with the stuffed animal he calls 'an emblem of the writer's voice'.[117] In the same way that, as Geoffrey puts it, 'Félicité found consolation in her assembly of stray objects, united only by their owner's affection', he himself finds comfort in the items that he sees on display in the little pavilion in Croisset, the only remains of Flaubert's house. Among these objects are a tumbler from which Flaubert is said to have taken a sip of water just before he died and a handkerchief with which, as Geoffrey says, he allegedly 'mopped his brow in perhaps the last gesture of his life'.[118] 'Such ordinary props', he adds, 'made me feel I had been present at the death of a friend'.[119]

In the novel's closing chapter, Geoffrey returns to what Flaubert's parrot has come to mean to him. '[T]o Félicité, it was a grotesque but logical version of the Holy Ghost', he says, 'to me, a fluttering, elusive emblem of the writer's voice.'[120] To the owner of Loulou, the parrot was a force of stability, the material shape of the certainty that comes with faith and, thence, the purveyor of religious consolation. For Geoffrey, however, Flaubert's parrot proves 'elusive', as he says, the more so once he discovers that there is no way of proving (except by some or other leap of faith) which of the two 'original' parrots that he saw in Rouen and Croisset were actually standing on Flaubert's writing desk as he was working on the story of Félicité and Loulou. Does it *really* matter? It would seem to do from the perspective of Geoffrey, for whom the writer's voice, however elusive or fluttering, turns out to be a guiding force in his frantic search for meaning. Whether that meaning is an actual source of comfort remains for Geoffrey to say. But read in conjunction with the epistolary discussion between Flaubert and Sand that we have been looking at in this chapter, Geoffrey's story may help us to understand more properly how bibliotherapy – defined, here, as a search for literary consolation – works.

The actual outcome of the bibliotherapeutic process lies beyond the scope of Barnes' novel. Is Geoffrey really helped in his struggle with grief? *Flaubert's Parrot* ends before we can tell, and it does so in an open way that precludes an educated guess. However, the outline of Geoffrey Braithwaite's story does sketch a reading situation that differs significantly from those that I identified in my earlier analyses of the accounts that Joseph Luzzi and Katharine Smyth, among others, gave of their comfort reading. In their cases, as we could see, the guiding presence of the writer (Dante and Virginia Woolf, respectively) was made possible by a proper balance between the right amount of identification these readers could forge between their own situations and those portrayed in the books at hand, and an equally right amount of distance that not only kept reminding them that books are somehow different from life but also that, on the basis of that distance, the possibility of change could be revealed to their depressed minds.

The problem with Geoffrey's reading of Flaubert may well be that he identifies too strongly with what he sees as the author's voice. He is clearly craving for Flaubert's wisdom, the accuracy of which he also takes for granted. Flaubert is a master, for Geoffrey, endowed with the authority of what Lacan calls a 'sujet supposé savoir' ['subject supposed to know'], the sort of authority that, as we saw, Flaubert felt uncomfortable with: 'As for revealing my own opinion of the people I bring on stage', he wrote to George Sand on 6 February 1876, 'no, no! a thousand times no! I don't recognize my *right* to do so.'[121] The readerly position that Geoffrey is after seems better served by the sort of author that Sand aims to be, a moral prophet, bringer of the right sort of message, bringer of consolation.

## The Limits of Bibliotherapy

'You can define a net in one of two ways', Geoffrey Braithwaite quips in one of his more philosophical moments. 'Normally, you would say that it is a meshed instrument designed to catch fish. But you could, with no great injury to logic, reverse the image and define a net as a jocular lexicographer once did: he called it a collection of holes tied together with string.'[122] The discussion between Sand and Flaubert that we have looked at suggests that something similar could be said of 'consolation'. George Sand's perspective offers a positive definition, which sees consolation as an attempt (successful or not) to attune oneself to the fundamental ambiguities of life, accepting the realities of pain and loss without losing sight of the possibilities of joy and love. Flaubert's more sceptical perspective, by contrast, labels consolation as wishful thinking, the patching up of a problem instead of its solution.

Those who hunger for an art that consoles, Flaubert argues, ultimately fall prey to the same illusion as religious believers: they crave a palliative or even a sedative that prevents them from experiencing life as it is. The only real solution for Flaubert, as we have seen, is to stare despair in the face and to continue writing. After Sand's death, as he told Madame Roger des Genettes, memories of his friendship with the great writer 'made [him] review the course of [his] life'. '[Y]our friend has become more stoical during the past year', Flaubert writes. 'In short, after an afternoon given over to days gone by I *willed* myself to think of them no longer, and went back to work.'¹²³ The passage echoes the letter to Ernest Feydeau in which Flaubert first talks about his 'religion of Despair'. That letter – to which I referred earlier – is followed a month later by another one, in which Flaubert asks his friend how things are going ('Are you a little less sad?'¹²⁴). Adding yet another injunction for Feydeau to keep working – 'Life is short and Art long!', Flaubert exclaims – he ends his letter with a telling story about Socrates, who still wanted to learn to play the lyre on the eve of his death.¹²⁵ 'What good is that?', the philosopher's fellow prisoners wondered. 'To have known it before I die', Socrates replied. 'Truly, this is one of the most morally elevated things I have ever heard', Flaubert writes. 'I would have preferred having said this to having captured Sébastopol.'¹²⁶

By extolling Art's truth over life's worthless illusions, Flaubert, as we will see in the next chapter, runs the risk of being taken for a mere aesthete, not so much a believer in the religion of Despair as an apostle for a new religion of Style. Whether or not it is correct or fair, the criticism is understandable. But it does fail to appreciate the extent to which Flaubert remained focused on the representation of what in his letter to Ernest Feydeau he called 'the black pit'. Interestingly, the term returns in one of Flaubert's later letters to Madame Roger des Genettes. Its date is uncertain – sometime in 1861, apparently.¹²⁷ In it, Flaubert sings the praise of Lucretius, whose work provides him with an occasion to compare the worldview of Antiquity with that of modernity. Flaubert favours the former, obviously. 'The melancholy of the ancient world', he writes, 'seems to me more profound than that of the moderns, all of whom more or less imply that beyond the dark void lies immortality. But for the ancients that "black hole" was infinity itself; their dreams loom and vanish against a background of immutable ebony. No crying out, no convulsions – nothing but the fixity of a pensive gaze.'¹²⁸ That gaze is the gaze of indifference (*impassibilité*), in matters philosophical as well as aesthetic.

While Flaubert's correspondence with George Sand seems to suggest that the very idea that his work could be framed as consoling was beyond him, passages like these ally him quite closely with ancient theories of comfort, the Stoic variety most notably, provided that it be tinged with a sufficient degree of scepticism. What he dislikes about Lucretius, he confesses to Edma Roger des Genettes, is 'that he didn't *doubt* enough that he is weak: he wanted to explain, to conclude'.¹²⁹ Overt didacticism and opinionated certainty, as his discussion with Sand shows, is not the stuff of Flaubert's art.

There are, as we have seen, other ways of framing the opposing definitions of our key concept. Some define consolation as diversion, the (temporary) escape from pain, while others limit their use of the word to actions and experiences that enable them to confront the feelings of pain and loss that define life and learn from them. While there is no intrinsic reason to prefer one definition over the other – the experience of pain is wide enough to contain both meanings of consolation, to paraphrase Valéry[130] – the inclination to value the latter one more greatly and to consider 'diversion' as not truly consoling is apparently not always that easy to avoid. This is clearly the case in the book by Michaël Fœssel to which I have been referring in the previous chapter. As Fœssel puts it:

> The hypothesis according to which consolation (both as a need and as a practice) has a positive ethical significance gains in credibility the moment when we distinguish between consolation and diversion. While the latter boils down to an act of escapism that leaves our anxiety untouched, the former confronts our loss in an attempt to change its perception. Even if the act of consolation does not put an end to our suffering, it does give us something new, a kind of supplement to our unhappiness. More precisely, while the person who delivers comfort is not capable of bringing back what we lost, he does give us something else.[131]

As the last sentence of this quotation suggests, Fœssel's belief in a supreme form of consolation seems to be inspired by Freud's analysis of the work of mourning in 'Trauer und Melancholie'. True consolation goes together with a healthy form of grief in which the mourner eventually manages to accept the loss of the loved and move on with their life without having the feeling that the process involves a form of betrayal towards the loved one. What Freud sees as a less healthy form of grief – melancholy, in the oppositional scheme of the essay – is marked, as we have seen in our analysis of *Hamlet*, by a distinct resistance to accept the loss incurred, Patricia de Martelaere's 'desire to remain inconsolable'. As Fœssel puts it: 'the melancholic pretends to know what he has lost: that certainty renders him deaf to all possible consolations.'[132]

While Fœssel's conclusion seems apt in the case of Hamlet's mourning, Geoffrey Braithwaite seems to be a different type of *inconsolé*. He is far from pretending to know what he has lost. On the contrary even: the secret behind his wife's death is a truth which his obsessive interest in Flaubert enables him to keep deferring. Geoffrey's 'Trauerarbeit' is hardly over at the end of Barnes' novel. Halfway through *Flaubert's Parrot*, we may consider it still likely that Geoffrey's obsession with the author of *Madame Bovary* will enable him to finally confront the truth behind his wife's suicide. 'Three stories contend within me', Geoffrey says at one point in the book's seventh chapter, '[o]ne about Flaubert, one about Ellen, one about myself.'[133] The second story is the hardest to tell, he admits, but also the one which he needs his audience to be prepared for, in the double sense of that word:

> by the time I tell you her story I want you to be prepared: that's to say, I want you to have had enough of books, and parrots, and lost letters, and bears, and the opinions of Dr Enid Starkie, and even the opinions of Dr Geoffrey Braithwaite.

The remaining sentences of the paragraph already make it doubtful that the hoped-for confrontation will follow. 'Books are not life,' Geoffrey goes on to say, 'however much we might prefer it if they were. Ellen's is a true story; perhaps it is even the reason why I am telling you Flaubert's story instead.'[134]

The capital word is 'instead', obviously, even though Geoffrey's recurrent use of 'perhaps' and other hedging modifiers – 'the hesitating narrator' he calls himself[135] – is also striking. Geoffrey's anecdotes about Flaubert continue to defer his wife's story, even in the novel's thirteenth chapter, which begins, nevertheless, with the suggestion that the pure truth of Ellen Braithwaite will finally be revealed. But even here, Geoffrey's love for 'the hermit of Croisset' manages to reduce the retired doctor to silence when it comes to the secret life of the wife whom he describes, significantly, as 'someone I feel I understand less well than a foreign writer dead for a hundred years'.[136] 'Is this an aberration, or is it normal?', he wonders. Since the question is a rhetorical one, it can do without an answer. Instead, Geoffrey offers a further reflection in which he returns to the difference between Art and Life that Flaubert proclaimed as the central foundation of his poetics. At this point in the novel, however, the dogma in question clearly undercuts whatever therapeutic effect the reading of Flaubert may have on this specific reader. Geoffrey's conclusion makes sense, no doubt, but not the sort of sense upon which bibliotherapy is founded:

> Books say: she did this because. Life says: she did this. Books are where things are explained to you; life is where things aren't. I'm not surprised some people prefer books. Books make sense of life. The only problem is that the lives they make sense of are other people's lives, never your own.

What Geoffrey describes, here, as a fundamental problem is the actual foundation of many successful forms of bibliotherapy: readers learn from books not in spite of the fact that they make sense of other people's lives, but *because* they do. Bibliotherapy involves making sense of your own problems through the interpretation of other people's problems. It is by understanding their problems as not dissimilar but not fully identical to your own that you begin to see your own problems in new and productive ways. Such an understanding requires an act of negotiation – an interpretive dynamic that is opened up by the recognition of likeness *and* difference, as we saw in the example of Joseph Luzzi's reading memoir and as we will continue to see in the next chapter. While it could be said that this is indeed what Flaubert's work has in store for Geoffrey, this reader's mind is too much set on identification, driven by the strictest of analogies between life and art. For this sort of reader, Flaubert may well be one of the worst possible guides. One of the many ironies of Barnes' novel is that in this respect Geoffrey Braithwaite would probably have been served better by the Ambulance George Sand.

## Notes

1. Barnes, *Flaubert's Parrot*, 168.
2. Barnes, *Flaubert's Parrot*, 95.
3. Barnes, *Flaubert's Parrot*, 13.
4. Barnes, *Flaubert's Parrot*, 166.
5. 'Post-menopausal' he calls it: Barnes, *Flaubert's Parrot*, 180.
6. Barnes, *Flaubert's Parrot*, 181.
7. Barnes, *Flaubert's Parrot*, 164.
8. Barnes, *Flaubert's Parrot*, 103.
9. Barnes, *Flaubert's Parrot*, 168.
10. The essay was first published in the *New York Review of Books* of 10 June 1993, as a review of the English translation of the Flaubert-Sand *Correspondance* (Knopf, 1993; translation by Francis Steegmuller and Barbara Bray); it was later collected in Julian Barnes, *Something to Declare*, 215–34.
11. Barnes, *Flaubert's Parrot*, 181.
12. Barnes, *Flaubert's Parrot*, 181.
13. Barnes, *Flaubert's Parrot*, 181.
14. The letter to Feydeau is dated 26 October 1859. I will come back to it later in this chapter. In what follows, references to Flaubert's letters are, as far as possible, to *The Letters of Gustave Flaubert: Volumes I and II (1830–1880)*, selected, edited and translated by Francis Steegmuller.

In the case of letters that are not included in Steegmuller's edition, I made my own translations of the French originals as found in Gustave Flaubert, *Correspondance*. References to the letters that Flaubert and Sand exchanged are to *Flaubert-Sand: The Correspondence*, translated by Francis Steegmuller and Barbara Bray.

15. Barnes, *Flaubert's Parrot*, 181.
16. Barnes, *Flaubert's Parrot*, 180, 181.
17. Starkie, *Flaubert the Master*, 302.
18. Hutcheon herself gives Barnes' novel as an example (alongside Eco's *The Name of the Rose*, Fowles' *A French Lieutenant's Woman*, Doctorow's *Ragtime* and Rushdie's *Midnight's Children*) in *A Poetics of Postmodernism*, 44. See, also, Guignery, *The Fiction of Julian Barnes*, 43 and Lee, *Realism and Power*, 36. See also Guignery, '"My wife ... died": une mort en pointillé dans *Flaubert's Parrot* de Julian Barnes'; Bernard, '*Flaubert's Parrot*: le reliquaire mélancolique'.
19. Capet et al., 'Julian Barnes in Conversation', 126. The interview is also included in *Cercles*, 4, 2002, 255–69 and in Guignery and Roberts (eds), *Conversations with Julian Barnes*, 1010–14.
20. Barnes, *Levels of Life*, 102–3.
21. Interestingly, in *Levels of Life*, Barnes mentions that he read out a passage from *Flaubert's Parrot* at Pat Kavanagh's funeral. 'Nearly thirty years ago, in a novel, I tried to imagine what it would be like for a man in his sixties to be widowed.' However, as he goes on to say, '[m]y fictional widower had a different life – and love – from mine, and quite a different widowing.' Barnes, *Levels of Life*, 114–15.
22. See, for instance, *Flaubert's Parrot*, 164.
23. Barnes, *Flaubert's Parrot*, 166.
24. *The Letters of Gustave Flaubert*, 246 ('mon monsieur est d'une nature tempérée': Flaubert, *Correspondance*, II, 238).
25. The second one is that in which he rips apart (so to speak) Enid Starkie, who was convinced that she had exposed a number of mistakes in Flaubert's description of Emma Bovary's eyes. Barnes, *Flaubert's Parrot*, 74–5; the passage that provokes Geoffrey's ire can be found in Starkie, *Flaubert the Master*, 356. Geoffrey's criticism is not limited to Starkie's work, but also concerns what he calls her 'atrocious French accent (. . .) full of dame-school confidence and absolutely no ear, swerving between workaday correctness and farcical error, often within the same word' (74–5). It remains a mystery why Dr Braithwaite is so fiercely (and uncharacteristically) critical of Dr Starkie.
26. Barnes, *Flaubert's Parrot*, 38. Geoffrey is the first to reach for the book, but, as he puts it: 'I let him have the Turgenev, of course, if only to escape a discussion about the morality of possession' (39).
27. The aforementioned Edmond Ledoux even alleges that Juliet was Flaubert's 'fiancée' at one point. See Starkie, *Flaubert the Master*, 53. However, Starkie adds, '[i]t is impossible to know what [Juliet Herbert] was like and anything that is written about her can only be

invented.' The relationship between Flaubert and Juliet Herbert is the topic of Oliver, *Flaubert and an English Governess*. The French translation of Oliver's book is prefaced with an introduction by Julian Barnes.

28. This is the first mention of the narrator's name: Barnes, *Flaubert's Parrot*, 41.
29. Barnes, *Flaubert's Parrot*, 47.
30. Barnes, *Flaubert's Parrot*, 46–7.
31. Albeit not without making a final insulting remark – not, mind you, to Ed Winterton himself, but to the object of his biographical research: 'I think the remark I then made was deeply unfair to Mr Gosse both as a writer and as a sexual being; but I do not see how I could have avoided it' (Barnes, *Flaubert's Parrot*, 48).
32. Barnes, *Flaubert's Parrot*, 13.
33. Barnes, *Flaubert's Parrot*, 14.
34. Barnes, *Flaubert's Parrot*, 84.
35. See, for instance, Winock, *Flaubert*, 5.
36. Lottman, *Flaubert: A Biography*, 8. Barnes published a very critical review of Lottman's biography in the *London Review of* Books of 4 May 1989, later collected in *Something to Declare*, 147–53 (Section A of 'Flaubert's Death-Masks').
37. Barnes, *Flaubert's Parrot*, 15.
38. Barnes, *Flaubert's Parrot*, 15.
39. Barnes, Flaubert's Parrot, 136.
40. Barnes, *Flaubert's Parrot*, 136.
41. *Flaubert-Sand: The Correspondence*, 398.
42. *Flaubert-Sand: The Correspondence*, 400.
43. Barnes, *Something to Declare*, 232.
44. Geoffrey refers to the passage in Barnes, *Flaubert's Parrot*, 22, where it is transcribed slightly differently, without any apparent change of meaning, however: 'I had begun it solely on account of her, only to please her. She died while I was in the midst of this work. So it is with all our dreams.'
45. For an insightful analysis of the letters, see also Deutelbaum, 'Desolation and Consolation'.
46. The friendship between Sand and Flaubert is the subject of Tricotel, *Comme deux troubadours*. Had he known it, this is a book I'm sure Geoffrey Braithwaite would have liked a lot.
47. The portrait is reproduced in Starkie, *Flaubert the Master*, between pages 150 and 151.
48. See, for instance, Wall, *Flaubert: A Life*, 270. See also Starkie, *Flaubert the Master*, 95: Starkie quotes from Sand's account of the dinner in her *Journal*: 'Flaubert passionate and more sympathetic to me than the others, why I do not yet know.'
49. Winock, *Flaubert*, 465, 479, my translation.
50. *Flaubert-Sand: The Correspondence*, 272.

51. *Flaubert-Sand: The Correspondence*, 274. Also quoted in Wall, *Flaubert: A Life*, 321.
52. Starkie, *Flaubert the Master*, 96.
53. Winock, *Flaubert*, 373. Sand's biographers agree. Martine Reid, for one, labels their relationship 'epistolary for the main, of a rare quality', 'a true friendship'. Reid, *George Sand*, 290, 291, my translation. 'Few writers ever represented a more polar opposition', Joseph Barry comments: *George Sand ou le scandale de la liberté*, 463, my translation.
54. Wall, *Flaubert: A Life*, 269.
55. Wall, *Flaubert: A Life*, 269.
56. Barnes, 'Consolation v. Desolation', in *Something to Declare*, 218.
57. Barnes, *Flaubert's Parrot*, 16.
58. *Flaubert-Sand: The Correspondence*, 377. The little 'trifle', as I mentioned earlier, is 'La légende de Saint Julien Hospitalier', later to be part of Flaubert's *Trois contes*.
59. *Flaubert-Sand: The Correspondence*, 379.
60. *Flaubert-Sand: The Correspondence*, 379.
61. *Flaubert-Sand: The Correspondence*, 379 (emphasis by Sand).
62. *Flaubert-Sand: The Correspondence*, 379.
63. *Flaubert-Sand: The Correspondence*, 379.
64. *Flaubert-Sand: The Correspondence*, 379.
65. *Flaubert-Sand: The Correspondence*, 379 (emphasis by Sand).
66. Flaubert, *Correspondance*, III, 53, my translation.
67. Flaubert, *Correspondance*, III, 52, my translation.
68. Flaubert, *Correspondance*, III, 52, my translation.
69. Flaubert, *Correspondance*, III, 53, my translation.
70. Barnes, *Flaubert's Parrot*, 181.
71. Flaubert, *Correspondance*, III, 53, my translation.
72. Letter to Louise Colet, 9 December 1852: *The Letters of Gustave Flaubert*, 238.
73. The letter is dated 'about 31 December 1875'. *Flaubert-Sand: The Correspondence*, 380.
74. *Flaubert-Sand: The Correspondence*, 381.
75. *Flaubert-Sand: The Correspondence*, 381, emphasis by Flaubert. 'I aim at *Beauty* above all else', he adds.
76. *Flaubert-Sand: The Correspondence*, 385, emphasis by Sand.
77. *Flaubert-Sand: The Correspondence*, 385.
78. *Flaubert-Sand: The Correspondence*, 384.
79. *Flaubert-Sand: The Correspondence*, 383.
80. *Flaubert-Sand: The Correspondence*, 386.
81. *Flaubert-Sand: The Correspondence*, 388. 'For if a thing is True, it is good. Even obscene books are not immoral unless they lack truth. But that's not how it is in life' (388).
82. *Flaubert-Sand: The Correspondence*, 388.
83. Deutelbaum, 'Desolation and Consolation', 288.

84. *Flaubert-Sand: The Correspondence*, 398.
85. We know this from a letter that he wrote the day after to his niece Caroline, whom he addresses affectionately as 'mon Loulou', the very name given to the parrot that is a central presence in the story. Flaubert, *Correspondance*, V, 99, my translation.
86. Flaubert, *Correspondance*, V, 56, my translation.
87. Flaubert, *Correspondance*, V, 57, my translation.
88. Flaubert, *Correspondance*, V, 56–7, my translation.
89. The letter (to Léonie Brainne) is dated 28 July 1876 (Flaubert, *Correspondance*, V, 85). See also Starkie, *Flaubert the Master*, 258.
90. Starkie, *Flaubert the Master*, 258.
91. Flaubert, *Correspondance*, V, 86, my translation.
92. Flaubert, *Correspondance*, V, 78, my translation.
93. Barnes, *Flaubert's Parrot*, 16.
94. Barnes, *Flaubert's Parrot*, 16–17.
95. Barnes, *Flaubert's Parrot*, 17.
96. Letter of 19 June 1876. Flaubert, *Correspondance*, V, 56, my translation.
97. Barnes, *Flaubert's Parrot*, 21.
98. Starkie, *Flaubert the Master*, 260.
99. Barnes, *Flaubert's Parrot*, 74.
100. Barnes, *Flaubert's Parrot*, 17.
101. Flaubert, *Correspondance*, V, 57, my translation. 'George Sand's influence does not appear to have been decisive', writes Claude Tricotel (*Comme deux troubadours*, 221, my translation).
102. The central text is 'Transitional Objects and Transitional Phenomena' (1951), to be found in Winnicott, *Playing and Reality*. For a more thorough discussion of the concept see Chapter 5 of this book, pages 244–51.
103. Flaubert, *A Simple Heart*, trans. Roger Whitehouse. For the French original, see 'Un cœur simple', in *Oeuvres* II.
104. Flaubert, *A Simple Heart*, 39.
105. Flaubert, 'Un cœur simple', 613.
106. Flaubert, *A Simple Heart*, 43.
107. Flaubert, *A Simple Heart*, 46.
108. Flaubert, *A Simple Heart*, 47.
109. Flaubert, *A Simple Heart*, 48.
110. Flaubert, *A Simple Heart*, 48.
111. Barnes, *Flaubert's Parrot*, 17.
112. Johnson, *A Dictionary of the English Language*. The Greek word 'paraklètos' means 'advocate' rather than 'comforter'.
113. Flaubert, *A Simple Heart*, 50.
114. Flaubert, *A Simple Heart*, 51.
115. Flaubert, *A Simple Heart*, 53.
116. Flaubert, *A Simple Heart*, 56.
117. 'Perhaps that makes me as simple-minded as Félicité', he adds. Barnes, *Flaubert's Parrot*, 19.

118. Barnes, *Flaubert's Parrot*, 21.
119. Barnes, *Flaubert's Parrot*, 21.
120. Barnes, *Flaubert's Parrot*, 182–3.
121. *Flaubert-Sand: The Correspondence*, 388, emphasis by Flaubert.
122. Barnes, *Flaubert's Parrot*, 38.
123. *The Letters of Gustave Flaubert*, 616, emphasis by Flaubert.
124. Letter of 29 November 1859. Flaubert, *Correspondance*, III, 59, my translation.
125. Flaubert, *Correspondance*, III, 60, my translation.
126. Flaubert, *Correspondance*, III, 60, my translation.
127. Bruneau in the Pléiade edition gives the same vague, uncertain date: Flaubert, *Correspondance*, III, 191.
128. *The Letters of Gustave Flaubert*, 356.
129. *The Letters of Gustave Flaubert*, 356.
130. 'Et nous voyons maintenant que l'abîme de l'histoire est assez grand pour tout le monde.' Paul Valéry, 'La crise de l'esprit', 988.
131. Fœssel, *Le temps de la consolation*, 24.
132. Fœssel, *Le temps de la consolation*, 29.
133. Barnes, *Flaubert's Parrot*, 85–6.
134. Barnes, *Flaubert's Parrot*, 86.
135. Barnes, *Flaubert's Parrot*, 89.
136. Barnes, *Flaubert's Parrot*, 168.

Chapter 5

# Novels of Comfort: Woolf, Winnicott and the Work of Consolation

Perhaps there is one book for every life.
    One book with the power to reflect and illuminate that life; one book that will forever inform how we navigate the little strip of time we are given, while also helping us to clarify and catch hold of its most vital moments. For me, that book is *To the Lighthouse*, Virginia Woolf's novel about her parents, Julia and Leslie Stephen, who died when Virginia was thirteen and twenty-two, respectively. First published in 1927, it tells the story of the Ramsays, a family of ten who, along with an assorted group of friends, spends the summer on a remote island in the Hebrides. Tells the story of the Ramsays? I should rephrase: *To the Lighthouse* tells the story of everything.

Katharine Smyth, All the Lives We Ever Lived[1]

## Literature in Lockdown: Comfort Reading

'Our medicines are not something you'll find at the chemist', Ella Berthoud and Susan Elderkin write in their introduction to *The Novel Cure*, 'but at the bookshop, in the library, or downloaded onto your electronic reading device'.[2] Books, we should not forget, do not function in the way that pills are supposed to. They don't simply do their work once you've swallowed them whole. They require a specific mind-set in the reader, a willingness to interpret that goes beyond the idea that literary authors conceive of their writings as moral or other lessons that simply need to be put into practice. The books that bibliotherapists prescribe don't do the work for us. In that respect, bibliotherapy resembles the sort of psychotherapy in which the analyst is not intent upon giving answers to their patient, but by asking questions or making inquisitive suggestions means to guide the patient into finding their own answers. In the same way that they do not contain lessons to be simply applied, literary writings should not be considered by their readers as an author's answer to a given question (let alone to a reader's question), but as questions to which the reader is invited to discover their proper reply. 'The writer's work', as Proust famously said, 'is merely a kind of optical instrument which he offers to the reader to enable him to discern what, without this book, he would perhaps never have experienced in himself. And the recognition by the reader in his own self of what the book says is the proof of its veracity.'[3]

We tend to define literature – modern literature especially – in contra-distinction to the writings of authors whose primary aim is to give some or other form of advice or guidance. Of course, this in itself should not prevent readers from reading literary writings as if they were texts that offer moral guidance, as long as these readers realise that the difference between books and pharmaceutics, ultimately, comes with a warning: unlike 'regular', tested pills, books do not always have the curative effect readers hope for. Sometimes books are good for you, sometimes not. That, too, is a lesson Geoffrey Braithwaite could have learned from the author of *Madame Bovary*.[4]

The underlying chronology of this book's previous chapters – giving shape to a journey that lead us from Homer and Aristotle, through Boethius and Dante, to Shakespeare and, eventually, Flaubert – requires that the protagonists of the present chapter belong to a phase of the history of literature and poetics that comes after the great intervention of the latter's work. In the longer run of that history, Flaubert's impact turned out to be much greater than that of George Sand. In the decades after his death, the author of *Madame Bovary* and *Bouvard et Pécuchet* soon came to be seen as the godfather of Modernism, not only in France, but also internationally. His inspiration is notable in the work of several early twentieth-century giants: Joyce, Kafka, Proust, Svevo, Woolf.

Insofar as the previous chapters of this book provide an accurate outline of the joint histories of literature and consolation, the expectation at this point may well be that with Flaubert we have arrived at that grand narrative's (dead) end. Literature is literature, after all, and consolation is something different altogether. After Flaubert's decree that literature should first and foremost concentrate on being itself, the twain may well be expected no longer to meet. However, while in theory Flaubert's ideal of the autonomy of literature could easily have put an end to discussions of its comforting effects on readers, this is not what happened in practice. On the contrary, even: discussions of the consolatory nature of literary reading continued in the course of the twentieth century and in the first few decades of the twenty-first.

As it happens, the idea that literature brings consolation never seems to have been taken more as a given than it is today. In the weeks during which I am drafting this chapter, with the Covid-19 pandemic in full swing, most people remain locked inside their houses, with more time than ever to read books and worry. Even more so than before, it would seem, readers of all kinds, specialists and non-specialists alike, are sharing recommendations, both on social media and in magazines and newspapers, for what is commonly called 'comfort reading'.

In one of its weekly 'Bookmarks', the *Guardian* recently published a series of brief interventions in which a number of contemporary authors (Hilary Mantel, Max Porter, Alan Hollinghurst and Elif Shafak, among others) were being asked which books managed to comfort them in these difficult times. If their answers to the question are in any way representative, comfort reading appears to be provided best, in our long days of lockdown, by books that bring across messages of hope. Ideally, these books are tinged with a whiff of humour. Lockdown readers crave books that are generally considered 'uplifting': the word recurs throughout the series of interviews in the *Guardian*.

The same note strikes in a similar feature in the *New York Times*, where the interviewees – a group of American authors, this time – hold a plea for books that feed their readers with feelings of hope, equanimity and resilience, mainly. Incidentally, the newspaper's books service offers its readers the possibility to order a box of six classics of their series under the 'Uplifting' umbrella. The box contains titles that 'offer a welcome escape', the advertisement states, 'making for cozy reading that will make staying on your couch feel a little more like a choice' – and let you do a bit of world travelling without leaving home'.[5]

Interestingly, several of the interviewed authors in the *Guardian* and the *New York Times* also mention books that allow their readers to travel to different places and times. The appeal of 'novels of transport' is quite understandable: during times in which it is impossible to move around physically, we like to make long journeys in our minds. Historical novels, especially, seem to provide good comfort reading in that respect. As David Mitchell explains, novels that are set in the past remind us that despite our impression of being unique in unfortunate ways, we continue to be part of 'the human continuum', a chain of generations that is confronted, on and off, with minor and major crises, but which always proves resilient enough. 'In this time of crisis', Michiko Kakutani writes in a timely essay in the *New York Times* – 'Finding Solace, and Connection, in Classic Books' is the text's telling title – 'we are reminded that literature provides historical empathy and perspective, breaking through the isolation we feel hunkered down in our homes to connect us, across time zones and centuries, with others who once lived through not dissimilar events.'[6]

Reading the *Guardian* and *New York Times* interviews in tandem with the epistolary discussion that was central to this book's previous chapter, one might be tempted to conclude that George Sand's literature of hope must yield better results for most readers in their search for comfort reading than Flaubert's thorough yet disinterested analyses of human despair. While that may be so, we shouldn't forget that comfort reading is like comfort food (which is no doubt why we decided to call it so): we reach for it when we are in need of distraction. We know that the relief it will give us is temporary at best, but we also know that it will definitely make us feel better, if only for the time being. Like comfort food, comfort reading may not be really healthy, but it sure tastes good.

To be clear, the point that I'm trying to make, here, is in no way meant to slight the values of comfort reading. Even the most determined foodies are suckers for comfort food now and then. Montaigne, as we have seen – he is hardly the most superficial of guides – considered distraction a better strategy than most of the prescriptions found in classical consolatory writings. Likewise, in Boccaccio's *Decameron*, the consolatory function of storytelling is presented from the work's very beginning as an example of the idea that there is 'no better or more efficacious remedy against a plague than to run away from it'.[7] The comfort of diversion and distraction lies in the obvious fact that what causes you pain will then stop staring you in the face – for the time being, at least. But that is not the point, here.

My point, rather, is that Flaubert's literature of desolation ended up having a more 'positive' impact on the critical tradition of literary consolation than we would have expected on the basis of his denunciation of that tradition. As David James has shown, the example of Flaubert's modernist aesthetics lies behind the work of a new tradition in contemporary writing (of memoirs and novels, mainly) that tackles despair and desolation as realistically and dispassionately as possible, but still manages to do what in the subtitle of his book James calls 'the work of consolation'.[8] That work, to be clear, does not involve the soothing promise that things will get better, as in the Christian regime of consolation, but a direct and uncomfortably hard confrontation with the desolate reality of pain and suffering.

The idea that such a confrontation can be consoling rests on a framework that differs from that of Boethius and Dante in at least two respects. First, in the modern regime of comfort there is no longer a 'beyond' in which our losses will be truly repaired; hence the central presence in that regime of the notion of 'inconsolability'. While in the classical and Christian regimes people who cannot be consoled remain exceptions to be avoided, the figure that Michaël Fœssel calls the *inconsolé* is the iconic character of the modern regime, the norm rather than the exception. Secondly, in Dante's regime of comfort, the idea of beauty is a function of the metaphysical comfort that is in the hands of God. Beauty and consolation are intrinsically bound together, in this regime: that which is beautiful, is truly comforting. In the modern regime that we continue to look at in this chapter, the relationship between beauty and consolation comes under strain, to say the least. The soothing effect of beautiful things threatens to become a pseudo-solution for the insolvable problem of inconsolability. Beauty becomes an anaesthetic that covers up the reality of loss and despair, an all too comely form that prevents us from truly coming to terms with the chaos of our suffering.

As David James makes clear in the thought-provoking book at which I now want to take a closer look, the challenge for contemporary writers is to come up with a form of writing that, on the one hand, manages to address consolation without falling prey to the sort of critique that Flaubert levelled against George Sand, while on the other hand managing to escape the sort of critique that his own 'literature of desolation' began to provoke in later decades: did not Flaubert's celebration of the autonomy of style ultimately result in an empty consolation of form, some began to wonder,[9] a new religion in and of itself, with a consolation that turned out to be as hollow as that of the creed it tried to fight?

### Discrepant Solace

The writings of the authors that David James deals with in his book – David Grossman, J. M. Coetzee, Colm Tóibín, Joan Didion, and W. G. 'Max' Sebald are among the more famous – in no way qualify as the most obvious candidates for 'regular' comfort reading. Most of the works that are central to James' discussion deal with loss and grief, the sort of suffering that in itself can neither be solved nor forgotten. The loved one whom we have lost cannot return and neither can we simply divert our attention from their absence. The sort of comfort reading that we have just discussed and that provides temporary relief, is not really helpful in these cases.

What James refers to as 'the work of consolation' is related to the 'work of mourning' in the modern, Freudian sense of the word. What Freud labelled 'Trauerarbeit' aptly illustrates the modern idea of 'inconsolability', as I earlier made clear with reference to the work of the Flemish philosopher Patricia de Martelaere: the work of mourning begins with the desire not to be consoled, De Martelaere explains, since to a certain extent we do not want to move 'beyond' our love for the lost one. To be consoled would mean to give up the beloved, Freud suggested in 'Trauer und Melancholie'. In a later letter to Ludwig Binswanger (11 April 1929), he explains the mechanism further:

> Although we know that after such a loss the acute state of mourning will subside, we also know we shall remain inconsolable and will never find a substitute. No matter what may fill the gap, even if it be filled completely, it nevertheless remains something else. And actually this is how it should be. It is the only way of perpetuating that love which we do not want to relinquish.[10]

The challenge for authors writing novels or memoirs of grief is clear, in this respect: they need to come up with a form that addresses the reality of suffering in a way that does not feel like a comfortable cover-up for the pain that the loss induced. The ensuing work of art should in no way claim the status of substitute; it has to address the gap that Freud mentions, without presuming to fill it, let alone cover it up. Fortunately, as James reminds us, 'literature may not need to be comforting or dangerously distracting for it to be tangibly consoling'.[11]

Given his book's purpose, it makes sense that James insists on what he considers the need to distinguish between 'comfort' and 'consolation'. The former notion, to his mind, smacks too much of ease and complacency to be usefully related to the sort of suffering that is central to the texts he discusses. In a discussion of modern and contemporary writings, it is quite understandable that one would like to avoid the connotation between comfort and relative effortlessness; however, when Dante and Boccaccio refer to 'conforto' or Shakespeare talks of 'comfort', that connotation is not there, not yet at least, which is why I have treated the words 'comfort' and 'consolation' as non-problematically synonymous in the previous chapters.

The all too comforting connotation of 'comfort' appears to be present – if more latently – in the word 'consolation' as well. 'Hence consolation's hazy reputation in life as in art', James writes: it too, if more marginally, belongs to the vocabulary of idealism, somehow inevitably making promises that in the eye of most realists are naive. To them, the word seems to signal what Flaubert resented in George Sand's plea for a 'literature of consolation' – it threatens to function as what James calls 'a fable recasting what cannot be put right as something that might still be overcome'.[12] In the case of grief, more specifically, it threatens to cover up the loss in ways that run counter to the existential nature of the experience. Referring, in the epilogue to his book, to Freud's essay on 'Creative Writers and Day-Dreaming', James points out that literary texts (and other artistic products) may well, on the basis of what Freud calls their 'formal – that is, aesthetic – yield of pleasure', induce in readers this self-deluded form of consolation that the writers whose work features centrally in *Discrepant Solace* succeed in avoiding.[13] As James puts it in the introduction to his book:

> To be consoled in this way is to betray the very losses that dispose us to distraction. To allow oneself to be soothed in the eye of grief's storm is to diminish distress by self-deception. To seek refuge in visualizing how blighted events could otherwise have transpired is to entertain stories of speculation that deceive rather than edify, that threaten to attenuate the love for what we have lost, that coax us to retreat from the inexorable turbulence of experience altogether.[14]

The word that James prefers to use throughout his book is 'solace'. It shares the same Latin root (*solari*, 'to soothe') with 'consolation', for which it functions, therefore, as a near synonym (indeed, James uses them interchangeably at times). 'Solace', however, seems to have the advantage that it does not provoke the other word's immediate idealistic connotations. That is definitely the case in James' guiding notion, which also serves as his book's title: 'discrepant solace'. The phrase serves as a shorthand for the specific contribution which the authors who are central to James' book make to the history that I have outlined in the previous chapters: these authors continue Boethius' and Dante's search for a literary form that acknowledges man's need for consolation, while at the same time stressing – in contrast to the representatives of what I called the classical and Christian regimes of consolation – that this need is literally insatiable (to borrow, once more, Stig Dagerman's powerful description of the modern experience of consolation[15]).

To be clear, *Discrepant Solace* does not take the same broad historical perspective that I have taken in this book, even though James at times reminds his readers that different eras and cultures think differently about consolation.¹⁶ As I have indicated, the focus throughout James' book is on literature of the late twentieth and early twenty-first centuries, on the work of writers, more specifically, who, as we read on the book's inside cover, 'engage with consolation not as an aesthetic salve but as an enduring problematic'. In his book, James continues to shy away from the pseudo-medical jargon that one finds in bibliotherapeutic guides such as *The Novel Cure*: the writings that are central to *Discrepant Solace*, he points out in his introduction, '[p]rovid[e] few lasting tranquilizers'.¹⁷

The texts that James singles out for closer inspection do not lend themselves so easily to the assertive type of thematic interpretations with which *The Novel Cure* abounds. 'While you let the prose of this novel do its work on your troubled psyche, notice how turmoil coexists with calm in the world it describes', Ella Berthoud and Susan Elderkin typically claim in their prescription of a novel by Marilynne Robinson, an author who also features in James' book.¹⁸ The sentence exemplifies the money-back guarantee rhetoric that sustains the prescriptions of *The Novel Cure*, not only with respect to the effect that Robinson's prose will have on its every reader – 'your inner turmoil will be calmed'¹⁹ – but also with respect to what consolation is, always and ever: soothing. Unlike Berthoud and Elderkin, James is not so much interested in the actual effects which texts have on their readers. His question is not, as he puts it, 'whether literature today fortifies or assuages readers more effectively than at other points in its history'.²⁰ Warning potential readers of *Discrepant Solace* that they 'will find few soothers in this book', James intends to exchange the traditional 'calmative' conception of consolation with one in which the concept functions as 'an agent of contestation, one that signals rather than mitigates the implications of traumatic eloquence'.²¹ 'What might it mean', he wonders, 'to think of solace not as a phenomenon we estimate with rough calculations of how readers emotionally react to diegetic illustrations of consolation (or its privation and inadequacy), but as an affective state staged by the formal components of literary works themselves'.²²

The discrepancy that interests James, then, is not only between a text's form and its thematic or representational content, but also between what the text represents and the affective response a potential reader might have to it. In the process, he comes up with a much less stable conception of consolation than we can find in *The Novel Cure*. The texts that James discusses confront pain and suffering, head on, as it were, and in doing so they direct us to what he calls 'critical misgivings about consolation as commensurate with reckless denial, placid acceptance, or soothing escapism'.[23] Solace, here, is seen as what on the inside cover of James' book is described 'as a generative yet conflicted aspect of style'. It is the latter adjective that goes on to explain why James labels his central concept as 'discrepant': 'these writers invite us to consider that when literature reflects on its own capacity for consolation it reflects too on the disruptive comportments of style itself', James writes.[24] The writings of these authors, he goes on to say, 'dislodge solace from its etymological ancestry as a soothing remedy'.[25] In their work, they 'raise the critical stakes of discovering what it means to read for consolation as a paradoxical affordance of the formal operations of texts that may seem virtually antithetical to comfort'.[26]

What James calls the discrepancy of solace, then, cannot only be seen in the friction between content and form or representation and style; it can also be related to the tension between what Blumenberg in his analysis of the modern experience of consolation calls *Trostbedürfnis* and *Untröstlichkeit*. While James does not have the reference, the announcement, on the book's inside cover, of the impressive close readings that make up *Discrepant Solace* reads like an echo of Blumenberg's conceptual framework. The works discussed in James' book, it is said on the blurb, 'capture consolation's alternating desirability and contestation'; they 'turn consolation into a condition of expressional possibility without ever promising us relief'. *Discrepant Solace* delivers on that promise in a series of attentively careful textual analyses to which it is not my purpose in what follows to add (if that were possible, in the first place). Instead, I want to use James' exemplary analyses as an occasion to think about form in a number of bibliotherapeutic publications. My central case will be *All the Lives We Ever Lived*, Katharine Smyth's beautiful book on the solace of reading Virginia Woolf to which I referred in the introduction.

### Woolf on Flaubert

'Bleak truths can be purging', Julian Barnes is quoted as saying in the introduction to David James' *Discrepant Solace*: 'Describing things as they are rather than as we would like them to be can have a consoling effect.'[27] The direct occasion for the comment is Barnes' *Levels of Life*, one of the memoirs that exemplify the specific form of solace that James targets in his book. In it, James argues, Barnes 'suggests another way of thinking about consolation that's not solely based on the perception of it as the antidote to unresolved trauma but rather as an upshot of articulating raw, unsentimental 'truths' of experience'.[28] The quotation comes from an interview in which Barnes also refers to the epistolary discussion between Sand and Flaubert that was central to the previous chapter.[29] In fact, the statement that I just quoted is provoked by their exchange of letters on literary consolation: 'writing what George Sand would consider desolating literature is and can have a consoling effect', Barnes begins by saying.

The author of *Flaubert's Parrot* is not the only one to come to the conclusion that the opposing positions that Sand and Flaubert seem to assume in their discussion on literary consolation do not necessarily preclude the possibility of a third way, so to speak – not a *via media*, mind you, but one in which Flaubert's literature of desolation ends up being consoling, not on account of what it represents but on account of its formal build-up. Virginia Woolf, for one, was also fascinated by the exchange of letters between Sand and Flaubert, as we can see in a letter that she addressed in July 1906 to her friend Madge Vaughan, the daughter of John Addington Symonds, who married Will Vaughan, one of Woolf's nephews. Apparently, Madge had lent her friend an edition of the Flaubert-Sand letters, upon the return of which Woolf (still Virginia Stephen at the time) expressed her great interest in them in a way that enabled her not to choose parties in the grand debate between the two giants of French literature:

> I think no letters I have read interest me more, or seem more beautiful and more suggestive. I know his novels but I know them much better now. She brings out all his peculiar qualities so finely that no autobiography could tell so much as he tells almost unconsciously. I have read none of her novels: but only the autobiography. It is an immense lucid kind of mind, something like a natural force – with no effort or consciousness about it. I think I understand his artistic creed better: I knew all his features and boundaries – but I sink into her and am engulphed! I wanted to endorse, and add to, your pencil marks; whole passages seemed to start up as though writ in old ink. They penetrate so far and sum up so much that is universal as well as individual, and they say things that almost can't be said.[30]

While she admits that her literary affinity with Flaubert is greater ('I think I understand his artistic creed better'), Woolf in no way means to disparage Sand, whose great and convincing enthusiasm ('I sink into her and am engulphed') she claims to find endearing if not captivating. Woolf's deeper understanding of Flaubert's artistic creed becomes clearer in her famous 1922 essay 'On Re-reading Novels', in which she takes issue with Percy Lubbock's recently published *The Craft of Fiction*.[31] Woolf's central point of critique is that the author of that important book is too strict a formalist, so to speak. '[W]henever Mr. Lubbock talks of form it is as if something were interposed between us and the book as we know it', Woolf writes.[32] To her, form is not merely a textual property; it includes the emotion which it provokes in the reader and it serves as a signal of the author's artistic intentions. Woolf illustrates the former point in a brief but very astute reading of Flaubert's 'Un cœur simple'. The experience of reading a literary text is marked, in Woolf's view, by an accumulation of 'impressions' – 'Madame's character; the look of her house; Félicité's appearance; her love affair with Theodore; Madame's children; her visitors; the angry bull' – which at first point the reader in different directions, until '[a] sudden intensity of phrase, something which for good reasons or for bad we feel to be emphatic, startles us into a flash of understanding'.[33] At that point, the reader begins to grasp the author's design ('We see now why the story was written.'[34]). Interestingly, Woolf's sense that 'there is no more appropriate author than Flaubert' to illustrate her own more embracing conception of form seems to be premised on the author's aesthetics of invisibility.[35] On account of Flaubert's *impassibilité*, the reader is left to interpret for herself, sure, but the absence of a moralising perspective in this case allows Woolf to respond, simultaneously, to the story's 'pity' and 'irony' – its specific form, as it were, binds the two seemingly opposed responses together. While Woolf does not explain in any detail what it is in the form of the text that enables her to feel both 'pity' and 'irony' in Flaubert's narration, my guess is that – if we were to press her on the matter – she would be able to come up with the sort of analysis that James makes of the writings that he deals with in *Discrepant Solace*, a reading which is sensitive to the disjunctive relationship between narrative content and narrative form and which is, therefore, able to highlight how in the story's grotesque finale the impersonally neutral voice of the narrator manages to provoke in the reader both warm feelings of endearment towards Félicité and a more distanced awareness of the bitter ironies that can also be read in her vision of Loulou's ghost.

Contrary to the impression that I may have created earlier, Flaubert is not an immediately visible central presence in *Discrepant Solace*. Apart from the reference that Julian Barnes makes to him in the comment that I quoted earlier (see page 234), there is a second significant reference to him in James' book. It can be found at the beginning of the fourth chapter, where Flaubert briefly features as the high priest of the creed that gives that chapter its ominous title: 'The Religion of Style'. 'Style here is style as consolation, style as redemption, the grace of language', J. M. Coetzee is quoted as saying in the chapter's opening sentence. The 'here' in that quotation refers to Flaubert, whose 'idealist vision of style', in James' words, is seen by Coetzee as 'nothing if not consoling'.[36] Coetzee's comment on Flaubert comes from a brief essay on Beckett ('Beckett and the Temptations of Style'),[37] which in its closing paragraphs also touches upon what Coetzee sees as Beckett's 'repudiation' of Flaubert's 'religion of style'. In this essay, Coetzee tries to understand the 'zero' style of Beckett's later fictions, the reading of which, he feels, makes for an 'uncomfortable' experience.[38] Coetzee clearly shares what James calls 'Beckett's apparent suspicion' of Flaubert's aesthetic ideals, to the extent even that his description of Beckett's later works – 'they offer us none of the daydream gratification of fiction'[39] – reads like an auto-comment by the author of such bleak novels of comfort as *Age of Iron* and *Disgrace*. Indeed, while most readers of these novels will agree that they also make for 'uncomfortable' reading, that in itself, as James shows in the fourth chapter of his book, does not preclude their being consoling. In an attempt to 'complicate [the] received portrait of Coetzee as a dispassionate and unflinching artist who strips from his prose the solace his protagonists are denied', James manages to show that in Coetzee's writing 'solace can be ineluctable as well as out of place'.[40] Coetzee's style, James claims, 'performs the very solace that to all intents and purposes it strives to relinquish'[41] – not in the way of Flaubert's 'religion of style', obviously, but in the more discrepant way that Coetzee's style shares with the other authors who feature in James' book.

To be clear, my purpose here is not to save Flaubert or defend him against what could be seen as an unjust criticism, even though it should be pointed out that the aesthetic dogmas that Beckett and Coetzee refer to as the core of Flaubert's 'religion of style' predate the writing of *Madame Bovary* and are not necessarily representative of the author's entire oeuvre. As Leo Bersani has argued, Flaubert's later work, to which 'Un cœur simple' belongs, has a less high-flown conception of the redemptive power of art, stressing 'both the limitations and the necessity of art'.[42] The point that I'm trying to make aligns with the central thesis of David James: we would be mistaken if we failed to see the continuity between the generation of authors who represent the aesthetics of what James calls 'discrepant solace' and the modernist tradition opened up by Flaubert. While it is true that some of the representatives of the latter tradition had high claims about the power of autonomous art to repair and redeem – in our case: to bring consolation (and beauty) on the grounds of its formal make-up – we should not lose sight of the fact that in most cases the modernist advocates of what Bersani calls a 'redemptive aesthetic' – an aesthetic that, in our case, claims to have healing power – enclose in their writings a counterweight to that all too idealist belief. Proust is a good example of this central ambiguity: the *Recherche*, as Bersani shows in the opening chapter of his book, simultaneously expresses a belief in the reparative power of art and undercuts that belief by pointing at the categorical difference between the experiences that we have in life and those that we encounter in art.[43]

### Katharine Smyth on *To the Lighthouse*

One of the mediating figures between the proto-modernism of Flaubert and the generation of discrepant comforters to which Coetzee belongs is Virginia Woolf. In the first chapter of *Discrepant Solace*, James discusses Woolf's *To the Lighthouse* in relation to Ian McEwan's *Atonement*. The latter novel, James argues, takes up the theme of art's potential to bring comfort, but it does so in a way that is fundamentally questioning: *Atonement*, James claims, 'both generates and dismembers' solace and as such it is a true heir of 'modernism's concurrent assaying of and dispute with art as an antidote to devastation',[44] a dual process of which *To the Lighthouse* serves as a prime example. As James shows, convincingly in my view, Woolf's style runs counter to the narrative which the novel unfolds. 'At the level of events', James writes, 'the anguished arc of *To the Lighthouse* makes consolation a recurrent point on Woolf's diegetic compass, all the while unfulfillable, ultimately inconceivable.'[45] At the level of the novel's style, however, 'something else is going on', as James points out. The 'form' in which Woolf's writing results, he argues, 'testifies to irreparable loss' – it describes that which is lost with such astute descriptive force (with such precision) that we come to understand the loss as something which no consolation will be able to repair.[46]

*To the Lighthouse*, as I pointed out in the introduction, is the novel that is central to the bibliotherapeutic memoir in which Katharine Smyth tried to come to terms with the death of her father. I want to come back to Smyth's book, for a moment, in an attempt to find an answer to one of the questions that David James' insightful analysis of Woolf's novel provokes: irrespective of whether or not it manages to account for the discrepant solace that James sees at work in *To the Lighthouse*, how does bibliotherapy think about form?

Sometimes, apparently, it simply doesn't; and if it does, then usually in fairly general terms. In *The Novel Cure*, to give a first example, Woolf's *Mrs Dalloway* is treated by Berthoud and Elderkin in a prescription for readers who suffer from 'Monday Morning Feeling': 'If the thought of Monday fills you with doom', the authors of *The Novel Cure* write, in their typical upbeat parlance, 'if you emerge into wakefulness with the weight of a mountain pressing on your chest, pep yourself up with the first page (or two, or three, if you can't put it down) of *Mrs Dalloway*.'[47] Obviously, a one-and-a-half page book prescription does not provide the space for the sort of minute stylistic micro-analysis that James presents of Woolf's prose. To be fair, though, Berthoud and Elderkin do point out a specific formal characteristic of Woolf's style, 'a whole new way of writing' which Woolf 'invented', as they claim, and which consists of 'capturing thoughts in constant flux', directly presenting to the reader 'the vitality coursing through the veins of a woman, experiencing moment by moment, a day in June, in the London she loves, after the war has ended'.[48] What is most telling about Berthoud and Elderkin's conception of the form of Woolf's writing, is the somehow automatic effect it is taken to have on readers – on all readers. The novel is the utopian pill the pharmaceutical industry may have been dreaming of all the while: it only does what it is intended to do (make you feel better) and it has no unwilled side-effects at all. Focusing on one specific sentence from the novel's opening page in which Woolf describes how Clarissa Dalloway opens the French windows of her house, they simply assume – 'Can you not hear that squeak, feel the little shove as the doors give way, taste that clean, cold air?'[49] – that the book's reader cannot but read in the way in which they themselves are reading: the rhetorical question is the clear sign of that distinct certainty. The outcome of this self-evident reading perspective is also beyond dispute, as far as Berthoud and Elderkin are concerned: 'Then, receive, through your eyes and mind and into your body, Clarissa's appetite and love of life',[50] they go on to write, thinking aloud wishful thoughts of unproblematic communion. Woolf's words, here, appear to be given the same power that the host is given in Christian religious services – as the faithful take the wafer, they participate in the transubstantiated truth. (Berthoud and Elderkin are being ironical, sure, but only up to a certain point.)

The comfort of reading, here, is clearly defined by the feel-good effect that the opening pages of *Mrs Dalloway* cannot fail to have according to Berthoud and Elderkin. A closer look at the whole of *Mrs Dalloway* would, of course, also have to register the darker, more desolate notes in this literary text that ultimately also deals with the difficulties of holding on to what Berthoud and Elderkin call the 'appetite and love of life'.[51] In the end, Woolf's novel openly wonders whether suicide can ever be a rightful option in one's search for a life of true happiness, the absolute exclusion, that is, of ever still having to feel unhappy – 'did it not become consoling to believe that death ended absolutely?', Clarissa Dalloway wonders just a few pages in.[52] The question remains, then, as to how the novel's reflection in that less uplifting respect relates to the lesson which Berthoud and Elderkin expect Woolf's readers to draw from the example of *Mrs Dalloway*'s eponymous heroine: 'Become aware, as she is aware, of the presence of death – that all these scurrying people will one day just be bones and dust – and carry this awareness with you into your day.'[53]

Katharine Smyth's bibliotherapeutic analysis of Woolf's *To the Lighthouse* – my second and more extensive example – is obviously more elaborate than Berthoud and Elderkin's 500-word reading prescription of *Mrs Dalloway*. Conceptually speaking, however, Smyth's view of the novel's form is not all that different. Like the authors of *The Novel Cure*, Smyth also sees a straightforward relationship between what the text does and what the reader feels. In her case, aspects of formal analysis are often explicitly linked to comments on Woolf's artistic intentions or the biographical circumstances in which (and partly on account of which) the author wrote her text. The text's form, in other words, becomes a virtual meeting place, where the reader recognises the author's intentions (therapeutic and other) and on account of that recognition manages to relate the novel to their own life. In Smyth's memoir, however, the novel's power of exemplification and the reader's subsequent identification with the 'example' are less self-evident. As I pointed out in the introduction, Katharine Smyth keeps a steady eye on the significant differences between her own family life and that of the Ramsays in Woolf's novel. In *The Novel Cure*, the message is quite straightforward: 'if Clarissa can get out of bed and go buy the flowers herself, so can you, reader!' In Smyth's memoir, life's complications are presented with more attention to the fundamental ambivalence of human existence and to the ebb and flow of its ups and downs. As the book's title – *All the Lives We Ever Lived* – suggests, Smyth is also more attuned to the fact that the novel can bring comfort to different sorts of readers, each with their distinct problems, and, indeed, to readers at different times in their lives, times with different needs. '[O]ne of the wonders of Woolf's novel', Smyth writes, 'is its seemingly endless capacity to meet you wherever you happen to be'.[54] Already in the opening pages of her memoir, Smyth indicates that she has come to read *To the Lighthouse* differently over the years. Reading it for the first time 'as a moody, impressionable twenty-year-old',[55] during a year abroad in Oxford, it was only upon her second encounter with the text that she began to sense the role Woolf's novel could come to play in her life:

> *To the Lighthouse* is a work that rewards – that demands – reading and rereading; it was not until at least my second time through it that I had the impression of actually swimming round beneath its surface. But already, as I curled up with that book by the fire, it was beginning to reciprocate and even alter my experience, while also giving me a vocabulary by which to fathom that experience.[56]

Stressing that during her reading of it Woolf's novel began to 'reciprocate', Smyth makes clear that she does not take a merely instrumental view of the act of interpretation. A novel is not like a pill, utopian or other; one does not simply take and digest it. In the course of her successive readings, Smyth believes that even as her relationship to Woolf's novel changes, so does the text itself. While initially she engages with the character of Mrs Ramsay in a way that stresses the young reader's longing to identify – 'I wanted to be her', Smyth writes, 'that's how painful I found the distance between us, the distance between me and that text'[57] –, her later, more comforting insight into the novel seems to have grown from that very distance. 'For all my enchantment', Smyth writes, 'I would have done well to reflect further upon Mrs Ramsay's relationship to life, one I glossed over because I found it puzzling.'[58] It was only at a later stage that Smyth began to understand 'the tremendous blows that life has dealt her [Mrs Ramsay], that all lives are capable of dealing'.[59] It is to that more mature insight that Smyth relates the specific solace that she sought and found in what she calls Woolf's 'unrelenting search for meaning in the face of death':[60] the ultimately comforting thought that 'the complexities and contradictions of human experience' can never be reduced to 'simply one thing'.[61] Focusing on the phenomenon of marriage – that of the Ramsays, that of her parents, that of Leonard and Virginia Woolf, but also her own – Smyth comes to read *To the Lighthouse* as a novel that 'reveals the terrors that surround such sweetness'.[62] Inversely, looking more closely at her favourite sentence in the book (it occurs near the end of Chapter 11 of the novel's first part), she discovers in Mrs Ramsay's 'exalted affirmation of happiness' a premonition of the beloved character's impending death.[63]

The epiphanies that Woolf has in store for her readers deserve the eponymous epithet that Smyth bestows on them: they are indeed 'Woolfian', 'ambiguous, equivocal, and wholly fitting of a writer whose work is characterized above all by inconclusiveness'.[64] In a self-help guide like that of Berthoud and Elderkin, where novels are selected on account of the decisive lessons the bibliotherapists discover in them, such a characteristic is quite likely out of place. The biggest difference between *The Novel Cure* and *All the Lives We Ever Lived* lies in their conception of what both books refer to as the 'solace' that reading brings. For Berthoud and Elderkin, the solace of a good book resides in what in the introduction to *The Novel Cure* they describe as its 'showing you that you are not alone', in the fact that it allows the reader to 'see the world from a different point of view';[65] in practice, that different view turns out to be, mainly, a more positive, hopeful view, the sort of view that George Sand was aiming for. Bibliotherapy, in their book, involves primarily the prescription of what Berthoud in *The Art of Mindful Reading* labels 'calming books', a variety of the 'comfort reads' that one turns to in one's need for cheerfulness.[66]

Smyth's conception of solace comes closer to the meaning given to that term in David James' book. For Berthoud and Elderkin, to continue the pharmaceutical jargon that marks the introduction of *The Novel Cure*, many of the novels which they prescribe are seen to function as instant painkillers, the immediately soothing effect of which is temporary and very rarely a real contribution to the healing process. Smyth's approach is more oriented, as we have seen, to the reader's confrontation with the reality of suffering and the acceptance of the hard truths that cause it (the destructive impact of her father's alcoholism, his subsequent struggle with cancer and Smyth's grief after he dies).

## The Marquis de Lau Phenomenon

'Sometimes I think it's Woolf's mastery of moments like these – moments that hold up a mirror to our private tumult while also revealing how much we as humans share – that most draws me to her.'[67] In this single sentence, Smyth touches upon what is probably the key to successful bibliotherapy. The healing experience of reading requires that we begin to see our deeply personal problems ('our private tumult') more clearly through another person's story and that the insight that we derive from this newly found connection enables us to see our predicament simultaneously as our own (the book should manage to address us individually, in our specific singularity) and as part of a larger, shared problem.

The specific logic of exemplification upon which the success of Katharine Smyth's reading of Woolf's novel rests is similar to the one that underlies the Aristotelian idea that literary writings – in their capacity of products and producers of mimesis – function as concrete universals. In Sir Philip Sidney's *Apology for Poetry*, as one may recall, Aristotle's idea is used to explain the advantage of literature over philosophy and history writing. For Sidney as well as Aristotle, the advantage has to do with the specific form of knowledge that we derive from mimetic literature. Unlike historiography, 'poetry' (literature) does not talk about things that really happened and only once, moreover. But neither does it offer us general truths, like philosophy does. Giving us the best of both worlds, literature presents us with universal truths that are experienced concretely. '[O]nly poetry or fiction can create this sense of the singular you', the poet Harry Eyres writes in *Horace and Me*, his account (bibliotherapeutic to some degree) of a life-time of reading the Latin poet. 'Philosophy can't do it', Eyres argues, 'because philosophy always wants to generalise.'[68] Historiography can't do it, either, I would add, because it presents itself as a verifiable account of a series of singular events, the knowledge of which limits itself to those events. As a consequence, history writing's address to its readers does not entail an open invitation to relate what they read to what Smyth calls, in the sentence that I quoted earlier, their 'private tumult'. Of course, one can read a historical work in such a way, but that is not its prime purpose.

Literature – whether it be poems, plays or novels – does contain the invitation for readers to relate. When we read about Dante and Beatrice, see Hamlet onstage or follow the thoughts of Mrs Ramsay, we not only take an interest in these characters, but are drawn to them, sometimes even to the extent that we begin to identify – from a distance, obviously. Fiction does that with us, apparently: its engagement is such that we relate our own experience to that of the fictional characters we encounter. In the second chapter of *How Proust Can Change Your Life*, an early specimen of the bibliotherapy that he would later promote in the School of Life project that came to host Berthoud and Elderkin's work, Alain de Botton refers to this as 'the Marquis de Lau' phenomenon – the reference is to a friend of Proust's who according to the author of the *Recherche* bore a distinct resemblance to the carbuncle-nosed old man on a famous portrait by the Italian fifteenth-century painter Domenico Ghirlandaio.[69] Proust also made a habit of 'recognising' his friends and loved ones in literary writings. 'One cannot read a novel without ascribing to the heroine the traits of the one we love', the author of the *Recherche* is quoted as saying by De Botton, who is happy to adopt Proust's reading habit by claiming to recognise his girlfriend Kate in Proust's portrait of Albertine.[70]

De Botton's summary of what he sees as the two major 'benefits of the Marquis de Lau phenomenon' boils down to a rehearsal of some of the arguments that sustain our by now common claim that good literature can and does bring consolation. To see ourselves and our surroundings reflected in the books that we read – to see the marriage of one's parents in that of the Ramsays in *To the Lighthouse*, for instance, as Katharine Smyth does – may, firstly, help us feel less quaint or abnormal and therefore less alone. 'How comforting to witness a fictional person – who is also, miraculously, ourselves as we read – suffering the same agonies', De Botton writes, 'and, importantly, surviving'.[71] Secondly, De Botton argues, good novels 'sensitize' their readers, on account of their authors' prime ability 'to put a finger on perceptions that we recognize as our own, yet could not have formulated on our own'.[72] In books like the *Recherche*, we find new ways of expressing what it is that we feel and on the basis of these new expressions we also manage to arrive at new insights into our own experiences.

This is also the solace that Katharine Smyth derived from reading Woolf, whose novel, as she puts it at the very beginning of her book, gave her the 'vocabulary' that enabled her to 'fathom' with more depth the distress that she went through during her father's protracted struggle with alcohol and with the illness that ended his life. What the novel offered her – by way of the specific example that it set through the life-affirming character of Mrs Ramsay – was the suggestion that it was possible to 'relish [her] father's vices rather than cursing them'.[73] What Mrs Ramsay taught her (and kept teaching her with every successive rereading) was that given the 'complexities and contradictions of human experience, in which perception is not monolithic', it was worthwhile to keep looking out for the possibility of some light in life's darkest moments, while remaining aware that even in times of seemingly absolute bliss, one should remind oneself 'to never gloss over intricacy or inconsistency'.[74] 'The layers that accumulate, the memories we graft upon a place – these are sources of solace', Smyth writes in the penultimate chapter of her memoir.[75] For the memories to be truly consoling, they need to take into account the inherently contradictory nature of what it means to be human.

## Books as Comforters: Winnicott

*To the Lighthouse*, Katharine Smyth writes in the opening paragraph of *All the Lives We Ever Lived*, is the single most important book of her life. We all need such a book, she adds, in the passage that also serves as a motto to this chapter: 'One book with the power to reflect and illuminate [one's] life; one book that will forever inform how we navigate the little strip of time we are given, while also helping us to clarify and catch hold of its most vital moments.'[76] The title of Woolf's novel is quite inviting for the sort of bibliotherapeutic reflection Smyth's memoir has to offer. The right sort of novel can serve as a beacon whenever we feel adrift; it can serve as a compass that can help us find our way back; it can shed the light that we so desperately need when everything and everybody else fails. In doing all these things, novels provide us with the sense of direction, stability and clarity that we expect from the kind of experience to which Smyth refers in the subtitle of her book – whether we refer to that experience as 'solace', as she does, as 'consolation' or as 'comfort'.

If we define the experience in the way Doctor Johnson did in his famous *Dictionary of the English Language* – 'comfort', Johnson wrote, is 'the alleviation of misery' – bibliotherapy can be said to argue that novels (or poems, for that matter) function as 'comforters'. For Johnson, the latter word's usage seems to be limited in reference to a person, 'one that administers consolation in misfortunes'; 'one that strengthens and supports the mind in misery or danger'.[77] Thanks to the work of the British psychoanalyst Donald Winnicott, however, we can also understand the word 'comforter' in the specific sense of an object, whose function Winnicott first explained in 1953, in a ground-breaking paper on what he began to see as 'transitional phenomena'.[78] In the remainder of this chapter, I want to think through the conceptual analogy between books and Winnicott's comforters and suggest that their work consists in fuelling and guiding the transitional process of solace, leading readers to the novel perspective (the newly required insight) that is implied in any experience of consolation.

In his early paper on transitional phenomena, later republished as the opening chapter of the author's 1971 book *Playing and Reality*,

Winnicott focuses on the development of very young children (from month 4 to month 12, on average[79]) who begin to discover that they have a physical and mental existence apart from their mother, in an external world that holds the promise of joys as well as threats. In the process of that discovery, Winnicott suggests, children develop a specific attachment to what he calls 'transitional objects' – a teddy bear, say, or a doll, a piece of cloth, a blanket. The function of these objects is to facilitate the smooth transition in the child's mental disposition from a world in which its life is entirely dominated by the mother to a world that, as the child begins to learn, exists separately, from both its mother and itself.[80]

'The object' in question, Winnicott writes, 'represents the infant's transition from a state of being merged with the mother to a state of being in relation to the mother as something outside and separate.'[81] In calling them 'transitional', Winnicott also wants to point out that these objects have a material (objective) existence of their own, while at the same time being invested, subjectively, by their users (the children, in this case) with a singular meaning which these objects hold for them and only them. In the examples given by Winnicott, this meaning seems to relate to the function of these 'comforters' as instruments of 'defence against anxiety' or another means to calm down (and fall asleep).[82] Objects like these, Winnicott writes, function in 'an intermediate area of *experiencing*, to which inner reality and external life both contribute'.[83]

Indeed, the object's investment with subjective meaning is for Winnicott the central paradox of transitional objects, as he puts it in another paper: 'the baby creates the object, but the object was there waiting to be created and to become a cathected object'.[84] What is important, here, is the fact that the transitional object does not simply function as what Winnicott calls a 'projective entity': its function is not simply that of a thing onto which the child projects its own feelings. Quite the contrary: the object retains its autonomy, as 'an entity in its own right', as Winnicott writes, that to a certain extent resists appropriation. It is the very possibility of this resistance that forms the basis of the productive work of the transitional object: the object, as Winnicott puts it, is placed 'outside the area of the subject's omnipotent control'.[85] The object functions as a vehicle that raises the subject's awareness of an outside reality that is beyond its control. It comes to stand for an outside reality that may prove less willing to bend to our deepest wishes, but within which we will have to learn to live. 'All these transitional objects and transitional phenomena enable the child to stand frustrations and deprivations and the presentation of new situations', Winnicott claimed in a lecture delivered to the Nursery School Association in July 1950.[86] Transitional objects connect us to a world in which we will have to find our way and help us to navigate through it.

The function of my brief introduction to Winnicott's analysis of transitional objects will be self-evident: the excursion is meant to support the suggestion that novels of comfort (or other literary writings that we claim bring us consolation) work according to a similar logic, on the basis of what Paul Horton, in a discussion of Winnicott's work, calls our 'ability for transitional relatedness'.[87] Horton, an American psychiatrist who specialised in the mental mechanism of consolation, extends Winnicott's work on the function of transitional objects in the development of children to the life of adults. In his work, he wants to make clear how in the course of adult life, as he puts it,

> the treasured soothers, or 'transitional objects', of early childhood – exemplified by the blanket, stuffed animal, and favourite tune – are normally replaced by increasingly subtle and complex vehicles for growth and most especially solace through a lifelong series of progressive psychological transformations.[88]

Horton himself makes clear at several places in his book *Solace: The Missing Dimension in Psychiatry* that it is not at all farfetched to see novels and other literary texts as such 'vehicles for solace'. In one of these passages, he refers to Dickens' *David Copperfield*, 'a veritable exercise in transitional relatedness', as Horton writes.[89] Focusing on a passage in which the novel's hero explains how as a young boy of eight he found consolation in a selection of books that were left to him by his deceased father ('This was my only and my constant comfort', the narrator says[90]), Horton explains how these objects enable David – at this early stage of his life but continually so in later years – to adapt to a reality that, if handled the wrong way, may lead to severe trauma. 'Characteristically and in health', Horton writes, a person's proper relationship to their transitional objects 'facilitates engagement with novel, conflictual, even frightening circumstances and mediates or catalyzes psychological growth'.[91] In David's case – and in that of many others whose bibliotherapeutic confessions I have been quoting in the course of this book – good fiction seems to do the trick.

There are plenty of reasons why novels can serve as purveyors of transitional relatedness. 'If it seems perverse to suggest that literature is a teddy bear', Murray Schwartz writes in his contribution to a (rare) collection on the potential interest of Winnicott's work for literary scholars, 'I find it enlightening to realize what they have in common, the place of their meaningful experience for us, first as children, later as adults.'[92] Being products of the imagination that, in turn, require an imaginative response from their readers, literary writings' core business is the evocation of the sort of 'illusory experience' that is central to Winnicott's analysis of transitional phenomena.[93] Indeed, what Adam Phillips calls 'the play of imagination'[94] is an important element in what Winnicott sees as the lifelong process of human development. In his essay on 'Transitional Objects', Winnicott states that this process – described, there, as the 'task of reality acceptance' – is 'never completed'.[95] The phrase is apt for any discussion of consolation: as we have seen in each of the preceding chapters, the acceptance of an unwelcome fact (the loss of a loved one, the imminence of one's life ending) is a central given, one which the practice of consolation needs to strive for. Throughout our life, Winnicott believes, transitional phenomena continue to play an important role in this process, as they both force and enable us to relate our inner reality to the outer reality, the world that surrounds us. '[N]o human being is free from the strain of relating inner and outer reality', Winnicott argues, also surmising that 'relief from this strain is provided by an intermediate area of experience', to which religion and the arts contribute.[96]

In his paper on 'The Location of Cultural Experience' (originally published in 1967), Winnicott relates his early analysis of transitional objects (and the role played by these objects in the creation of an intermediate experience, that is, our nascent experience of being related to an outer world that exists apart from our inner reality) to what he calls 'the *potential space* between the individual and the environment'. 'This potential space', Winnicott writes, 'is at the interplay between there being nothing but me and there being objects and phenomena outside omnipotent control.'[97] 'Literature', Murray Schwartz contends, 'is written language located in potential space, the language *we* locate there'.[98] What Schwartz is right to stress, here, is the fact that the reading of a literary text is a *performance* of that text. The textual 'artefact' that is created by the text's author, to borrow Jan Mukařovsky's terms, is turned into an 'aesthetic object' by the reader.[99]

The specific type of object that books (especially fiction?) are, turns out to be apt to guide the mechanism of what in another later essay Winnicott calls 'of relatedness to usage'. In this text, first published in 1969, but delivered as a paper in November 1968,[100] Winnicott tries to analyse what happens in the actual 'use' of transitional objects, that is, after the subject managed to relate to it. Key to Winnicott's understanding of the process is what he describes as a specific and paradoxical form of 'destruction': as Winnicott sees it, the subject 'destroys' the object, figuratively speaking at least, and in doing so the subject confirms the object's autonomous status. As Winnicott puts it,

> [i]t is the destruction of the object that places the object outside of the area of the subject's omnipotent control. In these ways the object develops its own autonomy and life and (if it survives) contributes-in to the subject, according to its own properties.[101]

## Comfortably Unsettled?

Winnicott's description of the process in question is reminiscent of how several hermeneutically inspired theories of reading conceive of what Wolfgang Iser calls 'der Akt des Lesens'.[102] Readers invest the texts that they read with meaning – indeed, they are encouraged to do so by the texts themselves – but their interpretation of the text (the text's 'destructive' usage, in Winnicott's view) does not coincide with the textual object as such, and neither does it exhaust the text's power of signification. As in Winnicott's analysis of the use of transitional objects, the reader's personal interpretation both confirms the text's autonomy (as an object 'out there') and the reader's developing self.

The current conviction, central in many bibliotherapeutic reflections, that novels and other literary writings help readers develop their faculty of empathy may also be instructive here. As Winnicott's sees it, '[a] sign of health in the mind is the ability of one individual to enter imaginatively and accurately into the thoughts and feelings and hopes and fears of another person; also to allow the other person to do the same to us'.[103] Novels in particular are said to facilitate the development of powers of empathy in readers, since they give access, uniquely so according to some, to the perspective of other people. In real life we have no direct access to what another person feels, whereas in fiction we do – or so we say. The writing of fiction, as the Israeli author David Grossman argues, starts from 'the desire to know the other from within'.[104]

'[L]iterature does something deeper still than recover an inner voice', Josie Billington writes in *Is Literature Healthy?* '[L]iterature can "think" reality when ordinary human thought falls short', Billington argues: 'a book can have thoughts that humans *cannot* have'.[105] 'It can summon a voice that does not exist under the ordinary conditions of life.'[106] As we read George Eliot's *Middlemarch*, Billington shows, we come to understand Dorothea Brooks' most privately intimate thoughts as she struggles with her complex feelings regarding the imminent death of her sick husband. Our understanding of these feelings – provoked by Eliot's masterful use of free indirect discourse, as Billington makes clear – allows us to feel connected with Dorothea and with others finding themselves in similar situations.

Drawing on the work of the British psychoanalyst Wilfred Bion, Billington makes clear how Eliot's narrative technique 'shows human thought coming into being':[107] at specific moments in the novel – moments that involve pain and a feeling of imminent loss, for the most part – Dorothea seems to be unaware of truths which the novel's narrator already knows. Eliot's narrator, Billington writes, 'thinks Dorothea's half-thoughts for her'.[108] 'Free indirect discourse', she repeats after D. A. Miller, 'is the character's life as he or she cannot fully live it. Literary reading, we might say, is a person's life as he or she cannot fully *think* it, until the right book comes along.'[109] What Billington calls the 'right' sort of book, turns out to be especially productive in traumatic circumstances, in which the ailing reader's thoughts have been brought to a stand-still, fixed in fear for the unknown, uncertain about what will happen next. The right book, as we have seen in our discussion of the memoirs of Joseph Luzzi, Laura Bates and Katharine Smyth, is the book that enables us to think through our own situation in comparison with – that is, according to a balanced ratio of similarities and differences – the fictional universe at hand.

For Billington, Eliot's *Middlemarch* is clearly the right kind of book. It is the simultaneous disclosure of a series of truths and of the difficulties the female protagonist undergoes in the process of coming to grasp them that makes Eliot's novel a good diagnostic instrument, Billington believes, one that, as she puts it, 'might operate as an intermediary into human unhappiness'.[110] The phrase is an interesting one from the perspective of our central topic. If we feel the need to be comforted by a book, that does not necessarily mean that we want the book to feed us happy thoughts. Quite the contrary, Billington seems to suggest. Novels like Eliot's guide us into understanding better how we feel when we feel down; they assist us in what Billington considers 'the difficult task of real thinking'.[111]

The latter phrase contains an implicit reference to Bion's theory of mind. According to Bion, an unhealthy mental state is generally due to the fact that we do not use our potential to fully think consciously.

Mental suffering equals ignorance, for Bion: we suffer – from depression, say – because we do not know full well how we feel. In order to get better, we need to learn. In a crucial passage from his 1962 book *Learning from Experience* that Billington quotes, Bion describes the importance of 'thinking' as follows:

> If a person cannot 'think' with his thoughts, that is to say that he has thoughts but lacks the apparatus of 'thinking' which enables him to use his thoughts, to think them as it were, then the personality is incapable of learning from experience.[112]

Literary texts like Eliot's, Billington goes on to argue, enable readers to develop their thinking: they provide us with reflective models and scenarios.[113] Interestingly, Billington contrasts the role that novels such as *Middlemarch* can play in this process of learning to 'mindfulness manuals' and other 'modern self-help guides'. The former, Billington writes, 'offer (...) the unbalancing thought that in order to learn from experience, the evolutionary process may well have to be gone through at every new life stage'.[114] The latter, the implication seems to be, only provide us with the illusion of a solution, one that may be comforting for a while, but fails to deliver true insight, in the end. Billington doesn't refer to it directly, but the reading prescription of *Middlemarch* in *The Novel Cure* would seem to confirm her point. Readers who want to 'avoid ending up with Mr/Mrs Wrong' are advised to have a proper look at Eliot's novel. The parallel stories of Dorothea's and Dr Lydgate's unhappy relationships are the occasion of a characteristic piece of advice: 'Take great care to get to know both yourself and your intended before you tie the knot. If you forge ahead with only a partial understanding of their character, you may have some unpleasant surprises in store.'[115] Surely, one does not need to plough through an 800-page novel to come up with the sort of life lesson that just any story of a failed marriage could deliver.

Actually, Billington does refer to *The Novel Cure* in *Is Literature Healthy?*, albeit in a general way. One of the former's conceptual problems, she feels, lies in the fact that in prescribing literary texts, Berthoud and Elderkin also prescribe the effects these texts must have on their readers. In Billington's experience, bibliotherapy works better if the reading encounter is 'unpremeditated'.[116] In an illuminating empirical analysis that provides the material for the third chapter of her book, Billington shows that 'the most compelling thinking' that happens in therapeutic reading groups where participants read literary texts out loud occurs 'in the area *between* reader and book, not in any straightforward identification between reader and character or situation'.[117] Again, the difference with the reading model that underlies *The Novel Cure* is clear: as we have seen, Berthoud and Elderkin's prescriptions presuppose that readers fully identify with the protagonists of the reading suggestions. This book is not just for you, their recurrent suggestion seems to be, it *is* you.

The reading attitude that Billington prefers over 'identification' is one where 'there is no tidy alignment of story with the reader's personal experience'.[118] 'Overlap' – borrowed from Kenneth Burke's *Philosophy of Literary Form* – is the term that she uses: it presupposes the recognition of likeness, sure, but also the awareness of difference. Billington's model is the reading attitude that underlies the memoirs of Joseph Luzzi and Katharine Smyth that we discussed earlier; it involves the sort of engagement with texts that Geoffrey Braithwaite was no doubt looking for but failed to find.

Interestingly, in his early analysis of the work of 'comforters', Winnicott stresses that these transitional objects are instrumental in the developmental process 'of becoming able to accept difference and similarity' that he considers crucial in the realisation of one's individual self. We develop as individuals not just by recognising what distinguishes us from others, but also by acknowledging what we share with some. In this relational concept of individual identity, Winnicott suggests, our lifelong relatedness to transitional objects has an important and productive role to play, a role that I have associated in this chapter with the value of novels or other literary writings from which we claim to derive comfort. The examples that we have discussed in this chapter – some of the authors with whose writings David James deals in *Discrepant Solace*, but also Katharine Smyth on Virginia Woolf and Josie Billington on George Eliot – seem to suggest that the comfort in question is not of the variety that offers easy reassurance and says that all will be well in the end. These authors are experts in the specific sense that Adam Phillips wants to give to that inflated term: not only do they have 'the unusual capacity to both comfort and unsettle', they bear witness to what I take as a given of the modern regime of consolation: 'you can't have one without the other'.[119]

## Notes

1. Katharine Smyth, *All the Lives We Ever Lived*, 1.
2. Berthoud and Elderkin, *The Novel Cure*, 1.

3. Proust quoted in De Botton, *How Proust Can Change Your Life*, 25. The reference is to a passage from *Time Regained*, the closing book of *In Search of Lost Time*.
4. See also Moritz, *Die Überlebensbibliothek*, 303–5: 'In order to find out that reading does not automatically result in an improvement of one's personality, read: Gustave Flaubert, *Madame Bovary*.' (my translation)
5. Available at: <https://www.nyrb.com/collections/nyrb-book-boxes/products/uplifting-six-nyrb-classics>
6. Kakutani, 'Coronavirus Notebook', *New York Times*, May 5, 2020.
7. Boccaccio, *The Decameron*, 53.
8. James, *Discrepant Solace*.
9. A good example, mentioned by David James as well, is Bersani, *The Culture of Redemption*. I will come back to Bersani's book later in this chapter.
10. Freud to Binswanger, 11 April 1929, quoted by James on 19; also partly quoted in Samuel, *Grief Works*, 143.
11. James, *Discrepant Solace*, 9.
12. James, *Discrepant Solace*, 9.
13. James, *Discrepant Solace*, 213.
14. James, *Discrepant Solace*, 9.
15. See the discussion of Dagerman's text in Chapter 3 (pp. 120–1).
16. In the introduction to his book, James takes what he calls 'a short diachronic detour' in which he makes use of the work of George McClure and Ronald K. Rittgers, among others, to signal differences between early modern and contemporary ideas of consolation (*Discrepant Solace*, 22–4). In the former tradition, James writes, consolation is 'a mellowing agent in the wake of loss, an unbreachable safeguard against further onsets of despair' (23).
17. James, *Discrepant Solace*, 11.
18. Berthoud and Elderkin, *The Novel Cure*, 414. The reading prescription (of Robinson's novel *Home*) is for 'turmoil'. For James' discussion of Robinson's work (*Gilead* mainly, even though he also touches upon *Home*) see *Discrepant Solace*, 128–50. James' reading of *Home* is clearly much more targeted towards the text's internal dissonance than that of Berthoud and Elderkin.
19. Berthoud and Elderkin, *The Novel Cure*, 414.
20. James, *Discrepant Solace*, 7.
21. James, *Discrepant Solace*, 7.
22. James, *Discrepant Solace*, 7.
23. James, *Discrepant Solace*, 7.
24. James, *Discrepant Solace*, 23–4.
25. James, *Discrepant Solace*, 11.
26. James, *Discrepant Solace*, 6.
27. James, *Discrepant Solace*, 19.
28. James, *Discrepant Solace*, 19.

29. Guignery and Roberts, 'Julian Barnes: The Final Interview', 169. Also quoted in *Discrepant Solace*, 19.
30. Nicolson (ed.), *The Letters of Virginia Woolf, Volume I: 1888–1912*, 229.
31. Woolf, 'On Re-reading Novels', 122–30.
32. Woolf, 'On Re-reading Novels', 126.
33. Woolf, 'On Re-reading Novels', 125.
34. Woolf, 'On Re-reading Novels', 125.
35. Woolf, 'On Re-reading Novels', 125.
36. James, *Discrepant Solace*, 114.
37. Coetzee, *Doubling the Point*, 43–9.
38. Coetzee, *Doubling the Point*, 47, 49.
39. Coetzee, *Doubling the Point*, 49.
40. James, *Discrepant Solace*, 117.
41. James, *Discrepant Solace*, 117.
42. Bersani, *The Culture of Redemption*, 134. Bersani's case is the unfinished *Bouvard et Pécuchet*.
43. Bersani, *The Culture of Redemption*, 7–28. See also Bersani, *Marcel Proust: The Fictions of Life and Art*.
44. James, *Discrepant Solace*, 43.
45. James, *Discrepant Solace*, 46.
46. James, *Discrepant Solace*, 46.
47. Berthoud and Elderkin, *The Novel Cure*, 273.
48. Berthoud and Elderkin, *The Novel Cure*, 273.
49. Berthoud and Elderkin, *The Novel Cure*, 273.
50. Berthoud and Elderkin, *The Novel Cure*, 273.
51. Actually, that note already sounds on the novel's first page, a few lines down from the sentence that Berthoud and Elderkin quote, when the narrator hints at Mrs Dalloway's premonition that 'something awful was about to happen' (Woolf, *Mrs Dalloway*, 1).
52. Woolf, *Mrs Dalloway*, 6.
53. Berthoud and Elderkin, *The Novel Cure*, 274.
54. Smyth, *All the Lives We Ever Lived*, 47.
55. Smyth, *All the Lives We Ever Lived*, 66.
56. Smyth, *All the Lives We Ever Lived*, 2–3.
57. Smyth, *All the Lives We Ever Lived*, 67.
58. Smyth, *All the Lives We Ever Lived*, 67.
59. Smyth, *All the Lives We Ever Lived*, 68.
60. Smyth, *All the Lives We Ever Lived*, 119.
61. Smyth, *All the Lives We Ever Lived*, 89.
62. Smyth, *All the Lives We Ever Lived*, 46.
63. Smyth, *All the Lives We Ever Lived*, 118.
64. Smyth, *All the Lives We Ever Lived*, 120.
65. Berthoud and Elderkin, *The Novel Cure*, 2.
66. Berthoud, *The Art of Mindful Reading*, 122.
67. Smyth, *All the Lives We Ever Lived*, 243.

68. Eyres, *Horace and Me*, 185.
69. De Botton, *How Proust Can Change Your Life*, 25.
70. De Botton, *How Proust Can Change Your Life*, 24.
71. De Botton, *How Proust Can Change Your Life*, 28.
72. De Botton, *How Proust Can Change Your Life*, 28, 29.
73. Smyth, *All the Lives We Ever Lived*, 3.
74. Smyth, *All the Lives We Ever Lived*, 89.
75. Smyth, *All the Lives We Ever Lived*, 266.
76. Smyth, *All the Lives We Ever Lived*, 1.
77. Samuel Johnson, *A Dictionary of the English Language*, Vol. 1 (A-Kyd), no pagination.
78. Winnicott 'Transitional Objects and Transitional Phenomena'. The paper was first delivered at a meeting of the British Psycho-Analytical Society (May 1951). I made use of the (revised) republication in Winnicott, *Playing and Reality*, 1–34. For a good discussion of what he calls 'this most famous of Winnicott's papers' see Phillips, *Winnicott*, 113–20.
79. Winnicott, 'Transitional Objects and Transitional Phenomena', 6.
80. See also Chapter 25 ('First Experiments in Independence') of Winnicott, *The Child, the Family and the Outside World*, 167–72.
81. Winnicott, 'Transitional Objects and Transitional Phenomena', 19–20. The same definition occurs in Chapter 25 ('First Experiments in Independence') of Winnicott's *The Child, the Family and the Outside World*, 168.
82. Winnicott, 'Transitional Objects and Transitional Phenomena', 5.
83. Winnicott, 'Transitional Objects and Transitional Phenomena', 3, his italics.
84. Winnicott, 'The Use of an Object', in Winnicott, *Playing and Reality*, 119.
85. Winnicott, *Playing and Reality*, 120.
86. Published as Chapter 16 ('The Deprived Child and How He Can Be Compensated') in Winnicott, *The Family and Individual Development*, 211.
87. Horton, *Solace*, 59. For other examples of the relevance of Winnicott's concept of the transitional object for literary studies see Rudnytsky (ed.), *Transitional Objects and Potential Spaces*. See also Horton, Gerwitz and Kreutter (eds), *The Solace Paradigm*.
88. An idea that finds support in Winnicott's own work. As Adam Phillips writes in his discussion of it: 'Winnicott suggests that there is a continuity between the child's use of this first object and the adult's later use of the cultural tradition as it becomes meaningful to him.' Phillips, *Winnicott*, 115.
89. Horton, *Solace*, 76.
90. Quoted in Horton, *Solace*, 77.
91. Horton, *Solace*, 35.
92. Schwartz, 'Where is Literature', in Ludnytsky (ed.), *Transitional Objects and Potential Spaces*, 60.

93. Horton, *Solace*, 74; see, for instance, page 19 of 'Transitional Objects and Transitional Phenomena': 'Transitional objects and transitional phenomena belong to the realm of illusion which is at the basis of initiation of experience.'
94. 'The play of interpretation' is the title of the final chapter of Phillips' monograph on Winnicott (138–52).
95. Winnicott, 'Transitional Objects and Transitional Phenomena' 18.
96. Winnicott, 'Transitional Objects and Transitional Phenomena', 18.
97. Winnicott, *Playing and Reality*, 135.
98. Schwartz, 'Where is Literature?', 61, emphasis by Schwartz.
99. Mukařovsky, 'Die Kunst als semiologisches Faktum'.
100. Winnicott, 'The Use of an Object'.
101. Winnicott, 'The Use of an Object', 121.
102. Iser, *The Act of Reading*.
103. Winnicott, 'Transitional Objects and Transitional Phenomena', 12.
104. Grossman, *Writing in the Dark*.
105. Billington, *Is Literature Healthy?*, 44, emphasis by Billington.
106. Billington, *Is Literature Healthy?*, 106.
107. Billington, *Is Literature Healthy?*, 19.
108. Billington, *Is Literature Healthy?*, 31.
109. Billington, *Is Literature Healthy?*, 111. The reference is to D. A. Miller, *Jane Austen, or, The Secret of Style*.
110. Billington, *Is Literature Healthy?*, 20.
111. Billington, *Is Literature Healthy?*, 17.
112. Quoted in Billington, *Is Literature Healthy?*, 14. For the original see Bion, *Learning from Experience*, 84.
113. See also Davis, *Reading and the Reader*, ix. Davis' book offers a series of readings in the spirit of the same passage from Bion.
114. Billington, *Is Literature Healthy?*, 30.
115. Berthoud and Elderkin, *The Novel Cure*, 286.
116. Billington, *Is Literature Healthy?*, 105.
117. Billington, *Is Literature Healthy?*, 104, emphasis by Billington.
118. Billington, *Is Literature Healthy?*, 104.
119. Phillips, *Terrors and Experts*, xvii.

Chapter 6

# Fragments of a Consolatory Discourse: Sontag, Riley, Proust, Barthes

> After being abandoned by a lover who has expressed in the kindest way imaginable a need to spend a little more time on their own, how consoling to lie in bed and witness Proust's narrator crystallizing the thought that, 'When two people part it is the one who is not in love who makes the tender speeches.' How comforting to witness a fictional person [who is also, miraculously, ourselves as we read] suffering the same agonies of a saccharine dismissal and, importantly, surviving.
>
> Alain de Botton, *How Proust Can Change Your Life*[1]

## Against Consolation: Susan Sontag

'Throughout my life', Will Schwalbe writes in the introduction to *Books for Living*, 'I've looked to books for all sorts of reasons: to comfort me, to amuse me, to distract me, and to educate me.'[2] By now, it will no longer come as a surprise that a reader's list of what he sees as the prime functions of literature is headed by the one that has been central to this book all along. The previous chapters will also have made clear that the verb given pride of place by Schwalbe is somehow related to the ones that follow. Sometimes we are comforted by the sheer pleasure that reading provides, while at other times we find comfort in the distraction that our favourite books bring. But in almost all cases comfort comes with a form of learning, with an insight that is new and that we may well never have arrived at without reading these texts.

Schwalbe is probably best known for *The End of Your Life Book Club*, the touching bibliotherapeutic memoir to which I referred in the introduction. In it, Schwalbe recalls the numerous conversations that he had with his dying mother about the books they read and discussed during the treatment of her pancreatic cancer. The scene of some of these conversations is New York's Memorial Sloan Kettering Cancer Center, the same hospital where Susan Sontag was first treated for advanced breast cancer in the autumn of 1975. Sontag eventually died there, nearly thirty years later, of MDS, myelodysplastic syndrome, a form of blood cancer.[3] The story of Sontag's lengthy struggle with her disease is marked by a distinct refusal to be consoled, as we know from the memoir that David Rieff published of his mother's final years. In Sontag's view, to be consoled equalled giving up hope, and that meant allowing oneself to be reconciled with one's mortality, a prospect which Sontag just couldn't bring herself to adopt. As Rieff puts it, Sontag's 'fear of death was always far, far stronger than anything else – stronger even than her profound, and in the end inconsolable, sense of being always the outsider, always out of place'.[4]

'The fancy that I could have consoled her is itself presumptuous', Rieff admits in the opening chapter of his tribute to his mother.[5] Recalling the moment when a doctor from Sloan Kettering coolly mentioned the inevitable outcome of Sontag's medical situation ('a particularly lethal form of blood cancer'[6]), he writes:

> But how I would have liked to have been able somehow to console her, after that meeting with Dr. A. and through the months of her illness until her death. But instead, almost until the moment she died, we talked of her survival, of her struggle with cancer, never about her dying. I was not going to raise the subject unless she did. It was her death, not mine. And she did not raise it. To have done so would have been to concede that she might die and what she wanted was survival, not extinction – survival on any terms. To go on living: perhaps that was her way of dying.[7]

'Positive denial' Rieff calls his mother's standard response throughout her successive struggles with cancer. 'The sense that in ignoring bad news she could somehow stay strong, keep going, and, above all, keep writing was something that marked her as a person', he writes.[8] The situation in *The End of Your Life Book Club* and the tone which Schwalbe strikes throughout is entirely different, even if the pain of the loss that provoked the book's writing will have been no less unbearable. In comparison with Sontag, Schwalbe's mother seems to understand and accept her medical predicament from the beginning. Finding herself incurable, she soon discovers that she is able to exchange one form of hope (that of being cured) with other no less exhilarating variants of that same vital emotion. The very first books that he reads with his mother after her fatal diagnosis prove instrumental in that early discovery, Schwalbe suggests:

> they provided a different kind of hope than that which Dr. O'Reilly had given us. These two books [Roberto Bolaño's *The Savage Detectives* and Michael Thomas' *Man Gone Down*] showed us that we didn't need to retreat or cocoon. They reminded us that no matter where Mom and I were on our individual journeys, we could still share books, and while reading those books, we wouldn't be the sick person and the well person; we would simply be a mother and a son entering new worlds together. What's more, books provided much needed ballast – something we both craved, amid the chaos and upheaval of Mom's illness.[9]

'Reading isn't the opposite of doing,' Schwalbe quips in the opening pages of his memoir, 'it's the opposite of dying.'[10] Obviously, Sontag's illness didn't stop her from doing what she did most in her life – to read as well as write. But neither David Rieff's memoir nor Katie Roiphe's tender reconstruction of the author's final months contain any suggestions that Sontag turned to fiction for help or ease. In the spring of 2004, just after she received the MDS diagnosis, Sontag was mainly reading medical publications, following up her own advice (from *Illness as Metaphor*) that what a patient needed in order to heal was 'clarity, rational thought and medical information'.[11] Both Roiphe and biographer Benjamin Moser mention that Sontag's friend Peter Perrone read Tolstoy's *Death of Ivan Ilyich* to her in the last month of her final stay in Sloan Kettering.[12] Perrone had hoped the story would spark a conversation that could bring some consolation – the conversation didn't come, and neither did the consolation, it would seem.

When David Rieff talks about what the 'solace of art' meant to his mother, he cannot leave untouched the irony that the beauty that art had to offer made it even more difficult for his mother to leave the world behind.[13] The solace of art is also art's mendacity, Rieff adds, proving himself a worthy son to his always critical mother. In his reading memoir, Will Schwalbe, understandably, has no use in downplaying the fiction of artistic consolation, or in stressing the heavy truth of the inevitable end of his two-member venture. There is no doubt that many of the books that are mentioned in *The End of Your Life Book Club* would not have been to Sontag's taste, but for Schwalbe and his mother they apparently did what they were meant to do: they provided comfort and distraction, sometimes in conjunction, at other times separately. In the introduction to *Books for Living*, Schwalbe looks back on their joint reading sessions as follows: 'At times, the books gave us something to talk about when we wanted to talk about anything rather than her illness. But they also gave us a way to talk about subjects that were too painful to address directly.'[14]

'Of course', Schwalbe writes in the epilogue to *The End of Your Life Book Club*, 'the book club also gave us a welter of great books to read – books to savour and ponder, to enjoy, and to help Mom on her journey toward death and me on mine to life without her.'[15] In contrast to Sontag, Schwalbe's mother is a believer: the last words that she read before she drew her final breath appear to have been a reflection by Ruskin on the work needed to enter God's kingdom.[16] As Schwalbe is happy to report, his mother died surrounded by loved ones – and by books that 'had shown her the way', books she had enjoyed reading 'as she readied herself for the life everlasting that she knew awaited her'.[17] The contrast with David Rieff's record of his mother's last moments is stark. In the journals of the first period when Sontag was treated for breast cancer, he finds a series of characteristic injunctions to 'be cheerful, be stoic, be tranquil'.[18] Referring to a poem that Brecht wrote on his deathbed in a Parisian hospital, Rieff cannot but admit that his mother could not arrive at the final consolation that Brecht's poem has on offer, a variant of the classical consolatory topos that death is nothing to be afraid of. In the end, after all, death means nothing to us who will have become nothing ourselves:

> When in my white room at the Charité
> I woke towards morning
> And heard the blackbird, I understood
> Better. Already for some time
> I had lost all fear of death. For nothing
> Can be wrong with me if I myself
> Am nothing. Now
> I managed to enjoy
> The song of every blackbird after me too.[19]

So far for theory, Rieff feels sorry to admit: 'This was not the death she died.'[20]

## Times of Grief: Denise Riley

Contrary to what we might think, Michaël Fœssel writes, practices of consolation do not simply revolve around two participants, the person in need of comfort and the person providing that comfort. Rather, Fœssel argues, these practices are marked by a triangular grid in which the one in need of consolation is related by the one attempting to respond to that need to a third party.[21] That third party involved is not a person, but a collective frame of reference that founds the discourse of comfort and enables the consoler to 'tear away', in Fœssel's dramatic image, the person in need of consolation from their solitude. 'Society', 'nature' and 'language' are the examples that the author of *Le temps de la consolation* gives of that 'third party'. In the classical regime of consolation that we discussed in the first chapter of this book, the *sensus communis* functioned as such, as an 'instance that the person in distress can count on in spite of his distress'.[22] It is a reservoir of shared knowledge, in other words, that not only holds the promise of a moment 'beyond our suffering',[23] but also provides examples of earlier successful attempts at consolation. 'In time, you too will manage to rise above these difficult circumstances', the examples are meant to suggest.

There are three interlocking conditions which consolers need to meet in order to be successful, Fœssel claims. First, they should point the person in need of comfort, who in their present state of desolation only feels stuck in a meaningless chaos of pain, to the possibility of a more 'orderly' and less painful future. Second, the promise of that future needs to open up the possibility that the person in pain will be able to escape their isolation and return to the safe harbour of the collective. Third, comforters need to find a way of speaking that acknowledges and does justice to a suffering that feels unspeakable.[24] In Fœssel's words, 'the difficult ambition of the comforter consists in finding a way to relate a common discourse of suffering to the singularity of a specific case'.[25] The high stakes of that ambition, we have seen at its clearest in our discussion of *Hamlet*: as long as the individual in need of comfort feels that the common discourse does not apply to them, the discourse will fail.

The question, for our purposes, is fairly straightforward: if we say, as we have been doing all along, that books have the ability to bring comfort (the prime ability, even), what is it in them that enables them to meet the three conditions mentioned above? Which specific qualities do we ascribe to these favourite books of ours that we claim can offer soothing consolation? And which reading practice do these books require and set in motion? How do they succeed in addressing us, in our very pain, and in moving us along, bringing us to the novel insight that any successful practice of consolation seems to entail? While it is often argued that fiction enables readers to develop their potential for empathy, the question here seems to be the inverse one: how is it possible that we become convinced that books show empathy with our distress?

In an attempt to explain the comforts of reading, several readers point out that with respect to the first and second conditions that Fœssel lists, books can bring comfort because they oppose the formless and senseless chaos of pain with a meaningful construct that, in its form, provides the prospect of control. What comforters need to do, Fœssel argues, is to 'reconfigure experiential time':[26] they need to transform what to the person in need of comfort feels like an unending, undefined plain of pain and despair into a space that is temporally organised and bounded, not just by a 'before', but also by an 'after'. 'Consolatory writings', Fœssel argues, 'do not try to abolish the time of our distress, but to reorient it in an attempt to make the mourner understand that the passing of time can also become our ally.'[27]

Virginia Woolf's *To the Lighthouse*, Katharine Smyth writes, is a case in point, as the novel, in her experience, 'rectif[ied] grief's essential formlessness'.[28] In other words, the book enabled her to see more clearly into the shapeless misery that life had in store for her. It helped her to set things straight ('rectify'), to detect patterns of meaning in what, outside and without the book, was nothing more than a chaotic jumble of senselessness. Novels have plots and plots organise time, giving meaning to events by imposing an order on them that is not just chronological but also causal. Plots suggest the possibility of development, which in turn enables readers to rethink the chaos of what happened in their own lives in terms of possible closure. Of the examples that we discussed in this book, Luzzi's account of his reading of Dante is a further example: it is clear that the narrative drive of the *Divine Comedy* played a role in his reader's rediscovery of new meaning in the seemingly senseless moment of his wife's death. Luzzi's memoir, as we saw, also made clear that other structuring devices – of a non-narrative and more musical and acoustic nature – served a similar goal. The Dantean image that Luzzi developed in order to capture that process, readers may recall, was that of the turning around of time's arrow.

I want to pick up on that image, here, and relate it to a very potent self-analysis of mourning that David James also discusses in *Discrepant Solace*: Denise Riley's *Time Lived, Without Its Flow*.[29] In her text, as we will see, Riley tries to think through the idea that a text's formal apparatus – rhyme in a specific form of metrical poetry, in her case – might have an effect on a mourning reader's new conception of time. Originally published in 2012, Riley's essay offers a gripping reflection on the sudden death of her son Jacob, the devastating effect of which was also the topic of the author's 2016 collection of poems *Say Something Back*.[30] When death strikes and takes away a loved one, Joan Didion writes in *The Year of Magical Thinking*, 'life changes in the instant'.[31] Grief and mourning are traditionally defined as mechanisms of overcoming, Didion suggests,[32] yet for those in grief the very idea of a 'beyond' is usually far off. 'Grief, when it comes,' she adds, 'is nothing we expect it to be. (...) Grief is different. Grief has no distance. Grief comes in waves, paroxysms, sudden apprehensions that weaken the knees and blind the eyes and obliterate the dailiness of life.'[33] To be stuck in grief, in Denise Riley's apt phrase, is to experience time in a radical new way: time as one lives it, but without its flow.

In a note written ten months after Jacob died, Riley tries to articulate what her son's unexpected parting did to her own sense of temporality as follows:

> [A] sudden death, for the one left behind, does such violence to the experienced 'flow' of time that it stops, and then slowly wells up into a large pool. Instead of the old line of forward time, now something like a globe holds you. You live inside a circle with no rim. In the past, before J's idiotic disappearance, the future lay in front of me as if I could lean into it gently like a finger of land, a promontory feeling its way into the sea. But now I've no sense of any onward temporal opening, but stay lodged in the present, wandering over some vast saucer-like incline of land, some dreary wide plain like the banks of the river Lethe, I suppose. His sudden death has dropped like a guillotine blade to slice through my old expectation that my days would stream onwards into my coming life. Instead I continue to sense daily life as paper-thin. As it is. But this cut through any usual feeling of chronology leaves a great blankness ahead.
>
> Now you expect another death – a remaining child's – to be announced to you at any moment, and you try to steady yourself for it. It's not so much fearfulness as a life poised in acute suspension.[34]

To have to live in a timeless present, Riley comments, 'might sound like stoicism's programme', a variant of Zeno's idea that '[o]nly in the present moment is our happiness'. 'The irony is', Riley is understandably quick to point out, 'that now you've succeeded in living exclusively in the present, but only as the result of that death.'[35] Traditional ideas of mourning as overcoming or the Stoic ideal of endurance have become problematically void to her, Riley writes. 'What does your old philosophy of endurance mean, when there's no longer any temporality left in which to wait it out?'[36]

In his introduction to the 2019 edition of *Time Lived, Without Its Flow*, the novelist Max Porter praises Riley for having written what he describes as 'some of the best pages [he has] ever read on what poems are, on the "literature of consolation, what that could be or what it might do"'.³⁷ In the second half of that sentence, Porter is quoting from the 'Postscript' to Riley's essay, in the thirty pages of which the author tries to give a survey of what she has learned from the notes that she took in the three years of 'timeless time' that followed Jacob's death.³⁸ The notes, forty printed pages in all, are presented in twelve brief chapters, each of which are headed by an indication of the moment of their writing, relative to Jacob's parting ('Two weeks after the death', 'Six months after', 'Nine months after' . . . ). In an attempt to articulate more systematically what she sees as the 'vivid new sensation of a-temporality' that living with her son's death taught her,³⁹ Riley discusses two poems: one by Wordsworth ('A slumber did my spirit seal'), and one by Dickinson ('I felt a cleaving in my mind'). The poems are instances of 'what a literature of consolation might be', in the author's own view. They are 'sounding emblem[s]', Riley argues, which in their very form hint at the 'time of the dead' into which 'those who lose a child will go out with the lost one'.⁴⁰ The poems by Wordsworth and Dickinson are 'emblematic', she goes on to explain,

> of a loss at the moment when it's imperceptibly starting to shift; of the fact that there is change – you have been changed yourself, by your proximity to the death of an intimate – but also a return. This return is not to the same.⁴¹

The formal device that encapsulates the complex mechanism to which Riley refers is rhyme – repetition-in-difference, the return of the not-same. '[A] rhyme is close, but not identical', Riley argues,

> not an immaculate substitution but a recollection, while its sounding anticipates what's to come. This pulsating alteration-in-recognition comes close to the experience of a stopped time which is now unobtrusively, hesitantly – even reluctantly – finding a first breath of its future.⁴²

Rhyme projects possibilities which one can anticipate but not predict. What Riley is after, she is careful to remind us, is not 'a "therapeutics" or a curative aspect for rhyme'.⁴³ After all, there is, as she puts it, 'scarcely consolation for loss in a formally structured poem'.⁴⁴ Where, then, is the consolation in Riley's text? Max Porter – author of the critically acclaimed novel of mourning *Grief is the Thing with Feathers* (2015) – believes it is to be found in the new conception of 'maternal temporality' that Riley develops in the closing pages of her essay and that enables her to renew and continue her relationship with her departed son. 'In [this] new perception of time', Riley writes,

> there's this fresh kind of 'carrying forward'. Your previous history has been reshaped, as your being in time has now become demarcated differently yet again. Its boundaries are extended by and then after the death, as they had once been by and after the birth. Half bitten away by the child's disappearance, your time is nevertheless augmented – for the time of the dead is, from now on, freshly contained within your own.[45]

'What a wonderful idea', Porter exclaims. 'What a vital corrective to banal narratives of "moving on".'[46] Riley herself records her indebtedness to Freud's 'Mourning and Melancholia', but admits to prefer the 'less prescriptive, and more sympathetic' view of mourning that Freud develops in the letter to Binswanger to which I referred in the previous chapter. In that letter, written in reply to the sad news of the death of Binswanger's eldest son, Freud looks back on the death of his own daughter, Sophie, acknowledging that

> [a]lthough we know that after such a loss the acute state of mourning will subside, we also know we shall remain inconsolable and will never find a substitute, no matter what may fill the gap; even if it be filled completely, it nevertheless remains something else. And actually this is how it should be.[47]

To Riley, Freud's insight that 'this is the only way of perpetuating that love which we do not want to relinquish'[48] serves as the foundational inspiration for her consolatory reading of rhyme in the poems by Wordsworth and Dickinson that she selected for the occasion. 'Preservation through replacement', she calls the mechanism that relates mourning to rhyme: 'the familiar but then the differing, in the next breath':[49]

> Which is exactly what happens both in rhyme, and in your own gradual 'reanimation', so to speak, after you've been very near to a death. Nothing has changed, and yet it all has. You are returned after your brush with another's death, a brush that seemed to have stopped you, too – and you've been returned differently. You return, knowing more.[50]

## The Language of Comfort: *Sprezzatura*

'In Riley's delicate formation we might mourn better', Max Porter writes in conclusion of his praise for Riley's literature of consolation.

'We might speak to each other and make sense of things better if we know better how we are living with the dead.'[51] Porter's description of Riley's linguistic prowess brings us back to our discussion of what Michaël Fœssel considers to be the basic conditions to which comforters need to adhere, especially with respect to his analysis of the language that is required of them. It goes without saying that arguments in favour of the idea that books bring comfort tend to revolve around language use. We expect literary writings to excel linguistically; we take it that they give us language at its most flexible and effective. Given the pre-eminent importance of language in the practice of consolation, it makes sense, therefore, that we consider artists of language to be also, potentially at least, artists of comfort. But how do we describe this language? Which characteristics do we ascribe to it?

I want to relate some of the qualifications that Max Porter singles out in his praise of *Time Lived, Without Its Flow* to Fœssel's analysis of the language of comfort. For that language to work, Fœssel writes, 'consolation has to look for a *via media* between the literal sense of suffering, of which it has nothing to say, and another sense that needs to allow the suffering person to establish a new relationship with him- or herself'.[52] Most definitions of literature emphasise the fact that the writing that falls under this label typically explores the figurative potential of language. Also, these writings are usually taken to invite their readers to be active imaginatively, that is, to use their encounter with the literary text as an occasion to reflect upon – and depart from – their own situation.

In order to bring comfort, as we have seen, literary writings need to guide readers to new insights. The medium, in this respect, is what the message is all about. The prime function of the consolatory text, Fœssel points out, is to address us in such a way that we feel as if the language speaks to us directly. 'To bring comfort', he writes, 'is to speak *to* someone before speaking *about* something'.[53] In describing the 'brilliant exactitude' of Denise Riley's prose, Max Porter highlights precisely this quality. Riley's essay, he writes, 'has such an absence of writerly mannerism or manipulation that one feels one is being looked in the eye and must not turn away'.[54]

'Affective proximity' is the convenient phrase that Fœssel uses to label the ideal position of the comforter vis-à-vis the person in need of comfort.[55] The latter allow themselves to be comforted because the former succeed in giving the impression of being not only nearby but also understanding, empathetically so. Still, as Fœssel reminds us, comforters will always run the risk of being taken for flatterers.[56]

Flatterers, like comforters, need the attentive ear of the other person: but whereas the former crave that attention for their own sake – the feeling that the recipient of their words needs to hear exactly what they say is what they live for – the activity of the latter is not self-centred. Comforters who do not deserve to be called flatterers do not allow their words to be limited by what the person in need of comfort wants to hear. There is no end to flattery, whereas the prime goal of the act of comfort, as Fœssel argues, is to 'render itself useless' and to come to an end as quickly as possible.[57] Words of comfort that fail to become effective are immediately suspect, as Fœssel points out: they have the habit of drawing out the pain they are meant to alleviate.

Words of comfort should not draw attention to themselves or to the rhetorical tricks that underlie their working. The rhetoric of comforters is, like that of Baldassare Castiglione's ideal courtier, marked by *sprezzatura*: its artifice is hidden beneath a cloak of authenticity.[58] It doesn't cover up what needs to be said directly, it doesn't sugar-coat. Denise Riley's prose, Max Porter writes, is marked by 'a gorgeous no-nonsense technical virtuosity while dealing with strange and painful things'. That seemingly artless style enables the author to present herself and the reader with 'achingly beautiful conclusions without ever employing familiar, kitsch, or syrupy emotive strategies'.[59] Several critics described the success of Joan Didion's style in similar terms. 'Rawness' and 'precision' are words that recur in David James' analysis of *The Year of Magical Thinking* in *Discrepant Solace*,[60] whereas Deborah Nelson praises Didion for her 'clear-eyed and unsentimental prose'.[61] For Didion, as Nelson points out, 'sentimentality' is an 'aesthetic as well as moral flaw'.[62] The same thing could be said about Riley: her essay, Max Porter writes, 'is profoundly powerful without so much as a whiff of melodrama'.[63]

## The Language of Comfort: Metaphor and Re-description

The language of comfort threatens to fail once it discloses too clearly the comforter's intentions. Next to what I have called its *sprezzatura*-like quality, the language of comfort has a second characteristic that is also central in Fœssel's analysis of what he calls the 'grammar of consolation': its sustained use of metaphor. 'Consolations are not expected to be judged for their objectivity', Fœssel writes, 'but for what they do.'[64] Pragmatics supersedes semantics in the language of comfort, and it is in this domain, Fœssel claims, that we need to value the importance of metaphors. 'The metaphor is not only a rhetorical instrument of comfort,' he goes on to write, 'it is indicative of the consolatory gesture per se.'[65] Fœssel draws heavily on Paul Ricœur's analysis of the 're-descriptive' work of the metaphor:[66] metaphors invite us to look at familiar things with a new eye; in doing so they offer us new descriptions of the real.

In the specific case of consolatory writings, Fœssel argues, the metaphor opens up in the suffering mind the possibility of a new, less painful perspective. In Fœssel's words, it 'serves as an appeal to the imagination of the person addressed, to the extent in which it tries to re-describe the addressee's suffering with the help of unthought of meanings'.[67] That new perspective is consoling, Fœssel argues, in the sense that it diverts our mind without allowing the mind to forget – 'consolation', in Fœssel's felicitous phrase is 'diversion sans oubli', 'distraction without forgetting'.[68]

The key to the consolatory force of metaphors is the fact that they work according to the double-bind logic of identity and difference. The examples that Fœssel gives are taken from Boethius and Seneca. 'In saying that suffering or death is similar to "exile"', Fœssel writes, 'one is saying simultaneously what it is and what it is not; in short, one is redescribing the experience by means of a difference that is introduced through poetic language.'[69] Fœssel is talking about consolation proper, so to speak, not about the consolation of literature. But his remark about the metaphoric quality of poetic language – and his addition that the language of comfort is marked by a fundamental 'semantics of ambiguity'[70] – is an open invitation to relate his analysis of consolation proper to literary consolation, as is the remainder of his description of the linguistic predicament of the comforter, who is

> incapable of stating literally the loss that he has witnessed, but expresses that loss by the indirect means of the image. The metaphor inscribes a tension, internal to the phrase, between proper sense and figured sense. As such, it provokes the imagination of the addressee into searching out the resemblance between the figural term and the context.[71]

Of course, the books that we read are not, literally speaking, witness to the pain that we suffer. However, figuratively speaking, we do allow them to play that role. Some readers are convinced that these comforting books understand their pain better than the people who literally witness, on a day-to-day basis, their suffering. The comfort that these books have in store is the result, inevitably, of the linguistic prowess they display: these writings, readers believe, provide them with the words and images that enable them to see and understand their pain better, more productively.

We allow books to play that role because, unlike people who claim to bring the comfort that we need, books are beyond suspicion. There is little doubt that they will want to flatter us. More importantly, when we are reading a book we do not run the risk that Fœssel singles out as an important obstacle in consolatory encounters: the feeling that our pain is being usurped by our comforters instead of relieved. Texts that aim to console, as we have seen, need to have a forceful and inescapable appeal, but not an intrusive one. Their power of address is not coercive but generous. Their appeal is that of an open invitation to interpret, and to interpret as freely as one can.

For Wolfgang Iser and Jonathan Culler, this quality is a defining characteristic of literary writings – prose fiction in the case of Iser, lyric poetry in the case of Culler.[72] My concern here is not so much with the specifics of their respective theories as with their common idea of reading as performance. When we read literature, Iser and Culler claim, the cognitive process differs from when we read a newspaper article or a scientific paper. When we read literary fiction or a lyrical poem, we become the narrator of the story that we are reading (Iser) or we adopt the voice of the lyrical subject whose words are the poem (Culler), and in doing so we co-create the text that we are reading. At the same time, however, we remain aware of the distance between ourselves and the words on the page. In and of themselves, these words are what they are. While we didn't chose them, in our reading of them, as Iser points out, we make them 'concrete': we complement their 'indeterminate' potential with the specific meaning that we see in them, a meaning that is determined (i.e. made determinate) by our own individual perspective and situation. In Culler's take on lyrical poems, the reader's vocal performance of the written text (to read is to read aloud, in this conception) is a crucial element in a theory of the lyric that goes against traditional conceptions of the genre that either sees poems as expressions by authors or statements made by characters. In Culler's theory, readers literally make the poem into their own, not in the sense that they can simply interpret these texts in whichever way they see fit, but in the sense that the texts enable them to discover within themselves ideas, perspectives and subject positions they were not aware of.

Iser and Culler's conception of reading as performance calls to memory Fœssel's claim – in one of the many sharp definitions of the phenomenon that *Le temps de la consolation* contains – that the genre of the *consolatio* shares a number of rhetorical qualities with other classical texts that stage 'a dialogue of the soul with itself'.[73] The two subgenres overlap in their common goal, one could say. After all, the ultimate aim of consolatory writings, as Fœssel reminds us, is to make themselves useless, that is, to bring the addressee to the point where they no longer need the comforting words of the sender of the message.[74] When that point is reached, the person in need of comfort will be able to provide their own consolation and find strength in themselves, in a dialogue with self, as it were. Before that point is reached, however, in the depths of despair, comfort can only come from without. Moments of crisis, Fœssel writes, require 'words that are offered to us by another person and have the potential to relaunch us in a reasonable debate with ourselves'.[75]

Once again, what Fœssel writes about consolation in general terms offers an apt description of literary consolation, reminiscent, this time, of Proust's dictum that in reading we are indeed having a conversation with ourselves, 'au sein de la solitude' ('in the midst of solitude') as the author of the *Recherche* calls it in an oft-quoted passage of his famous essay on reading.[76] Interestingly, in that passage Proust is talking about what he calls the 'curative' potential of reading literature. Sometimes, he writes, in circumstances in which readers find themselves in a state of 'spiritual depression', books tend to have a healing effect. As such, Proust claims, they play 'a role similar to that of psychotherapists for certain neurasthenics'.[77] The analogy will be clear: the role is that of a mediating agent who enables the patient to come to new insights that lead to recovery, self-recovery even. In Proust's analysis of reading, books serve as this necessarily external impulse: they function to the reader's mind as 'an intervention which, while coming from another, takes place in our innermost selves'. But at the same time, they serve as an open invitation for readers to make into their own the reflections which the book has on offer. This process of internalisation, Proust writes, occurs 'in the midst of solitude': 'The indolent mind can obtain nothing from pure solitude since it is incapable of setting its creative activity in motion.'[78] To read, as Proust puts it elsewhere in his essay, is not to engage in a dialogue with the author of the text, but with oneself. The desired outcome of the process is not a simple confirmation of the reader's former beliefs or convictions, but the active (creative) discovery of new insights.[79]

## Roland Barthes and the Solitude of Mourning

As I see it, Proust's image of the solitary reader is relevant for a deeper understanding of literary comfort. The solitude of the reader is an example of the positively mature state which Winnicott – in his 1958 essay 'The Capacity To Be Alone' – describes as the ability to be alone in the presence of another, 'ego-relatedness' in Winnicott's jargon.[80] 'The capacity to be alone', Winnicott writes, 'depends on the existence of a good object in the psychic reality of the individual'.[81] This good object functions in very much the same way as Winnicott's transitional objects to which I referred in the previous chapter: their work, as we saw, consists of fuelling and guiding the transitional process of solace, leading readers to the novel perspective (the newly required insight) that is implied in any experience of consolation.

Whether or not the object is physically there is not relevant in Winnicott's view. What is important is that it works as 'an internal object', as a mediating force that enables us to find our bearings 'in a benign environment'.[82] In most of the examples that we have been discussing in this study, books and texts functioned in this way: as objects that enabled readers to come up with interpretations ('internal objects') that in turn enabled them, in difficult and trying circumstances, to calm down, think rationally and bear a reality that without the books and texts would very possibly have been unbearable, unliveable.

Winnicott's 'aloneness' – a solitude in the presence of someone else – also functions on the proviso that the other presence makes no demands.[83] This is, arguably, why books are such good companions for the solitary reader. As Proust writes, rehearsing a topos that can be traced back at least to Petrarch, books are the best of friends. They don't feel slighted when we lay them aside, and there is no way we need to feel embarrassed when we misunderstand them.[84] 'Perhaps that is why reading is one of the few things you do alone that can make you feel less alone', Will Schwalbe writes in *Books for Living*: 'Reading is a solitary activity that connects you to others.'[85] In each of the consolatory regimes and encounters that I discussed in the previous chapters, the connection between the person in need of comfort and the larger group for which the person bringing comfort functions as a spokesperson of sorts is a central issue. Consolation and solidarity share more than a single syllable. Looking back on a youth of voracious reading, Rebecca Solnit points out that this is precisely where for her the comfort of books lies: 'in recognizing my own condition or its equivalents and analogies in others, in not being alone in my loneliness and angst'.[86] 'Sometimes when you are devastated', Solnit writes, 'you want not reprieve but a mirror of your condition or a reminder that you are not alone in it.'[87] Some texts will bring their message of comfort gently, Solnit admits, while others 'loo[k] like a bandage but rea[d] like a wound'.[88]

The medical comparison may be extended even further: some texts will serve as bandages for some readers while stimulating the festering of wounds in others. In *Blue Nights*, Joan Didion recalls a discussion she had with her daughter Quintana about reading W. H. Auden's 'Funeral Blues' out loud at the memorial service for her husband John Gregory Dunne, Quintana's father. Didion wanted to include the poem because, as she writes, 'it spoke directly to the anger – the unreasoning fury, the blind rage – that I found myself feeling'; Quintana felt the poem was 'wrong'.[89] Interestingly, an early version of Auden's poem was originally meant to be satirical, but its inclusion in the movie *Four Weddings and a Funeral* made it a popular appearance at memorial services, where it undoubtedly comforted many.[90]

In the remainder of this chapter I want to have a look at a final reflection on the comforts of reading. My last case in this book is Roland Barthes, to whose *Fragments d'un discours amoureux* the title of this chapter sends a warm salute. My focus, however, is on Barthes' book on photography that followed his book on the language of love and that is also an *in memoriam* for Henriette Binger, the author's dearly beloved mother: *La chambre claire*. The book – *Camera Lucida* in the English translation – is the outcome of a period of mourning that follows the death of the author's mother. As Barthes puts it in the *Journal de deuil* that he wrote in his period of mourning: the 'livre sur la Photo' was the result of an attempt 'to integrate [his] suffering with [his] writing' ('d'intégrer mon chagrin à une écriture'[91]). Indeed, the actual writing of *La chambre claire* (15 April – 3 June 1979) coincides with the final months (and the last few pages) of the *Journal de deuil*, which Barthes had begun on 26 October 1977, his 'first mourning night (première nuit de deuil)',[92] the day after his mother died in their apartment in Paris at 11 rue Servandoni, peacefully, at 3.30 in the afternoon.[93]

Midway through his *Mourning Diary*, the inconsolable Barthes recounts a scene of failed consolation that I would like to take as the starting point of my joint reading of the *Journal* and Barthes' book on photography. It occurs in one of the entries dated 29 November (1977) in which Barthes explains to a certain AC (Antoine Compagnon, presumably) that the pain that the loss of his mother resulted in is 'chaotic, erratic' and therefore does not follow the regular process of what he calls 'a mourning subject to time': 'becoming dialectical, wearing out, "adapting"'. When AC reacts spontaneously that this is actually what mourning is all about ('c'est ça, le deuil'),

Barthes cannot but suffer from what he experiences as a painful generalisation of his pain: 'I can't endure my suffering being *reduced* – being *generalized* – (à la Kierkegaard): it's as if it were being stolen from me', he writes.[94] Mourning, as Simon Critchley and Jamieson Webster put it in a reflection on Freud's 'Mourning and Melancholia', 'demands a period of time that is absolutely individual'[95] – it is this time that Barthes feels deprived of.

As we have seen, the desire not to be consoled (Patricia de Martelaere) involves the attempt to bear witness to the absolute nature of one's love. To be able to go through a normal, regular process of mourning – one which comes to an end when the mourner is finally able to decide that this time has come – would take away the 'happiness' (so to speak) that results from what Barthes in his *Mourning Diary* describes as 'living in one's pain': 'I live in my suffering and that makes me happy. Anything that keeps me from living in my suffering is unbearable to me.'[96] Just over one month after his mother's death, Barthes wonders in his *Mourning Diary* whether the fact that he is able to continue life without her means that he loved her less than he thought.[97]

In *La chambre claire*, Barthes also refers to the fact that he was and remained inconsolable after the loss of his mother. The passage is part of his reflection, in the second part of the book, about the famous photograph that shows his mother as a young girl: it was taken in 1898 at the Jardin d'Hiver of the parental house in Chennevières, and shows five-year-old Henriette with her brother, Philippe, who was two years older.[98] In the passage, he is writing about photographic souvenirs that he has been going through in an attempt to recapture memories of his own childhood. But the attempt fails: in contrast to friends of his who were talking about cherished childhood memories, Barthes cannot but conclude that he no longer has them. Sadly, he writes, it is looking at these photographs that took the memories away: 'Surrounded by these photographs', he writes, 'I could no longer console myself with Rilke's line', and then he quotes one specific line from a love poem that Rilke wrote for Lou Andréas Salomé: 'Aussi doux que le souvenir, les mimosas baignent la chambre' ('Sweet as memory, the mimosas steep the bedroom').[99]

'I could no longer console myself', Barthes writes: the sentence suggests two interconnected ideas that I would like to develop here. The first is that photographs, in the specific way that Barthes thinks about them in *La chambre claire*, and at the specific moment in his life at which he is doing that thinking, do not bring comfort. The second is that poetry, in this case a poem by Rilke, obviously *does* have the power to bring comfort for Barthes – the fact that he says that the poem no longer consoles him must mean that it once did. It is clearly something in the photographs (something desolate) that takes away the powers of comfort that Rilke's poem used to have for Barthes. This brings me back to the question that is central to this chapter: What is it in literary texts that brings comfort? And what is it in the photographs of his mother – in the portrait of a loved one who is no longer there – that makes it difficult for Barthes, at this specific time, to find comfort?

Let me begin with the latter question, which on the basis of *La chambre claire* is probably easier to answer. The specific phase of mourning in which Barthes finds himself locked has something to do with it, obviously, but part of the answer also has to do with the 'ontology' (*le tel*) of the photograph, with what Barthes describes as the 'painful labor'[100] that these objects impose ('obligeait') on him, in an act of what he calls real violence.[101] Just before he writes about the line of Rilke's poem, as I have mentioned, Barthes discusses the famous photograph of the Jardin d'Hiver of which he had a reproduction made.[102] Here is the famous passage:

> I am alone with it, in front of it. The circle is closed, there is no escape. I suffer, motionless. Cruel, sterile deficiency: I cannot *transform* my grief, I cannot let my gaze drift; no culture will help me utter this suffering which I experience entirely on the level of the image's finitude (this is why, despite its codes, I cannot *read* a photograph): the Photograph – my Photograph – is without culture: when it is painful, nothing in it can transform grief into mourning.[103]

The two italicised words in this passage already hint at the point that I want to develop in my answer to the first of the above questions. The photograph cannot be read, Barthes argues: it doesn't seem to have the ability to provoke in the viewer (in this viewer at least) the power or the energy to transform the pain that he feels into something more productive, because it lacks the incentive to look elsewhere, to think differently, to imagine otherwise. To look at a photograph is painful because the photograph merely shows that which cannot be denied: the harsh reality of the mother no longer being there, whereas she once was there, at the time at least when the photograph was taken. What the photograph of his mother as a five-year-old shows – what it painfully points out – is the 'catastrophe'[104] that any photo-portrait shows and that Barthes relates to Winnicott: it is a signal of the fact that the catastrophe has already taken place:

'he is going to die',[105] 'she is going to die'.[106] The photograph's *punctum* relates to what Barthes labels 'the discovery of the equivalence' between '[t]his will be' and '[t]his has been'.[107] The photo shows a person who was alive at the time of its making but who no longer is – it gives 'an anterior future of which death is the stake'.[108]

## Alone Together: The Writing that Integrates

Back to my initial question: what is it in literary texts that allows them to function differently from photographs, as sources/purveyors/producers of comfort? Judging by the longer passage quoted above from *La chambre claire*, the answer to that question should be related to a text's transformative potential, the potential, that is, of offering its reader a perspective that does not only allow for the transformation of the reading self but also of what it is that is being represented in the text. The answer should also be related, obviously, to the 'medial' difference between photographs and texts, between *l'image* and *l'écriture*. As Barthes puts it a few pages after the discussion of the Winter Garden photograph to which I referred earlier:

> In the image, as Sartre says, the object yields itself wholly, and our vision of it is *certain* – contrary to the text or to other perceptions which give me the object in a vague, arguable manner, and therefore incite me to suspicions as to what I think I am seeing. This certitude is sovereign because I have the leisure to observe the photograph with intensity; but also, however long I extend this observation, it teaches me nothing. It is precisely in this *arrest* of interpretation that the Photograph's certainty resides: I exhaust myself realizing that *this has been*.[109]

Photographs put a stop to our interpretive efforts, they do not need to be read or scrutinised for an implicit meaning, because their meaning is obvious and the effect of that conclusion is a deadeningly tiring, 'exhausting' one ('je m'épuise', Barthes writes in the original). Writing, on the other hand, as Barthes famously puts it in the final paragraph of 'On échoue toujours à parler de ce qu'on aime' ('One Always Fails in Speaking of What One Loves'), the text of his that he had probably been typing out the morning of his near-fatal accident of Monday 25 February 1980, has the opposite effect – it is not exhausting (*épuisant*), it is, rather, 'a power' (*une puissance*), a form of empowerment, of energy, 'probable fruit of a long initiation, which annuls the sterile immobility of the amorous image-repertoire and gives its adventure a symbolic generality'.[110]

The first phrase that interests me in this passage is the one in which Barthes suggests that writing mobilises – at least, it undoes the immobility of one's imagination/imaginary. The phrase sounds like an echo of the passage about the photograph of the Winter Garden that I referred to earlier, in which Barthes recalls that sitting there in front of his mother's picture made him suffer, 'immobile'. The conjunction between the two passages allows me to come to what sounds like a logical conclusion: whereas photographs transfix you, render you immobile on account of their 'flatness',[111] good writing, the writing that possesses the power that Barthes has been after for most of his career, will transform you. It will enable you to see things differently, to assume a new perspective, maybe to begin a new life, a *vita nuova*. Good writing, to give the ultimate Barthesian example, would have to be Proust, I guess. Late July/early August 1978, Barthes is rereading Proust, as several entries in his *Mourning Diary* for that period show. Reading Proust reminds him of what the essence of literature is: 'Which is what literature is: that I cannot read without pain, without choking on truth, everything Proust writes in his letters about sickness, courage, the death of his mother, his suffering, etc.'[112] Whereas seeing photographs of his dead mother does not allow him to turn his pain into something else, Proust's writing does seem to have that effect, whether it be letters by Proust on the death of his mother, or passages in the *Recherche* that deal with the death of the narrator's grandmother. On that same day (1 August), he writes that he comes to understand that his pain is 'literally *endurable*', if only because he is able to express it in language:

> My culture, my taste for writing gives me this apotropaic or *integrative* power: I *integrate*, by language. My suffering is *inexpressible* but all the same speakable. The very fact that language affords me the word 'intolerable' immediately achieves a certain tolerance.[113]

This is what language does, apparently: it takes away the absolute certainty of a fixed meaning: it opens up new pockets of signification, resulting from the possibility of even the slightest distance between what is stated ('intolerable') and what can be understood by the statement ('a certain tolerance').

What language also does, the passage from the *Mourning Diary* seems to suggest, is that it socialises to a certain extent individual meanings and experiences, it invites us as individuals to become more than our singular selves, and to understand our experiences as having more than the idiosyncratic meaning that we single-mindedly see, without however nullifying our individual experience. Barthes adds a footnote to his statement about the 'integrative' function of language: 'I *integrate* – enter into a whole – federate – socialize, communize, gregoriate'.[114] The footnote seems to echo some of the concerns that Barthes develops in his 1977 course at the Collège de France on the theme of 'comment vivre ensemble' ('how to live together'), where he is clearly on the outlook for specific forms of 'idiorrhythmic' communality that do not impede the individual in the development of their individuality.[115] The phrase is also important because it echoes what to me is the programme of the *Journal de deuil* and *La chambre claire*: Barthes' attempt 'd'intégrer [s]on chagrin à une écriture' ('to integrate [his] suffering with [his] writing').[116]

I want to come back, in that respect, to a second aspect of Barthes' definition of writing in the final paragraph of his last text: writing, he states there, as we have seen, mobilises, and it does so by confronting our imaginary with what he calls 'une généralité symbolique'.[117] In the context of what I have been saying, the word 'généralité' echoes the passage from the *Mourning Diary* that I quoted earlier and in which Barthes complained about one of his friends 'stealing' away his pain from him by making generalising remarks about the natural course of mourning. That type of generalisation was negative in the sense that it deprived Barthes of something that he clearly wanted to call his own; by contrast, the 'généralité symbolique' that he talks about in his text on Stendhal is positive, in the sense that it integrates – without reducing the integrity of one's own experiences it reaches out to include those experiences in a more collective form. It allows us to see that the idiosyncrasies of our personal pain and our individual grief can be both acknowledged and shared, in the way that we have seen Hans Blumenberg describe the mechanism of consolation, whereby we are enabled to 'delegate' our grief for others to share it in a mechanism of 'fictive diffusion'.

The 'symbolic generality' that Barthes refers to is also one of the key components of Aristotle's analysis of mimesis: mimetic art enables us to recognise in what we see or read a variant of our own predicament ('this is me, in a certain way'), one that makes us aware of the fact that this predicament can be seen from a different perspective. Not only does this perspective open up the possibility of change – it makes us aware, in the sort of circumstances that we have been talking about, that our pain can be experienced more productively – it also gives us the impression that our pain can be shared, 'delegated' as Blumenberg would have it.[118] The act of reading a literary text, as Barthes conceives of it in its most ideal form, works according to a similar logic: it allows grieving readers to be both confirmed and mobilised in their arresting pain. This seems to be the insight that Barthes came to during his struggle with grief in the aftermath of his mother's death. As in most of the other cases that we dealt with in the course of this study – Daniel Mendelsohn, Joseph Luzzi, Rod Dreher, Larry Newton, Katharine Smyth, Denise Riley – the insight resulted from a meaningful encounter with literature, one that appealed to the reader on an idiosyncratically individual level ('this book was especially written for me') and fuelled the process of socialisation on which practices of comfort rest.

In Barthes' case the encounter was with Proust. In *How Literature Saved My Life*, the American critic David Shields talks about a similar encounter, not with the author of the *Recherche*, but with J. D. Salinger:

> When I can't sleep, I get up and pull a book off the shelves. There are no more than thirty writers I can reliably turn to in this situation, and Salinger is still one of them. I've read each of his books at least a dozen times. What is it in his work that offers such solace at 3:A.M. of the soul? For me, it's how this voice, to a different degree and in a different way in every book, talks back to itself; how it listens to itself talking, comments upon what it hears, and keeps talking. This self-awareness, this self-reflexivity, is the pleasure and burden of being conscious, and the gift of his work – what makes me less lonely and makes life more livable – lies in its revelation that this isn't a deformation in how I think; this is how human beings think.[119]

'I wanted literature to assuage human loneliness', Shields writes in conclusion to his book, 'but nothing can assuage human loneliness. Literature doesn't lie about this – which is what makes it essential.'[120] What Shields considers the quintessence of literature is to Barthes the quintessence of literary consolation: in not lying about what they do, literary texts create the space that enables one to find a way of being alone together – the sort of space that practices of comfort, literary or not, seem to require.

## Notes

1. De Botton, *How Proust Can Change Your Life*, London: Picador, 1997, 28.

2. Schwalbe, *Books for Living*, 4.
3. Moser, *Sontag*, 367 and 695, respectively. The first chapter of Roiphe, *The Violet Hour*, 25–76 also deals with Sontag's illness and death.
4. Rieff, *Swimming in a Sea of Death*, 74.
5. Rieff, *Swimming in a Sea of Death*, 16.
6. Rieff, *Swimming in a Sea of Death*, 7.
7. Rieff, *Swimming in a Sea of Death*, 17.
8. Rieff, *Swimming in a Sea of Death*, 92.
9. Schwalbe, *The End Of Your Life Book Club*, 31–2.
10. Schwalbe, *The End Of Your Life Book Club*, 7.
11. Roiphe, *The Violet Hour*, 32.
12. Tolstoy's novella is a classic in medical humanities courses: see Billington, *Is Literature Healthy?*, 32–44.
13. Rieff, *Swimming in a Sea of Death*, 170.
14. Schwalbe, *Books For Living*, 4.
15. Schwalbe, *The End Of Your Life Book Club*, 323.
16. Schwalbe, *The End Of Your Life Book Club*, 321.
17. Schwalbe, *The End Of Your Life Book Club*, 320.
18. Rieff, *Swimming in a Sea of Death*, 179.
19. Brecht, *Poems: Part Three* (this poem translated by Michael Hamburger), 451–2, partly quoted in Rieff, *Swimming in a Sea of Death*, 168.
20. Rieff, *Swimming in a Sea of Death*, 179.
21. Fœssel, *Le temps de la consolation*, 36, my translation.
22. Fœssel, *Le temps de la consolation*, 37, my translation.
23. Fœssel, *Le temps de la consolation*, 37, my translation.
24. Fœssel, *Le temps de la consolation*, 35–8.
25. Fœssel, *Le temps de la consolation*, 81, my translation.
26. Fœssel, *Le temps de la consolation*, 43, my translation.
27. Fœssel, *Le temps de la consolation*, 49, my translation.
28. Smyth, *All the Lives We Ever Lived*, 211.
29. Riley, *Time Lived, Without Its Flow*.
30. James also deals with Riley's work in the epilogue of his book: *Discrepant Solace*, 219–23.
31. Didion, *The Year Of Magical Thinking*, 3.
32. Didion, *The Year Of Magical Thinking*, 34–5.
33. Didion, *The Year Of Magical Thinking*, 26–7.
34. Riley, *Time Lived, Without Its Flow*, 31–2.
35. Riley, *Time Lived, Without Its Flow*, 32.
36. Riley, *Time Lived, Without Its Flow*, 32–3. Riley further discusses Stoicism in *Impersonal Passion*, 38–42.
37. Max Porter, 'Introduction' to Riley, *Time Lived, Without Its Flow*, 7.
38. Riley, *Time Lived, Without Its Flow*, 56. The sentence that Porter quotes is on page 67.
39. Riley, *Time Lived, Without Its Flow*, 58.
40. Riley, *Time Lived, Without Its Flow*, 78, 60.

41. Riley, *Time Lived, Without Its Flow*, 78.
42. Riley, *Time Lived, Without Its Flow*, 78.
43. Riley, *Time Lived, Without Its Flow*, 77.
44. Riley, *Time Lived, Without Its Flow*, 78.
45. Riley, *Time Lived, Without Its Flow*, 83.
46. Porter, 'Introduction' to Riley, *Time Lived, Without Its Flow*, 8.
47. Letter of 11 April 1929, quoted in Riley, *Time Lived, Without Its Flow*, 74.
48. Freud to Binswanger, cited in Riley, *Time Lived, Without Its Flow*, 74.
49. Riley, *Time Lived, Without Its Flow*, 75.
50. Riley, *Time Lived, Without Its Flow*, 75.
51. Porter, 'Introduction' to Riley, *Time Lived, Without Its Flow*, 9.
52. Fœssel, *Le temps de la consolation*, 74, my translation.
53. Fœssel, *Le temps de la consolation*, 79, my translation and emphasis.
54. Porter, 'Introduction' to Riley, *Time Lived, Without Its Flow*, 5.
55. Fœssel, *Le temps de la consolation*, 45, my translation.
56. Fœssel, *Le temps de la consolation*, 83.
57. Fœssel, *Le temps de la consolation*, 83, my translation.
58. Castiglione, *The Book of the Courtier*, 66–8.
59. Porter, 'Introduction' to Riley, *Time Lived, Without Its Flow*, 6.
60. James, *Discrepant Solace*, 162–5.
61. Nelson, *Tough Enough*, 144.
62. Nelson, *Tough Enough*, 145.
63. Porter, 'Introduction' to Riley, *Time Lived, Without Its Flow*, 5. In the case of Didion, as Nelson shows, this rhetoric of precise sparsity is aimed at avoiding, at all costs, the reproach of self-pity. See also Didion, *The Year of Magical* Thinking, 196–8. The issue is also central in C. S. Lewis' classic analysis of grief: 'the bath of self-pity', Lewis writes, 'the wallow, the loathsome sticky-sweet pleasure of indulging it – that disgusts me' (C. S. Lewis, *A Grief Observed*, 4). As we have seen in Chapter 2, to indulge in self-pity is a trait of the selfish mourner, as Laelius argues in Cicero's *De amicitia*.
64. Fœssel, *Le temps de la consolation*, 74.
65. Fœssel, *Le temps de la consolation*, 74.
66. Fœssel, *Le temps de la consolation*, 90; the reference is to Ricœur's *La métaphore vive* (1975).
67. Fœssel, *Le temps de la consolation*, 90n1, my translation.
68. Fœssel, *Le temps de la consolation*, 75, my translation.
69. Fœssel, *Le temps de la consolation*, 90, my translation.
70. Fœssel, *Le temps de la consolation*, 90, my translation.
71. Fœssel, *Le temps de la consolation*, 90, my translation.
72. For Iser, see, for instance, *The Implied Reader*. For Culler, see *Theory of the Lyric*; also: Van der Haven and Pieters, 'Lyric Address'.
73. Fœssel, *Le temps de la consolation*, 81, my translation.
74. Fœssel, *Le temps de la consolation*, 83.
75. Fœssel, *Le temps de la consolation*, 81, my translation.

76. Proust's essay ('De la lecture') serves as an introduction to his translation of Ruskin's *Sesame and the Lilies*: Marcel Proust, 'On Reading', 99–129. The reference is to page 117. See also Pieters, *De tranen van de herinnering*, 36–48.
77. Proust, 'On Reading', 116.
78. Proust, 'On Reading', 117.
79. Proust, 'On Reading', 114.
80. Winnicott, 'The Capacity To Be Alone', 29–36.
81. Winnicott, 'The Capacity To Be Alone', 31–2.
82. Winnicott, 'The Capacity To Be Alone', 32.
83. Winnicott, 'The Capacity To Be Alone', 34.
84. Proust, 'On Reading', 123.
85. Schwalbe, *Books for Living*, 7.
86. Solnit, *Recollections of My Non-Existence*, 107.
87. Solnit, *Recollections of My Non-Existence*, 108.
88. Solnit, *Recollections of My Non-Existence*, 107.
89. Didion, *Blue Nights*, 157.
90. The poem is included in Paterson (ed.), *The Picador Book of Funeral Poems*, 54 and it is referenced in Anthony and Ben Holden (eds), *Poems That Make Grown Men Cry*, 117.
91. Barthes, *Mourning Diary*, 105. For the original, see Barthes, *Journal de deuil*. For an astute reading of Barthes' reflections on grief in *The Mourning Diary* and *Camera Lucida* see Badmington, *The Afterlives of Roland Barthes*, 13–60.
92. Barthes, *Mourning Diary*, 3.
93. Samoyault, *Roland Barthes*, 634.
94. Barthes, *Mourning Diary*, 71.
95. Critchley and Webster, *The Hamlet Doctrine*, 119.
96. Barthes, *Mourning Diary*, 173.
97. Barthes, *Mourning Diary*, 68.
98. Barthes also writes about the photograph in his *Mourning Diary*, 143 and 226.
99. In Rilke's original: 'So milde wie Erinnerung / duften im Zimmer die Mimosen'. The poem, 'Dir zur Feier', was begun in 1897 and finished in 1898, the year of the Winter Garden photograph. The passage occurs in Barthes, *Camera Lucida*, 91.
100. Barthes, *Camera Lucida*, 66.
101. Barthes, *Camera Lucida*, 91.
102. The *Mourning Diary* shows that he received it on 28 December 1978 (220). He discovered the photograph on 13 June 1978 (*Mourning Diary*, 143). See also Samoyault, *Roland Barthes*, 673.
103. Barthes, *Camera Lucida*, 90.
104. Barthes, *Camera Lucida*, 96.
105. Barthes, *Camera Lucida*, 96.
106. Barthes, *Camera Lucida*, 96.

107. Barthes, *Camera Lucida*, 96.
108. Barthes, *Camera Lucida*, 96.
109. Barthes, *Camera Lucida*, 106–7.
110. Barthes, 'One Always Fails in Speaking of What One Loves', in Barthes, *The Rustle of Language*, 305.
111. Barthes has a lot to say about their 'platitude' in *Camera Lucida*; see, for instance, 106.
112. Barthes, *Mourning Diary*, 177.
113. Barthes, *Mourning Diary*, 175.
114. Barthes, *Mourning Diary*, 175.
115. Barthes, *Comment vivre ensemble*, translated as Barthes, *How To Live Together*. See also Pieters and Pint (eds), *Reading Barthes Retroactively* and Pint, *The Perverse Art of Reading*.
116. Barthes, *Mourning Diary*, 105.
117. Barthes, 'One Always Fails', 305.
118. See also Fœssel, *Le temps de la* consolation, 84: 'the consolatory discourse is sustained by a rhetoric of verisimilitude ('le vraisemblable')', my translation.
119. Shields, *How Literature Saved My Life*, 176–7.
120. Shields, *How Literature Saved My Life*, 188.

# Epilogue: The Library of Comfort

> Where, in what blessed, endlessly irrigated gardens, on what trees,
> from what delicately unpetalled calyces
> do the fruits of solace ripen?
> Those rare, superb fruits that you stumble upon
>
> in the trampled meadow of your loss, each new find
> a marvel in its size, its firm, smooth rind,
> in its somehow escaping the whim
> of the bird, the envy of the worm.
>
> 'Solace', Don Paterson (after Rainer Maria Rilke)[1]

Now that the time has come to round off this book, I hope that the painting on its cover reflects what I have tried to express in these pages: the library of comfort has plenty of titles in store – many more, in any way, than can be dealt with in the bounds of a single study like this. Each and every one of us has our very own comfort reads. Taken together, that is a lot of books, indeed. Even if we grant that several of the consoling titles on our individual lists will also feature on those of fellow readers, the library of comfort comes close to being as limitless as Borges' Library of Babel.[2] By now, the experience is a familiar one to me. Whenever I have given a talk on the topic of this book, whether for academic or more general groups of listeners, members of the audience would happily volunteer new titles, books which they believed I could and should also deal with. In the personal experiences of these readers, the books in question had done exactly that which they took it I was talking about: they had provided serious literary comfort.

The painting on my book's cover was made by the Viennese artist Friedrich Frotzel (1898–1971). Its title – 'The Old Bookcase' – makes it even more appropriate. The library of comfort, as we have seen, is a very old bookcase indeed.[3] The period that we traversed in the course of six chapters – from Homer to the present – is dauntingly long, to say the least. Each of the moments that I selected from that vast literary history warrants a closer study in itself. Other moments, focusing on the work of still different authors, could have been added. In the lengthy preparation of this book, there were times when I considered writing several other chapters: on Petrarch's *Invective Contra Medicum*, for instance, on Rilke's *Sonnets to Orpheus*, or on the contemporary French writer Michel Houellebecq, the consolatory potential of whose work is the surprising topic of a recent monograph.[4]

However, since my own book was already expanding beyond the terms that I had agreed upon with the publisher, I had to be selective. Fortunately, the exhaustive treatment of a topic no longer seems to be a realistic goal in our scholarly culture. There is simply too much information, too much history, too many possible data. As I mentioned in the introduction to my book, my goal was not to survey the entire history of the inter-relationships between literature and consolation. What I wanted to do, basically, was to show how the idea that readers derive consolation from the books that they turn to in moments of distress – a critical intuition that we hear quite often nowadays – was itself underpinned by ideas and notions that derive from a dual conceptual history, that of literature and poetics on the one hand, and that of consolation on the other. Representing specific moments in which these two historical trajectories were shown to intersect, my selected case studies are meant to teach us something about the development of the two concepts considered in isolation. The moments and texts under scrutiny teach us something about what literature is and can do, but also about what consolation is and can do. The point that I wanted to make, above all, is that the historical development of Western ideas of consolation tells us something of how we think about the reading of literature; inversely, my argument went, our ideas of what literature is and does shed light on the rhetorical and fictional nature of proper linguistic expressions of comfort.

The woman in the painting, in my predictable reading of Frotzel's beautiful image, is looking for comfort in the books that she finds assembled in the old bookcase in front of her. She may well have found it in the volume that she is visibly engrossed in. The white handkerchief that is lying on the ground – it must have dropped – is clearly meant to catch our attention. I take it this female reader does not simply have a cold. She must be sad, for whatever reason. Could it be that she is in mourning? The black dress that she is wearing is surely not sufficient proof in itself. Also, since the painter has allowed her to turn her back on us, it is impossible to detect in her facial expression further signs of distress.

Still, the book that is sitting in the young woman's lap clearly renders her handkerchief rather useless. Whether or not it really alleviates her sadness, we can only guess. But even if she turned around for a moment to look us in the eye, smiling or not, the outcome of her consolatory reading would still be for her to decide. Books *can* bring comfort, as we have seen, but whether or not they actually do may well depend less on their intrinsic qualities than on the will of the person in need of comfort to be comforted.

Frotzel's painting remains silent on the identity of the books and other writings that are collected in this library of comfort. While the spines of a few of the books on the painting seem to be adorned with titles or the names of authors, none of these are legible – understandably so. After all, the library of comfort centres upon readers, not writers. It is rather useless, therefore, to try to imagine which book of comfort the young woman is reading. The painting is dated 1929. Some Rilke perhaps? Who knows? As we have seen in the course of the previous chapters, different books have different effects on different types of readers. Some will manage without fail to provide comfort for numerous readers, but still leave others unresponsively cold. Some books will provide comfort to different readers for different reasons or in different respects. Joseph Luzzi and Rod Dreher, as we saw, were both consoled by Dante's *Divine Comedy*, but the same book clearly did not result in a common consolatory experience.

Other readers, still, will suddenly find consolation in texts that had no comforting effect at all when they read them on previous occasions. In order to be comforted by books, we need first of all to be responsive to their effects. Once we understand literature's potential to console better, we might even find comfort in texts that first appear to be anything but comforting. At one particularly interesting moment in his *Paris Review* interview, Adam Phillips briefly turns the tables on his interviewer, asking him what he thinks of the Randall Jarrell line 'The ways we miss our lives is life' that Phillips discusses in the 'Prologue' to his book *Missing Out*.[5] 'I don't know what it's about', the interviewer says, 'but it strikes me as true, and painful because it's true.'[6] 'What's painful about it?', Phillips wonders. 'It could be extremely comforting, couldn't it?'[7] Since the interviewer doesn't seem convinced right away, Phillips goes on to explain: 'I'm saying there could be comfort in that line. And the comfort would be something like, "You don't have to worry too much about trying to have the lives you think you're missing. Don't be tyrannised by the part of yourself that's only interested in elsewhere.'"[8]

The issue is not so much whether or not Jarrell's line is or is not consoling, but rather that in matters of literary consolation it is up to readers to decide whether or not they want to be comforted, even though putting it like this might be overstressing the impact of the will in matters of consolation. Quite often, being comforted is something that happens to us, unexpectedly. This is especially the case when we chance to come across a passage in a literary text that moves us in the way that comfort can. The young woman in Frotzel's painting may well be on the verge of experiencing such a moment. Whether or not the author she is reading intended to write words of comfort is not really relevant. What matters is that the words on the page, in the full ambiguity that we like our literary texts to display, reach out to this reader and allow her to come to a new insight that makes life more bearable.

The large majority of visual representations of comfort that I know generally picture two people. One of them, the person in need of comfort, is visibly sad. The other person, the comforter to be, stands or sits nearby, usually within reach. More often than not, the latter is putting an arm around the former, or laying a hand on their shoulder. The comfort of reading is much harder to visualise, but Friedrich Frotzel's painting does the job better than most. If we look at the painting through the lens of the topic that was central to this book, it does not take too much imagination to see that the book in the young woman's lap is, likewise, holding its sad reader in a consoling embrace. Chances are that in this very book she will stumble upon one of the rare 'fruits of solace' that Don Paterson writes about in his beautiful translation of Sonnet 17 in the second part of Rilke's *Sonnette an Orpheus*. The poem's first two stanzas fit as a motto to my epilogue, and thence, to this entire book. Their message is as clear as the painting that Frotzel made. Every time we show our sadness to our friends and relatives, many will come to comfort us, often to no avail. Most likely, they will leave unwanted traces in what Rilke calls 'the trampled meadow of our loss'. One of modernism's most staunch believers in the powers of literature, the poet of the *Sonnette an Orpheus* believed that in many respects literature could make a meaningful difference. Good poems, Rilke was convinced, were true and untouched fruits of solace. The point of my book was not to assert that Rilke was right, but to offer a critical survey of the arguments that he could and did use to sustain that conviction. It will be a relief – if not a comfort – if the book turns out to be of some use to some readers.

## Notes

1. Paterson, *Orpheus*, 47.
2. Borges, 'The Library of Babel'.
3. Frotzel, 'Der alte Bücherkasten' (1929), oil on canvas, Vienna, Schloss Belvedere.
4. Novak-Lechevalier, *Houellebecq, l'art de la consolation*.
5. Phillips, *Missing Out*, xii. The line is from 'A Girl in a Library', where it reads: 'And yet, the ways we miss our lives are life': Jarrell, *The Complete Poems*, 15–18.
6. Phillips, 'The *Paris Review* Interview', in *In Writing: Essays on Literature*, 255. Originally published as 'The Art of Nonfiction No. 7' in *The Paris Review*, 208, spring 2014; the interviewer is Paul Holdengräber.
7. Phillips, 'The *Paris Review* Interview', 255.
8. Phillips, 'The *Paris Review* Interview', 255–6.

# Bibliography

Abrams, M. H., *Natural Supernaturalism: Tradition and Revolution in Romantic Literature*, New York and London: W. W. Norton and Company, 1971.

Alfonsi, Luigi, *Dante e la Consolatio Philosophiae di Boezio*, Como: Marzorati, 1944.

Arendt, Hannah, *The Human Condition: A Study of the Central Dilemmas Facing Modern Man*, New York: Doubleday and Company, 1959.

Aristote, *La poétique*, ed. and trans. Roselyne Dupont-Roc and Jean Lallot, Paris: Seuil, 1980.

Aristotle, *The 'Art' of Rhetoric*, trans. John H. Freese, London and Cambridge, MA: Heinemann and Harvard University Press (Loeb Classical Library), 1947.

Aristotle, *The Nicomachean Ethics*, trans. Harris Rackham, London and Cambridge, MA: Heinemann and Harvard University Press (Loeb Classical Library), 1956.

Aristotle, *Poetics*, ed. and trans. Stephen Halliwell, London and Cambridge, MA: Harvard University Press (Loeb Classical Library), 2005.

Aristotle, *Poetik*, ed. and trans. Manfred Fuhrmann, Stuttgart: Reclam, 1994.

Ascoli, Albert, *Dante and the Making of a Modern Author*, Cambridge: Cambridge University Press, 2010.

Astell, Ann W., *Job, Boethius, and Epic Truth*, Ithaca, NY and London: Cornell University Press, 1994.

Auden, W. H., *Lectures on Shakespeare*, ed. A. Kirsch, Princeton: Princeton University Press, 2000.

Auerbach, Erich, *Dante: Poet of the Secular World*, New York: New York Review Books, 2007.

Auerbach, Erich, 'Figura', in Auerbach, *Scenes from the Drama of European Literature*, Manchester: Manchester University Press, 1984, 11–76.

Badmington, Neil, *The Afterlives of Roland Barthes*, London: Bloomsbury, 2016.

Baltrušaitis, Jurgis, *Anamorphoses ou perspectives curieuses*, Paris: Perrin, 1955.

Baltrušaitis, Jurgis *Les perspectives dépravées: Tome 2: anamorphoses*, Paris: Flammarion, 2008.

Baltussen, Han, 'Cicero's Consolatio ad se: Character, Purpose and Impact of a Curious Treatise', in Baltussen (ed.), *Greek and Roman Consolations: Eight Studies of a Tradition and its Afterlife*, Swansea: The Classical Press of Wales, 2013, 67–92.

Baltussen, Han (ed.), *Greek and Roman Consolations: Eight Studies of a Tradition and its Afterlife*, Swansea: The Classical Press of Wales, 2013.

Barnes, Julian, *Flaubert's Parrot*, London: Picador, 1984.

Barnes, Julian, *Levels of Life*, London: Jonathan Cape, 2013.

Barnes, Julian, *Something to Declare*, London: Picador, 2002.

Barolini, Teodolinda, *Dante's Poets: Textuality and Truth in the Comedy*, Princeton: Princeton University Press, 1984.

Barry, Joseph, *George Sand ou le scandale de la liberté*, Paris: Seuil, 1982.

Barthes, Roland, *Camera Lucida: Reflections on Photography*, trans. Richard Howard, London: Flamingo, 1984.

Barthes, Roland, *La chambre claire: Note sur la photographie*, Paris: Gallimard, 1980.

Barthes, Roland, *Comment vivre ensemble: Cours et séminaires au Collège de France (1976–1977)*, Paris: Seuil, 2002.

Barthes, Roland, *How to Live Together: Novelistic Simulations of Some Everyday Spaces*, trans. Kate Briggs, New York: Columbia University Press, 2012.

Barthes, Roland, *Journal de deuil: 26 octobre 1977 – 15 septembre 1979*, ed. Nathalie Léger, Paris: Seuil/Imec, 2009.

Barthes, Roland, *Mourning Diary: October 26, 1977 – September 15, 1979*, ed. Nathalie Léger, trans. Richard Howard, New York: Hill and Wang, 2010.

Barthes, Roland, *The Rustle of Language*, trans. Richard Howard, Berkeley: University of California Press, 1989.

Bates, Laura, *Shakespeare Saved My Life: Ten Years in Solitary with the Bard*, Naperville, IL: Sourcebooks, 2013.

Bernard, Catherine, '*Flaubert's Parrot*: le reliquaire mélancolique', *Etudes anglaises*, 54, 4, 2001, 453–64.

Bersani, Leo, *The Culture of Redemption*, Cambridge, MA: Harvard University Press, 1990.

Bersani, Leo, *Marcel Proust: The Fictions of Life and Art*, New York: Oxford University Press, 1965.

Berthoud, Ella, *The Art of Mindful Reading: Embracing the Wisdom of Words*, London: Leaping Hare Press, 2019.

Berthoud, Ella, and Elderkin, Susan, *The Novel Cure: An A to Z of Literary Remedies*, London: Canongate, 2013.

Billington, Josie, *Is Literature Healthy?*, Oxford: Oxford University Press, 2016.

Billington, Josie (ed.), *Reading and Mental Health*, London: Palgrave/MacMillan, 2019.

Bion, Wilfred, *Learning from Experience*, London: Maresfield Library, 1962.

Blackwood, Stephen, *The Consolation of Boethius as Poetic Liturgy*, Oxford: Oxford University Press, 2015.

Bloom, Allan, *Shakespeare on Love and Friendship*, Chicago and London: University of Chicago Press, 2000.

Bloom, Harold, *Shakespeare: The Invention of the Human*, London: Fourth Estate, 1999.

Blumenberg, Hans, 'Trostbedürfnis und Untröstlichkeit des Menschen', in Blumenberg, *Beschreibung des Menschen*, Frankfurt: Suhrkamp, 2006, 623–55.

Boccaccio, *The Decameron*, trans. G. H. McWilliam, Harmondsworth: Penguin, 1977.

Boethius, *The Consolation of Philosophy*, trans. David R. Slavitt, Cambridge, MA and London: Harvard University Press, 2008.

Bonnet, Pierre-André, *La bibliothérapie en médecine générale*, Montpellier: Sauramps Médical, 2013.

*The Book Lovers' Anthology: A Compendium of Writing about Books, Readers and Libraries*, Oxford: The Bodleian Library, 2015.

Borges, 'The Library of Babel' (1941), in Borges, *Labyrinths: Selected Stories and Other Writings*, trans. James E. Irby, Harmondsworth: Penguin, 1985, 78–86.

Borsuk, Amaranth, *The Book*, Cambridge, MA: MIT Press, 2018.

Bosco, Umberto (dir.), *Enciclopedia Dantesca*, Roma: Istituto dell' Enciclopedia Italiana, 1970.

Boyce, Benjamin, 'The Stoic Consolatio and Shakespeare', *PLMA*, 64, 4, 1949, 771–80.

Boys-Stones, 'The *Consolatio ad Apollonium*: Therapy for the Dead', in Han Baltussen (ed.), *Greek and Roman Consolations: Eight Studies of a Tradition and its Afterlife*, Swansea: The Classical Press of Wales, 2013, 123–38.

Brecht, Bertolt, *Poems: Part Three, 1938–1956*, ed. John Willett and Ralph Manheim, London: Eyre Methuen, 1976.

Caldwell, John, 'The *De Institutione Arithmetica* and the *De Institutione Musica*', in Margaret Gibson (ed.), *Boethius: His Life, Thought and Influence*, Oxford: Basil Blackwell, 1981, 135–54.

Calvino, Italo, 'Gerolamo Cardano', in Calvino, *Why Read the Classics?*, trans. Martin McLaughlin, London: Jonathan Cape, 1999, 77–81.

Campbell, Jen, *Weird Things Customers Say in Bookshops*, London: Constable, 2012.

Campbell, Jen, *The Bookshop Book*, London: Constable, 2014.

Campbell, Lily B., *Shakespeare's Tragic Heroes: Slaves of Passion*, Cambridge: Cambridge University Press, 1930.

Capet, Antoine, Romanski, Philippe, Terrien, Nicole, and Sy-Wonyu, Aïssatou (eds), 'Julian Barnes in Conversation', in Flaubert's Parrot *de Julian Barnes: 'Un symbole du logos?'*, Mont Saint-Aignan: Presses Universitaires du Rouen et du Havre, 2002, 119–33.

Cardano, Girolamo, *The Book of My Life*, introduction by Anthony Grafton, trans. Jean Stoner, New York: New York Review Books, 2002.

Cardanus, Hieronymus, *De Consolatione Libri Tres*, Venice: Hieronymus Scotus, 1542.

*Cardanus Comforte, translated into Englishe. And published by commaundement of the right honourable Earl of Oxenford*, London: Thomas Marshe, 1573.

Carson, Anne, *Nox*, New York: New Directions, 2010.

Castiglione, Baldassare, *The Book of the Courtier*, trans. George Bull, Harmondsworth: Penguin, 1981.

Chadwick, Henry, *Boethius: The Consolations of Music, Logic, Theology, and Philosophy*, Oxford: Oxford University Press, 1981.

Chong-Gossard, James H. Kim, 'Consolation in Euripides' *Hypsipyle*', in J. R. C. Crousland and James R. Hume (eds), *The Play of Texts and Fragments: Essays in Honour of Martin Cropp*, Leiden/Boston: Brill, 2009, 11–22.

Chong-Gossard, James H. Kim, On 'Mourning and Consolation in Greek Tragedy', in Han Baltussen (ed.), *Greek and Roman Consolations: Eight Studies of a Tradition and its Afterlife*, Swansea: The Classical Press of Wales, 2013, 37–66.

Ciani, Maria Grazia, *La consolatio nei tragici greci: elementi di un topos*, Roma: L'Erma di Bretschneider, 1975.

Cicero, *De amicitia*, trans. W. A. Falconer, London and Cambridge, MA: Heinemann/Harvard University Press (Loeb Classical Library), 1954.

Cicero, *Tusculan Disputations*, trans. J. E. King, London and Cambridge, MA: Heinemann and Harvard University Press (Loeb Classical Library), 1966.

Coetzee, J. M. *Doubling the Point: Essays and Interviews*, ed. D. Atwell, Cambridge, MA and London: Harvard University Press, 1992.

Courcelle, Pierre, *La consolation de philosophie dans la tradition littéraire*, Paris: Etudes Augustiniennes, 1967.

Crabbe, Anna, 'Literary Design in the *De Consolatione Philosophiae*', in Margaret Gibson (ed.), *Boethius: His Life, Thought and Influence*, Oxford: Basil Blackwell, 1981, 237–74.

Craig, Hardin, 'Hamlet's Book', *The Huntington Library Bulletin*, 6, 1934, 17–37.

Critchley, Simon, *The Greeks and Us*, London: Profile Books, 2019.

Critchley, Simon, and Webster, Jamieson, *The Hamlet Doctrine*, London/New York: Verso, 2013.

Culler, Jonathan, *Theory of the Lyric*, Cambridge, MA and London: Harvard University Press, 2015.

Curtius, Ernst Robert, *European Literature and the Latin Middle Ages*, trans. Willard R. Trask, London: Routledge and Kegan Paul, 1955.

Cushman, Robert E., *Therapeia: Plato's Conception of Philosophy*, Chapel Hill: University of North Carolina Press, 1958.

Dagerman, Stig, 'Our Need for Consolation is Insatiable', trans. Steven Hartman, *Little Star: A Journal of Poetry and Prose*, 5, 2013, 301–7.

Dante, *Convivio*, ed. P. Cudini, Milano: Garzanti, 2005.

Dante, *The Divine Comedy*, trans. Jean Hollander and Robert Hollander, New York: Anchor Books, 2004.

Dante, *Vita Nuova*, intro. Edoardo Sanguinetti, notes Alfonso Berardinelli, Milano: Garzanti, 1999.

Dante, *La Vita Nuova*, trans. David R. Slavitt, Cambridge, MA and London: Harvard University Press, 2010.

Davis, Philip, *Reading and the Reader*, Oxford: Oxford University Press, 2013.

De Botton, Alain, *How Proust Can Change Your Life*, London: Picador, 1997.

De Botton, Alain, and Armstrong, John, *Art as Therapy*, London: Phaidon, 2013.

De Grazia, Margeta, Hamlet *without Hamlet*, Cambridge: Cambridge University Press, 2007.

De Martelaere, Patricia, *Een verlangen naar ontroostbaarheid: Over leven, kunst en dood*, Amsterdam/Leuven: Meulenhoff/Kritak, 1993.

De Waal, Frans, *The Age of Empathy: Nature's Lessons for a Kinder Society*, New York: Three Rivers Press, 2009.

Derrida, Jacques, 'La pharmacie de Platon', in Derrida, *La dissémination*, Paris: Seuil, 1972, 77–213.

Derrida, Jacques, *Politics of Friendship*, trans. George Collins, London: Verso, 1997.

Detambel, Régine, *Les livres prennent soin de nous: Pour une bibliothérapie creative*, Arles: Actes Sud, 2015.

Deutelbaum, Wendy, 'Desolation and Consolation: The Correspondence of Gustave Flaubert and George Sand', *Genre*, 15, 1982, 281–302.

Didion, Joan, *Blue Nights*, New York: Alfred A. Knopf, 2011.

Didion, Joan, *The Year Of Magical Thinking*, London: Fourth Estate, 2005.

Donato, Antonio, *Boethius' Consolation of Philosophy as a Product of Late Antiquity*, London: Bloomsbury, 2013.

Douce, Francis, *Illustrations of Shakespeare, and of Ancient Manners: With Dissertations on the Clowns and Fools of Shakespeare; on the Collection of Popular Tales Entitled Gesta Romanorum; and on the English Morris Dance*, London: Longman, Hurst, Rees, and Orme, 1807.

Dreher, Rod, *How Dante Can Save Your Life: The Life-Changing Wisdom of History's Greatest Poem*, New York: Regan Arts, 2015.

Ebbesen, Sten, 'The Aristotelian Commentator', in John Marenbon (ed.), *The Cambridge Companion to Boethius*, Cambridge: Cambridge University Press, 2009, 34–55.

Ellrodt, Robert, *Montaigne and Shakespeare: The Emergence of Modern Self-Consciousness*, Manchester; Manchester University Press, 2017.

Eyres, Harry, *Horace and Me: Life Lessons from an Ancient Poet*, London: Bloomsbury, 2013.

Fantham, Elaine et al., *Seneca: Hardship and Happiness*, Chicago: University of Chicago Press, 2014.

Ferrari, G. R. F., 'Plato and Poetry', in George Kennedy (ed.), *Classical Criticism*, Vol. 1 of *The Cambridge History of Literary Criticism*, Cambridge: Cambridge University Press, 1997, 92–148.

Ferris, Joshua, review of Don DeLillo, *Zero K*, *New York Times*, 2 May 2016.

Flaubert, Gustave, 'Un cœur simple', in *Œuvres*, II, ed. A. Thibaudet and R. Dumesnil, Bibliothèque de la Pléiade, Paris: Gallimard, 1952, 589–622.

Flaubert, Gustave, *Correspondance*, 5 vols. ed. Jean Bruneau, Paris: Gallimard, 1973–2007.

*Flaubert-Sand: The Correspondence*, trans. Francis Steegmuller and B. Bray, London: Harvill/Harper Collins, 1993.

*The Letters of Gustave Flaubert: Volumes I and II (1830–1880)*, ed. and trans. Francis Steegmuller, London: Picador, 2001.

Flaubert, Gustave, *A Simple Heart*, trans. Roger Whitehouse, London: Penguin Books, 2015.

Fœssel, Michaël, *Le temps de la consolation*, Paris: Seuil, 2015.

Forker, Charles R. (ed.), *King Richard II: The Arden Shakespeare*, London: Bloomsbury, 2002.

Foucault, Michel, *Surveiller et punir: Naissance de la prison*, Paris: Gallimard, 1975.

Freccero, John, *Dante: The Poetics of Conversion*, ed. and intro. by Rachel Jacoff, Cambridge, MA and London: Harvard University Press, 1986.

Freeman, Laura, *The Reading Cure: How Books Restored My Appetite*, London: Weidenfeld and Nicolson, 2019.

Freud, Sigmund, 'Mourning and Melancholia', in James Strachey (ed.), *The Standard Edition of the Complete Psychological Works of Sigmund Freud*, Vol. 14, London: The Hogarth Press, 1956–74, 243–58.

Gerk, Andrea, *Lesen als Medizin: Die wundersame Wirkung der Literatur*, Berlin: Rogner und Bernhard, 2015.

Gibbons, Brian (ed.), *Romeo and Juliet: The Arden Shakespeare*, London: Bloomsbury, 1997.

Gibson, Margaret (ed.), *Boethius: His Life, Thought and Influence*, Oxford: Basil Blackwell, 1981.

Gilman, Ernest B., *The Curious Perspective: Literary and Pictorial Wit in the Seventeenth Century*, New Haven and London: Yale University Press, 1978.

Gilman, Ernest B., '*Richard II* and the Perspectives of History', *Renaissance Drama*, 7, 1976, 85–115.

Golomb, Alain, *Petit guide de lectures qui aident à vivre*, Paris: Payot, 2010.

Graver, Margaret, *Cicero on the Emotions:* Tusculan Disputations *3 and 4*, Chicago and London: University of Chicago Press, 2002.

Graver, Margaret, *Stoicism and Emotion*, Chicago and London: University of Chicago Press, 2009.

Graver, Margaret, 'The Weeping Wise: Stoic and Epicurean Consolations in Seneca's 99th Epistle', in Torsten Fögen (ed.), *Tears in the Graeco-Roman World*, Berlin: De Gruyter, 2009, 235–52.

Greenblatt, Stephen, *Renaissance Self-Fashioning from More to Shakespeare*, Chicago: University of Chicago Press, 1980.

Greenblatt, Stephen, *Shakespearean Negotiations: The Circulation of Social Energy in Renaissance England*, Berkeley: University of California Press, 1988.

Greenblatt, Stephen et al. (eds), *The Norton Shakespeare, Based on the Oxford Edition*, New York and London: W. W. Norton Company, 1997.

Greene, Roland (ed.), *The Princeton Encyclopedia of Poetry and Poetics*, Fourth Edition, Princeton: Princeton University Press, 2012.

Groskop, Viv, *The Anna Karenina Fix: Life Lessons from Russian Literature*, London: Penguin Books, 2018.

Grossman, David, *Writing in the Dark: Essays on Literature and Politics*, New York: Farrar, Strauss and Giroux, 2008.

Gruber, Joachim, *Kommentar zu Boethius*, De Consolatione Philosophiae, Berlin and New York: De Gruyter, 2006.

Guignery, Vanessa, *The Fiction of Julian Barnes*, London: MacMillan, 2006.

Guignery, Vanessa, '"My wife . . . died": une mort en pointillé dans *Flaubert's Parrot* de Julian Barnes', *Etudes britanniques contemporaines*, 17, 1999, 57–68.

Guignery, Vanessa, and Roberts, Ryan (eds), *Conversations with Julian Barnes*, Jackson: University Press of Mississippi, 2009.

Halliwell, Stephen, *The Aesthetics of Mimesis: Ancient Texts and Modern Problems*, Princeton: Princeton University Press, 2002.

Halliwell, Stephen, 'Antidotes and Incantations: Is There a Cure for Poetry in Plato's *Republic*?', in Pierre Destrée and Fritz-Gegor Herrmann (eds), *Plato and the Poets*, Leiden/Boston: Brill, 2011, 241–66.

Halliwell, Stephen, 'Tragedy and the Emotions', in Halliwell, *Aristotle's Poetics*, Chicago: University of Chicago Press, 1988, 168–201.

Halliwell, Stephen, 'Tragic Pity', in Halliwell, *The Aesthetics of Mimesis: Ancient Texts and Modern Problems*, Princeton: Princeton University Press, 2002, 207–33.

Harrison, Robert Pogue, *The Body of Beatrice*, Baltimore: Johns Hopkins University Press, 2000.

Heitsch, Dorothea B., 'Approaching Death by Writing: Montaigne's *Essais* and the Literature of Consolation', *Literature and Medicine*, 19, 1, 2000, 96–106.

Holden, Anthony, and Holden, Ben (eds), *Poems That Make Grown Men Cry: 100 Men on the Words that Move Them*, London: Simon and Schuster, 2014.

Hollander, Robert, *Studies in Dante*, Ravenna: Longo Editore, 1980.

Holloway, Paul, *Consolation in Philippians: Philosophical Sources and Rhetorical Strategy*, Cambridge: Cambridge University Press, 2001.

Horton, Paul C., *Solace: The Missing Dimension in Psychiatry*, Chicago: University of Chicago Press, 1981.

Horton, Paul C., Gerwitz, Herbert, and Kreutter, Karole J. (eds), *The Solace Paradigm: An Eclectic Search For Psychological Immunity*, Madison, CT: International Universities Press, Inc., 1988.

Homer, *The Iliad*, trans. Peter Green, Oakland: University of California Press, 2015.

Hunter, Joseph, *New Illustrations of the Life, Studies, and Writings of Shakespeare*, 2 vols, London: J. B. Nichols and Son, 1843.

Hutcheon, Linda, *A Poetics of Postmodernism: History, Theory, Politics*, London: Routledge, 1988.

Iser, Wolfgang, *The Act of Reading: A Theory of Aesthetic Response*, Baltimore: Johns Hopkins University Press, 1981.

Iser, Wolfgang, *The Implied Reader: Patterns of Communication in Prose Fiction from Bunyan to Beckett*, Baltimore: Johns Hopkins University Press, 1974.

Jack, Belinda, 'The Rise of the Medical Humanities', *Times Higher Education*, 22 January 2015. Available at: <https://www.timeshighereducation.com/features/the-rise-of-the-medical-humanities/2018007.article>

Jaeger, Werner, *Paideia: die Formung des griechischen Menschen*, Berlin: De Gruyter, 1934.

James, David, *Discrepant Solace: Contemporary Literature and the Work of Consolation*, Oxford: Oxford University Press, 2019.

Jarrell, Randall, *The Complete Poems*, New York: Farrar, Straus and Giroux, 1969.

Johann, Horst-Theodor, *Trauer und Trost: eine quellen- und strukturanalytische Untersuchung der philosophischen Trostschriften über den Tod*, München: Fink, 1968.

Johnson, Samuel, *A Dictionary of the English Language*, Facsimile of the 1755 edition in 2 volumes, Hildesheim: Georg Olms Verlagsbuchhandlung, 1968.

Josipovici, Gabriel, Hamlet *Fold on Fold*, New Haven and London, 2016.

Kakutani, Michiko, 'Coronavirus Notebook: Finding Solace, and Connection, in Classic Books', *New York Times*, 5 May 2020.

Kassel, Rudolf, *Untersuchungen zur griechischen und römischen Konsolationsliteratur*, München: Beck, 1958.

Kastan, David Scott, *A Will to Believe: Shakespeare and Religion*, Oxford: Oxford University Press, 2014.

Kastely, James L., *The Rhetoric of Plato's* Republic: *Democracy and the Philosophical Problem of Persuasion*, Chicago and London: University of Chicago Press, 2015.

Kästner, Erich, *Doktor Erich Kästners Lyrische Hausapotheke*, München: dtv, 2016.

Kierdorf, Wilhelm, 'Consolatio as a Literary Genre', in H. Cancik and H. Schneider (eds), *Brill's New Pauly: Encyclopaedia of the Ancient World: Antiquity*, Vol. 3, Leiden and Boston: Brill, 2003, 704.

Kirsch, Arthur, 'Virtue, Vice, and Compassion in Montaigne and *The Tempest*', *Studies in English Literature, 1500–1900*, 37, 1997, 337–52.

Konstan, David, *The Emotions of the Ancient Greeks: Studies in Aristotle and Classical Literature*, Toronto: University of Toronto Press, 2006.

Konstan, David, 'The Grieving Self: Reflections on Lucian's *On Mourning* and the Consolatory Tradition', in Han Baltussen (ed.), *Greek and Roman Consolations: Eight Studies of a Tradition and its Afterlife*, Swansea: The Classical Press of Wales, 2013, 139–52.

Konstan, David, *Pity Transformed*, London: Duckworth, 2001.

Korsten, Frans-Willem, *A Dutch Republican Baroque*, Amsterdam: Amsterdam University Press, 2017.

Lacan, Jacques, *Les quatre concepts fondamentaux de la pyschanalyse* (Séminaire XI), Paris: Seuil, 1973.

Laín Entralgo, Pedro, *The Therapy of the Word in Classical Antiquity*, ed. and trans. L. J. Rather and J. M. Sharp, New Haven and London: Yale University Press, 1970.

Latacz, Joachim, *Homer: der erste Dichter des Abendlands*, München: Artemis, 1989.

Leader, Darian, *The New Black: Mourning, Melancholia and Depression*, London: Penguin, 2009.

Lee, Alison, *Realism and Power: Postmodern British Fiction*, London: Routledge, 2014.

Lerer, Seth, *Boethius and Dialogue: Literary Method in* The Consolation of Philosophy, Princeton: Princeton University Press, 1985.

Lever, J. W. (ed.), *Measure for Measure: The Arden Shakespeare*, London: Bloomsbury, 1998.

Lewis, C. S., *A Grief Observed*, London: Faber and Faber: 2015.

Lottman, Herbert, *Flaubert: A Biography*, Boston: Little, Brown and Company, 1989.

Lupton, Julia Reinhard, *Thinking with Shakespeare: Essays on Politics and Life*, Chicago and London: University of Chicago Press, 2011.

Luzzi, Joseph, *In A Dark Wood: What Dante Taught Me about Grief, Healing and the Mysteries of Love*, London: William Collins, 2015.

Maguire, Laurie, *Shakespeare als therapeut*, Amsterdam: Nieuw Amsterdam Uitgevers, 2007.

Maguire, Laurie, *Where There's A Will There's A Way: Or, All I Really Need to Know I Learned from Shakespeare*, London: Nicholas Brealey Publishing, 2007.

Manguel, Alberto, *Homer's* The Iliad *and* The Odyssey: *A Biography*, Vancouver: Douglas and McIntyre, 2007.

Marenbon, John (ed.), *The Cambridge Companion to Boethius*, Cambridge: Cambridge University Press, 2009.

Martha, Constant, 'Les Consolations dans l'Antiquité', in Martha, *Etudes Morales sur l'Antiquité*, Paris: Hachette, 1883, 135–89.

Matthews, John, 'Anicius Manlius Severinus Boethius', in Margaret Gibson (ed.), *Boethius: His Life, Thought and Influence*, Oxford: Basil Blackwell, 1981, 25–43.

McChord Crothers, Samuel, 'A Literary Clinic', *The Atlantic Monthly*, 118, Sept. 1916, 291–301.

McClure, George, *Sorrow and Consolation in Italian Humanism*, Princeton: Princeton University Press, 1991.

McGirr, Michael, *Books That Saved my Life: Reading for Wisdom, Solace and Pleasure*, Melbourne: Text Publishing, 2018.

MacLeod, C. W. (ed.), *Iliad: Book XXIV*, Cambridge: Cambridge University Press, 1982.

McMillin, Scott, 'Shakespeare's *Richard II*: Eyes of Sorrow, Eyes of Desire', *Shakespeare Quarterly*, 35, 1, 1984, 40–52.

McNicol, Sarah, and Brewster, Liz (eds), *Bibliotherapy*, London: Facet Publishing, 2018.

Maus, Katharine Eisaman, *Inwardness and Theater in the English Renaissance*, Chicago and London: University of Chicago Press, 1995.

Means, Michael H., *The Consolation Genre in Medieval English Literature*, Gainesville: University of Florida Press, 1972.

Mendelsohn, Daniel, *An Odyssey: A Father, a Son and an Epic*, London: William Collins, 2017.

Modesto, Filippa, *Dante's Idea of Friendship: The Transformation of a Classical Concept*, Toronto: University of Toronto Press, 2015.

Montaigne, Michel de, 'Of Diverting or Diversion', in Stephen Greenblatt (ed.), *Shakespeare's Montaigne: The Florio Translation of the Essays: A Selection*, New York: New York Review of Books, 2014, 226–38.

Montserrat-Cals, Claude, *Consolation à Dagerman*, Paris: Les Belles Lettres, 2009.

Moore, Jeanie Grant, 'Queen of Sorrow, King of Grief: Reflections and Perspectives in *Richard II*', in Dorothea Kehler and Susan Baker (eds), *In Another Country: Feminist Perspectives on Renaissance Drama*, Metuchen, NJ and London: The Scarecrow Press, 1991, 19–35.

Moorhead, John, 'Boethius' Life and the World of Late Antique Philosophy', in John Marenbon (ed.), *The Cambridge Companion to Boethius*, Cambridge: Cambridge University Press, 2009, 13–33.

Moritz, Rainer, *Die Überlebensbibliothek: Bücher für alle Lebenslagen*, Zürich: Piper, 2006.

Moser, Benjamin, *Sontag: Her Life*, London: Allen Lane, 2019.

Mueller, Janel M., and Scodel, Joshua (eds), *Elizabeth I: Translations 1592–1598*, Chicago: University of Chicago Press, 2009.

Mukařovsky, Jan, 'Die Kunst als semiologisches Faktum' (1934), in Mukařovsky, *Kapitel aus der Ästhetik*, Frankfurt: Suhrkamp, 1970, 138–47.

Murari, Rocco, *Dante e Boezio: Contributo allo Studio delle Fonti Dantesche*, Bologna: Zanichelli, 1905.

Nauta, Lodi, 'A Humanist Reading of Boethius's Consolatio Philosophiae: The Commentary by Murmellius and Agricola (1514)', in Lodi Nauta and Arjo Vanderjagt (eds), *Between Demonstration and Imagination: Essays in the History of Science and Philosophy: Presented to John D. North*, Leiden: Brill, 1999, 313–38.

Nehamas, Alexander, 'Pity and Fear in the *Rhetoric* and the *Poetics*', in Amélie Oksenberg Rorty (ed.), *Essays on Aristotle's* Poetics, Princeton: Princeton University Press, 1992, 291–314.

Nelson, Deborah, *Tough Enough: Arbus, Arendt, Didion, McCarthy, Sontag, Weil*, Chicago and London: University of Chicago Press, 2017.

Newman, Sandra, *The Western Lit Survival Kit: How to Read the Classics Without Fear*, London: Penguin Books, 2012.

Nicolson, Adam, *The Mighty Dead: Why Homer Matters*, London: William Collins, 2014.

Nicolson, Nigel (ed.), *The Letters of Virginia Woolf, Volume I: 1888–1912 (Virginia Stephen)*, New York and London: Harcourt Brace Jovanovich, 1977–1982.

North, John, *The Ambassador's Secret: Holbein and the World of the Renaissance*, London: Hambledon Continuum, 2005.

Novak-Lechevalier, Agathe, *Houellebecq, l'art de la consolation*, Paris: Stock, 2018.

Nussbaum, Martha C., 'Poetry and the Passions: Two Stoic Views', in Jacques Brunschwig and Martha C. Nussbaum (eds), *Passions and Perceptions: Studies in Hellenistic Philosophy of Mind: Proceedings of the Fifth Symposium Hellenisticum*, Cambridge and Paris: Cambridge University Press/Editions de la Maison des Sciences de l'Homme, 1993, 97–149.

Nussbaum, Martha, 'Tragedy and Self-sufficiency: Plato and Aristotle on Pity and Fear', in Amélie Oksenberg Rorty (ed.), *Essays on Aristotle's Poetics*, Princeton: Princeton University Press, 1992, 261–90.

O'Daly, Gerard, *The Poetry of Boethius*, Chapel Hill, NC and London: University of North Carolina Press, 1991.

Oliver, Hermia, *Flaubert and an English Governess: The Quest for Juliet Herbert*, Oxford: Clarendon Press, 1980.

Ouaknin, Marc-Alain, *Bibliothérapie: lire, c'est guérir*, Paris: Seuil, 1994.

Paster, Gail Kern, 'Montaigne, Dido, and *The Tempest*: "How came that widow in?"', *Shakespeare Quarterly*, 35, 1, 1984, 91–4.

Paterson, Don, *Orpheus: A Version of Rilke*, London: Faber and Faber, 2006.

Paterson, Don (ed.), *The Picador Book of Funeral Poems*, London: Picador, 2012.

Pavesich, Vida, 'Hans Blumenberg: Philosophical Anthropology and the Ethics of Consolation', in Phillip Honenberger (ed.), *Naturalism and Philosophical Anthropology*, London: Palgrave MacMillan, 2015, 66–93.

Pensalfini, Rob, *Prison Shakespeare: For these Deep Shames and Great Indignities*, Basingstoke: MacMillan/Palgrave, 2016.

Perez-Bill, Judith, 'Priam ou la conscience endeuillée', in Perez-Bill, *Apprendre à philosopher avec Homère*, Paris: Editions Ellipses, 2018, 154–71.

Phillips, Adam, *In Writing: Essays on Literature*, London: Hamish Hamilton, 2016.

Phillips, Adam, *Missing Out: In Praise of the Unlived Life*, New York: Farrar, Straus and Giroux, 2012.

Phillips, Adam, *Terrors and Experts*, London: Faber and Faber, 1995.

Phillips, Adam, *Winnicott*, London: Penguin Books, 2007.

Pieters, Jürgen, 'Coornhert en Calvijn over Job: De lijdzaamheid van de vrije mens versus de almacht van de afwezige God', in Jaap Gruppelaar and Jürgen Pieters (eds), *'Un certain Holandois:' Coornhert en de vragen van zijn tijd*, Hilversum: Verloren, 2014, 55–74.

Pieters, Jürgen, *De tranen van de herinnering: Het gesprek met de doden*, Groningen: Historische Uitgeverij, 2005.

Pieters, Jürgen, 'Facing History, or the Anxiety of Reading: Holbein's "The Ambassadors" according to Greenblatt and Lyotard', in Tamsin Spargo (ed.), *Reading the Past: Literature and History*, London: Palgrave, 2000, 88–102.

Pieters, Jürgen, 'Normality, Deviancy, Critique: Toward a 'Governmental' Reading of Shakespeare's *Measure for Measure*', in Marc Boone and Marysa Demoor (eds), *Charles V in Context: The Making of a European Identity*, Brussels: VUB University Press, 2003, 189–205.

Pieters, Jürgen, *Speaking with the Dead: Explorations in Literature and History*, Edinburgh: Edinburgh University Press, 2005.

Pieters, Jürgen, and Kris Pint (eds), *Roland Barthes Retroactively: Reading the Collège de France Lectures*, Paragraph, 31, 1, 2008.

Pietrobelli, Antoine, 'Soigner par les lettres: bibliothérapie des Anciens', in Claude Calame (ed.), *Dossier: Soigner par les lettres: La bibliothérapie des Anciens*, special issue of *Métis*, 15, 2017, 7–20.

Pint, Kris, *The Perverse Art of Reading: On the Phantasmatic Semiology in Roland Barthes' Cours au Collège de France*, Amsterdam: Rodopi, 2010.

Plato, *Republic*, ed. and trans. Chris Emlyn-Jones and William Preddy, London and Cambridge, MA: Harvard University Press (Loeb Classical Library), 2013.

(Ps-)Plutarch, 'Consolatio ad Apollonium', in Plutarch, *Moralia*, trans. Frank Cole Babbitt, London and Cambridge, MA: Heinemann and Harvard University Press (Loeb Classical Library), 1927.

Price, Leah, *Unpacking my Library: Writers and Their Books*, New Haven and London: Yale University Press, 2011.

Proust, Marcel, 'On Reading', in Proust, *On Reading Ruskin*, ed. and trans. Jean Autret, William Burford and Phillip J. Wolfe, New Haven and London: Yale University Press, 1987, 99–129.

Quintilian, *The Institutio Oratoria*, trans. Harold Edgeworth Butler, London and Cambridge, MA: Heinemann and Harvard University Press (Loeb Classical Library), 1958.

Rabinow, Paul, *Unconsolable Contemporary: Observing Gerhard Richter*, Durham, NC and London: Duke University Press, 2017.

Redfield, James M., *Nature and Culture in the* Iliad: *The Tragedy of Hector*, Chicago and London: University of Chicago Press, 1975.

Reid, Martine, *George Sand*, Paris: Gallimard, 2013.

Relihan, Joel C., *The Prisoner's Philosophy: Life and Death in Boethius's Consolation*, Notre Dame, IN: University of Notre Dame Press, 2007.

Riddehough, Geoffrey B., 'Queen Elizabeth's Translation of Boethius' 'De consolatione philosophiae', *The Journal of English and Germanic Philology*, 45, 1, 1946, 88–94.

Rieff, David, *Swimming in a Sea of Death: A Son's Memoir*, London: Granta, 2008.

Riley, Denise, *Impersonal Passion: Language as Affect*, Durham, NC and London: Duke University Press, 2005.

Riley, Denise, *Time Lived, Without Its Flow*, London: Picador, 2019.

Rittgers, Ronald, *The Reformation of Suffering: Pastoral Theology and Lay Piety in Late Medieval and Early Modern Germany*, Oxford: Oxford University Press, 2012.

Roiphe, Katie, *The Violet Hour: Great Writers at the End*, New York: The Dial Press, 2016.

Rudnytsky, Peter L. (ed.), *Transitional Objects and Potential Spaces: Literary Uses of D. W. Winnicott*, New York: Columbia University Press, 1993.

Ryan, Kiernan, *Shakespeare*, Houndmills: Palgrave, 2002.

Samoyault, Tiphaine, *Roland Barthes*, Paris: Seuil, 2015.

Samuel, Julia, *Grief Works: Stories of Life, Death and Surviving*, London: Penguin Books, 2017.

Schaeben, Ulrike, *Trauer im humanistischen Dialog: Das Trostgespräch des Giannozzo Manetti und seine Quellen*, Berlin: De Gruyter, 2011.

Scheible, Helga, *Die Gedichte in der Consolatio Philosophiae des Boethius*, Heidelberg: C. Winter, 1972.

Schorn, Stefan, 'Tears of the Bereaved: Plutarch's Consolatio ad uxorem in Context', in Thorsten Fögen (ed.), *Tears in the Graeco-Roman World*, New York and Berlin: De Gruyter, 2009, 335–65.

Schwalbe, Will, *Books for Living: A Reader's Guide to Life*, London: Two Roads, 2017.

Schwalbe, Will, *The End of Your Life Book Club*, London: Two Roads, 2012.

Scott-Douglass, Amy, *Shakespeare Inside: The Bard Behind Bars*, London: Continuum, 2007.

Scourfield, J. H. D., *Consoling Heliodorus: A Commentary on Jerome Letter 60*, Oxford: Clarendon Press, 1993.

Scourfield, J. H. D., 'Towards a Genre of Consolation', in Han Baltussen (ed.), *Greek and Roman Consolations: Eight Studies of a Tradition and its Afterlife*, Swansea: The Classical Press of Wales, 2013, 1–36.

Searle, John, 'The Logical Status of Fictional Discourse', *New Literary History*, 6, 2, 1975, 319–32.

Sels, Nadia, '"A heart that can endure" Hans Blumenberg's Anthropology of Solace', *Image and Narrative*, 14, 1, 2013. Available at: <http://www.imageandnarrative.be/index.php/imagenarrative/article/view/293>

Shields, David, *How Literature Saved My Life*, London: Notting Hill Editions, 2013.

Sieghart, William, *The Poetry Pharmacy: Tried-and-True Prescriptions for the Heart, Mind and Soul*, London: Particular Books, 2017.

Sieghart, William, *The Poetry Pharmacy Returns: More Prescriptions for Courage, Healing and Hope*, London: Particular Books, 2019.

Simmel, Georg, *Fragmente und Aufsätze*, ed. G. Kantrorowicz, München: Drei Masken Verlag, 1923.

Smith, Rebecca, *Jane Austen's Guide to Modern Life's Dilemmas*, Lewes: Ivy Books, 2012.

Smyth, Katharine, *All the Lives We Ever Lived: Seeking Solace in Virginia Woolf*, London: Atlantic Books, 2019.

Soellner, Rolf, *Shakespeare's Patterns of Self-Knowledge*, Columbus: Ohio State University Press, 1972.

Solnit, Rebecca, *Recollections of My Non-Existence*, London: Granta, 2020.

Sontag, Susan, *Regarding the Pain of Others*, London: Penguin Books, 2003.

Sophocles, *Antigone, Oedipus the King, Electra*, trans. Humphrey D. F. Kitto, ed. Edith Hall, Oxford: Oxford University Press, 1994.

Sorabji, Richard, *Emotion and Peace of Mind: From Stoic Agitation to Christian Contemplation*, Oxford: Oxford University Press, 2000.

Southworth, John, *Shakespeare the Player: A Life in the Theatre*, Stroud: Sutton Publishing, 2000.

Stanley, Jacqueline, *Reading to Heal: How to Use Bibliotherapy to Improve Your Life*, Boston: Element Books, 1999.

Starkie, Enid, *Flaubert the Master*, London: Weidenfeld and Nicolson, 1971.

Sweeney, Megan, *Reading Is My Window: Books and the Art of Reading in Women's Prisons*, Chapel Hill: University of North Carolina Press, 2010.

Sweeney, Megan (ed.), *The Story Within Us: Women Prisoners Reflect on Reading*, Champaign: University of Illinois Press, 2012.

Targoff, Ramie, *Posthumous Love: Eros and the Afterlife in Renaissance England*, Chicago: University of Chicago Press, 2014.

Treggiari, Susan, *Terentia, Tullia and Publilia: The Women of Cicero's Family*, London and New York: Routledge, 2007.

Tricotel, Claude, *Comme deux troubadours: Histoire de l'amitié Flaubert-Sand*, Paris: Société d'Edition d'Enseignement Supérieur, 1978.

Tukhareli, Nathalia, 'Bibliotherapy-based Wellness Program for Healthcare Providers: Using Books and Reading to Create a Healthy Workplace', *Journal of the Canadian Health Libraries Association*, 38, 2, 2017, 44–50.

Tukhareli, Nathalia, *Healing Through Books: The Evolution and Diversification of Bibliotherapy*. Lewiston, NY: Edwin Mellen Press, 2014.

Valéry, Paul, 'La crise de l'esprit' (1919), in Valéry, *Œuvres*, I, ed. Jean Hytier, Paris: Gallimard (Bibliothèque de la Pléiade), 1957, 988–1000.

Van der Haven, Cornelis, and Pieters, Jürgen, 'Lyric Address: By Way of an Introduction', in Van der Haven and Pieters (eds), *Lyric Address in Dutch Literature 1250–1800*, Amsterdam: Amsterdam University Press, 2018, 7–20.

Verhoeven, Cornelis, *Het leedwezen: Beschouwingen over troost en verdriet, leven en dood*, Bilthoven: Ambo, 1971.

Vidal-Naquet, Pierre, *Le monde d'Homère*, Paris: Perrin, 2002.

Wall, Geoffrey, *Flaubert: A Life*, London: Faber and Faber, 2001.

Walmsley, Ann, *The Prison Book Club*, London: Viking, 2015.

Weil, Simone, and Bespaloff, Rachel, *War and* The Iliad, intro. Christopher Benfey, New York: New York Review Books, 2005.

Wells, Stanley, and Taylor, Gary (eds), *The Oxford Shakespeare: The Complete Works*, Oxford: Oxford University Press, 1988.

White, Stephen A., 'Cicero and the Therapists', in Jonathan Powell (ed.), *Cicero the Philosopher: Twelve Papers*, Oxford: Clarendon Press, 1995, 219–46.

White, James Boyd, *When Words Lose Their Meaning: Constitutions and Reconstitutions of Language, Character, and Community*, Chicago and London: University of Chicago Press, 1984.

Wilson, Marcus, 'Seneca the Consoler? A New Reading of his Consolatory Writings', in Han Baltussen (ed.), *Greek and Roman Consolations: Eight Studies of a Tradition and its Afterlife*, Swansea: The Classical Press of Wales, 2013, 93–122.

Winnicott, Donald W., 'The Capacity To Be Alone' (1958), in Winnicott, *The Maturational Processes and the Facilitating Environment*, New York: International Universities Press, Inc., 1965, 29–36.

Winnicott, Donald W., *The Child, the Family and the Outside World* (1964), London: Penguin 1991.

Winnicott, Donald W., *The Family and Individual Development* (1965), London: Routledge, 2006.

Winnicott, Donald W., *Playing and Reality* (1971), London and New York: Routledge, 2005.

Winnicott, Donald W., 'Transitional Objects and Transitional Phenomena', in Winnicott, *Playing and Reality*, London and New York: Routledge, 2005, 1–34.

Winnicott, Donald W., 'The Use of an Object and Relating through Identifications', in Winnicott, *Playing and Reality*, London and New York: Routledge, 2005, 115–27.

Winock, Michel, *Flaubert*, trans. Nicholas Elliott, Cambridge, MA: Harvard University Press, 2016.

Woolf, Virginia, 'On Re-reading Novels', in *Collected Essays*, Volume 1, London: Hogarth Press, 1966, 122–30.

Woolf, Virginia, *Mrs Dalloway*, London: Penguin Books, 2018.

Žižek, Slavoj, *Looking Awry: An Introduction to Jacques Lacan through Popular Culture*, London and Cambridge, MA: MIT Press, 1991.xcv

# Index

Note: 'n' indicates chapter notes.

acceptance, 16, 28, 32, 45, 47, 53, 122, 125, 217, 247
aesthetics, 10, 70, 100–2, 194, 206, 216, 228, 235, 236; *see also* beauty; form; style
allegory, 47, 72, 88, 93
Ambrose, 71
*anamnesis*, 161
anamorphosis, 140–3, 145, 151
animals, 119, 188n
*apatheia* (suppression of emotions), 38, 40, 44, 177
Aristotle, 46–54, 56, 194, 242, 276
  *Nicomachean Ethics*, 27
  *Poetics*, 49–52, 55
  *Rhetoric*, 30, 49
Armstrong, John, and Alain De Botton, *Art as Therapy*, 12
Ascoli, Albert, 94, 107n
Astell, Ann, 98, 108n
*Atlantic Monthly, The*, 4–5
Auden, W. H., 170, 271
Auerbach, Erich, 88
authenticity, 183–5

Bach, Johann Sebastian, 70–1
Baltussen, Han, 36, 38
banishment, 146–7, 172–6; *see also* exile
Barnes, Julian, 101, 108n
  *Flaubert's Parrot*, 193, 194–201, 202, 210–15, 217–19, 221n, 226
  *Levels of Life*, 197–8, 220n, 233
  review of *Flaubert-Sand: The Correspondence*, 200–2
  *Something to Declare*, 196, 219n
Barolini, Teodolinda, 97
Barthes, Roland, 269–77
  *Camera Lucida*, 271–6
  *The Mourning Diary*, 271–2, 275–6
Bates, Laura, *Shakespeare Saved My Life: Ten Years in Solitary with the Bard*, 112–16, 151–2
beauty, 10, 13, 70, 89–90, 101, 229, 237
Beckett, Samuel, 236
  *Waiting for Godot*, 183
Bersani, Leo, 236–7
Berthoud, Ella
  *The Art of Mindful Reading*, 241
  and Susan Elderkin, *The Novel Cure: An A-Z of Literary Remedies*, 11–12, 182, 194, 225, 232, 238–9, 241, 250–1, 252n, 253n
Bespaloff, Rachel, 58n
bibliophilia, 3
bibliotheraphy, 3–6, 7, 10–11, 14, 21n, 22n, 63, 67–8, 110–17, 182, 194, 196–7, 199, 214, 215–19, 225, 232, 233, 238, 241–2, 244, 250
Billington, Josie, *Is Literature Healthy?*, 11, 248–51
Binswanger, Ludwig, 230, 264
Bion, Wilfred, 249–50

Blackwood, Stephen, 77
Bloom, Allan, 158, 167
Bloom, Harold, 116, 163, 191n, 192n
Blumenberg, Hans, 16, 119–20, 125, 136, 183–5, 233, 276–7
Boccaccio, Giovanni, *The Decameron*, 228, 230
Boethius, 41, 73, 79–82, 118, 133, 194, 231, 267
  *The Consolation of Philosophy* (*De consolatione philosophiae*), 71, 72–80, 82–7, 90–3, 96, 97, 103, 107n, 110, 111, 113, 152–3, 161
  *De Institutione Musica*, 79, 106n
Bonaparte, Mathilde, 210
Brecht, Bertolt, 259

Calvin, John, 135
Cardano, Girolamo, *De Consolatione Libri Tres* (*Cardanus Comforte*), 122–8, 134, 135
*caritas*, 82–3
Castiglione, Baldassare, *The Book of the Courtier*, 266
Cavalcanti, Guido, 66
change, 35, 125, 132, 215, 276
character, 114–17
Chong-Gossard, James H. Kim On, 44, 45, 46
Christian regime of literary comfort, 15–16, 62–104
  *versus* the classical regime, 35, 39, 71–3
  *versus* the modern regime, 118–22, 127–8, 132–5, 144, 154–5, 157, 158, 161–2, 173, 183, 229, 231
  see also Boethius; Dante Alighieri; God; Job
Chrysippus, 54–5
Cicero, 37, 38, 79–83, 118, 127–8
  *Consolatio*, 37–9, 41, 71
  *De amicitia*, 80–1, 127
  *Tusculan Disputations*, 40–1, 78, 82, 129–30, 147, 155
classical regime of literary comfort, 15, 23–57
  *versus* the Christian regime, 35, 39, 71–3
  *versus* the modern regime, 35, 39–42, 46, 118–22, 126–30, 132–3, 135, 137, 139–40, 145, 153–5, 161–2, 164–5, 180, 182–3, 205, 216, 229, 231, 260, 269
  see also Aristotle; Cicero; Homer; Plato; Plutarch; Stoicism
Coetzee, J. M., 'Beckett and the Temptations of Style', 236
Colet, Louise, 206
comfort reading, 225–9
communal/collective experience (*sensus communis*), 39–41, 45, 46, 118, 122, 126, 132, 136, 139–40, 145, 260
*consolationes*, 37–9, 41, 71, 268–9
Covid-19 pandemic, 225–9
Crabbe, Anne, 79
Craig, Hardin, 122–3
Crantor of Soli, 37–8, 39, 40, 177
Critchley, Simon, 131, 272
critical detachment, 55–6
Crothers, Samuel McChord, 'A Literary Clinic', 4–5
Culler, Jonathan, 268
Curtius, Ernst Robert, 73
Cushman, Robert, 53
Cyprian, 71

Dagerman, Stig, 'Our Need for Consolation', 120–1, 231
Dante Alighieri, 79–103, 107n, 115, 118, 121, 194, 229, 230, 231
  *Convivio*, 73, 79–80, 82–90, 92–5, 97, 107n
  *Divine Comedy*, 15, 16, 62–71, 81, 88, 93–103, 133, 261, 284
  *La Vita Nuova*, 66, 70, 82, 83, 85–90, 92, 93, 96, 97
  see also Dreher, Rod, *How Dante Can Save Your Life*; Luzzi, Joseph, *In A Dark Wood: What Dante Taught Me about Grief, Healing, and the Mysteries of Love*

De Botton, Alain
  *How Proust Can Change Your Life*, 242, 256
  and John Armstrong, *Art as Therapy*, 12
De Martelaere, Patricia, 125, 171, 175, 217, 230, 272
De Waal, Frans, 188n
dead, the, conversations with, 67–71, 198
DeLillo, Don, *Zero K*, 7
Derrida, Jacques, 14, 82
desolation, 118, 194, 196, 204–8
despair, 195, 197, 203, 204–8, 215–16
Deutelbaum, Wendy, 208
Dickens, Charles, *David Copperfield*, 246
Dickinson, Emily, 263, 264
didacticism, 70, 102, 216
Didion, Joan
  *Blue Nights*, 271
  *The Year of Magical Thinking*, 262, 266, 279n
Dinesen, Isak, 53
Diogenes of Babylon, 54–5
discourse of consolation (*logos paramuthètikos*), 31–4, 37, 43
distraction and diversion, 70, 102–3, 176–82, 228
Donato, Antonio, 78, 79, 92
Douce, Francis, 123
Dreher, Rod, *How Dante Can Save Your Life*, 3, 62, 65–6, 99–103, 115, 284
Dupont-Roc, Roselyne, 50, 51

Elderkin, Susan, and Ella Berthoud, *The Novel Cure: An A-Z of Literary Remedies*, 11–12, 182, 194, 225, 232, 238–9, 241, 250–1, 252n, 253n
*eleos* (pity), 28–31, 32, 49–50, 53
Eliot, George, *Middlemarch*, 249–50
Ellrodt, Robert, 146
emotional intelligence, 40

emotions, 40, 43, 44, 54, 81–2, 89, 139–40
  suppression of (*apatheia*), 38, 40, 44, 177
empathy, 248, 261
*energeia*, 69
escapism, 56
Euripides, 44, 48
exile, 64, 65, 74, 84, 85, 107n, 113, 267; *see also* banishment
Eyres, Harry, *Horace and Me*, 242

failure of comfort, 41–6, 56, 85, 117–86, 194, 271–2
false comfort, 17, 20, 56, 76, 130, 143–4, 157, 162–7, 178, 180, 182, 184
fear (*phobos*), 49–50
Ferrari, John, 77
Ferris, Joshua, 7
Feydeau, Georges, 197, 204–6, 216, 219n
flattery, 265–6, 268
Flaubert, Gustave, 15, 16, 186, 193–219, 220n, 222n, 226, 228, 229, 231, 233–7
  *A Simple Heart* ('Un cœur simple'), 208–14, 223n, 235, 236
  *see also* Barnes, Julian
Fœssel, Michaël, *Le temps de la consolation*, 118, 120, 131, 137, 162, 183, 185, 217, 229, 259–61, 265–9
Forker, Charles, 140, 148
form, 8, 13, 42, 52, 55, 64, 74, 77, 78, 102, 193, 194, 229, 230, 231, 232–3, 235–9, 261, 263; *see also* plot; style
Foucault, Michel, 118, 131, 191n
fraudulent comfort *see* false comfort
Freccero, John, 96
Freeman, Laura, *The Reading Cure*, 6, 10, 11
Freud, Sigmund, 66, 230, 231
  'Trauer und Melancholie', 124–5, 175, 217, 230, 264
friendship, 27, 53, 80–2

Frotzel, Friedrich, 'The Old Bookcase', 282–5
Fuhrmann, Manfred, 50
funeral poems, 8–9, 12

Genettes, Edma Roger des, 209, 212, 215, 216
God, 66, 71, 72, 74, 91, 97, 99, 103, 118, 119, 128, 133, 135, 153, 154, 156, 162, 189n, 229; *see also* salvation
Goethe, Johann Wolfgang von, 183
Greenblatt, Stephen, 116, 161
Grossman, David, 248
*Guardian, The*, 227

Halliwell, Stephen, 49, 50, 51, 54
Harrison, Robert Pogue, 85
Heitsch, Dorothea, 181
help, 185
Herbert, Juliet, 198–9, 220n
Hippocrates, 43, 44
historiography, 242
Holbein, Hans the Younger, 'The Ambassadors', 140–1, 143, 145
Hollander, Robert, 97
Holloway, Paul, 37, 39
Holy Ghost/Spirit, 211, 213, 214
Homer, 15, 16, 23–8, 118, 121
  *The Iliad*, 23–36, 42–8, 52–3, 57n, 58n, 121, 189n
  *The Odyssey*, 23–6, 31–2, 42–3
  *see also* Manguel, Alberto, Homer's The Iliad *and* The Odyssey; Mendelsohn, Daniel, *An Odyssey: A Father, a Son and an Epic*
honesty, 159–62, 179
hope, 158, 203, 204–8, 257–8
Horton, Paul, 246
Houellebecq, Michel, 283
human experience, 243–4
humanism, 126–7, 132, 135
Hunter, Joseph, 123
*Huntington Library Bulletin, The*, 122
Hutcheon, Linda, 197, 220n
Huygens, Constantijn, 69

identity, 114–17, 132, 267
imagination, 70, 185, 247, 248, 265, 275, 276
inconsolability, 34, 119, 120, 127, 130–7, 167–76, 184, 217, 229–30, 257, 271–2
indifference, 205–7
individuality, 132, 276
insight, 31, 47, 50, 52–3, 55–7, 120, 243, 256, 265, 269, 277
inwardness, 138–48, 151, 184
Iser, Wolfgang, 248, 268

Jack, Belinda, 7–8, 12
James, David, *Discrepant Solace*, 228, 229–33, 235–8, 241, 252n, 261, 266
Jarrell, Randall, 284–5, 286n
Jerome, 71
Job, 71–2, 100, 103, 108n, 122, 133–5
Johnson, Samuel, *A Dictionary of the English Language*, 213, 213n, 244
Josipovici, Gabriel, 134

Kakutani, Michiko, 227–8
Kastan, David Scott, 132–3
Kastely, James, 53
*katharsis*, 43, 49–53, 54, 56, 194
Konstan, David, 30, 39
Korsten, Frans-Willem, 135, 136

Lacan, Jacques, 141–3, 215
Laín Entralgo, Pedro, 42–3
Lallot, Jean, 50, 51
language of comfort, 264–6, 266–9, 275–6; *see also* words of comfort
Leader, Darian, 175
Lear, Jonathan, 51–2
learning, 256
Lerer, Seth, 77, 79, 92–3
Lever, J. W., 155, 158
literary comfort
  concept of, 6–12, 282–5
  topology of, 12–16
  *see also* Christian regime; classical regime; modern regime

lockdown, 225–9
*logos paramuthètikos* (discourse of consolation), 31–4, 37, 43
Lubbock, Percy, *The Craft of Fiction*, 235
Lucian, 'On Mourning', 39
Lucretius, 216
Luhrmann, Baz, dir. *Romeo and Juliet*, 162–3, 167, 169, 175–6
Lupton, Julia Reinhard, 134
Luther, Martin, 132, 135
Luzzi, Joseph, *In A Dark Wood: What Dante Taught Me about Grief, Healing, and the Mysteries of Love*, 62–71, 99–103, 214–15, 219, 251, 261, 284

McClure, George, 72, 161
McEwan, Ian, *Atonement*, 237
Machiavelli, Niccolò, 69
Machiavellianism, 138
MacLeod, C. W., 31, 32
Maguire, Laurie, *Where There's A Will There's A Way: Or, All I Really Need to Know I Learned from Shakespeare*, 110, 114–17, 160–1, 183
Manceau, Alexander, 201–2
Manguel, Alberto, *Homer's* The Iliad *and* The Odyssey, 25–6, 47
manipulation, 159–62
Maus, Katharine Eisaman, 138
Mendelsohn, Daniel, *An Odyssey: A Father, a Son and an Epic*, 23–6
metaphor, 266–9
Miller, D. A., 249
mimesis, 51–2, 54, 194, 242, 276
Mitchell, David, 227
modern regime of literary comfort, 15, 16, 110–86, 193–219, 225–51, 256–77
    *versus* the Christian regime, 118–22, 127–8, 132–5, 144, 154–5, 157, 158, 161–2, 173, 183, 229, 231
    *versus* the classical regime, 35, 39–42, 46, 118–22, 126–30, 132–3, 135, 137, 139–40, 145, 153–5, 161–2, 164–5, 180, 182–3, 205, 216, 229, 231, 260, 269
    *see also* Barthes, Roland; Flaubert, Gustave; James, David; Riley, Denise; Sand, George; Shakespeare, William; Sontag, Susan; Winnicott, Donald; Woolf, Virginia
Modesto, Filippa, 82, 83
Montaigne, Michel de, 146, 228
    'On Diverting or Diversion', 179–82
mortality, 119, 257
Moser, Benjamin, 258
mourning, 230, 261, 272–3
Mukařovsky, Jan, 247
music, 64, 79, 102, 106n, 153, 181
myth, 92

narrativity, 35, 52–3
Nelson, Deborah, 266, 279n
*New York Times, The*, 7, 227–8
Newton, Larry, 112–16, 152
Nicolson, Adam, 35
Nietzsche, Friedrich, 119
Nussbaum, Martha, 53–6

Orpheus, 36, 42–3, 79, 90–3, 97–9
Ouaknin, Marc-Alain, 7
Ovid, 74, 91

*paraklètos*, 213, 223n
passions, the, 53–4
Paster, Gail Kern, 179
Paterson, Don
    ed. *Picador Book of Funeral Poems*, 8, 12
    'Solace', 282, 285
patience, 134–5
Pensalfini, Rob, 186n, 187n
Peripatetics, 40
Perrone, Peter, 258
perspective, 9, 10, 31, 40–1, 44, 51, 55, 118, 125–6, 140–5, 150–1, 182, 248, 267, 275, 276

Petersen, Wolfgang, dir. *Troy*, 35, 52, 58n
Petrarch, 69, 161, 283
Phillips, Adam, 247, 251, 284
philosophy, 36–40, 43, 48, 72–9, 84–5, 87, 92–8, 118, 174, 216, 242
*phobos* (fear), 49–50
photographs, 272–5
pity (*eleos*), 29–31, 32, 49–50, 53
Plato, 36–7, 40, 43, 44, 46–9, 51–4, 57, 73, 76, 92, 161
  *The Republic*, 47–9, 53–5, 77
  *Timaeus*, 79
plot, 35, 55, 261
Plutarch, 39, 41, 118, 127–8
  'Consolatio ad Apollonium' (Ps-), 32, 39, 176–7, 179
  *De Exilio*, 147
poetry, 7–8, 72–9, 86–97, 194, 268, 272–3, 285
  classical/Greek tragedy, 36–7, 42–57
  funeral poems, 8–9, 12
Porter, Max, 262–6
Posidonius, 54–5
Prison Shakespeare, 110–17
prosimetric form (*prosimetrum*), 74, 78
Proust, Marcel, 226, 237, 242–3, 269–70, 275, 277; *see also* De Botton, Alain: *How Proust Can Change Your Life*
psychology, 29, 115, 116, 118
purification, 43, 49–50

Quintilian, *The Institutio Oratoria*, 26

Rabinow, Paul, 120
reading, 277
  attitude, 250–1
  as performance, 247, 268–9
realism, 231
reality, 203–4, 215, 247
reason, 15, 31–4, 36–41, 43–5, 47, 48, 53, 76, 118–20, 126–30, 132, 137, 139, 152–4, 162, 164–5, 170

re-description, 266–9
Reformation, 122, 132, 133, 135
religion, 97–101, 118, 120–2, 153–4, 159, 162, 205–6, 215–16
resilience, 203
revenge, 27, 34, 44, 125–6
revision, 92–4
rhyme, 263–4
Ricœur, Paul, 267
Rieff, David, *Swimming in a Sea of Death*, 257–9
Riley, Denise, *Time Lived, Without Its Flow*, 259–66
Rilke, Rainer Maria, 272, 280n, 283, 285
Rittgers, Ronald, 72, 132
Robinson, Marilynne, 232
Roiphe, Katie, 258
rosemary, 166, 191n

Saint Augustine, 71, 73, 118, 161
Salinger, J. D., 277
salvation, 74, 97, 101, 103, 118, 135, 157
Sand, George, 186, 193–219, 222n, 228, 231, 234, 241
Schwalbe, Will
  *Books for Living*, 256, 258–9, 270
  *The End of Your Life Book Club*, 3, 256–9
Schwarz, Murray, 247
Scott-Douglas, Amy, *Shakespeare Inside: The Bard Behind Bars*, 111
Searle, John, 185–6
self, 132, 146
self-comfort, 152, 153
self-fashioning, 116
self-help, 114–17
self-loss, 137
self-love, 127
self-pity, 279n
Seneca, 39, 41, 71, 118, 127–8, 267
  *Consolatio ad Helviam Matrem*, 146
  *Hercules Furens*, 93

*sensus communis* (communal/
  collective experience), 39–41,
  45, 46, 118, 122, 126, 132, 136,
  139–40, 145, 260
Shakespeare, William, 15, 16,
  110–86, 194, 203, 230
  Prison Shakespeare, 110–17
  *Hamlet*, 121, 122–38, 144–6, 151,
    155, 156, 160, 174, 182, 184,
    186, 189n, 217, 260
  *King Lear*, 139
  *Measure for Measure*, 121, 122,
    153–62, 163, 164, 167, 168,
    184, 191n
  *Richard II*, 121, 122, 136–53,
    155, 160, 184, 190n
  *Romeo and Juliet*, 121, 122,
    125, 162–76, 184, 191n,
    192n
  *The Tempest*, 121, 176–82
  *Twelfth Night*, 145
  see also Bates, Laura, *Shakespeare Saved My Life: Ten Years in Solitary with the Bard*; Maguire, Laurie, *Where There's A Will There's A Way: Or, All I Really Need to Know I Learned from Shakespeare*
Shields, David, *How Literature Saved My Life*, 277
Sidney, Sir Philip, *Apology for Poetry*, 242
Sieghart, William, *The Poetry Pharmacy*, 5–6
Simmel, Georg, 119, 185, 188n
sincerity, 131–2
Smyth, Katharine, *All the Lives We Ever Lived: Seeking Solace in Virginia Woolf*, 1–2, 3, 6, 9–10, 13, 214–15, 225, 233, 237–44, 261
Socrates, 47–9, 53, 54, 76–7, 180, 216
solace, 231, 233, 241, 243, 258
solidarity, 8–9, 10, 32, 35, 46, 122, 132, 136, 162

solitude, 269–74
Solnit, Rebecca, 270–1
Sontag, Susan, 146, 256–9
Sophocles, 43–6, 48
  *Electra*, 44–7, 53, 137
Sorabji, Richard, 49
Stanley, Jacqueline, 4
Starkie, Enid, 197, 209, 211, 220n
Stoicism, 38, 40, 53–6, 127, 133, 177, 216, 262
style, 7, 64, 69, 94, 204, 206, 211, 216, 229, 233, 235–8, 266; see also form; plot

Targoff, Ramie, 166, 176
*terpnos logos* ('cheering speech'), 42–3
texts, 247–8, 274
thinking, 249–50
time/temporality, 261–4
*Times Higher Education*, 7
Tofteland, Curt, 'Shakespeare Behind Bars', 111
Tolstoy, Leo, *The Death of Ivan Ilyich*, 258, 278n
tragedy, Greek, 44–54, 56
transitional objects, 212–14, 244–8, 251, 254n, 270
trust, 160
truth, 145, 161, 164, 178–9, 180
truths, 100, 145, 202, 234, 241, 242, 249
Tukhareli, Natalia, 4, 7

'uplifting' novels, 227

Valéry, Paul, 217
Vaughan, Madge, 234
Verhoeven, Cornelis, 119–20, 183, 184
Virgil, 74, 91, 96, 98, 103, 121

Wall, Geoffrey, 202n
Webster, Jamieson, 131, 272

Weil, Simone, 58n
Winnicott, Donald, 212, 213, 244–8, 251, 254n, 270, 273–4
Winock, Michel, 202
women, 44
Woolf, Virginia, 233–41
   *To the Lighthouse*, 237–41, 243–4, 261
   *Mrs Dalloway*, 238–9, 253n
   'On Re-reading Novels', 235
   *see also* Smyth, Katharine, *All the Lives We Ever Lived: Seeking Solace in Virginia Woolf*
words of comfort, 42–3, 131–2, 145, 148–51, 163, 180–1, 185–6, 266; *see also* language of comfort
Wordsworth, William, 263, 264

Žižek, Slavoj, 140–3

EU representative:
Easy Access System Europe
Mustamäe tee 50, 10621 Tallinn, Estonia
Gpsr.requests@easproject.com